Information Technology: Social Issues

Information Technology: Social Issues

A Reader

Edited by
Ruth Finnegan, Graeme Salaman and
Kenneth Thompson

Hodder & Stoughton

A MEMBER OF THE HODDER HEADLINE GROUP

in association with The Open University

ISBN 0 340 41669 6

First published 1987
Impression number 15 14 13 12 11 10 9 8 7 6
Year 1999 1998 1997 1996 1995 1994

Typeset by Print Origination, Formby, Merseyside.
Printed in Great Britain for Hodder & Stoughton Educational, a division of Hodder
Headline Plc, 338 Euston Road, London NW1 3BH by Athenæum Press Ltd,
Newcastle upon Tyne.

Contents

Acknowledgements

The editors and publishers would like to thank the following for permission to reproduce papers in this volume:

C. Freeman for Chapter 1 'The Case for Technological Determinism', previously unpublished conference paper; Harvard University Press for Chapter 2 'Electronics Takes Command' by Ithiel de Sola Pool from *Technologies of Freedom* (1983); John Wiley & Sons Ltd for Chapter 3 'Models of "Computer Literacy"' by B. Street from Gill, K. S. (ed.) *Artificial Intelligence for Society* (1986) (chapter originally entitled 'Literacy – comparative perspectives: "autonomous" and "ideological" models of "computer literacy"'); Association for Computing Machinery Inc for Chapter 4 'Value Conflicts and Social Choice in Electronic Payment Systems' by R. Kling from *Communications of the ACM*, 21, 8, 1978 (article abridged and originally called 'Value conflicts and social choices in electronic funds transfer system developments'); J. Monk and C. Bissell for Chapter 5 'Defence and the Electronics Industry', previously unpublished; Gower Publishing Group for Chapter 6 'New Technology and the Labour Process' by J. Child from Knights, Wilmott and Collinson (eds.) *Job Redesign* (1985); Croom Helm Ltd for Chapter 7 'New Technology and Bank Work: Banking on IT as an "Organizational Technology"' by S. Smith and D. Wield from Harris, L. (ed.) *New Perspectives as the Financial System*; W. H. Melody for Chapter 8 'Telecommunication – Policy Directions for the Technology and Information Services' (abridged) from Zorkoczy, P. (ed.) *Oxford Surveys in Information Technology*, 3, 1986; Michael Joseph for Chapter 9 'Surveillance, Computers and Privacy' by Duncan Campbell and Steve Connor from *On the Record* (1986); F. Webster and K. Robins for Chapter 10 'Dangers of Information Technology and Responsibilities of Education', specially written – revised from an earlier Oxford Polytechnic paper; Ellis Horwood Limited, Chichester for Chapter 11 'Information Technology and the North-South Divide' by J. Bessant from Burns, A. (ed.) *New Information Technology* (1984, updated figures 1987); W. Dutton for Chapter 12 'Decision-Making in the Information Age: Computer Models and Public Policy' from Dervin and Voigt (eds.) *Progress in Communication Services*, 5, 1984; N. D. Jayaweera for Chapter 13 'Communication Satellites, a Third World Perspective' from *Media Development*, 30, 4, 1983; Sage Publications for Chapter 14 'The Social Economics of Information Technology' by I. Miles and J. Gershuny from Ferguson, M. (ed.) *New Communication Technologies and Public Policy* (1986); The Controller of Her Majesty's Stationery Office for Chapter 16 'IT Futures in Households and Communities' by J. Bessant, K. Guy, I. Miles and H. Rush from *IT*

Futures, NEDO (1985); American Psychological Association for Chapter 17 'Social Psychological Aspects of Computer Mediated Communication' by T. W. McGuire, S. Kiesler and J. Siegel from *The American Psychologist*, 39, 10, 1984; Grafton Books for Chapter 18 'Computers and the Human Spirit' by S. Turkle from *The Second Self* (1985); IEEE for Chapter 19 'Engineers and the Work that People Do' by H. Rosenbrock from *IEEE Control Systems Magazine*, Vol. 1, No. 3, September 1981; Penguin Books Ltd (1984)/W. H. Freeman & Co., San Francisco (1986) for Chapter 20 'Artificial Intelligence' by J. Weizenbaum from *Computer Power and Human Reason*.

This Reader is produced in association with an Open University Course (the second level interdisciplinary course DT200 *Introduction to Information Technology: Social and Technological Issues*) and we are indebted to the course team for all the background work necessary to produce this collection of readings. In particular, we would like to thank the following members or associates of the course team for help and suggestions: James Anderson, Peter Braham, Hedy Brown, Stuart Hall, Nick Heap, Diana Laurillard, John Stratford, Ray Thomas, Peter Zorkoczy, and also, outside the Open University, John Davis (University of Kent) and William Melody (Simon Fraser University and the Economic and Social Research Council, London). We are also most grateful to Jo Doherty and Mandy Ellis for their invaluable help in processing the manuscript.

Introduction

The fact that it has become acceptable to refer to developments in information technology as an 'Information Revolution' should mean that it will come as no surprise to find social scientists turning their attention to analysing some of the social issues raised by this revolution. Indeed, some social scientists have acted as the heralds of this particular revolution, hailing it as ushering in a 'Post-Industrial Society' (Daniel Bell), and as proceeding at such a dizzying pace as to induce 'future shock' (Alvin Toffler). Others have been more critical, or at least more circumspect, examining the negative consequences as well as the positive effects of advances in information technology. Usually, books dealing with these social issues are not conceived as part of an educational course in information technology itself, but are more likely to feature in social science courses on topics such as the mass media, economic development, or the sociology of work and industrial relations. Courses on information technology tend to confine themselves to technical issues and the inculcation of practical skills, offering only the barest hint of the social context and consequences of IT. In this respect, the educational aim of developing 'computer literacy' and 'IT awareness' is often defined narrowly, with a consequent neglect of these broader social and educational considerations.

We would not be so bold as to claim that this book is unique in its origins, but it is relatively unusual in its conception as part of an interdisciplinary *Introduction to Information Technology* course, designed to complement teaching materials on technical issues and practical skills. Because of this, our selection of papers on social issues has been made according to their relevance to IT application areas that are featured in the course, including the home, service industries (banking and retailing), manufacturing, education and government. They are also issues chosen to illustrate the implications of IT applications at different social levels: international, national, organizational, small group and household, and the individual.

Because this is a fairly new area of study, there is no single discipline or theoretical framework that adequately encompasses the broad range of social issues that are raised by the information revolution. It requires interdisciplinary collaboration and open-mindedness, while recognizing that many of the perspectives and concepts developed in the past may still serve as an initial guide to understanding this new area of development. After all, IT is not a special impervious 'thing', but a social phenomenon, and therefore analysable through social science insights and methods rather than being left to engineers as 'their' thing.

The battery of social science concepts that have been applied and refined in other areas are thus also relevant to the understanding of IT and its social implications – concepts like power and authority, development and dependency, the labour process and deskilling, education versus training, ideology and social construction of knowledge, class and gender, pluralist democracy versus technocratic or capitalist hegemony, the self and social interaction. These ideas are drawn from various competing or complementary theoretical perspectives and relate to long-standing debates about the nature of society, its development and functioning: cultural variability and political choice versus technological determinism; social evolution based on an unfolding logic of increasing efficiency versus cyclical crises arising from inherent contradictions; pluralistic decision-making versus class domination; modernization versus imperialism; individual agency versus social structural determinants, and so on. The primary purpose of this book is not to enter directly into those theoretical debates, but to draw on their conceptual resources in order to pose some of the key social issues concerning IT, and to bring their insights to bear on how IT is shaped by social factors and how its application carries social and not just technical implications and consequences.

While drawing on established social science concepts and theoretical perspectives, we are conscious of the need for social scientists to expand their traditional horizons, often in an interdisciplinary context (including technological disciplines and IT specialists), in order to take account of new developments occurring in and through information technology, such as the challenge to traditional perspectives on the mass media presented by new interactive and 'narrowcast' electronic media. There has to be some interest in looking not just *back* to the 'industrial revolution' and its debatable consequences, but also to current and (possibly) future developments which, some would argue, constitute a new kind of revolution. In this context, social scientists cannot afford to indulge in armchair criticism of IT developments, or be content with an assigned role of 'battlefield padre' or technology's social worker, attending to the casualties of the 'cruel necessities' of progress. Social science needs to fulfil its rightful role and capacity, not merely to describe what IT does, but also to explain how it develops and why it is used. The shape taken by various forms of IT, the investment they receive, and the way in which they are utilized, are influenced by social factors such as power, ideology, economic interests, organizational hierarchies and their processes of decision-making, and social psychological factors at the level of the small group and individual subjective perceptions. In analysing these social determinants, the papers included in this volume tend to be rather critical of many widely accepted notions about IT, such as those of the 'Gee, Whiz!' and 'marvels of science' variety, or those which suggest IT will save Britain's economy or remedy the defects of its educational system, while at the same time ensuring world peace (for example, through the 'Star Wars' defence system) and solving the problems of the Third World (for example, through satellite broadcasting). This apparently critical stance is not necessarily tied to any particular moral or political position, but stems from the mode of enquiry typical of social science, which is sceptical and questioning of taken-for-granted wisdom. The popular belief is itself a social product, as is IT, and requires critical analysis to discern the social influences and interests that have moulded it.

Because of these considerations, the issues addressed in this book do not always correspond to popular or political conceptions of the most pressing issues concerning IT. In part this is also due to the fact that in some cases the papers were written as research reports or reviews of academic studies. However, we have sought to select and edit the chapters in such a way as to cover issues that are formulated in terms of general theoretical insights and

Acknowledgements

The editors and publishers would like to thank the following for permission to reproduce papers in this volume:

C. Freeman for Chapter 1 'The Case for Technological Determinism', previously unpublished conference paper; Harvard University Press for Chapter 2 'Electronics Takes Command' by Ithiel de Sola Pool from *Technologies of Freedom* (1983); John Wiley & Sons Ltd for Chapter 3 'Models of "Computer Literacy"' by B. Street from Gill, K. S. (ed.) *Artificial Intelligence for Society* (1986) (chapter originally entitled 'Literacy – comparative perspectives: "autonomous" and "ideological" models of "computer literacy"'); Association for Computing Machinery Inc for Chapter 4 'Value Conflicts and Social Choice in Electronic Payment Systems' by R. Kling from *Communications of the ACM*, 21, 8, 1978 (article abridged and originally called 'Value conflicts and social choices in electronic funds transfer system developments'); J. Monk and C. Bissell for Chapter 5 'Defence and the Electronics Industry', previously unpublished; Gower Publishing Group for Chapter 6 'New Technology and the Labour Process' by J. Child from Knights, Wilmott and Collinson (eds.) *Job Redesign* (1985); Croom Helm Ltd for Chapter 7 'New Technology and Bank Work: Banking on IT as an "Organizational Technology"' by S. Smith and D. Wield from Harris, L. (ed.) *New Perspectives as the Financial System*; W. H. Melody for Chapter 8 'Telecommunication – Policy Directions for the Technology and Information Services' (abridged) from Zorkoczy, P. (ed.) *Oxford Surveys in Information Technology*, 3, 1986; Michael Joseph for Chapter 9 'Surveillance, Computers and Privacy' by Duncan Campbell and Steve Connor from *On the Record* (1986); F. Webster and K. Robins for Chapter 10 'Dangers of Information Technology and Responsibilities of Education', specially written – revised from an earlier Oxford Polytechnic paper; Ellis Horwood Limited, Chichester for Chapter 11 'Information Technology and the North-South Divide' by J. Bessant from Burns, A. (ed.) *New Information Technology* (1984, updated figures 1987); W. Dutton for Chapter 12 'Decision-Making in the Information Age: Computer Models and Public Policy' from Dervin and Voigt (eds.) *Progress in Communication Services*, 5, 1984; N. D. Jayaweera for Chapter 13 'Communication Satellites, a Third World Perspective' from *Media Development*, 30, 4, 1983; Sage Publications for Chapter 14 'The Social Economics of Information Technology' by I. Miles and J. Gershuny from Ferguson, M. (ed.) *New Communication Technologies and Public Policy* (1986); The Controller of Her Majesty's Stationery Office for Chapter 16 'IT Futures in Households and Communities' by J. Bessant, K. Guy, I. Miles and H. Rush from *IT*

Futures, NEDO (1985); American Psychological Association for Chapter 17 'Social Psychological Aspects of Computer Mediated Communication' by T. W. McGuire, S. Kiesler and J. Siegel from *The American Psychologist*, 39, 10, 1984; Grafton Books for Chapter 18 'Computers and the Human Spirit' by S. Turkle from *The Second Self* (1985); IEEE for Chapter 19 'Engineers and the Work that People Do' by H. Rosenbrock from *IEEE Control Systems Magazine*, Vol. 1, No. 3, September 1981; Penguin Books Ltd (1984)/W. H. Freeman & Co., San Francisco (1986) for Chapter 20 'Artificial Intelligence' by J. Weizenbaum from *Computer Power and Human Reason*.

This Reader is produced in association with an Open University Course (the second level interdisciplinary course DT200 *Introduction to Information Technology: Social and Technological Issues*) and we are indebted to the course team for all the background work necessary to produce this collection of readings. In particular, we would like to thank the following members or associates of the course team for help and suggestions: James Anderson, Peter Braham, Hedy Brown, Stuart Hall, Nick Heap, Diana Laurillard, John Stratford, Ray Thomas, Peter Zorkoczy, and also, outside the Open University, John Davis (University of Kent) and William Melody (Simon Fraser University and the Economic and Social Research Council, London). We are also most grateful to Jo Doherty and Mandy Ellis for their invaluable help in processing the manuscript.

concepts, and that can be analysed in terms of empirical evidence. The various section headings give some indication, in relatively untheoretical terms, of what those general issues are:

Part 1, The Shaping of Information Technology: Determinism or Choice?, introduces some different conceptions and aspects of a central theoretical topic in the social sciences: What are the key determining factors in social development and how much scope is left for human choice? Is social development determined by technology, or is technology a cultural product that is shaped by other cultural factors such as values and political or moral choices? In particular, the papers address, in their different ways, the issues of 'technological determinism'.

Part II, The Shaping of Information Technology: Some Actors in the Drama, can be viewed as a focusing down of the broader issue of the previous section concerning determinism or choice, and as being concerned with the relative contributions of social actors (individuals and groups) and social structures (for example, economic and technological imperatives) in specific IT developments. Are these developments part of an inevitable structural trend in certain social systems, or do some actors' perceptions and choices play a more important part than others in shaping those developments?

Part III, Some Critical Issues for the Information Age: Control and Power, asks who controls information technology and what power does this bring? Does IT tend to be developed and used for the good of all, increasing individual freedom and reducing inequalities of power and wealth, or does it threaten to have the opposite effect unless checked? This is a field in which social scientists, and even some investigative journalists, have done much work that is relevant to understanding the effects and control of IT, particularly in studies of political processes, ideology in education, and economic development.

Part IV, Some Critical Issues for the Information Age: Access and Participation, is also concerned with power and inequality, but from the perspective of groups or societies who would like to participate in the IT revolution, and be empowered by it, but whose prospects with regard to access and participation are difficult to forecast. Forecasting the future, not in visionary terms, but in terms of predictions based on analyses of empirical trends, might be taken to be the underlying theme of these papers.

Part V, The Future of the Human Spirit: Depersonalization or New Development? is also about trying both to forecast the future and to interpret the present, but here the question is not about IT as such, but about the nature and the future of the human being, or what IT means for the person or 'self'. What do such analyses tell us about the implications of IT for our personhood and for our modes of social interaction?

Much current writing on IT is very generalized, often representing extreme optimistic or pessimistic views with little empirical content, or, alternatively, so specifically focused on just one particular aspect (for example, employment) that it misses any perspective on wider issues or on the controversial nature of our assessment of IT. The selection of papers in this Reader is designed to avoid these two extremes. Instead it aims to pull together specific and documented studies which at the same time exemplify (either in themselves or as juxtaposed here) both an awareness of wider questions and controversies and some explicit discussion of the problems and issues posed by IT in the modern world.

No book can expect to cover all the important issues in such a broad topic as information technology. We are conscious of the fact that some topics are under-represented in this collection; for example the resistance or participation of shopfloor workers in IT developments. In some cases this is because the topic is already well covered elsewhere and readers are likely to have access to these sources. However, we have tried to give a broad representation of the major issues, including a sample of different theoretical perspectives and a range of positions from the pessimistic/critical to the optimistic/enthusiastic. In the case of students taking the Open University course *Introduction to Information Technology*, this set of readings is complemented by other teaching materials, including course units, supplementary reading, computers and software, television and audio programmes. However, we hope that the collection of papers in this volume will be seen to be an essential ingredient in any comprehensive introduction to information technology.

Readers may disagree with specific positions (the more so that differing viewpoints are deliberately included) but our aim is to provide some conspectus of the debates and the issues in what is inevitably a controversial area – inevitably, but not often enough recognized as such. The hope is that the papers here, and thus the Reader as a whole, will lead to wider discussion of the issues, not just among academic social scientists (though this is one central aim), but also among educators, industrialists, politicians, theologians, and moralists. These issues are not just something for the technicians, but raise questions for debate among us all as citizens.

Ruth Finnegan, Graeme Salaman and Kenneth Thompson
Open University, 1987

PART I

The Shaping of Information Technology: Determinism or Choice?

Introduction to Part I

The existence and spread of information technology are often taken for granted, as an inevitable part of modern life, whether for good or ill. But as this part illustrates, there are a number of different viewpoints on what shapes it and how far we have some choice in its development.

Christopher Freeman's provocative 'Case for Technological Determinism' opens the discussion. He takes the view that some changes in technology systems – steam power in the last century, information technology in this – are so overwhelmingly important that they affect the entire economy.

Freeman sees such revolutions as taking place seldom, in the framework of the 'long cycles' in economic development envisaged by Schumpeter and others, and followed up in many writings by himself and his associates (for example, Freeman *et al.*, 1982; Freeman, 1986). His theory is thus in part an economic one, so that, despite the paper's title, his position here might better be called 'technological-cum-economic determinism'. Within this determinism, he allows some small leeway for social and political choice (for example, between socialist and capitalist responses to developments in information technology), but overall sees the general trend of world technology as irreversible and irresistible.

Ithiel de Sola Pool also sees technology as providing the impetus for current developments through the 'electronic revolution', but at the same time considers that its precise direction can be partially influenced by human choice. This is a position which he has described as 'soft technological determinism' (1983, p. 5), since, as he puts it here, 'Technology shapes the structure of the battle but not every outcome' (below p. 32). He takes the example of the new forms of communication made possible by the convergence between print, telephones and broadcasting. These trends have indeed been started off by technological developments, but whether the new media are to be used for centralized control or increased democratic participation is also a matter for legal and political decisions.

Brian Street takes up a quite different position. He attacks technological deterministic views, in particular the assumptions that technology is in some way 'autonomous' or must lead to inevitable results. Instead he sees the crucial factors as social and political. He argues that the historical development of print/written literacy was determined by social and political not technological processes, and suggests that the same is therefore likely to be true of 'computer literacy'. In his view, what determines the development of computer learning is the effect of those in power propagating ideologies about literacy which suit their own needs, and are thus more to do with current political relationships and ideologies than with real pedagogic or technological issues.

But technological development can also be seen not as the result of technological determinism (hard or soft) or of sweeping economic or power relations, but as shaped by a whole range of both general and specific factors of the kind traditionally considered by many social scientists. This is the general line adopted in Rob Kling's paper. He takes the particular example of the electronic transfer of money. This is indeed one important form of modern information technology, but the issues he raises are also more general and abiding ones. In his discussion of the introduction, aims, design, reliability or security of electronic systems, he stresses how such decisions are, and must be, crucially affected by the values held by policy makers – values which differ in different organizations and circumstances and on which there are genuinely different positions. He also points to the importance of competition between differing interest groups and organisations, and to the crucial contribution made by *people*: those who do – or do not – choose to use the available technologies, or to use them in particular ways. In this interpretation values and social choice are of the essence.

The four views exemplified here do not exhaust the possible positions, nor are they in every respect contradictory (to some extent they may move at different levels of analysis). Nevertheless they do represent different and influential viewpoints on how information technology is ultimately shaped, and on the room for human choice. The development of information technology raises crucial issues for society – among them many already mentioned in this section, like employment, democratic control, or privacy. In order to consider these issues seriously, we need to recognize and confront, even if we cannot fully decide, the disputes about how far we can or cannot shape this development.

1

The Case for Technological Determinism[1]

Christopher Freeman

1 Introduction

In his book on *Explaining Technical Change*, Jon Elster (1983) describes two main approaches:

> First, technical change may be conceived of as a rational, goal directed activity, as the choice of the best innovation among a set of feasible changes. Secondly, technical change may be seen as the cumulative addition of small and largely random modifications of the production process. Any serious student of technology will agree that technical change exhibits both these aspects, but there are strong differences in emphasis between the contending explanations. (p. 9)

This paper argues that there is a third approach to technical change, which, while recognizing that both the other approaches have a domain of validity, allows also for paradigm changes in technology, which arise neither exclusively from rational choice nor yet from cumulative small modifications but from new combinations of radical innovations related both to major advances in science and technology and to organizational innovations. Such 'new technological systems' can offer such great technical and economic advantages in a wide range of industries and services that their adoption becomes a necessity in any economy exposed to competitive economic, social, political and military pressures. Increasingly this century, the world-wide diffusion of such new techno-economic paradigms dominates the process of technical change for several decades and powerfully influences economic and social developments even though it does not uniquely determine them. In other words, the paper argues the case for a limited autonomy of science and technology in determining the scope and direction of some major new developments in the economy. It does so in the first place on the basis of a review of the debate on 'demand-pull' and 'technology-push' in technical innovation, secondly on the historical evidence relating to the development of the electronic computer and the associated new 'information technology' paradigm.

It does not follow from this analysis, even if it is valid, that fatalism is the only possible response to new developments in science and technology. On the contrary, efforts to shape and to humanize new developments in technology are all the more important. But such efforts are only likely to be successful if they are based on an understanding of the strength of the thrust which accompanies the diffusion of a new techno-economic paradigm.

2 'Demand-pull' and 'technology-push' theories

For many years there has been a continuing but rather ill-structured debate, mainly among economists and historians of science and technology, about the determinants of technical change in industrialized societies. On the one hand are those who stress the autonomous development of technology and the increasingly strong influence of both science and technology in innovation. On the other hand there are those who claim that it is the market and other economic and social influences which primarily determine the scale, the rate and the direction of invention and innovation activity, and in some cases even of science itself.

It is no surprise to sociologists of science that studies sponsored by agencies responsible for basic science (such as the National Science Foundation) have come up with findings that tend to support the science and technology-push hypothesis, while studies sponsored by market-oriented agencies tend to support the alternative emphasis. This does not necessarily justify a cynical view of the debate, since the issues are extremely complex and there is some justification in the empirical evidence for both types of explanation, and for an interplay between them.

Partly for this reason too, the protagonists in this debate do not correspond precisely to the ideological schools familiar in other fields of economics or social sciences. Thus, for example, there are neo-classical economists, who lay great stress on the exogenous and unpredictable influences of science and technology on economic development (see, for example, Salter, 1960), while others emphasize the demand-driven features of technical change and the rational choice between alternative combinations of labour and capital in the traditional production function or the 'production possibilities frontier'.

Very different emphases are also to be found in the Marxist literature. Hessen (1931) and his Soviet colleagues at one extreme stressed demand-pull as the decisive influence not only on technology, but also on basic science, while Bernal (1953) stressed the relatively autonomous development of fundamental research, the tendency for new developments in science to give rise to entirely new industries and indeed at least at one time the tendency for scientists to take over the world and the universe (Bernal, 1928).

'Demand-pull' theories and 'technology-push' theories do not correspond exactly to Elster's 'rational choice' and 'evolutionary trial and error' models, but there is a considerable overlap. Those economists and others who have stressed the role of 'demand-pull' tend to assume, if not a neo-classical omniscience of 'perfect information' about prices, markets, costs and alternative combinations of factors of production, at least some fairly reliable information and signals about what the market 'wants' as the main guiding force for inventive and innovative activities.

Those economists (or historians, or technologists) who have stressed science and technology 'push' on the other hand have tended to emphasize the uncertainties of technical innovation, the experimental nature of R and D, the difficulties of getting precise information about markets which often are only vaguely foreshadowed, and which are themselves in a state of flux. While they stress the inherently unpredictable nature of basic scientific research, they also point to 'technological trajectories' which may follow scientific or technological breakthroughs, and which encompass the improvement of various technical characteristics as well as the enlargement of the range of potential applications. Nelson and Winter (1982) may be taken as characteristic of this type of neo-Schumpeterian economist with their 'evolutionary theory of economic change'.

As in the case of Elster's two theories of technical change and as also in the analogous case of explanations of inflation in terms of 'cost-push', or 'demand-pull', it is possible to subscribe to both types of explanation in differing social situations, or to hybrid theories. Nevertheless, the distinction is an important one and, as with Elster's categories, economists and historians tend to be recognisable as putting the main emphasis on one set of explanations or the other.

Thus, for example, despite his disclaimer for basic science, it is not unreasonable to regard Schmookler (an economist who made a great contribution to the history of inventions) primarily as an advocate of a demand-pull explanation of technical change. In his major work on *Inventions and Economic Growth* (1966), he sought to demonstrate with the use of very detailed patent statistics that generally speaking the peaks and troughs of *invention* activity lagged behind the peaks and troughs of *investment* activity in a number of key US industries in the nineteenth century.

From this he drew the conclusion that the main stimulus to invention and innovation came from the changing pattern of demand as measured by investment in new capital goods in railways and other industries. In his own words:

> The possibility that the results reflect the effect of capital goods inventions on capital goods sales is grossly implausible. In the time series comparisons, trend turning points tend to occur in sales before they do in patents and long swing troughs in sales in the industries examined are adequately explained on other grounds . . . . The fact that innovations are usually made because men want to solve economic problems or capitalize on economic opportunities is of overwhelming importance for economic theory. Hitherto, many economists have regarded invention – and technological change generally – as an *exogenous*, and some even thought an *autonomous* variable . . . These views insofar as they were of a substantive nature rather than merely a methodological convenience, are no longer tenable . . . the production of inventions and much other technological knowledge, whether routinized or not . . . is in most instances as much an economic activity as the production of bread. (pp. 204-8)

He also rejected the idea that this analysis might be valid only for the large numbers of routine secondary patents which were concerned with the follow-through of key inventions and innovations.

Schmookler certainly succeeded in demonstrating a strong association between investment activity and inventive activity in a number of industries. However, he was less successful in demonstrating a consistent time lag of the series on invention, for, as he frankly admitted, there were occasions when the time series on patents appeared to lead the investment statistics. He therefore did not rest his case exclusively on a consistent lead of the investment and sales series, but on the argument that investments usually lead the upswing from troughs and the movement of investment could be better explained by external events than by 'invention-push'.

Schmookler's work was followed by a series of studies in the 1960s and 1970s, which attempted to show that innovation was mainly or exclusively led by market demand. In their review paper criticizing these studies, Mowery and Rosenberg (1979) pointed out that there was considerable confusion in many of them between 'demand' and 'need'. Since human 'needs' are almost infinite and often long-felt, they cannot explain the emergence of a particular innovation at a certain time. There is also a considerable difference between anticipating a possible or potential future demand and responding to an effective market demand articulated today. Whereas Schmookler's work would possibly be classified in the second category at least in the sense of the immediate stimulus to invention activity, some of the other studies could not be so classified, since they dealt with the imaginative anticipation of a future market for a new product.

Mowery and Rosenberg also pointed out that the authors of some of these studies did not in fact agree with the tendency to interpret their results as evidence of market demand leadership in the generation of innovations. Particularly in the case of the 'Queen's Award' study at Manchester and the SAPPHO project at the Science Policy Research Unit, University of Sussex, the authors had specifically emphasized that they regarded innovation success as the result of an interplay between science and technology push factors and user-need and demand, with each factor sometimes predominating in particular instances.

This powerful critique of demand-led theories by Mowery and Rosenberg may be complemented by a critique based on the application of Schmookler's own methods but in different industries and in different circumstances, and using some additional measures. With a group of colleagues (Walsh, 1984), we attempted to test Schmookler's theory in the case of some sub-sectors of a 'science-related' industry – the chemical industry. We chose that industry for a variety of reasons but perhaps the main one was that we wished to test Schmookler's hypothesis not only for a more recent period (the last half century), but also for an industry which could be described as R & D intensive or even 'science-intensive' – at least in some sectors. Although, in their time, all of the four industries on which Schmookler concentrated his efforts (railways, paper, petroleum, and agriculture) were certainly the focus of considerable inventive and innovative activity, none of them could be described as 'science-intensive', with the possible exception of petroleum-refining after 1920. We also believed it probable that 'demand-pull' theories had much greater validity in the nineteenth century than in the twentieth century (Lilley, 1970).

Ideally, we would have liked to investigate several other industries but we were restricted by limitations of time and resources. As Schmookler and his PhD students found, the extraction, classification and enumeration of patents is extremely time-consuming. However, in some respects we went beyond what Schmookler attempted since we were interested not just in 'demand-pull' and 'technology-push' but also in 'science-push'.

We not only made use of long time series of patent statistics, as Schmookler did, we also attempted to use time series of statistics relating to the publication of relevant scientific papers. These bibliometric techniques were pioneered by a historian of science, Derek de Salla Price (1963) and again, while we recognize that there are serious methodological problems, we nevertheless believe that, as in the case of patent statistics and inventive activities, some rough measure of the direction and scale of scientific activities can be derived from the use of these techniques. We also included the principal European countries in our analysis, in addition to the United States.

Although we made use of statistics of patents and scientific papers and related these to measures of output, investment, and sales after the manner of Schmookler, we were very much aware of the dangers of the simplistic use of such aggregative measures and correlation techniques which may obscure as much as they reveal. In each sub-sector which we analysed (synthetic materials, petro-chemicals, drugs and dyestuffs) we were interested also in the *major* scientific discoveries and *key* inventions and innovations, since we did not accept Schmookler's view that aggregate trends also reflect the trend of the most important discoveries and inventions. We therefore tried to understand the history of each sector in *qualitative* as well as in *quantitative* terms, and to take account (as Schmookler also did) of major external social and economic events, which influenced the development of each sector and the process of technical change, such as the demand for synthetic materials for the war economy of the Third Reich.

In our research project we sought to test both a 'strong' and a 'weak' demand-pull hypothesis. In fact, as we have seen, Schmookler did not find a consistent time lag of inventive activities behind investment activities, but taken together with other evidence of factors influencing investment and related demand, he thought that he had enough evidence to justify his conclusions. In our case, if we had found a 'Schmookler' pattern in which the patent statistics series consistently lagged behind indicators of sales, output and investment, then we would have regarded this as rather strong supporting evidence for his theory, since it extended the analysis to a science-based industry and to other industrial countries. But we did not find such a consistent pattern. If we had found, further, that not only did the 'demand' time series lead the 'invention' time series but both led the 'science' series, then this would have been supporting evidence for an even stronger version of 'demand-pull' affecting both technology and science à la Hessen. But, again, we did not find such a consistent pattern.

If on the other hand, our results showed that a wave of scientific publication in a new field preceded a wave of invention activity (as measured by patents) and that both were followed by a wave of investment in the production of new types of chemicals, then this would provide evidence of a 'counter-Schmookler' pattern of technical change based on science and technology 'push'.

As in Schmookler's own work the pattern of leads and lags was by no means so clear-cut as to put the issue beyond all doubt. But as with his work we did find evidence of synchronicity in the pattern of economic and technical developments, i.e. the major upsurge of production and investment in each sector was accompanied by a remarkable increase both in the numbers of patents and in the output of related scientific publications. The pattern of cyclical downturns was less clear-cut but such troughs were less important than in Schmookler's industries until the most recent period.

The most interesting result of our work, however, was the evidence tentatively suggesting that a 'counter-Schmookler' pattern was characteristic of the early stages in synthetic materials, drugs and dyestuffs, changing to something more closely resembling a 'Schmookler' type pattern once the industry 'took off'. Qualitative analysis in all four cases confirmed the importance of scientific and technological breakthroughs permitting and triggering an upsurge of inventive activity and technical innovations.

This is consistent with a Schumpeterian interpretation postulating a close interdependence between technical, scientific and market developments, but with exogenous science and new technology often predominating in the early stages, and market demand, process innovations and secondary inventions dominating in the mature industry. It should be noted that in purely quantitative terms the number of patents and papers in the late stages will be far greater than in the early stage. There are analogies here with the Kuhnian concepts of change of paradigm and 'normal science' (Kuhn, 1962). The next section considers the case of the change of paradigm based on the electronic computer.

3   Major radical innovations and paradigm change

One of the major criticisms of the demand-pull hypothesis and of the related 'rational choice' decision-making in generating technical change relates to the origins and early development of those innovations which could hardly be construed as the cumulative addition of small modifications to existing products and processes. Thus, for example, there is no way that nuclear reactors could have emerged from incremental improvements to earlier ways of generating electricity or that nylon could have emerged from improvements in natural textile materials. Schumpeter pointed out that railways could not easily emerge from a combination of stage coaches and maintained that radical innovations, so far from being introduced by 'rational' entrepreneurs on the basis of accurate knowledge of 'demand' from consumers, were usually imposed on an initially unreceptive and unwilling market, by rather unusual entrepreneurs.

This Schumpeterian debate may be illustrated by the example of the electronic computer, which almost everyone would agree is one of the most important, if not the most important innovation of the twentieth century. In their account of the early history of the US computer industry, Katz and Phillips (1981) make some interesting comments on the reasons why private funds were not committed to the commercialization of the electronic computers which had been developed and used on a very small scale during the Second World War for code cracking, ballistic and design calculations:

> the general view prior to 1950 was that there was no commercial demand for computers. Thomas J. Watson Senior, with an experience dating from at least 1928, was as well acquainted with both business needs and the capabilities of advanced competitive devices as any business leader. He felt that the one SSEC machine which was on display at IBM's New York offices 'could solve all the scientific problems in the world involving

scientific calculations'. He saw no commercial possibilities. This view, moreover, persisted even though some private firms that were potential users of computers – the major life insurance companies, telecommunications providers, aircraft manufacturers and others were reasonably informed about the emerging technology. A broad business need was not apparent.

Even later, after IBM had produced a small batch of computers for the US Government during the Korean war, the Product Planning and Sales Department forecast no civil market for the model 650 computer. Against their opposition the Applied Science Group persuaded T.J. Watson Junior (who had taken over) to back the 650 model and forecast a sale of 200. In fact, 1800 machines were sold.

Cases such as this surely knock a hole in any 'pure' theory of market-led invention and innovation. A much more plausible version would relate to the role of military demand and military sponsorship of R and D. However, it would be perverse to overlook the 'push' from technologists and scientists who wished to promote technical advance and imagined new applications in many different directions. As Katz and Phillips (1981) describe it:

In a real sense the technologist users (in government) and the technologist suppliers (in private firms), had coincident interests and were members of a cognisable 'fraternity'. They attempted to prevail on their respective host organisations to supply funds to meet their technological and scientific objectives. The demand, that is, was more in the form of budget requests by this group for funds for investment in R and D – without regard to immediate economic returns on investment – then it was a demand for marketable computer hardware.

There were certainly visionary scientists and technologists, such as Norbert Wiener and John Diebold, who foresaw most of the contemporary applications of computers in every branch of the economy. But successful commercial exploitation of these opportunities depended on many new radical innovations in software, in computer memories, and integrated circuits and in telecommunications as well as on the 'creation' of new markets by organisational innovations and imaginative entrepreneurs. The study of major innovations and their diffusion has led 'Schumpeterian' economists, such as Katz and Phillips, Nelson and Winter or Nathan Rosenberg, to a very different view of technical change than that postulated by 'demand-pull' theories.

Dosi (1985) has summed up the 'Stylised facts' which have emerged from this stream of 'innovation research', over the past two decades:

First, the innovative process has some rules of its own which at least in the short and medium-term, cannot be described as simple and flexible responses to changes in market conditions. It is the nature of technologies themselves that determine the range within which products and processes can adjust to changing economic conditions and the possible directions of technical progress.

Second, scientific knowledge plays, and increasingly in this century, has played a crucial role in opening up new possibilities of major technological advances.

Third, the increasing complexity of research and innovative activities has militated in favour of institutional organizations (R and D laboratories of big firms, government labs, universities, etc.) as opposed to individual innovators, as the most conducive environments for the production of innovations.

Fourth, in addition to the previous point, and in many ways complementary to it, a significant amount of innovation and improvements is originated through 'learning by doing' and is generally embodied in people and organizations (primarily firms). The same can be said for R and D which is generally incorporated and linked with the productive activities of the firms.

Fifth, notwithstanding the increasing institutional formalization, research and innovation activities maintain an intrinsic *uncertain nature*. The technical (and even more so the commercial) outcome of research activities can hardly be known *ex ante*.

Sixth, technical change does not occur randomly, for two main reasons, in the sense that (i) in spite of considerable variations with regard to specific innovations, the directions of technical change are often defined by the state-of-the-art of the technologies already in use, and (ii) it is generally the case that the probability to make technological advances of firms, organizations and often countries, is among other things, a function of the technological levels already achieved by them. In other words technical change is a cumulative activity.

Consideration of this Schumpeterian literature on technical change and innovation, as well as the 'demand-pull' literature, suggests the need for a taxonomy of innovation which distinguishes between incremental innovation, radical innovation, new technical systems and new technological paradigms. In our own work on technical change in the post-war UK economy, we (Freeman and Soete, 1986; Soet, 1985) found that in all sectors, despite the great variety of specific incremental and radical innovations in almost every industry, there was evidence of a change of 'paradigm' from the energy-intensive, inflexible, mass and flow production technology of the 1950s and 1960s to an information-intensive, flexible, computerized technology in the 1970s and 1980s. Such pervasive shifts in technology affecting many or all branches of the economy, clearly require attention as well as the individual innovations which are the focus of most innovation research. We therefore define four categories of innovation:

(i)   Incremental innovation

These occur more or less continuously in any industry or service activity although at differing rates in different industries, depending upon a combination of demand pressures and technological opportunities. These innovations may often occur, not so much as the result of any deliberate research and development activity, but as the outcome of inventions and improvements suggested by engineers and others directly engaged in the production process, or as a result of initiatives and proposals by users. Many empirical studies have confirmed their great importance in improving the efficiency in use of all factors of production, for example, Hollander's study of productivity gains in

Du Pont rayon plants or Townsend's study of the Anderton shearer loader in the British coal mining industry. They are particularly important in the follow-through period after a radical breakthrough innovation (see below) and frequently associated with the scaling-up of plant and equipment and quality improvements to products and services for a variety of specific applications. Although their combined effect is extremely important in the growth of productivity, no single incremental innovation has dramatic effects, and they may sometimes pass unnoticed and unrecorded. However, their effects are apparent in the steady growth of productivity which is reflected in input-output tables over time by major changes in the coefficients for the existing array of products and services. The evidence of demand-led inventions and innovations relates primarily to this category and they account for the vast majority of patents.

(ii)   Radical innovations

These are discontinuous events and in recent times are usually the result of a deliberate research and development activity in enterprises and/or in university and government laboratories. They are unevenly distributed over sectors and over time, but our research did not support the view of Mensch (1975), that their appearance is concentrated particularly in periods of deep recessions (Freeman, Clark and Soete, 1982), in response to the collapse or decline of established markets. But we would agree with Mensch that, whenever they may occur, they are important as the potential springboard for the growth of new markets, or in the case of radical process innovations, such as the oxygen steelmaking process, of big improvements in the cost and quality of existing products. They may often involve a combined product, process and organizational innovation. Over a period of decades a radical innovation, such as nylon or the pill, may have fairly dramatic effects, but in terms of their economic impact they are relatively small and localized, unless a whole cluster of radical innovations are linked together in the rise of entire new industries and services, such as the synthetic materials industry or the semiconductor industry (see (iii) below). Strictly speaking, at a sufficiently disaggregative level, radical innovations would constantly require the addition of new rows and columns in an input-output table. But in practical terms, such changes are introduced only in the case of the most important innovations and with long time lags, when their economic impact is already substantial. Evidence of market-led radical innovation is much weaker than in the case of incremental innovation, since by definition usually no established market exists. Clearly, however, those technologists and scientists who are primarily responsible for inventing and developing radical innovations *do* have a potential market in mind and are influenced by social and economic developments. As Carlota Perez puts it: the search is always to turn base metals into gold and not vice versa. Moreover the evidence of innovation case studies is strong that those innovators who take a lot of trouble to identify potential users and study their needs are more likely to succeed than those who do not.

(iii)   Changes of 'technology system'

These are far-reaching changes in technology, affecting several branches of the economy, as well as giving rise to entirely new sectors. They are based on a combination of radical and incremental innovations, together with organizational innovations affecting more than one or a few firms. Keirstead (1948) in his exposition of a Schumpeterian theory of economic development, introduced the concept of 'constellations' of innovations, which were technically and economically interrelated. An obvious example is the cluster of synthetic materials innovations, petro-chemical innovations, innovations in injection moulding and extrusion machinery, and innumerable application innovations for synthetics introduced in the 1930s, 1940s and 1950s (Freeman, Clark and Soete, 1982).

(iv)   Changes in 'techno-economic paradigm' ('technological revolutions')

Some changes in technology systems are so far-reaching in their effects that they have a major influence on the behaviour of the entire economy. These are the 'creative gales of destruction' which are at the heart of Schumpeter's theory of long cycles in economic development. The diffusion of steam power and of electric power are obvious examples of such deep-going transformations. So too, we would claim, is the combination of innovations associated with the electronic computer. The expression 'techno-economic paradigm' implies a process of economic selection from the range of the technically feasible combinations of innovations, and indeed we are suggesting that it takes a relatively long time (a decade or more) for a new paradigm to crystallize and still longer for it to diffuse right through the system. This diffusion involves a complex interplay between technological, economic and political forces which we discuss further below. Here we insist only on the requirement that a new techno-economic paradigm is one that affects the structure and the conditions of production and distribution for almost every branch of the economy.

Dosi (1983) has used the expression 'change of technological paradigm' and made comparisons with the analogous approach of Kuhn (1962) to 'scientific revolutions' and paradigm changes in basic science. In these terms 'incremental innovation' along established technological trajectories may be compared with Kuhn's 'normal science'. Several other authors have also used the expression 'technological paradigm' to connote broadly similar ideas.

While there are similarities in all these concepts, the approach of Carlota Perez (1983, 1985) is the most systematic and has some important distinguishing features. She argues that the development of a new 'techno-economic paradigm' involves a new 'best practice' set of rules and customs for designers, engineers, entrepreneurs and managers, which differ in many important respects from the previously prevailing paradigm. Such technological revolutions give rise to a whole series of rapidly changing production functions for both old and new products. While the exact savings in either labour or capital cannot be precisely foreseen, the general economic and technical advantages to be derived from the application of the new technology in product and process design become increasingly apparent and new 'rules of thumb' are gradually established. Such changes in paradigm make possible a 'quantum leap' in potential productivity, which, however, is at first realized only in a few leading sectors. In other sectors such gains cannot usually be realized without organizational and social changes of a far-reaching character.

The new 'information technology' paradigm, based on a constellation of industries, which are among the fastest growing in all the leading industrial countries, such as computers, electronic components and telecommunications, has already resulted in a drastic fall in *costs* and a counter-inflationary trend in prices in these sectors as well as vastly improved technical performance. This combination is relatively rare in the history of technology and it means that this new paradigm satisfies all the requirements for a Schumpeterian revolution in the economy. Our research showed that this technological revolution is now affecting, although very unevenly, all other sectors, because of its actual or potential economic and technical advantages. In considering this technological revolution, we must take into account not only particular products or processes, but the changes in organization and structure of both firms and industries, which accompany the introduction of IT. Several commentators, in emphasizing the deep-going transformation which is involved in large firms (such as General Motors), have described the changes as a 'Cultural Revolution'. In addition to these fundamental changes in management structure of large firms, and in their procedures and attitudes, there are many other parallel effects of the spread of IT through the economy: the capability which it confers for more rapid changes in product and process design; the much closer integration of design, production and procurement functions within the firm; the reduced significance of economies of scale based on dedicated capital-intensive mass production techniques; the reduction in numbers and weight of mechanical components in many products; the much more integrated networks of component suppliers and assemblers of final products and the related capital-saving potential; the growth of new 'producer services' to supply manufacturing firms with the new software, design, technical information, and consultancy which they increasingly require; and the extremely rapid growth of many small new innovative enterprises to supply these services and new types of hardware and components.

Thus, changes of techno-econonic paradigm are based on combinations of radical product, process and organizational innovations. They occur relatively seldom (perhaps twice in a century) but when they do occur they necessitate changes in the institutional and social framework, as well as in most enterprises if their potential is to be fully exploited. They give rise to major changes in the organizational structure of firms, the skill mix and the management style of industry.

The overwhelming importance of such technological transformations is that, *if* the problems of institutional adaptation and structural change can be overcome, they offer tremendous scope for new employment-generating investment as well as labour-saving productivity gains. These opportunities arise both in the provision of new and improved consumer goods and services and in the provision of a new range of capital equipment for all sectors of the economy.

Characteristically, they facilitate savings in all factors of production, although initially their effects may be concentrated on one or other factor.

Perez (1983) has suggested that big boom periods of expansion occur when there is a 'good match' between a new techno-economic 'paradigm' or 'style' and the socio-institutional climate. Depressions, in her view, represent periods of mis-match between the emerging new paradigms (already quite well advanced during a previous long wave of expansion) and the institutional framework. The widespread generalization of the new paradigms, not only in the 'leading' branches of the upswing but also in many other branches of the economy, is possible only after a period of change and adaptation of many social institutions to the requirements of the new technology. Whereas technological change is often very rapid, there is usually a great deal of inertia in social institutions, buttressed by the political power of established interest groups, as well as by slow response times of many individuals and groups. The structural crisis of the 1980s is in this perspective a prolonged period of social adaptation to this new paradigm. This approach is reminiscent of Marx's theory of tension between the 'productive forces' which have a certain degree of autonomy based on technical change and 'production relations' which tend to reinforce and preserve existing social arrangements.

Each successive structural crisis raises problems of institutional adaptation, but Perez is not suggesting that 'socialism' is the only possible outcome. On the contrary, socialist economies are also confronted with the need for profound institutional changes as well as the capitalist societies.

She insists that there is scope for a variety of alternative social and political solutions, which might offer a 'good match', and sees the present period as one of social and political 'search' for satisfactory solutions. The outcome will depend on the lucidity, strength and bargaining force of the conflicting social groups involved. However, all the potential 'solutions' would be based on the widespread use of information technology throughout the economic system. This assumption seems realistic in the light of the current world-wide diffusion of the new technology, as well as in terms of the general experience of international diffusion of technology over the past two centuries. This experience suggests that the competitive pressures in the world economy are so strong that it is very hard to be 'non-conformist' once a paradigm has crystallized. Technological choices become increasingly constrained, even though an element of social and political choice remains. Even socialist countries, which have attempted initially to opt out of a pattern of technology characteristic of the capitalist countries, have after a decade or so generally been obliged to fall in with the world-wide trend, with relatively minor differences. This was the case with the USSR after intense controversy in the 1920s, which adopted Fordist assembly line technology and even Taylorism in an effort to overhaul the capitalist countries. It is apparently now also the case with China, which after a rather more determined attempt to develop and diffuse alternative technological systems, is now falling into line with the general trend of world technology.

Note

1 The author gratefully acknowledges support from the ESRC for two research projects which are discussed in the text. The paper draws on some earlier publications reporting the results of these projects (see References).

References

Bernal, J.D. (1928) *The World, the Flesh and the Devil*, London: Cape.

Bernal, J.D. (1953) *Science and Industry in the Nineteenth Century*, London: Routledge and Kegan Paul.

Dosi, G. (1983) 'Technological Paradigms and Technological Trajectories: the Determinants and Direction of Technical Change', in C. Freeman (ed.) (1984) *Long Waves in the World Economy*, 2nd edition, London: Frances Pinter.

Dosi, G. (1985) 'The micro-economic sources and effects of innovation', paper, CNR Conference, Rome (mimeo), Science Policy Research Unit, University of Sussex.

Elster, J. (1983) *Explaining Technical Change*, Cambridge: Cambridge University Press.

Freeman, C. (1984) 'Prometheus Unbound', *Futures*, October 1984, pp. 494-507.

Freeman, C., Clark, J. and Soete, L.L.G. (1982) *Unemployment and Technical Innovation: A Study of Long Waves in Economic Development*, London: Frances Pinter.

Freeman, C. and Soete, L.L.G. (eds) (1986) *Technical Change and Full Employment*, Oxford: Blackwell.

Hessen, B. (1931) 'The social and economic roots of Newton's Principia', in N. Bukharin (ed.) *Science at the Crossroads*, revised edition, London: Frank Cass.

Hollander, A. G. (1965) *The Sources of Increased Efficiency: A Study of Du Pont Rayon Plants*. Cambridge, Mass.: MIT Press.

Katz, B.G. and Phillips, A. (1981) 'Government, technological opportunities and the emergence of the computer industry' (mimeo Kiel Conference).

Keirstead, B.G. (1948) *The Theory of Economic Change*, Toronto: Macmillan.

Kuhn, T. (1962) *The Structure of Scientific Revolutions*, Chicago and London: Chicago University Press.

Lilley, S. (1970) 'Technological progress and the industrial revolution 1700-1914' in C.M. Cipolla (ed.) (1973) *The Industrial Revolution*, London: Fontana.

Mensch, G. (1975) *Das Technologische Patt*, Frankfurt: Umschau.

Mowery, D. and Rosenberg, N. (1979) 'The influence of market demand upon innovation', *Research Policy*, Vol.8 No.2, pp. 102-53.

Nelson, R.R. and Winter, S.G. (1982) *An Evolutionary Theory of Economic Change*, Cambridge, Mass. and London: Harvard University Press.

Perez, C. (1983) 'Structural Change and the Assimilation of New Technologies in the Economic and Social System', *Futures*, October 1983, pp. 357-75.

Perez, C. (1985) 'Micro-electronics, Long Waves and World Structural Change: New Perspectives in Developing Countries', *World Development*.

Price, D. (1963) *Little Science, Big Science*, New York: Columbia University Press.

Rosenberg, N. (1976) *Perspectives on Technology*, Cambridge: Cambridge University Press.

Salter, W. (1960) *Productivity and Technical Change*, Cambridge: Cambridge University Press.

Schmookler, J. (1966) *Inventions and Economic Growth*, Cambridge, Mass.: Harvard University Press.

Soete, L. (ed.) (1985) *Technological Trends and Employment: Volume 3, Electronics and Communications*, Aldershot: Gower Press. (See also Volumes 1, 2, 4 and 5 in the same series.)

Townsend, J. F. (1976) *Innovation in Coal-Mining Machinery: 'The Anderton Shearer Loader' – the role of the NCB and supply industry in its development*, SPRU Occasional Paper No. 3, University of Sussex.

Walsh, V. (1984) 'Invention and Innovation in the Chemical Industry: Demand-Pull or Discovery Push?', *Research Policy*, Vol.13, No.6, pp. 211-41.

2

Electronics Takes Command

Ithiel de Sola Pool

Once upon a time companies that published newspapers, magazines, and books did very little else; their involvement with other media was slight. They reviewed plays and movies, they utilized telephones and telegraphs, they reported on the electrical industry, but before about 1920 they had limited business ties with any of those industries. This situation is changing, and with implications adverse to freedom.

A process called the 'convergence of modes' is blurring the lines between media, even between point-to-point communications, such as the post, telephone, and telegraph, and mass communications, such as the press, radio, and television. A single physical means – be it wires, cables, or airwaves – may carry services that in the past were provided in separate ways. Conversely, a service that was provided in the past by any one medium – be it broadcasting, the press, or telephony – can now be provided in several different physical ways. So the one-to-one relationship that used to exist between a medium and its use is eroding. That is what is meant by the convergence of modes.

The telephone network, which was once used almost entirely for person-to-person conversation, now transmits data among computers, distributes printed matter via facsimile machines, and carries sports and weather bulletins on recorded messages. A news story that used to be distributed through newsprint and in no other way nowadays may also be broadcast on television or radio, put out on a telecommunication line for printing by a teletype or for display on the screen of a cathode ray tube (CRT), and placed in an electronic morgue for later retrieval.

Technology-driven convergence of modes is reinforced by the economic process of cross-ownership. The growth of conglomerates which participate in many businesses at once means that newspapers, magazine publishers, and book publishers increasingly own or are owned by companies that also operate in other fields. Both convergence and cross-ownership blur the boundaries which once existed between companies publishing in the print domain that is protected by the First Amendment and companies involved in businesses that are regulated by government. Today, the same company may find itself operating in both fields. The dikes that in the past held government back from exerting control on the print media are thus broken down.

1 The electronic revolution

The force behind the convergence of modes is an electronic revolution as profound as that of printing. For untold millennia humans, unlike any other animal, could talk. Then for four thousand years or so their uniqueness was not only that they could move air to express themselves to those immediately around them, but also that they could embody speech in writing, to be preserved over time and transported over space.[1] With Gutenberg a third era began, in which written texts could be disseminated in multiple copies. In the last stage of that era phonographs and photographs made it possible to circulate sound and pictures, as well as text, in multiple copies. Now a fourth era has been ushered in by an innovation of at least as much historical significance as the mass production of print and other media. Pulses of electromagnetic energy embody and convey messages that up to now have been sent by sound, pictures, and text. All media are becoming electronic.

The word 'electronic' implies more than electrical. The dictionary tells us that electronics is the science of the behavior of electrons in gases, vacuums, or semiconductors. Long before the vacuum tube was invented, telegraph and telephone messages flowed over electrical wires, but the flow was not subject to much control. Except for noise and attenuation, the current that went in was the current that came out. From Lee de Forest's vacuum tube of 1906, through computers, to today's computers on a chip, progress in electronics has allowed manipulations such as storing, amplifying, and transforming electrical signals. In today's electronic communication, the electrical pulses are stored in computer memories as arrays of on-off switches, which are usually represented in verbal explanations as zeros or ones and called bits. Transmission from sender to receiver also flows in such digital codes. To say that all media are becoming electronic does not deny that paper and ink or film may also continue to be used and may even be sometimes physically carried. What it does mean is that in every medium – be it electrical, like the telephone and broadcasting, or historically nonelectrical, like printing – both the manipulation of symbols in computers and the transmission of those symbols electrically are being used at crucial stages in the process of production and distribution.

Each revolutionary technology – writing, printing, and electricity – was clumsy and limited in its early stages. Writing on cuneiform tablets could not compete with alphabetic writing on paper, nor could Gutenberg's press compete with a rotary one. The seeds of the electronic revolution lay in the late eighteenth century when scientists found that electric currents could travel far. One of the first uses of this phenomenon that occurred to them was for signaling. A variety of telegraphs was invented. In 1774 in Geneva, George-Louis Le Sage strung a circuit for each letter between two rooms, in one of which a switch could be opened or closed on each circuit, thus agitating in the other room a pith ball labeled with a letter. By watching the sequence of jiggling balls, the receiver could read an alphabetic message. In 1807-1808, Samuel T. von Soemmering built a similar device in Munich with water jars instead of pith balls. Whenever a circuit was closed in one room, electrolysis started in one of the letter-labeled jars in the other room, causing bubbles to rise.[2]

To Samuel Morse goes credit not for having the telegraphic idea, which was widespread, but for launching in 1844 an economic form of telegraph which actually caught on. His competitors, Royal E. House and David Hughes, like Le Sage, had made alphabetic systems that would mechanically reproduce each letter; but with the technology of the day, such equipment was clumsy and prone to break down. Morse adopted a simple key to make and break a circuit, producing dots and dashes of sound depending on the operator's timing. The rugged device required highly trained operators, but labor in his day was cheap. What would be the wrong solution for today was the right solution for then.

Even with Morse's simple device, early telegraphy was expensive. One message at a time traveled over hundreds of miles of electrical wires strung on poles across the countryside. At a high cost per word, only the most valuable messages were telegraphed, and they were transmitted in the most cryptic form possible. Code was used to abbreviate common phrases into words. In newspapers the front page often had a short column of telegraph 'bulletins', each about an inch long. Lengthier analytic coverage waited for stories sent by the more economical mails. The practical uses for telegraphy in its early form were therefore limited.

The cost of telegraphy could be cut if several messages could be sent at once at different tones over the same wire. This was called a multiple telegraph. Venture capitalists funded Alexander Graham Bell to invent such a device. In the process he developed the telephone, using varied tones to do more than carry a few simultaneous telegraph signals.

The early telephone, too, was a crude and limited device. To keep costs down, a fidelity level was accepted well below that at which music could be enjoyed or the phone used for entertainment. The system was optimized for its single most marketable use, conversation.

Broadcasting became economically possible only half a century later. Music and entertainment of tolerable quality were delivered at costs people could afford by using the free airwaves instead of expensive wires and switches. Such open broadcasting was not adapted to private person-to-person communication, and even communication for small audiences was impracticable for early radio and television. A few stations were all that the system then allowed, and these were allocated to uses of high priority. Such uses included point-to-point communication for ships at sea or for the armed forces. For the general public in a democratic country another high priority was broadcasting for mass audiences.

The technological constraints on electronic communication are now becoming less confining. Alternative transmission systems such as the telephone network, cable systems, and microwaves can all be used in a great variety of ways. They can be used at low cost with low fidelity if that is sufficient to the need, or at higher cost for higher fidelity. They can be used point-to-point or broadcast. They can be encrypted for privacy or transmitted in the clear. The design of communications systems today need not follow a cookbook recipe for each purpose to be served but is more a matter of optimizing among the several alternatives for which a multipurpose system may be used in a mix of markets. Rarely will the optimum arrangement be a wholly separate system for each purpose. More often, different uses and groups of users will share many of the same facilities.

For the first three-quarters of the twentieth century the major means of communications were neatly partitioned from each other, both by technology and by use. Phones were used for conversation, print for mass distribution of text, movies for dramatic entertainment, television for entertainment too, radio for news and music and phonograph records for music. No law of nature said that it had to be that way. Other approaches were proposed and tried. For a quarter of a century from 1893 phones carried music and news bulletins to homes in Budapest, Hungary. Thomas Edison thought that the main use for the phonograph he had invented would be for mailing records as letters. Drums and bugles have been used not just for music but to send messages to distant auditors. But there were good reasons for the success of one device for one use and another device for another use. Cost, hability, and the existence of better alternatives all determined what a device would be used for.

The fact that different technologies were consecrated to different uses protected media enterprises from competition from firms using other technologies. Newspaper publishers did not worry about the growth of phonograph records; each kept to its own turf. The separation of modes was never complete, but it created significant moats.

Now the picture is changing. Many of the neat separations between different media no longer hold. IBM and AT&T, which once thought themselves giants of different industries, now compete. Each can provide customers with the means for sending, storing, organizing, and manipulating messages in text or voice. Cable television systems no longer just distribute broadcast programs but also transmit data among business offices and sell alarm services, movies, news, and educational courses. Enterprises that in the past saw themselves as in quite different businesses now find themselves in competition.

The explanation for the current convergence between historically separated modes of communication lies in the hability of digital electronics. Conversation, theater, news, and text are all increasingly delivered electronically. Electronic methods have proved superior not just for exotic new uses but also for communications that in the past were done by the physical impact of ink on paper. Sound and images can be sampled and transmitted as digital pulses. Using computer logic on such arrays of bits, large complicated patterns representing text, voice, or pictures can be manipulated by computer with far more flexibility than was possible with paper or earlier electrical but analog records. Such digital records can be preserved in electronic memories, converted in format, and transmitted instantaneously to remote destinations. Thus all sorts of communications processes that in the past were handled in unique and cumbersome nonelectronic ways may now be mimicked in digital code. All sorts of communications can therefore be carried on the same electronic network.

Depending on circumstances, either intensification of competition or monopoly among carriers may follow from this fact. With the fences down, battles are fought for what were once separate turfs. Whether an enlarged monopoly emerges or competition remains the norm is determined partly by policy, but also very largely by the characteristics of the technology. The emerging technology is likely to foster only a few small islands of monopoly, since many alternatives exist for the delivery of every service.

There is nothing new about attempts to use communications technologies for a variety of purposes. The savings in doing so are obvious. The problems were technical, and it is these problems that digital electronics is overcoming. It is thereby bridging three main technical separations that existed between established industries – between the telegraph and telephone, between the telephone and radio, and between print and electrical delivery. Through these mergers electronic technology is bringing all modes of communications into one grand system.[...]

2   Convergence of print and electronics

In the past, a broad moat separated the print media from the electrical ones. These two technologies did things differently enough to limit competition between them, though to a degree they competed in news, fiction, and pictures, The competition and convergence of electrical media with print began with telegraphy, continued with broadcasting, and today is most striking with data or computer networks.

From the infancy of radio, newspapers wondered how broadcasting would affect them.[...] It was easy to speculate that this new and easy way of keeping informed might kill or at least injure newspapers. An alternative hypothesis held that a short newscast would stimulate interest and lead listeners to read newspapers more. Research demonstrated that the second proposition was closer to the truth.[3] There are some people in the world who are interested in news and others who are not. Most of the people who listened to newscasts, as well as those who read the newspapers, were the ones who were interested. Radio and the printed page were not substitutes for each other but opportunities for the news-hungry, who used them both. And insofar as following news built a habit, the media supported each other. The same sort of relationship existed between radio sports and attending games, records and attending concerts, radio drama and taking related books out of the library. Indeed, it became somewhat of a cliché among communication researchers to say that different media did not displace but reinforced each other.

Then came television. The motion picture industry, though it survived, was fundamentally transformed. Attendance plummeted. And when a football game was shown on the air, the stands were often empty. Clearly the relationship among media is more complicated than always giving mutual support or always displacing one another. The question now is which pattern applies to newspapers, magazines, and books in confrontation with computer information services. Is the relationship one of reinforcement, like that between newspaper and radio news, or is it one of cataclysmic reconstruction, like that between movies and television?

A major factor determining whether the mechanism of support or displacement predominates is the degree to which the new medium fully serves those needs that its rival medium satisfied. Hearing a radio report of a ball game is a lesser experience than watching it. But watching it on television may be every bit as exciting as being there, perhaps more so. The functions that a medium serves are not just its ostensible ones but also latent ones, frequently unrecognized. A pioneer British study, for example, found television to be a substitute for movies more for young children than for adolescents; for adolescents, going to the movies was a chance to leave home and go out on a date.[4] Nor is the interaction between media encompassed merely by the complementary or substitutive reactions of the audience. For example, in the United States, television combined with rising postal rates killed such general magazines as *Life*, not because people would not consume both, but because both media sought support from the same advertisers, and the advertising pie was not large enough to feed both.

For the past century there has thus been continual ebb and flow among media as changes in price, technology, and character have interacted on one another. The development of photography in the nineteenth century gave magazines a giant boost. Newspapers responded with telephotographs and rotogravure sections. Those sections were then killed by movie newsreels. The newsreel in turn could not survive television. Newspapers used to carry serialized fiction, which in many countries they no longer do because magazines and television outdo them in that function.

But while television beats the print media in some domains, it also sustains the print media. The broadcasting industry has its trade journals. Newspapers run broadcasting schedules, thereby winning readers. *TV Guide* has the biggest weekly circulation of any magazine in the United States, and *Radio Times* and *TV Times* have the largest magazine circulations in England. In the pretelevision era, movie magazines were among the most successful ones.

Media react on each other not only in their rise and decline but also in change of character. In an era in which broadcasters get the news out fastest, newspapers have had to give their readers features and analysis that the broadcasters do not provide.[5] Newspapers now rush less to bring out the news of the minute; they no longer issue extras. But they do much more of what weeklies also do in filling in background and examining the news in depth.

Though there has been both convergence of and competition between electronic and nonelectronic media for some time, now something is new. It appears likely that digital electronic networks may, in the twenty-first century, carry the bulk of what is today delivered as printed paper. The output may still often end up as words on paper, but the paper is likely to be spewed out at a terminal to which the information has flowed electronically. The old totally separated system of print publishing, in which hard copy is produced by the mechanical pressing of ink on paper and the copy is delivered by physical carriage, is being challenged by electronic technologies.

Today, as yesterday, mail is still for the most part carried physically by vehicles and men. Printed publications too are physically moved, sometimes by the post. But such physical portage of text is rapidly giving way to electronic transmission. Already within companies a large part of the message traffic comes off computer terminals. There are few functions for which the classical technology of print remains unconnected to electronic transmission, or will long remain so. The costs at almost every stage of electronic publishing and record keeping are becoming lower than those for hard copy. The time is fast approaching when handling information on paper rather than by computer will be an extra cost alternative done only for taste or convenience.

Not too far in the future hardly anything will be published in print that is not typed on a word processor or typeset by use of a computer. The long and bitter struggle of compositors' unions to protect linotyping is over. Periodicals and publishing houses compose their text on computer terminals and edit it that way too.

The electronic transformation of printing has been most dramatic in newspapers. For a century, news services have sent text to the editorial room electrically, but in the past the electrical representation was lost as fast as hard copy sheets rolled out of the teletypewriter. Now the news service feeds not only a printing terminal but also a computer's memory where the text is retained for editing. On many papers reporters no longer type their stories on paper at all. They type at a cathode ray tube (CRT) and edit right on the screen, leaving the story in the computer for further processing. The editor reviews the stories at his CRT. The formating, headlining, placement, and composition of ads are also done on computer terminals that have been developed specially for the newspaper industry. Ironically, the first paperless offices in the world, if there are any, may be in newspapers.

One result is that the entire newspaper exists in computer readable form before it ever rolls off the presses in print. The computer tape need not be and probably is not thrown away. It has many uses. For one thing, newspapers can now be indexed by programs that search the tape for key words. This is useful in the market for information services. The publisher can sell to a researcher a compilation of all the stories that have dealt with some specified topic. So newspapers can move into the information retrieval business. The first outstanding example was the *New York Times* Information Bank.

Soon everything that gets printed will exist also in computer form, and filing will be more efficient in the electronic than the manual form. With electronic publishing there are also writings that in the Gutenberg sense never get printed at all. Texts entered on one processor can be read on a screen at that or another linked processor without ever being printed. These are only the early steps in the electronic transformation of publishing.

In the coming era, the industries of print and the industries of telecommunication will no longer be kept apart by a fundamental difference in their technologies. The economic and regulatory problems of the electronic media will thus become the problems of the print media too. No longer can electronic communications be viewed as a special circumscribed case of a monopolistic and regulated communications medium which poses no danger to liberty because there still remains a large realm of unlimited freedom of expression in the print media. The issues that concern telecommunications are now becoming issues for all communications as they all become forms of electronic processing and transmission.

3   Cross-ownership

The technological convergence of modes is the major force bringing publishing into the regulated electronic environment. A contributing factor is the development of conglomerates which are in the business of both print and electronic communications. These have been largely separate businesses in most democratic countries, sometimes because of laws and regulations restricting cross-ownership between communication modes. In most countries the electronic media are government monopolies, but the print media are private. The post, telephone, and telegraph are usually in one ministry, though more often than not the 'P' and 'T' parts of the ministry hardly talk to each other. Broadcasting is often a separate government monopoly, and where commercial broadcasting exists, sometimes there may be restrictions on cross-ownership between publishing and broadcasting.

The partitions to the communications industry are more numerous in the United States than elsewhere. An elaborate attempt has been made by the

FCC, the Department of Justice, and the courts to encourage pluralism by partitioning communications. There are half a dozen main partitions that they have tried to preserve against convergent trends in the technology, but with limited success. More often than not, the barriers have not lasted. Technology frequently makes the separations inefficient, and entrepreneurs seek to expand their empires' sectors.

One separation that the American government long tried to maintain was between telegraphy and the competing media of telephony and the mails. Since 1913 the federal government has sought to preserve Western Union against entry of the Bell System into telegraphy. But with the decline of telegraphy and the growing cost of messengers, Western Union has been forced to rely on the postal service and AT&T for its delivery system. Mailgrams, which by 1977 exceeded telegrams in words sent by a factor of five, go by teletype to a post office near their destination for delivery from there by the postal service. Ordinary telegrams are now mostly phoned. The sender of a telegram from Boston to New York dials a Boston phone number but is connected to a clerk in a Western Union office in New Jersey. The clerk transcribes the text and phones it to the New York addressee. The system is an anachronism.

With the arrival of computer data transmission, the advantage of using the phone network for computer traffic became so obvious, and vested interests in computer use so strong, that the government no longer tried to exclude the phone company from that business. The traditional separation was broken. In prospect is an ever larger role of the phone network in text transmission. Today numerous companies compete to provide long-distance service for both voice and text. These include not only AT&T but also Satellite Business Systems, International Telephone and Telegraph, and MCI Communications Corporation. The number continues to grow.

Another separation that the government tried long to maintain was between domestic and international carriers. That border too has now been breached. In 1960 Western Union was compelled to divest itself of Western Union International and was given a monopoly in domestic telegraphy by the FCC; a set of companies called international record carriers – specifically WUI, RCA, ITT, and TRT – were given by the FCC the international cable business to themselves. Both the FCC and Congress have changed their minds about the wisdom of that arrangement, and Congress has changed the law. The Record Carrier Competition Act of 1981 allows Western Union and the international record carriers to compete both domestically and internationally, and they are doing so.

Until the 1980s, AT&T, which did handle both domestic and international voice traffic, was not permitted to use the telephone lines for international data traffic. However, technology in the form of acoustic couplers, which enables users to connect any computer terminal to an ordinary telephone, made that regulation unenforceable. The FCC has abandoned it, so AT&T is now both domestically and internationally in both the voice and data communications business.

A domestic-international division has also been maintained in satellite communications. The United States is committed by treaty to using Intelsat, the international satellite organization, for international satellite transmission. For domestic satellite traffic, however, the FCC has adopted an 'open skies' policy. Within the United States, a competing set of companies have been licensed to provide communication by satellite; these include RCA, Western Union, the American Satellite Corporation, Satellite Business Systems, Hughes, and Comsat General.

Technically, the segregation between international and domestic satellite transmission is artificial. The perimeter of a satellite's beam does not follow national boundaries, and a beam can cover as much as one-third of the earth. There may be political reasons but there are no engineering reasons to bar anyone from using a satellite to communicate anywhere within its beam. So the distinction between domestic and international satellites has not been consistently maintained. For example, Intelsat now provides domestic satellite service for at least seventeen countries. Algeria was the first. Its towns deep in the Sahara had no telephone service to the cities along the Mediterranean shore. By putting a ground station in each of these towns and also near the capital and contracting with Intelsat for circuits, Algeria instantly established communication without the expense of constructing a line of microwave towers through the desert. Conversely, Canada's Anik 1 domestic satellite provides international communication. Canada led the United States by a year in having a domestic communication satellite, during which time some American customers used Anik for communication between points in the United States. They have done so since in periods of transponder shortage on American domestic satellites.

Various proposals are currently being made that would further blur the distinction between domestic and international satellites. Satellite Business Systems, an American specialized common carrier with a satellite of its own, is negotiating with Canada to offer service there too. Indonesia's Palapa satellite is being used also by the Philippines, Malaysia, and Thailand. Regional satellite systems are being proposed for the Middle East, the Andean bloc, East Asia, and other groups of nations. Both the limit to the number of satellites that can be placed on the geostationary orbit under present frequency allocations and the cost of satellites make shared use attractive for small or medium-sized countries. And in the United States the philosophy of deregulation makes the FCC more willing to allow a process whereby domestic and international carriers can go into competition with each other.

Another partition that regulators have tried unsuccessfully to make stick is that between communications and computing. What made that distinction impossible was the evolution in the 1960s of time sharing, in which many different users at scattered locations all use the same computer at once. Such computing systems are also telecommunication systems. Almost every time-sharing system has a mailbox program that allows persons on the system to send messages to each other. Under the Communications Act of 1934, telecommunications carriers have to be licensed by the FCC, but the FCC was neither empowered nor eager to turn the computer industry into a regulated industry or to take upon itself the task of regulating it. The FCC therefore had to find a way to distinguish time-sharing systems from communications networks. In 1971, in Computer Inquiry I, the FCC announced official definitions distinguishing computing from communications. But the distinctions failed. Every digital communication system that stores and forwards messages does things that fall squarely under the definition of computing, and conversely, every time-sharing system with its mailboxes and access from a distance does things that fall squarely under the definition of communications.

So in 1976 the FCC made a second try. In Computer Inquiry II, the dichotomy between computing and communication was dropped. Instead, a distinction was drawn between 'basic' and 'enhanced' communications services, which is also an uncertain distinction. New inquiries have been started to try to draw lines in the borderland between them.

In the meantime, companies in the business of communications and computing are each invading the terrain of the other. IBM is a partner in Satellite Business Systems. Other computer manufacturers, such as Control Data Corporation, have formed data networks to service their customers. Telecommunications companies, particularly those that introduce new digital switches, which are themselves computers, may offer their customers computing services on their facilities. This is the kind of 'enhanced' service that AT&T will increasingly offer now that the 1982 consent decree and Computer Inquiry II have freed it from the 1958 prohibition against engaging in any business but common carrier communications. The divested local operating companies will still be prevented by the new consent decree from marketing the powerful computing capabilities of their digital switches for other computer services, but for how long?

4   Cross-ownership of publishing and broadcasting

Since the 1920s the most lively cross-ownership issue for the press has been its involvement with broadcasting. Radio and television were the media that threatened the press and regarding which it sought to hedge its bets. Now on the horizon is a new set of threats arising from entirely new media. Information retrieval systems, such as the on-line business news services found in brokers' offices or the videotex being experimented with in many parts of the world, are new competition for the press. The publishers are worried. One group of newspapers in Texas recently went to court to stop AT&T from running a videotex experiment. Newspaper publishers have been trying to persuade Congress, and have succeeded in persuading the judge in the Bell System antitrust case, to prohibit AT&T from publishing informative kinds of electronic yellow pages.

The first defensive tactic by the owners of an old medium against competition by a new one is to have the new one prohibited. If this does not work, the next defensive tactic is to buy into the attacker. Newspapers tried to limit radio news. In Great Britain, at the newspapers' behest, the British Broadcasting Corporation (BBC) was forbidden for years to do anything with news except read a short wire-service bulletin: no detail, no drama, no effects, just a drab announcement. But in the United States, where the tactic of prohibition was not available, cross-ownership was tried. Print publishers became media conglomerates. Broadcasters for years tried to stop cable television; now they want to be cablecasters too.

5   Cross-ownership of cablecasting and other media

In cable television, cross-ownership is evolving rapidly. American cable enthusiasts generally wanted to keep that medium out of the hands of broadcasters and phone companies, two competitors with motives to stifle its challenge to their established way of doing things. In 1970 the FCC banned phone companies from owning cable systems in their geographic area of operations and banned television networks from owning cable systems anywhere. In 1971 the FCC also banned television stations from owning cable systems within their reception area. The networks are now fighting those rules, and telephone companies may be expected to fight them in the future. In 1981 the FCC granted CBS a modest exception, allowing it to buy cable systems for up to 90,000 homes for experimentation. In 1982 the FCC issued a notice of proposed rulemaking to eliminate the prohibition on network ownership of cable systems.

A still more important issue about cross-ownership is whether the owner of a physical cable may be the programmer of the system or must be only a common carrier. The consequences of allowing a cable system to be owned by a company from some other medium of communications depend critically on whether cablecasting is a business of carriage only or of content too. On the one hand, the physical cable along the streets is likely to be a monopoly. If the company which has this monopoly also controls the programing, there is reason for concern, and even more so if the company also controls other media. On the other hand, there is no inherent limit on the number of channels of cable programing. One company's having a channel does not prevent another company from having a competing channel. Policy considerations regarding cross-ownership of the physical plant and the channels for use are thus quite different.

In the 1980s the issue of how to organize a mature cable system is likely to be a major national controversy. Cable is now organized as a broadcasting system rather than as a common carrier. Much more money is to be made by selling movies and sports on pay television than by leasing channels for others to program. Cablecasters therefore prefer to see themselves less in the communications engineering business than in the entertainment business. Investors in cable systems are largely companies in mass media rather than in electronics.[...]

While the notion of having the physical cable run by a common carrier is popular among thoughtful observers of cable in the United States, the assumption is widespread that it would be a carrier other than the telephone company. The expectation in Great Britain has been the reverse, though the issue is now being debated. The time will come when broadband digital phone systems can provide the same service as a cable system. When this happens, there will no longer be any need for two feeds into each home, one for voice and one for video. The telephone company will become an obvious carrier for video as well as voice. The issue of cross-ownership restrictions on telephony and cable will then become acute.

When the time comes, whether with optical fibers or with cable, that hundreds of channels of video can reach each home, there will no longer be any justification for banning cross-ownership of individual channels or of programing so long as the number of channels is kept above the number normally in demand for lease at reasonable cost. If a newspaper wishes to improve its service by coupling its print offering with an on-line data base, or with a newsreel, one could only cheer this result. Certainly the preservation of the press, a goal that everyone proclaims, is better served by encouraging the print media to make imaginative use of multimedia opportunities than by enjoining them from doing anything but putting ink on paper in an obsolete conventional way.

The death of American railroads occurred partly because they saw themselves as being in the business of moving trains over steel rails rather than of moving goods by whatever technology was most efficient. Newspapers can face the same sort of fate. Imaginative newspapers today know this and are seeking to be in the information business regardless of the channel. Their health may easily depend on being in the dissemination business via a cable carrier as well as via print on paper, and via other sorts of delivery media too. This is one reason that the issue of whether cable systems have common carrier obligations or are instead monopoly broadcasters or publishers is so important, and will be so fiercely fought between the conflicting information industries in the near future.

6   Implications for a free press

The regulations on cross-ownership of electronic media are striking testimony to the extraordinary pervasiveness of government regulation. Some of the segmentations seem sensible, while others seem absurdly wrong-headed. Some are designed to diversify sources of information in the community, while others serve no purpose but to protect an established vested interest. But useful or not, these requirements are in principle at odds with the First Amendment tradition of no government authority. They would be totally unconstitutional as applied to print. Yet over the electronic media, government has exercised its authority in ponderous detail.

More often than not, however, the bars on cross-ownership have proved ineffective. Despite government attempts to prevent it, cross-ownership reinforces a convergence among modes that is drastically changing the structure and legal status of communications industries. Neither competition among modes nor convergence between them is new; what is new is the scope of the convergence. Today, thanks to science's mastery of the mechanics of transmission of electronic and optical energy, engineers are able to transform and retransform the frequencies and amplitudes of signals at will. They can convert signals between analog and digital mode to utilize the advantages of each; they can convert to whatever frequencies are most convenient. Communications of all kinds, when transformed into digitized form, can not only be transmitted but also stored and modified as desired. Computers can manipulate communications in all media so as to synthesize graphic patterns or voice, to edit text or video tapes, to write abstracts without a human author, to draw inferences, or to find proofs. Thus a broadband digital communication system is likely in the end to become a vehicle not only for data communication but also for other kinds of communication, including voice and pictures, publishing, broadcasting, and mail.

It is misleading to ask where all this will lead, for there is no steady state to which the process of unification and differentiation will lead. The trend as far ahead as anyone can see is toward a convergence among media, with great communications institutions working in many modes at once in interconnected ways. Convergence does not mean ultimate stability, or unity. It operates as a constant force for unification but always in dynamic tension with change. New devices will be invented to serve specialized needs. There will always be specialization, innovation, and attempts to do differently and for some purposes better what a universal telecommunication system does, and there will always also be a return to the universal system because of the extraordinary convenience of universality.

There is no immutable law of growing convergence; the process of change is more complicated than that. Nonetheless, a particular trend of convergence has been set in motion by the development of electronic communication. Before that, a series of institutions existed based on the printing press, namely newspapers, magazines, and books. Over the centuries a legal tradition developed that protected these from government control. Electronic communication has not been equally well protected by its newer tradition. The extension of electronic means to do better and faster what the older modes of communication did with lead, ink, and paper has inadvertent consequences for the sustenance of freedom.[...]

7   Policies for freedom

In all issues of communications policy, the courts and legislatures will have to respond to a new and puzzling technology. The experience of how the American courts have dealt with new nonprint media over the past hundred years is cause for alarm. Forty years ago Zechariah Chafee noted how differently the courts treated the print media from newer ones: 'Newspapers, books, pamphlets, and large meetings were for many centuries the only means of public discussion, so that the need for their protection has long been generally realized. On the other hand, when additional methods for spreading facts and ideas were introduced or greatly improved by modern inventions, writers and judges had not got into the habit of being solicitous about guarding their freedom. And so we have tolerated censorship of the mails, the importation of foreign books, the stage, the motion picture, and the radio.'[6] With the still newer electronic media the problem is compounded. A long series of precedents, each based on the last and treating clumsy new technologies in their early forms as specialized business machines, has led to a scholastic set of distinctions that no longer correspond to reality. As new technologies have acquired the functions of the press, they have not acquired the rights of the press. On print, no special excise taxes may be applied; yet every month people pay a special tax on their telephone bill, which would seem hardly different in principle from the old English taxes on newspapers. On print, the court continues to exercise special vigilance for the preferred position of the First Amendment; but other considerations of regulatory convenience and policy are given a preferred position in the common carrier and electronic domains.

Since the lines between publishing, broadcasting, and the telephone network are now being broken, the question arises as to which of these three models will dominate public policy regarding the new media. There is bound to be debate, with sharp divisions between conflicting interests. Will public interest regulation, such as the FCC applies, begin to extend over the conduct of the print media as they increasingly use regulated electronic means of dissemination? Or will concern for the traditional notion of a free press lead to finding ways to free the broadcast media and carriers from the regulation and content-related requirements under which they now operate?

Electronic media, as they are coming to be, are dispersed in use and abundant in supply. They allow for more knowledge, easier access, and freer speech than were ever enjoyed before. They fit the free practices of print. The characteristics of media shape what is done with them, so one might anticipate that these technologies of freedom will overwhelm all attempts to control them. Technology, however, shapes the structure of the battle, but not every outcome. While the printing press was without doubt the foundation of modern democracy, the response to the flood of publishing that it brought forth has been censorship as often as press freedom. In some times and places the even more capacious new media will open wider the floodgates for discourse, but in other times and places, in fear of that flood, attempts will be made to shut the gates.

The easy access, low cost, and distributed intelligence of modern means of communication are a prime reason for hope. The democratic impulse to regulate evils, as Tocqueville, warned, is ironically a reason for worry. Lack of technical grasp by policy makers and their propensity to solve problems of conflict, privacy, intellectual property, and monopoly by accustomed bureaucratic routines are the main reasons for concern. But as long as the First Amendment stands, backed by courts which take it seriously, the loss of liberty is not foreordained. The commitment of American culture to pluralism and individual rights is reason for optimism, as is the pliancy and profusion of electronic technology.

Notes

1   Innis, Harold A. (1951) *The Bias of Communication*. Toronto: University of Toronto Press.
2   Harlow, Alvin F. (1936) *Old Wires and New Waves*, pp. 40-3. New York: D. Appleton-Century.
3   Lazarsfeld, Paul P. (1940) *Radio and the Printed Page*. New York: Duell, Sloan and Pearce.
4   Himmelweit, Hilda (1958) *TV and the Child*. London: Oxford University Press.
5   The growth of radio news and particularly of shortwave reception compelled the Communist Party of the Soviet Union in 1963 to redefine the respective role of Pravda and radio broadcasters. Until then, all media, including radio newscasters, had had to wait for the Pravda story to learn how to treat a news item. This delay gave foreign broadcasters an edge on up-to-the-minute news. So the instructions were changed, giving radio newscasters the mission of first announcement of news, while Pravda was given the mission of its fuller interpretation (Pool, Ithiel de Sola and Schramm, Wilbur (1974) (eds) *Handbook of Communication*, p. 452. Chicago: Rand McNally.).
6   Chafee, Zechariah (1941) *Free Speech in the United States*, p. 361. Cambridge, Mass.: Harvard University Press.

3

Models of 'Computer Literacy'

Brian V. Street

Attempts to spread the uses of computing beyond specialist areas are currently being referred to as 'computer literacy'. The intention is clearly to draw an analogy with better known forms of literacy and to assert that what has happened there, in terms of mass literacy campaigns and attempts to break elite monopolies of the forms of reading and writing, should also be attempted with relation to computing. It is claimed that the population as a whole should be given access to at least the 'technical' skills involved in basic programming and keyboard familiarity just as, it is assumed, formal education systems now provide access for all to the 'mysteries' of the written word. I would like to argue, however, that the analogy is not as simple as it seems, but rather raises a whole series of problems which have only recently been confronted in relation to literacy in general. Those wishing to spread computing to a wider public – and I would endorse their aims – need to recognize that it is not a simple matter of following the path of school literacies, as though they had forged the tools and solved the problems already. Computer teachers and organizers should not, in fact, expect to find a ready-made model in literacy practice, to which they can hitch their own aims and objectives and then wait for results. Rather, the whole issue of literacy in the conventional sense is currently being rethought and newly theorized in ways which challenge the everyday 'common sense' conceptions of it that I suspect are being assumed when the analogy is applied to computing. I would like to explore some of these recent debates within literacy studies and suggest that they are very relevant to the issues raised here, even though the terminology and assumptions may be unfamiliar to those directly involved in computing. To some extent I will leave it to readers to make many of the links for themselves, since I am not a computer 'buff' and would hesitate to tread too far into the field itself. The question of 'applications', though, seems to me one that requires some dialogue between the two fields of computer studies and literacy studies.

For present purposes I shall use the term 'literacy' as a shorthand for the social practices and conceptions of reading and writing. I have attempted elsewhere to describe some of the theoretical foundations for a description of such practices and conceptions and to challenge assumptions, whether implicit or explicit, that until recently dominated the field of literacy studies.[1] I contend that what the particular practices and concepts of reading and writing are for a given society depends upon the context – that they are already embedded in an ideology and cannot be isolated or treated as 'neutral' or merely 'technical'. What practices are taught and how they are imparted depends upon the nature of the social formation. The skills and concepts that accompany literacy acquisition, in whatever form, do not stem in some automatic way from the inherent qualities of literacy, as some authors would have us believe, but are aspects of a specific ideology. Faith in the power and qualities of literacy is itself socially learnt and is not an adequate tool with which to embark on a description of its practice.

Many representations of literacy, however – and, I suspect, of 'computer literacy' – rest on the assumption that it is a neutral technology that can be detached from specific social contexts. I shall argue that such claims, as well as the literacy practices they purport to describe, in fact derive from specific ideologies which are mostly not made explicit. This failure to analyse the use and consequences of literacy and to theorize just what is the nature of the practice which is assumed to produce these 'uses and consequences', is particularly crucial when we come to consider comparisons of literacy practice across different cultures or across different cultural groups within a given society or nation state. Yet it is precisely such a 'cross-cultural' comparison that is occurring when members of a 'literate' group attempt to spread their practice to others – to 'non-literates' or 'illiterates' as they are referred to in this society, terms which already demonstrate the cultural loading and assumptions that underly statements about literacy. If we take literacy as referring to a set of conceptualizations and beliefs, rather than simply a technical skill, then it becomes clear that the imparting of this to others is a matter of 'culture transfer' rather than simply of 'technology transfer'.[. . .]

In order to clarify the differences between these different approaches to the analysis of literacy, I shall characterize them as the 'ideological' model and the 'autonomous' model of literacy respectively.

I deal first with the 'autonomous' model. This model is often at least partially explicit in the academic literature, though it is more often implicit in that produced as part of practical literacy programmes. The model tends to be based on the 'essay-text' form of literacy and to generalize broadly from what is in fact a narrow, culture-specific literacy practice. The model assumes a single direction in which literacy development can be traced, and associates it with 'progress', 'civilization', individual liberty and social mobility. It attempts to distinguish literacy from schooling. It isolates literacy as an independent variable and then claims to be able to study its consequences. These consequences are classically represented in terms of economic 'take-off' or in terms of 'cognitive' skills. The main outlines of the model occur in similar form across a range of different writers both in the literacy field and, I would hazard a guess, in the field of 'computer literacy'.[. . .]

An influential example of the 'economic' case for literacy, for instance, and one which obviously has close links with assumptions currently being made about the implications of computing for society at large, is the claim by Anderson[2] that a society requires a 40 per cent literacy rate for economic literacy programme outlines. What is not specified is what specific literacy practices and concepts 40 per cent of the population are supposed to acquire. Yet comparative material, some of which Anderson himself provides, demonstrates that such practices and conceptions are very different from one culture to another. The homogenization of such variety, which is implied by the statistical measures and the economic reductionism of these approaches, fails to do justice to the complexity of the many different kinds of literacy practice prevalent in different cultures. It also tends implicitly to privilege and to generalize the writer's own conceptions and practices, as though these were what 'literacy' is.

The theory behind these particular conceptions and practices becomes apparent when we examine the claims made for the 'cognitive' consequences of literacy by many writers in the field. These claims, I argue, often lie beneath the explicit statistical and economic descriptions of literacy that are currently dominant in much of the development literature. The claims are that literacy affects cognitive processes in some of the following ways: it facilitates 'empathy', 'abstract context-free thought', 'rationality', 'critical thought', 'post-operative' thought (in Piaget's usage), 'detachment' and the kinds of logical processes exemplified by syllogisms, formal language, elaborated code, etc. It would be interesting to explore how far similar assumptions are being made about the 'cognitive' consequences of computer literacy.

Against these assumptions I have posed an 'ideological' model of literacy.[1] Those who subscribe to this model concentrate on the specific social practices of reading and writing. They recognize the ideological and therefore culturally embedded nature of such practices. The model stresses the significance of the socialization process in the construction of the meaning of literacy for participants, and is therefore concerned with the general social institutions through which this process takes place and not just the explicit 'educational' ones. It distinguishes claims for the consequences of literacy from its real significance for specific social groups. It treats sceptically claims by Western liberal educators for the 'openness', 'rationality' and 'critical awareness' of what they teach, and investigates the role of such teaching in social control and the hegemony of a ruling class. It concentrates on the overlap and interaction of oral and literate modes rather than stressing a 'great divide'.

The 'ideological' model has the following characteristics:

1 It assumes that the meaning of literacy depends upon the social institutions in which it is embedded.
2 Literacy can only be known to us in forms which already have political and ideological significance and it cannot, therefore, be helpfully separated from that significance and treated as though it were an 'autonomous' thing.
3 The particular practices of reading and writing that are taught in any context depend upon such aspects of social structure as stratification (such as where certain social groups may be taught only to read) and the role of educational institutions (such as in Graff's[3] example from nineteenth century Canada where they function as a form of social control).
4 The processes whereby reading and writing are learned are what construct the meaning of it for particular practitioners.
5 We would probably more appropriately refer to 'literacies' than to any single 'literacy'.
6 Writers who tend towards this model and away from the 'autonomous' model recognize as problematic the relationship between the analysis of any 'autonomous', isolable qualities of literacy and the analysis of the ideological and political nature of literacy practice.

The writers and practitioners I am discussing do not necessarily couch their arguments in the terms I am adopting. Nevertheless, I maintain that the use of the term 'model' to describe their perspectives is helpful since it draws attention to the underlying coherence and relationship of ideas which, on the surface, might appear unconnected and haphazard. No one practitioner necessarily adopts all of the characteristics of any one model, but the use of the concept helps us to see what is entailed by adopting particular positions, to fill in gaps left by untheorized statements about literacy, and to adopt a broader perspective than is apparent in any one writer on literacy. The models serve in a sense as 'ideal types' to help clarify the significant lines of cleavage in the field of literacy studies and to provide a stimulus from which a more explicit theoretical foundation for descriptions of literacy practice and for cross-cultural comparison can be constructed.

The models are not logically equivalent, in that the 'ideological' model actually subsumes the assumptions implicit in what I term the 'autonomous' model. Those who subscribe to the 'autonomous' model are, in fact, being ideological, but in covert and often subconscious ways. They are, in fact, responsible for the polarity by their attempt to abstract supposedly 'neutral', 'technical' aspects of literacy from the cultural and ideological context, as though these could be considered independently and the 'cultural bits' added on later. The 'ideological' model, on the other hand, does not attempt to deny technical skills or cognitive aspects, but rather recognizes that they cannot be handled independently of the cultural whole which gives them meaning. It makes explicit, as far as possible, the specific ideological assumptions being made rather than denying that they exist in this context and thereby simply disguising them.

I use the term 'ideological' to describe this approach, rather than the less contentious or loaded terms 'cultural' or 'sociological', etc. in order to signal quite explicitly that literacy practices are located not only within cultural wholes but also within power structures – the very emphasis on the 'neutrality' and 'autonomy' of literacy by many writers is ideological in the sense of veiling this power dimension. I do not use the term in its old-fashioned Marxist (and current anti-Marxist) sense of 'false consciousness' and simple-minded dogma, but rather in the sense employed within contemporary studies of discourse (e.g. within cultural studies, social anthropology, sociolinguistics, etc.) where ideology is a site of tension between authority and power on the one hand and individual resistance and creativity on the other. This tension operates through the medium of a variety of cultural practices, including particularly language and – I would add – literacy. It could be argued that it has been lack of attention to this complexity of cultural practices and the tensions between them that has led to the well-documented 'failure' of so many literacy campaigns.

At a recent conference on literacy, called precisely to analyse this failure and to suggest new conceptualizations and theories for handling the question that might be applied by Unesco and national agencies in the field of both adult and child education, a speaker suggested that the reason why governments continued to pour so much money and resources into programmes that had such a poor 'success' rate was not that they held overoptimistic assumptions about what literacy could do, which is currently a major argument in the field.[4] Rather, he claimed, it was precisely because governments knew that literacy on its own could not achieve the aims laid out in the 'autonomous' model – economic take-off, social mobility, cognitive improvement, etc. – that they continued to give it such a high profile: it enabled them to avoid the real issues that such aims involve, issues of power and of the political relations between those in authority, with the power to define others and their 'needs', and the various competing groups and cultures in a given society or state. No one can easily stand up and argue that literacy campaigns are not necessary (my own position would be that some programmes are essential but that the way in which they are conducted is the crucial point), and so through their literacy programmes governments can give an appearance of appropriate action and good intentions that would be difficult to challenge, while at the same time maintaining and disguising the real power relations and forms of exploitation that create the problems they claim literacy can solve.

This may be a somewhat cynical view for an English audience socialized into believing that governments are relatively well meaning and even, in matters of education and literacy, 'non-political', but it might help to put into perspective some of the policy decisions currently being made in the areas respectively of technology and education in this country. I am thinking in particular of the increase in resources for technological and computing 'hardware', which is what has helped to make 'computer literacy' a major issue in relation to both schooling and remedial education, and the decline in resources for the 'humanities' and social sciences in those same sectors. Questions about 'computer literacy' and how it can be widely disseminated can, it seems to me, only be confronted meaningfully after prior analysis and scrutiny of the bases of such policy decisions.

These decisions arise out of deeper and often hidden ideological and cultural assumptions and it is to these that I would direct the attention of those concerned with computing and education, rather than to the technical and pedagogic 'problems' it raises. Within this society current debates about the 'spread' of computer literacy to working class groups and ethnic minorities are clearly related to differences of power and ideology between the various groups concerned, rather than to simply their relative 'educability' or cognitive competence. I am arguing, therefore, that it is both intellectually ill-founded and politically naive to attempt to conduct a discussion about 'computer literacy' in terms simply of technology transfer and pedagogic technique.

Notes

1 Street, B.V. (1984) *Literacy in Theory and Practice*. Cambridge: Cambridge University Press.
2 Anderson, C.A. (1966) 'Literacy and schooling on the development threshold: some historical cases', in Anderson, C.A., and Bowman, M. (eds) *Education and Economic Development*. London: Frank Cass.
3 Graff, H.J. (1979) *The Literacy Myth: Literacy and Social Structure in the 19th Century City*. New York: Academic Press.
4 Ahmed, M. (1987) 'Adult literacy in cultural context', in Wagner, D. (ed.) *The Future of Literacy in a Changing World*. Oxford: Pergamon Press.

4

Value Conflicts and Social Choice in Electronic Payment Systems

Rob Kling

1 What issues do electronic funds transfer systems raise?

During the last decade, bankers, other members of the financial community, and computer specialists have been planning payment systems based on electronic impulses rather than cash, credit card chits, and paper cheques and receipts. These Electronic Funds Transfer (EFT) systems[1] promise to cut the cost of paper processing, reduce petty theft, and support convenient add-on services such as automatic payroll deposits (Arthur D. Little, 1975; Cox and Giese, 1972; Federal Reserve Bank of Boston, 1974; National Commission on Electronic Fund Transfers, October 1977). EFT systems include networks for automatically clearing checks while debiting and crediting individual accounts, directly debiting and crediting individual bank accounts from point-of-sale (POS) terminals in retail stores, and providing cash on demand 24 hours a day through automatic tellers.[. . .]

EFT developments raise complex legal, social, and technical issues and a fragmented literature devoted to EFT systems has grown at an enormous pace during the last few years. A few studies investigate a broad range of opportunities and problems that EFT systems may foster (Arthur D. Little, 1975; National Commission on Electronic Fund Transfers, October 1977). However, most of the published articles and proprietary reports address the special interests of financial, business and technical groups that directly benefit from particular EFT arrangements. This pattern is due, in part, to the sheer complexity and variety of issues that EFT systems raise. In addition, most EFT experts owe their intimacy to working with an enterprise which has some stake in a particular form of EFT development. These commitments help create a literature in which analysis and advocacy are subtly intertwined.

Many analysts view EFT systems as 'economic instruments' whose costs and benefits may be assessed adequately in dollars. This article balances the literature on EFT systems by viewing them as both economic and political instruments. As political instruments, EFT systems may exacerbate conflicts of social values, which, because they are relatively intangible, are difficult to assess.

The analytic framework developed in section 2 utilizes idealized value positions to provide criteria for social choices. Some social activities that may be catalyzed by EFT systems, such as regulatory impediments to EFT developments, consumer indifference to EFT-related services, 'credit blackouts', large scale theft, or political surveillance, are substantially more troublesome for parties that hold one value position than for parties that hold another. In fact, certain patterns of EFT development exacerbate major value conflicts in American society.

Section 3 indicates how some criteria for social choice lead many organizations to develop EFT systems. Section 4 analyses several major unresolved social and technical problems in EFT developments – maintaining consumer sovereignty in markets within which EFT-based services are provided, developing reliable systems, and protecting individual privacy.[2] Since the importance of these issues, and the sense one makes of them, depends upon one's values, these analyses are linked to major value positions that underlie discussions of EFT developments. Section 5 addresses two fundamental issues in shaping pro-social policies for EFT developments: how the public can learn about the ramifications of different EFT arrangements and what pace of development is most sensible. The article also points the reader to the rather dispersed literature on EFT systems.

2   Value positions for assessing EFT systems

EFT systems are a technical instrument; a means to some end. Proposals for preferred EFT arrangements often assume that certain social goods should be maximized. Five major value orientations are implicit in the published discussions of EFT systems.

(i)   *Private Enterprise Model.*   The preeminent consideration is profitability of the EFT systems, with the highest social good being the profitability of the firms providing or utilizing the systems. Other social goods such as users' privacy or the need of the government for data are secondary (Rule, 1975).

(ii)   *Statist Model.*   The strength and efficiency of government institutions is the highest goal. Government needs for access to personal data on citizens and needs for mechanisms to enforce obligations to the state always prevail over other considerations (Rule, 1975).

(iii) *Libertarian Model.*   The civil liberties as specified by the US Bill of Rights are to be maximized in any social choice. Other social purposes such as profitability or welfare of the state are to be sacrificed if they conflict with the prerogatives of the individual (Rule, 1975).

(iv)   *Neopopulist Model.*[3]   The practices of public agencies and private enterprises should be easily intelligible to ordinary citizens and be responsive to their needs. Societal institutions should emphasize serving the common man.

(v)   *Systems Model.*   The main goal is that EFT systems be technically well organized, efficient, reliable, and aesthetically pleasing.

In different instances, these positions may support, conflict with, or be independent of each other. Except for the Systems Model, each has a large number of supporters and a long tradition of support within this country. Thus EFT developments which are congruent with these positions might be argued to be in 'the public interest'.

Perceptions of benefits and problems depend upon one's values and commitments. For example, diminishing the cost of cheque processing is congruent with the Private Enterprise position articulated above, but is indifferent to Libertarian and Neopopulist positions. On the other hand, government regulations requiring financial institutions using EFT systems to keep detailed archival records of the transactions processed would be most congruent with a Statist position. These regulations compromise both Libertarian and Private Enterprise positions. This would especially be the case if the records kept at the expense of the businesses using EFT systems are occasionally searched by government agencies wishing to audit the activities of selected persons or groups.[. . .]

3   Incentives for EFT developments

Some analysts identify emerging EFT systems with social progress. For example, Long claims that:

> EFTS is happening because it is a better way. All arguments about the sufficiency of the present paper system are meaningless. Television did not come about because the radio system was overloaded or breaking down, nor did radio or the telephone develop because the mail was about to collapse. Neither were these systems built because the public was crying for their development. They came about simply because they represented a 'better way' of communication. (Long, 1974a, p. 2)

Even if EFT systems can foster some form of social progress, they are costly ('A retreat from the cashless society', 1977; Benton, 1977; National Commission on Electronic Fund Transfers, 1977) and will be developed by organizations with specific incentives. While many EFT systems are to be used by the larger public, they are selected, financed, and developed by financial institutions, retail firms and public agencies which embed them in their own operations. It should not surprise anyone that EFT systems have been designed to provide attractive benefits to those organizations that utilize them directly (Backman, 1976; Clayton, 1972; Cox and Giese, 1972; Federal Reserve Bank of Boston, 1974; Long, 1974a, 1974d; Richardson, 1970). Thus EFT systems have been most forcefully advocated and developed by groups which employ predominantly Private Enterprise or Statist criteria for social choice.[4] The following examples include three that illustrate predominantly Private Enterprise criteria and two that illustrate Statist criteria.

1   In general, savings and loan associations are prohibited by law from providing checking accounts. Direct linkages between POS terminals and banks might afford customers the convenience of checking accounts without violating current laws. Such innovations might enable savings and loan banks to draw customers (and thus deposits) away from commercial banks.

2   Supermarkets and small business suffer large losses from bad checks. Computer-based credit authorization services enable a merchant to diminish his losses.

3   Firms that advertise by mail often define potential customers by certain demographic characteristics (National Commission on Electronic Fund Transfers, October 1977, pp.128-130). Knowledge that a person recently purchased a similar service is a better predictor of the likelihood that he will purchase a given service than is his membership in some demographically defined group. As financial transactions become automated, the pool of potential market data either for internal use by large retail firms or for sale by credit card firms could increase substantially and provide merchants with finer mailing lists.

4   In 1970, the Federal Reserve Board (Fed) processed 7.7 billion checks (Kaufman, 1973) for member banks, and the volume has been growing at 7 per cent each year. But it is barred from passing its costs back to the banks. In addition, banks have been steadily leaving the Federal Reserve System since World War II (Boehne, 1974). The Fed provides special loans and market information in exchange for member banks maintaining relatively high reserve funds on account without interest in the reserve system. If the Fed administered a national EFT system, it could increase the accuracy and timeliness of its data about transactions in the economy. If automated check processing systems could lower the cost of check handling,[5] the Fed could diminish its overheads. Improved information and reduced reserve requirements might entice banks to re-enter the Federal Reserve System and thereby help increase the Fed's effective control over monetary policy (Kaufman, 1973).

5   By the end of 1975, more than 32 million people were receiving Social Security benefits. Automating the transfer of credit to social security recipients could save a large fraction of the costs of preparing and mailing monthly checks. In addition, theft of checks from post boxes would be eliminated.[...]

The little publicly available data on which to assess the claims for cost savings indicates that most EFT systems become cost effective only with very high transaction volumes (Arthur D. Little, 1975; Benton, 1977; National Commission on Electronic Fund Transfers, October 1977). Benton (1977) estimates that a typical check verification system requires 600,000 verifications per month to be economically viable. While over 6,000 automated teller machines are reported in use ('A Retreat from the Cashless Society', 1977), recent surveys of their operating costs indicate that, on the average, they cost between $1.50 and $2.50 per transaction, given current levels of use (Benton, 1977). Ernst estimates that a nationwide automated clearing house network would need between 180 million and one billion transactions per year to be economically viable (Jurgen and Ernst, 1977). The high capital costs of EFT systems and the high volumes of business which they require makes consumer acceptance vital.[6]

Some incentives are more important than others in EFT-using organizations. It is unlikely that individual banks would save a substantial portion of the cost of paper handling with EFT systems (Arthur D. Little, 1975; Benton, 1977). Rather, fear and hope drive many private organizations into developing EFT systems. A firm that develops EFT-related services may gain new customers; one that delays much longer than its competitors may lose out (Long, 1974a).

While Private Enterprise and Statist criteria encourage many organizations to develop specific EFT arrangements, some consumer convenience (a Neopopulist value) may accrue from them. However, no one argues that enhancing Libertarian values are either a major incentive or likely consequence of large-scale EFT developments. Lastly, Systems criteria and consumer convenience, a Neopopulist criterion, may favor more integrated services (for example, fewer cards and terminals).

The relatively few incentives offered by EFT developments for advocates of Libertarian or Neopopulist criteria for EFT developments may be underscored by reversing our analysis. EFT technologies may help solve some of the problems faced by profit-making firms or public agencies in carrying out their activities. But advocates of Neopopulist criteria, who stress institutional and legislative reforms to render large organizations more accountable to the public, are unlikely to view EFT systems as an important strategic instrument. Similarly, Libertarian analysts, who are concerned about minimizing the intrusiveness of organizations into people's private lives, are unlikely to consider EFT technologies to be important means for protecting individual liberties. As we shall see in the next section, some EFT technologies do not threaten these value positions if they are embedded in particular market arrangements or are accompanied by special legal safeguards. But this is far different from saying that EFT technologies provide new means for Libertarian or Neopopulist social reforms.

4   EFT developments and social values

During the last decade, the intellectual climate surrounding EFT developments has altered dramatically. Until the mid-1970s, Private Enterprise, Statist, and Systems criteria dominated the analyses of EFT operations. However, during the last few years, policy analyses of EFT developments have been addressed from a wider variety of perspectives including Neopopulist and Libertarian positions (Kling, 1976a, 1976b; National Commission on Electronic Fund Transfers, October 1977; Privacy Protection Study Commission, 1977; Schuck, 1975; Turoff and Mitroff, 1975; Wessel, 1974). Public policies are developed by political actors in a context of competing values (and interests) (Kling, 1978b). Policy analyses may be informed by 'objective' studies, such as empirical studies of EFT operating costs or studies of the state of the art in computer security. But anticipating the likely effects of future technologies relies upon analogies with similar situations and hypothetical cases. One's values help decide which analyses are most attractive and which features of the technology and social setting should be included in the hypothetical cases. More generally, personal values play a central role in helping a policymaker when there is little empirical data to inform decisions (Kling, 1978b), a situation characteristic of emerging technologies. Of course, some analyses may be particularly biased by ignoring or heavily discounting competing value concerns.

Many policy analyses, regardless of quality, are also political documents which reflect workable compromises among parties who represent conflicting interests and values. This is the best way to view the recent detailed reports of the National Commission on Electronic Fund Transfers (NCEFT) (National Commission on Electronic Fund Transfers, February and October 1977) or the Privacy Protection Study Commission (PPSC, 1977). Both reports address relevant competing values. There are, in addition, explicit conflicts regarding market arrangements and consumer protection in the majority and minority reports of the NCEFT.[. . .]

4.1   Consumer convenience and protection

Firms that offer EFT services, such as automated tellers and POS terminals linked to banks, provide new services that enhance the convenience of consumers and thereby attract new business. Thus viewed, these EFT systems illustrate the pro-social action of free markets. Consumers will vote with their dollars for the better quality services.

Since 1971, the American Bankers Association has commissioned several market studies of people's acceptance of EFT technologies (Arthur D. Little, 1975). Most people appear satisfied with their current payments media (for example, cash, credit cards, checks) and have shown little interest in shifting to real-time payments. Most consumers seem particularly interested in maintaining their float and controlling the size and timing of their payments. Thus they will occasionally opt for preauthorized deposits into their accounts (for example, payrolls) and show little interest in preauthorized debits (for example, telephone or utility bills). Generally, consumers manifest the same kind of economic rationality as do business enterprises: they want to increase the speed with which they receive income, control the speed at which they pay for goods and services, and are unwilling to accept convenience for its own sake without asking what it will cost. Of course, individual levels of control may vary with different EFT technologies. For example, one maintains control over payments with automated tellers and relinquishes control with preauthorized debits which exclude stop-payment mechanisms.

Approximately 20 per cent of American households do not utilize checking accounts (Arthur D. Little, 1975). While many of these people tend to be poorer than account users, some of them simply prefer to transact business on a cash basis. However, certain government initiatives may force many of these people to utilize checking accounts or related banking arrangements. If the major federal agencies that provide monetary payments such as the Veterans Administration, Social Security Administration, and selected welfare agencies rely upon automated check processing systems to reduce their overhead costs, then they can force their clients into holding bank accounts. Such actions would compromise Libertarian values for Statist values.

Difficulties also arise when business conditions do not meet free market assumptions. For example, if the public depends upon a particular set of arrangements which originally offered convenience, consumer exit becomes difficult, and suppliers may raise their prices or lower the quality of service (Eichner, 1976).

Recent credit card practices illustrate the point. During the late sixties, many banks provided charge cards easily. Since the cards offered a convenient service, many people enthusiastically adopted them and there are now over 75 million bank cards in circulation (Privacy Protection Study Commission, 1977, p.57). For certain transactions, such as renting a car, possession of a bank card (or a similar quality card) has become essential. In 1976, the bank card companies began to alter the arrangements for card services by (a) charging a minimum monthly fee, even if the card is unused, and (b) replacing the carbon copy card receipts enclosed with the monthly bill with a simplified listing of transactions. Service charges to the customer have increased. Consumer ease, a Neopopulist value, has been diminished since card customers must expend additional energy to verify their transactions or provide receipts for other purposes.

In consumer protection, as in other market issues, the positions taken by various parties seem to hinge in large part on a prior value commitment. People who trust current market structures or who view the recent history of regulation as inimical to their interest or to a broader public interest, advocate reliance upon current market forces to select the best services. In their view, Neopopulist and Private Enterprise values can be jointly served (Federal Reserve Bank of Boston, 1974). Other analysts view the American economy as becoming increasingly controlled by several hundred large corporations (Blair, 1972) which are usually protected by the regulatory agencies that were charged to balance their institutional interests against legislative mandates and broader public interests (Mintz and Cohen, 1976; Reid, 1976; Wilcox and Shephard, 1975). According to these analysts, reliance upon current market and regulatory arrangements would not further serve the broad public, and they point to the vigor with which specific industries have fought consumer reforms such as truth-in-advertising laws and the Fair Credit Reporting Act. These Neopopulist critiques emphasize the ways in which particular markets differ from the neoclassical model of perfect competition, and they seek various forms of corrective action to recreate those special settings where there is a relative harmony between Neopopulist and Private Enterprise criteria.

4.2   Reliability

In theory, unreliable EFT systems serve no legitimate interest. Individuals and organizations could lose valuable capital and credibility. In addition, the theft of sensitive data could threaten Libertarian values by invading the privacy of data subjects. The Systems position also supports computer systems which can easily be rendered secure from theft and be dependable (Steifel, 1970). However, security measures may compromise the Neopopulist position if increased security requires more complex procedures for ordinary people to verify their identities.

During the last decades we have learned that increasing the scale of a computer system leads to a more than linear increase in the difficulty of maintaining it reliably. While most of the existing EFT prototypes seem relatively reliable, it is hard to extrapolate from their behaviour to systems that are considerably more complex without careful study. Unfortunately, many EFT advocates minimize the problems of large scale theft or system failure when addressing lay audiences (including public officials) who are satisfied with the current payments systems (Clayton, 1976; Cox and Giese,

1972; Federal Reserve Bank of Boston, 1974; Long, 1974a; Simpson, 1976). Reliable systems would be more costly; advertising potential problems would discourage people from adopting EFT services casually: both would impede the acceptance of EFT systems.

4.2.1   THEFT AND SABOTAGE (SECURITY)

Lucrative thefts and embezzlements have been carried out on computer-based systems (Allen, 1975; Parker, 1976; Whiteside, 1978). Many EFT advocates portray the existing paper-based payments system as inefficient (Long, 1974a). It is also relatively secure. The maximum theft is limited by the amounts of cash or securities that are stored in any one place. In the paper-based system, the money is physically distributed over thousands of banks. Some security is built into the current system of decentralized and weakly coupled banks since theft requires physical presence. Perhaps an occasional Brinks robbery will net a million dollars every few years. However, in automated check processing (ACP) systems the maximum theft is only limited by all the funds on account in a particular bank. If an intruder is sufficiently clever to 'enter' via a remote terminal, he could gain access to all the funds in the system!

For a theft to be successful with ACP systems, credits need not exit from the system. A successful thief might simply transfer funds into his account and transform them into services by transacting legitimate business and allowing other businesses to legitimately debit his account in exchange for goods and services. Alternatively, if he wished to leave the country with substantial cash, he might extract it by normal means after surreptitiously siphoning funds into several medium-sized accounts. He might also extract funds through automated tellers.

While strategies for enhancing system security are receiving substantial attention, the task of developing thoroughly secure software systems is immense. In a recent review of system security, Linde noted 26 different generic functional flaws in software systems (Linde, 1975). These range from strategies for authenticating users to the strategies for checking the appropriateness of various parameters that are passed between system modules. In addition, he noted 18 distinct strategies that an interloper could use in attempting to gain illegitimate access to privileged system commands and password files and then to 'free' access to a system. The current situation may be summarized as follows:

1   Most contemporary computer systems are insecure and it is currently impossible to prove that a given computer system is technically secure.
2   The body of techniques for developing technically secure systems is growing rapidly (Hoffman, 1977; Linde, 1975; Peterson and Turn, 1967; Saltzer and Schroeder, 1975; Weissman, 1975). These schemes vary in cost and influence the design of dozens of system features.
3   Any computer system is as secure as its weakest component. Most of the larger computer systems have several features that enhance security, but these may be bypassed by clever intruders who exploit other design weaknesses (Linde, 1975).
4   The strategies for insuring a high level of protection require dozens of features in each system to be appropriately designed. These special

features may only coexist on a few experimental systems and a few systems used within the intelligence community.

5   A heavily protected system is relatively costly and each additional security feature adds to the system overhead (Hoffman, 1977). The former adds to the cost of frequent checking while the latter limits the ease with which certain resources such as data files may be shared.

6   Most security flaws in computer systems are detected after the system is implemented. They are usually found: (a) after a penetration has been discovered, (b) through a systematic and costly security check, (c) by accident.

7   The preceding remarks apply primarily to computer systems with a centralized processor. The state of knowledge about strategies for developing secure networks, such as those required for EFT systems, is even more primitive.

Computer-based systems can be rendered relatively secure through deft design and extensive testing (Linde, 1975). Most security flaws in computer systems are currently found by accident, one bug at a time. However, systems can be shaken down through 'war games' to help understand their flaws and develop countermeasures for successful penetration. In the case of EFT systems, various components may have to be installed in operational settings for some period of time before they are shaken down for technical flaws. During periods of installation or alteration they remain relatively vulnerable.

Secure systems also depend upon complete, well-specified and carefully enforced administrative procedures. Passwords, for example, must not only be restricted to people with 'need to know', but also altered when people change jobs. Physical security of a site to exclude unauthorized persons [without] identification (badges) is inappropriate when they walk through sensitive areas. Procedures such as these, even when sufficient in principle, are often not enforced with thorough and uniform efficiency. Most organizational life continues 'effectively' with some slippage in the efficacy of internal surveillance and control. However, levels of internal surveillance and control that are sufficient for manual record systems or decoupled and simple computer-based services, may not be sufficient to offer adequate protection for larger scale, or highly coupled, EFT systems.

Theft by insiders or by people with inside connections remains a constant problem in the most technically secure system (Parker, 1976; Whiteside, 1978). Given the potential gains, thieves may attempt to extort as well as bribe or co-opt employees of financial institutions who know sensitive details of EFT operations. Since there are over 14,000 commercial banks and 5,000 savings and loan associations (excluding branches) in this country, there would be tens of thousands of potential points of entry and people who might assist such entry. Maintaining the integrity of people who have sensitive knowledge of EFT systems operations and insuring the thorough enforcement of administrative controls may far exceed the technical problems of system security in both magnitude and difficulty.

4.2.2 SYSTEM AVAILABILITY

To the public, computing represents a reliable technology. They are concerned with the problems of inaccurate data or organizational procedures (such as billing errors) rather than with system crashes (Sterling and Laudon,

1976). The closer one gets to the terminals of an online system, the more one lives in the 'up' and 'down' world of computing. The more complex the architecture of a computer system and its associated software, the more likely it is to fail. Small dedicated machines often run without crashing for months, while many large computer centers expect at least a few crashes every week.[7] While many crashes require only minutes to recover from, occasional crashes can keep a system down for hours or days. All this is tolerable when anyone who depends upon the system can let a transaction slip for an hour or two without major cost or inconvenience.

The dynamics of real-time EFT networks deserve special attention. Real-time debiting schemes will probably change the time constant of the current payments system by several orders of magnitude. Tremendous differences can therefore be expected in the characteristic behaviour of the system to inputs or disturbances. It would help to have concrete studies of EFT dynamics to draw strong conclusions. However, hypothetical examples can help illustrate the dynamics that merit attention in simulations or in real systems.[8]

Consider the following examples.

1   A major urban bank developed a small network of automated teller machines in a downtown area. Some people became accustomed to relying upon the system for spare cash when they were entertaining themselves downtown. One night the network crashed, but no notices were posted at the automated tellers. When some people found one machine inoperable, they hailed cabs and began an unsuccessful tour of the automated tellers seeking cash. The next morning the bank received irate calls from several cabbies who had trouble collecting their fares.

2   Under current arrangements, if a bank makes a clerical error, and a customer's account is not properly credited, the person can still conduct his normal business affairs while he and the bank investigate the problem. It might come to his attention via an overdraft notice by mail, and checks he has just written are probably still passing through the chain of payee and banks that normally take several days. While this system is slow, it is relatively tolerant of certain errors. A real-time system is likely to be less tolerant. If a person relies upon a real-time POS network as the medium for doing his business and a data processing or clerical error occurs while he is on a weekend trip, he may suddenly find himself unable to buy gas, food, or pay for his hotel.

3   A large firm with several hundred thousand employees deposits its payroll in employee accounts late on a Friday afternoon. Suppose that due to either a clerical error or program malfunction, these payroll transfers are not properly made and each employee receives only several dollars. During the evening, other institutions may attempt to debit these employee accounts for preauthorized payments such as insurance premiums. In addition, employees may be transacting their regular business and expect their payroll to be available as a credit base. If some of these transactions bounce, and then transactions upon which they are based begin to bounce, we may see 'poor credit' propagate through EFT systems. Such a stream of poor credits may propagate through thousands of accounts before it is noticed. Could such an event, however unlikely, lead to a 'credit black-out'

somewhat analogous to the Northeast power black-out of 1965 and the New York City blackout of 1977?

The first is a real example illustrating equipment failures which are relatively well understood. The other two are hypothetical examples which illustrate special problems with recordkeeping procedures. The effects of equipment failure of recording procedures may be similar – losses of service: but their causes differ. Individual errors and system failures may be rare, but they can be very disruptive. While these particular conditions may not occur, are there other conditions that could precipitate system failures in nationwide real-time EFT systems?

4.3   Privacy of personal transactions

Privacy connotes a complex array of issues: what information shall be collected about a person; how shall a person know about, complete, or correct a record (due process); to whom and under what conditions shall personal records be made available (confidentiality). A common view treats privacy as an elementary social exchange (Westin and Baker, 1972). People that wish a service relinquish certain information so that the provider may make a sound decision.

In a society where most individuals conduct their business with small scale local institutions, few formal records are needed. An individual may have some knowledge of and control over those records that are kept. During the last century, American society has become one in which people transact a large fraction of their business with regional or national organizations. The emergence of new government agencies (for example, Social Security Administration, state motor vehicle agencies) and large regional and nationwide firms has increased the number of occasions that people need relinquish written information about their personal histories and practices.

Many organizations routinely share information about their clients to help improve their own decisions (Privacy Protection Study Commission, 1977; National Commission on Electronic Fund Transfers, October 1977). Credit histories, medical records, and personnel information exemplify the records that circulate, often with the tacit consent or encouragement of the data subject. People applying for a service with one organization often want the provider to know of successful similar transactions completed elsewhere. Since records are costly to routinely collect, store, and transfer, little information is collected frivolously (Westin and Baker, 1972).

While people have been asked to provide more information (Privacy Protection Study Commission, 1977, pp. 6-13) about their personal activities to organizations less subject to local control, they have not gained commensurate legal protection. Regulations restricting the kind of data collected and occasions over which information provided for one purpose may be used for another have not evolved as rapidly as have new recordkeeping practices (Privacy Protection Study Commission, 1977, pp. 10-11; US Dept. HEW, 1973). In fact, most people do not know all the occasions on which their records are shared or the uses to which they are put (Privacy Protection Study Commission, 1977, pp. 12-13).

Libertarian criteria emphasize system designs, organization practices and laws which minimize intrusiveness, maximize fairness, and maximize the control individuals have over the content and confidentiality of their records unless there are major, competing concerns (Privacy Protection Study Commission, 1977, pp. 13-28). Advocates of Statist and Private Enterprise positions emphasize the needs that large organizations have for information, the costs of implementing due process procedures, and of the infrequency of abuse (Rossman, 1976). Recordkeeping practices, surveillance, and control over access will be addressed in the next three sections.

4.3.1 RECORDKEEPING PRACTICES

While there are many EFT technologies which could be used by many kinds of organizations, ACP systems and bank records illustrate the way in which privacy issues generally arise. Any ACP system would record to whom each person writes each check. This information, along with the date of the transaction, a check identifier and the amount of transaction would appear in one's local bank record. Record of each payee is necessary to provide a possible receipt and to enable the check writer to audit his account. All this information is available now, since each bank microfilms every check cashed against one of its account holders. However, the cost of finding out whether a particular individual wrote a check to a particular party or group is prohibitively expensive. The checks are filmed as they are processed and each person's checks are randomly distributed through the thousands of other checks processed by his bank each month. Privacy of transactions is now ensured under all but the most unusual circumstances by the sheer cost and inconvenience of manual search. (Some surveillance is possible: a bank can easily keep track of the checks written by particular individuals as they clear. However, it is extremely expensive to search for records of those checks after they have been returned to the checkwriter.) In the current system, the microfilm records are kept on file for six years. With ACP systems, they would be neatly filed in machine-readable form for six years.

In EFT systems, disclosure of information is the primary privacy issue. This situation contrasts with credit-reporting systems in which the accuracy of information about a person and his right to audit his own file, contest its contents, and control its access are all salient issues (US Department HEW, 1973). In most financial transactions, the first three are the normal rights of any creditor or debtor. A critical issue is designating the owner of the set of data describing an individual's transactions with financial institutions. Recent court rulings have tended to place ownership of records in the hand of the record keeper and to hold that the data subject has no legal interest in them (Privacy Protection Study Commission, 1977, pp. 6-8).

4.3.2 SURVEILLANCE AND ORGANIZATIONAL EFFECTIVENESS

Some of the organizations that would use large scale EFT systems transact business with tens of thousands or even millions of clients. In order to manage their large volume of transactions and clients, they need personally specific information. Also clients will need detailed accounting of their transactions (for example, for what, with whom, when, for how much) to audit their own records. Different kinds of data will be carefully collected by organizations to help carry out socially sanctioned activities. However, the range of information available through integrated large scale EFT systems creates a tremendous social resource.

Rule (1974, pp.269-77; 1975) defines the 'surveillance capacity' of an information system by 'the sheer *amount* of meaningful personal data available on those with whom the system must deal . . . , the effective *centralization* of data resources . . . the *speed* of information flow and decision-making within the system . . . and the *points of contact* between system and clientele'. Any of the major EFT systems increase at least the last three characteristics of surveillance capacity. Institutions which utilize EFT systems may increase their effectiveness by exerting more control over their clients who deviate from their preferred practices. For example, most businesses that use POS terminals linked to a banking network could insure that each customer is able to pay his bill when services are rendered. Currently, credit card verification and check verification cards only attest that a customer is a good credit risk in general, but not that he is creditworthy at the time of a particular transaction. Thus, increases in the speed of information flow may help businesses decrease their losses through poor credit decisions.[. . .]

4.4   Value positions and public interests

The issues here reflect some of the fundamental value conflicts in the debates over preferred EFT arrangements. It may appear simplistic to emphasize the conflicts between Libertarian analysts with Private Enterprise and Statist analysts; one may wonder about the issues and conditions under which Neopopulists would concur with people using Private Enterprise arguments. However, these cleavages consistently recur in debates over preferred EFT arrangements (Dowling, 1976; National Commission on Electronic Fund Transfers, October 1977; Privacy Protection Study Commission, 1977; Rossman, 1976). One does not find consumer advocates insisting that EFT systems be rapidly developed with the same vigor that they sought truth-in-advertising laws or the Freedom of Information Act (Schuck, 1975). Nor do civil libertarians suggest that EFT technologies provide important new means for protecting personal freedom (Privacy Protection Study Commission, 1977).

These conflicts do not mean that Neopopulist and Libertarian values necessarily suffer under all EFT arrangements. Both Libertarian and Neopopulist values are best served when EFT developments meet special criteria and are covered by protective covenants. (However, even Libertarian and Neopopulist criteria suggest different policies for sharing EFT facilities.) Parties using Systems criteria also prefer special EFT technologies – those that are particularly elegant, efficient, and reliable (Backman, 1976; Mazzetti, 1976). Laissez-faire EFT developments are only consistent with certain Private Enterprise and Statist analyses.

Even though the NCEFT has published a rich set of policy recommendations to help foster benign EFT developments, one should not expect a single bundle of policies to provide a complete, coherent, and consistent framework for pro-social EFT developments. Even the NCEFT has hedged in some of its proposals; for example, it has recommended a policy of 'pro-competitive' sharing in which individual cases are to be resolved in the courts.

It is unlikely that a complex, fragmented, and diffuse technology, like EFT systems, will develop through any more coherent decisions than have more focused technologies such as communications satellites (Kinsley, 1976) or television (Bunce, 1976). It is commonly assumed that some combination of market discipline, regulatory oversight, and professional self-control will insure technical and social arrangements that best serve a broad public (Kling, 1978a). However, technologies that are developed in complex and fragmented markets (Kling and Gerson, 1977), support services which are mediated by large organizations, and which serve disorganized publics, do not fit these 'models of accountability' very well (Kling, 1978a). Traditionally, policies for technology development have emphasized multiple goals (for example, employment and technological advance) and reflect major concessions to established interests which support conflicting means, if not ends (Bunce, 1976; Kinsley, 1976). The net effect is that EFT developments will serve some value positions more strongly than others. That makes computer specialists who develop particular EFT systems tacit partisans of the value positions their developments best support (Kling, 1974).

5   EFT developments and social choice

Many new technologies exacerbate conflicts of interests, and conflict alone should not discourage innovation. Groups that can exploit technical innova-tions often fare better than competitive groups which do not. In retrospect, the replacement of blacksmiths by automechanics is simply a 'cost' of switching from horses to cars. Only romantic sentiment would lead us to yearn for the vanishing blacksmith. However, value conflicts are more subtle. It may be easy to say that groups which develop market-supported innova-tions best serve the public interest. But it is harder to assert that public life is improved, say, if legitimate opportunities for freedom of individual expres-sion are sacrificed for administrative efficiency.

Value conflicts may be the unintended long-term byproducts of conflicts fought between more tangible interests. For example, the development of large scale highly integrated EFT systems by private enterprises may threaten Libertarian values. However, the organizations that advocate large-scale EFT systems seem to be more concerned with short-term competition with each other than with weakening Libertarian values. It is fairer to say that their technical strategists are indifferent to competitive values than that they are opposed to competitive values.

The analyses in section 4 indicated how certain EFT developments can easily lead to fundamental conflicts between the five value positions intro-duced earlier. These conflicts cannot easily be resolved by some simple cost/benefit calculus. While a single organization might use a cost analysis to decide how best to exploit the potentials of different EFT systems, public policies to balance competing interests, encourage competitive markets, protect consumers, ensure reliable systems, and protect individual rights to privacy are not easily accommodated by simple quantitative analyses. Some calculations, such as the expected costs of different policies, or the number of people or transactions to be influenced, may inform policy decisions. How-ever, there is simply no overall calculus into which such values can be substituted that would mechanically choose 'optimal' policies. When calculi, such as cost/benefit analyses, are proposed, they are often based upon tacit social and philosophical assumptions which render them ethically 'incomplete' (Goodpaster and Sayre, 1977).

Nevertheless, public policies to shape EFT developments are likely to be more sensible if the public learns to understand the social dynamics of EFT arrangements. Public policies are more likely to be effective if EFT developments move at such a pace that they do not rapidly antiquate new administrative or legal arrangements. We now turn to these two issues, learning and the pace of development.

5.1 Learning

Many of the policy questions raised by EFT might be better answered with greater information about the opportunities provided and problems raised by alternative EFT technologies and arrangements. But it is not clear how the public will learn about preferential EFT arrangements before some systems are developed on such a large scale that they are too costly to revise (Kling, 1976a; 1976b). It is tempting to propose experimental systems to be studies. In fact, there are now several [. . .] small-scale 'experiments' such as those initiated by the savings and loans associations which have placed terminals in supermarkets (Long, 1974b). While these efforts might produce helpful data about system reliability and consumer-business relations, their results are now treated as proprietary.

It may also be difficult to extrapolate from small-scale EFT prototypes to larger-scale operations. After all, if one 'experimented' with private automobiles in 1910 by placing 2,500 cars in Los Angeles, would they have helped us understand the long-range problems of roadway congestion and pollution in the city several decades later? Simply building relatively small-scale prototype systems and extrapolating their behavior in some near linear fashion may provide little insight into the dynamics of a society which depends on digital debits and credits.

An alternative to experimentation is to turn to the imperfect methods utilized by 'futures' researchers (Linstone and Simmonds, 1977). One strategy, that of speculative scenarios, has been explored in some EFT studies (Arthur D. Little, 1975). Another promising, but difficult, approach uses explicit social theory and an explicit 'design space' for predicting the likely impacts of alternative (EFT) technologies (Kling, 1978c).

There is compelling evidence from the BART development that when technical choices are made to alter social behavior, without good social theory, poor and irrevocable choices may result (Webber, 1976). Unfortunately, theories to help understand and predict the kinds of social behavior influenced by EFT advances are poorly developed (Kling, 1978c). And tragically, the value of such theory is often disparaged within the technical and business communities.

While these approaches, scenarios, and theories are influenced by the sensitivity, imagination, and biases of the investigator they provide some understanding of the potential impacts of larger scale EFT arrangements. In addition, futures researchers readily acknowledge that complex technical forecasts and technology assessments are value laden (Linstone and Simmonds, 1977). Thus, the value positions identified here should also appear in 'futures' studies of EFT arrangements (Arthur D. Little, 1975; Kling, 1978c).

5.2 Pace of EFT developments

Despite these normative considerations, EFT developments are emerging in an industrial system and under existing legal and regulatory arrangements which encourage large enterprises to expand their operations. Growth is a dominant feature of large enterprises (Eichner, 1976) and both the computer and financial industries are highly concentrated. For expansion-seeking suppliers of computing equipment, EFT systems offer a lucrative new market.

EFT systems offer financial institutions strong potential for increasing their market share. Firms in both industries may gain from large-scale EFT systems which provide many services. Such EFT designs need not evolve through long-term planning. Rather, on the margin, most EFT suppliers, providers, users, and consumers reduce their costs and increase their convenience by incremental integration of the EFT services.

Many American industries (Goodpaster and Sayre, 1977; Lawless, 1977) use a 20 year period for planning and amortizing major investments. While 20 or 30 year intervals are sensible planning periods for financial analysts, they may be too short for serious social analysis. In addition, both private enterprises and legislative bodies utilize much shorter time frames in analyzing policy alternatives (Lawless, 1977). But many major technologies are woven into the fabric of social life over a period of several decades. When the period of foresight is much smaller than the period over which serious social repercussions are felt, the 'tyranny of small decisions' easily leads to an overall arrangement which no one would have sought had the long run designs been initially made explicit. For example, 20 years ago the Los Angeles freeway system promised freedom and convenience. At each choice point, it was 'rational' for developers to create bedroom enclaves and regional shopping centers that paralleled the freeways. Today, Southern Californians are locked into a pattern of transportation and land use which does not meet their needs very well and which is hard to drastically alter. Similarly, current market arrangements and dispersed regulatory responsibilities encourage EFT providers, users, and regulators to continue making attractive incremental choices. As EFT services spread, failing to integrate several related services that are manually linked by different users or consumers may appear oddly 'inefficient'. Thus, the highly integrated and pervasive nature of EFT systems may be less the product of a grand design than the byproduct of many small 'locally rational' decisions. EFT systems are being developed at a rapid pace. As Long notes, 'The fear of being out of the marketplace is one of the strongest in our present day environment' (Long, 1974a). Sometimes, this fear is turned into the claim that EFT systems are 'essential' and 'inevitable', and thus there is little reason to consider, let alone regulate, the pace of development. However, as we have indicated in section 3, there is little evidence to indicate that EFT technologies are 'essential' aside from the competitive pressures felt by businesses in sectors where EFT developments may alter market shares. EFT technologies may provide interesting and convenient services; but interest and convenience are less persuasive criteria.

If EFT technologies are 'inevitable', the public certainly can afford to wait a few more years for them to be developed. More importantly, arguments about inevitability obscure both the mad scramble of financial institutions for preferential market positions behind the scenes and our ability to choose which EFT technologies best serve a broad range of public interests. The fact that many large-scale technical developments seem to emerge without explicit public choice leads some analysts to reify technology and argue that complex technical developments are out of control (Ellul, 1964). Our ability to select and even to reverse large-scale technical developments may provide the most serious refutation of this vision of technological imperialism (Winner, 1977).

In the short run, active EFT development in 1978 undermines the proposals of the NCEFT and PPSC to help resolve some of the value conflicts which are easily exacerbated by EFT developments (National Commission on Electronic Fund Transfers, October 1977; Privacy Protection Study Commission, 1977). Traditionally, legal and regulatory protections lag behind new technological developments, even when potential problems could have been averted easily with early action (Lawless, 1977, p.521). Active development and implementation of major EFT components today simply places our society again in a position of placing our faith in new technologies and hoping for the best (Kling, 1978a). We need to enhance our abilities to purposefully shape EFT systems in a way that deals with the long-term problems that may be faced by many, in addition to the short-term gains accrued by the few.

6   Conclusion

This paper has introduced many complex issues that the public will face as EFT systems become widespread. While they have been addressed in greater detail elsewhere, few have been satisfactorily resolved.

This paper has, in fact, underlined the problematic character of certain 'solutions'. Because large-scale EFT developments raise many complex technical, legal, and social issues, neat answers to the dilemmas examined here are unlikely. And no small list of 'solutions' (for example, technically secure networks, encrypted data, 'correct programming' laws which provide people with legally assertable interests in financial data about them, EFT regulatory agencies) would be sufficient to insure benign EFT developments. Such 'solutions' might improve the ease, convenience, and quality of certain EFT arrangements. But reliance upon them ignores the profound social character of different EFT technologies and their institutional settings.

Acknowledgments

Paul Armer, Russell Dewey, Bernard Galler, C.C. Gotlieb, Lance Hoffman, and Dan McCracken provided helpful comments on an earlier version of the analysis presented here (Kling, 1976a). Robert Ashenhurst, Bruce Gilchrist, James Meehan, James Rule, and the referees provided helpful comments on a more recent version.

Notes

1   EFT systems connote those technologies used to transmit credits, debits or related

business information with computing and/or communications technologies. 'EFT' is often used loosely to denote various computer-based technologies used by banks and businesses to process and store financial transactions and related information.

2   This paper treats only a few major issues catalyzed by EFT developments. Many issues, such as the impacts of EFT systems on the US Postal Service are outside its scope.

3   This position is also close to the spirit of Jeffersonian democracy and the sensibilities of Common Cause, the 'citizen's lobby'.

4   EFT systems have also captured the imaginations of people who judge computer systems by their technical merits (Backman, 1976; Mazzetti, 1976; Walker, 1975).

5   Checks alone were estimated to cost $5 billion to process in 1973.

6   While many organizations publicly announce new EFT developments, withdrawals are more quiet. One exception is the decision of Glendale Federal Savings and Loan to remove a network of 137 POS terminals from 20 supermarkets after two years of development and trial. Apparently, consumers routinely cashed their payroll checks through the terminals, but did not increase their bank deposits sufficiently to allow the bank to turn a profit ('A retreat from the cashless society', 1977).

7   One may also buy reliability with backup equipment such as extra processors, core, and secondary storage: the costs increase accordingly.

8   Before disasters occur, emphasis upon errors seems misplaced. However, studies of computer error indicate that often there are no organizational procedures for correcting errors because the errors in question were never considered possible (Sterling and Laudon, 1976; Wessel, 1974, 97-108).

References

'A retreat from the cashless society' (April 1977), *Business Week*, pp. 80-90.

Allen, B. (July-Aug 1975) 'The embezzler's guide to computer systems', *Harvard Business Rev. 53*, pp. 79-89.

Arthur D. Little Inc. (Jan 1975) 'The consequences of electronic funds transfer – a technology assessment of movement towards a less cash/less check society', Rep. C-76397, Cambridge, Mass.

Backman, F. (1976) 'Are computers ready for the checkless society?'. Proc. AFIPS, NCC. Vol.45 AFIPS Press, Montvale, New Jersey, pp.147-56.

Benton, J. (July-August 1977) 'Electronic funds transfer: pitfalls and pay-offs', *Harvard Business Rev*, pp. 16-19, 28-9, 164-73.

Blair, J.M. (1972) *Economic Concentration: Structure, Behaviour and Public Policy*. New York: Harcourt, Brace Jovanovich.

Boehne, E. (July 21, 1974) 'The Fed's job is getting harder', Financial Sect., *New York Times*.

Bunce, R. (1976) *Television in the Corporate Interest*. New York: Praeger.

Clayton, R.E. (Sept 1972) 'Electronic funds transfer is coming'. *Banking 65*, pp. 42-6.

Cox, E.B. and Giese, P. (Nov-Dec 1972) 'Now it's the "less-check society"'. *Harvard Business Rev.50*, pp. 6-18.

Dowling, R. (Oct 27, 1976) 'Congress urged to enact access curbs before EFT development', *American Banker CXLI*, 209, 1, 24.

Eichner, A. (1976) *The Megacorp and Oligopoly: Micro Foundations of Macro Dynamics*. New York: Cambridge University Press.

Ellul, J. (1964), *The Technological Society*. New York: Knopf.

Federal Reserve Bank of Boston (Oct 1974) 'The economics of a national electronic funds transfer system'. Conf. Ser. No. 13, Boston, Mass.

Goodpaster, K. and Sayre, K. (1977) 'An ethical analysis of power: company decision-making', in *Values in the Electric Power Industry*, Sayre, K. (ed.) U of Notre Dame Press, Notre Dame, Ind.

Hoffman, L. (1977) *Modern Methods for Computer Security and Privacy.* New Jersey: Prentice Hall, Englewood-Cliffs.

Jurgen, D. and Ernst, M. (May 1977) 'Electronic funds transfer: too much, too soon?', *IEEE Spectrum 14*, 5, pp. 51-7.

Kaufman, G. (1973) *Money, the Financial System, and the Economy.* Chicago, Ill.: Rand McNally.

Kinsley, M. (1976) *Outer Space and Inner Sanctums: Government, Business and Satellite Communication.* New York: Wiley.

Kling, R. (Fall 1974) 'Computers and social power', *Computers and Society 5*, 3, pp. 6-11.

Kling, R. (June 1976a) 'Passing the digital buck: unresolved social and technical issues in electronics funds transfer systems', TR87, Inform. and Comptr. Sci. Dept., University of California, Irvine, California.

Kling, R. (Fall 1976b) 'EFTS; social and technical issues', *Computers and Society 7*, 3, pp. 3-10.

Kling, R. (Summer 1978a) 'Six models for the social accountability of computing', *Computers and Society 9*, 1.

Kling, R. (March 1978b) 'Information systems and policymaking: computer technology and organizational arrangements', *Telecommunications Policy* 2, 6, pp. 22-32.

Kling, R. (1978c) 'EFT and the quality of life', Proc. AFIPS, NCC, Vol. 47, AFIPS Press, Montvale, New Jersey, pp. 191-7.

Kling, R. and Gerson, E. (Dec 1977) 'The social dynamics of technical innovation in the computing world', *Symbolic Interaction* 1,1, pp. 132-46.

Lawless, E. (1977), *Technology and Social Shock.* New Brunswick, New Jersey: Rutgers University Press.

Linde, R.R. (1975) 'Operating system penetration', Proc. AFIPS, NCC, Vol. 44, AFIPS Press, Montvale, New Jersey, pp. 361-8.

Linstone, H.A. and Simmonds, W.C. (1977) *Futures Research: New Directions.* Reading, Mass.: Addison-Wesley.

Long, R.H. (Oct 1974a) 'Discussion Paper. Federal Reserve Bank of Boston. The economics of a national electronics funds transfer system'. Conf. Ser. No. 13, Boston, Mass., pp. 32-8.

Long, R.H. (1974b) 'EFT systems, banking, and regulation J: A report by the ACT division of BAI', Bank Administration Inst., Park Ridge, Il.

Mazzetti, J.P. (1976) 'Design considerations for electronic funds transfer switch development', Proc. AFIPS 1976, NCC, Vol. 45, AFIPS Press, Montvale, New Jersey, pp. 139-46.

Mintz, M. and Cohen, J. (1976) *Power Inc.* New York: Viking Press.

National Commission on Electronic Fund Transfers (Feb 1977) 'EFT and the public interest'. Washington D.C.: US Government Printing Office.

National Commission on Electronic Fund Transfers (Oct 1977) 'EFT in the United States: policy recommendations and the public interest'. Washington D.C.: US Government Printing Office.

Parker, D.B. (1976) *Crime by Computer.* New York: Scribners.

Peterson, H.E. and Turn, R. (1967) 'System implications of information privacy', Proc. AFIPS SJCC, Vol. 30, AFIPS Press, Montvale, New Jersey, pp. 291-300.

Privacy Protection Study Commission (July 1977) 'Personal privacy in an information society', Washington D.C.: US Government Printing Office.

Reid, S. (1976) The New Industrial Order: Concentration Regulation and Public Policy. New York: McGraw Hill.

Richardson, D.W. (1970) Electric Money: Evolution of an Electronic Funds Transfer System. Cambridge, Mass.: MIT Press.

Rossman, L.W. (Oct 28, 1976) 'Financial industry sees EFT privacy laws adequate', American Banker CXLI, 210, pp. 1,11.

Rule, J. (1974) Private Lives and Public Surveillance. New York: Schocken Books.

Rule, J. (Oct 1975) 'Value choices in electronic funds transfer policy', Office of Telecommunications Policy, Executive Office of the President, Washington D.C.

Saltzer, J. and Schroeder, M. (Sept 1975) 'The protection of information in computer systems', Proc. IEEE 65, 9 pp.1278-308.

Schuck, P.H. (1975) 'Electronic funds transfer: a technology in search of a market', Maryland Law Review 35, 1, pp. 74-86.

Simpson, R.C. (Winter 1976) 'Money transfer services', Computers and Society 7, 4, pp. 3-9.

Steifel, R.C. (Oct 1970) 'A checkless society or an unchecked society?', Computers and Automation 19, pp. 32-5.

Sterling, T. and Laudon, K. (Dec 1976) 'Humanizing information systems', Datamation, 22, 12, pp. 53-9.

Turoff, M. and Mitroff, I. (1975) 'A case study of technology assessment applied to the "cashless society" concept', Technol. Forecasting Soc., Change 7, pp. 317-25.

US Dept. HEW. (1973) Secretary's advisory committee on automated personal data systems, 'Records computers, and the rights of citizens', Washington D.C.

Walker, G.M. (July 24 1975) 'Electronic funds transfer systems', Electronics, pp. 79-85.

Weissman, C. (1975) 'Secure computer operation with virtual machine partitioning', Proc. AFIPS, NCC, Vol. 44, AFIPS Press, Montvale, New Jersey, pp. 929-34.

Webber, M. (Fall 1976) 'The BART experience – what have we learned?', The Public Interest, Vol. 45, pp. 79-108.

Weizenbaum, J. (1976) Computer Power and Human Reason. San Francisco: Freeman.

Wessel, M. (1974) Freedom's Edge: The Computer Threat to Society. Reading, Mass.: Addison Wesley.

Westin, A. and Baker, M. (1972) Databanks in a Free Society. New York: Quadrangle Books.

Whiteside, T. (1978) Computer Capers. New York: Crowell.

Wilcox, C. and Shephard, W. (1975) Public Policies Towards Business (fifth ed.). Homewood: Richard D. Irwin.

Winner, L. (1977) Autonomous Technology: Technology Out of Control as a Theme in Political Thought. Cambridge, Mass.: MIT Press.

PART II

The Shaping of Information Technology:
Some Actors in the Drama

Introduction to Part II

If IT is of concern, and this book suggests that it matters greatly, probably more than we have yet appreciated, then it matters that we are able to understand and explain what it is, what it does, and how it is developed and applied. This book is committed to the conviction that these questions are inherently and irredeemably social, and that they must be addressed in terms of the theories and concepts of the social sciences. This part of the Reader represents the application of social science to the analysis of the ways in which the design and application of IT is shaped.

It thus follows the first part, but involves a deliberate shift of gear. Here we are concerned not with the grand issues of theory, but with the concrete, complex and highly mediated processes by which particular aspects and applications of IT are developed, selected, and refined.

Four substantive areas are addressed. Necessarily, therefore, others have been left out. 'Actors' covered include firms, management, white collar workers, government, the defence industries. We could not cover every group (for example, engineers, customers, shop floor workers). The accounts are offered not as comprehensive coverage but as a means of identifying the various forms the process of technological selection and use can take. Of particular interest is the complex, incomplete, even contradictory quality of the process of selection and use and control of IT. Frequently in these papers we find intentions producing unintended consequences; we find a variety of relationships replacing the apparent simplicity of the grand theory; we find a choice of strategies rather than simplistic determination.

The expression 'actors' itself pinpoints an element of this complexity. The expression is used here in the sense of *dramatis personae* – the main figures (or some of them) involved in the shaping and selection of IT. The expression is *not* used to imply that these people are in any sense fulfilling the requirements of a societal role or script – creatures of a total social system. These 'actors' are acting freely in the light of what they identify as available options, critical circumstances and key objectives. The precise degree of choice cannot be assumed, but itself constitutes a significant focus of these papers. As Child remarks, apropos managerial strategies with respect to IT: 'in capitalist economies corporate managerial strategies will *necessarily reflect a consciousness of certain general objectives* which are normal conditions for organisational survival'.

But as Smith and Wield point out, such general objectives do not offer or identify clear and unequivocal means for their achievement. The choice of means (and within closer limits the choice of short-term ends and the ways in which these are assessed and measured) is open to choice, is influenced by the state of knowledge and understanding. A significant implication of this is obvious: that those choosing the means of goals achievement may be muddled, confused, mistaken.

If the analysis of the origins of IT itself must take place against the backdrop of the questions Marx asked about the nature and functions of science and technology, then the analysis of the process of selection and use of

IT, and the relationship between this process and the goals it is intended to serve brings us, once again, back to the underlying questions addressed by the sociologist Max Weber in his classification of forms of organizational rationality, and his distinction between the assessment of profit and loss by precise calculation and accounting, and the development of expertise with bureaucratic structures. However, there are a number of problems with these sources of rationality, which Weber himself appreciated: the uncertain relationship between formal accounting and the ultimate objectives of economic activity; the potential mismatch between technical expertise and hierarchical authority, the range of problems analysed in terms of 'dysfunctions of bureaucracy', and the capacity of those with managerial functions to deploy institutional power resources towards sectional interests (Hyman, 1985, p.10). In various forms the papers in this part can be seen to be addressing this question of the rationality of management, government, or other decision-making with respect to IT, and the possible bases of inherent irrationality.

The paper by Monk and Bissell addresses an issue which, as they demonstrate, is more editorialized about than studied. The defence industries have played a crucial role in the development of IT. What is much less clear is *how* military research and development has influenced the civil electronics industry. This paper seeks to classify some of these issues and relationships.

Child's paper analyses the process of management selection and use of IT at work. This requires the use of the concept of management strategy – i.e. an understanding of what managers wish to achieve and of how they seek to achieve it. While these strategies are developed within the context of 'fundamental capitalist objectives', they cannot simply be 'read-off' from these objectives, any more than they can be assured of success. Usefully, this paper relates strategies with respect to IT to management objectives (reduction of costs) and to their consequences for labour force segmentation, skill and status, and to the capacity of organized labour to defend the interests of the workforce. The analysis can be seen to reflect, in its conclusions, the continuing importance of a class analysis: the structural opposition of the interests and strategies of management and labour.

Smith and Wield's paper describes recent applications of IT within banking work and organization. The intriguing aspect of this paper is the argument that the application of IT in this area has 'not markedly increased productivity but has instead generated some new problems in place of those they were intended to solve' (Smith and Wield, p.98). This finding has implications for broader discussions of management strategy, organizational rationality, and management–worker relationships.

Finally, the paper by Melody addresses the nature and role of government policy and their impact on the development of telecommunications and services. As well as demonstrating the complexity and significance of the relationship between State and IT, this paper argues that at a time when the development and application of IT is of increasing national economic importance, the development of policy becomes more important, even during a period of ostensible 'deregulation'. Again here is an area where objectives, strategies and choice are crucial.

Reference

Hyman, R. (1985) 'Managerial strategies in industrial relations and the control of labour', in K. Lilja *et al.* (eds) *Problems in the Redescription of Business Enterprises.* Helsinki School of Economics.

5

Defence and the Electronics Industry: Civil Exploitation of Defence Electronics

John Monk and Chris Bissell

The association between the UK electronics industry and the defence industry is close and long-standing. Developments in one area continue to have a great influence on the other. This close link, together with the recent poor performance of the British electronics industry has led to many calls for better civil exploitation of defence electronics technology. This discussion will look at the background to this recent preoccupation with military 'spin-off' – the term often used for the (positive) influence of one area of technology on another. A detailed and comprehensive analysis of the situation will not be attempted, however; neither have we marshalled the mass of statistics on the subject. Rather, we shall try to identify some of the issues and problems involved, and question some of the assumptions implicit in much of the spin-off debate.

1   Generalities

First, it is not always clear what is meant by 'spin-off'. The most common notion appears to be something along the following lines. Some new discovery is made by staff working on a military project; a civil or commercial application is perceived, and a product eventually results. The advantage, of course, is that Research and Development (R & D) effort in the military field bears fruit in other areas, with benefits for the non-military sector and the country as a whole. This common perception of 'spin-off', however, seems to be very rare, and despite various efforts to encourage the phenomenon over the years, concrete examples are hard to come by. This does not mean, however, that concrete examples are not claimed as spin-off: it is not unusual to hear, for example, that liquid crystals are a 'spin-off' from British military R & D, or that the spin-off from the US military and space programmes of the 1960s was a whole range of products, from Teflon to microprocessors. Closer examination of such claims, however, shows that interaction between military and civilian areas is more complicated than might appear at first sight. Indeed, the question of spin-off can only properly be considered in the complete technological and economic context of military and civil activities; and rather than use the term spin-off, which seems to imply a flow in a single direction (from military research and development to civil exploitation) it is more reasonable to try to identify various areas of interaction between military and civil/commercial sectors.

Some of the most important of these areas are:

Ideas: Fundamental research can be and often is carried out by primarily military organizations. For example, British government laboratories carry out such fundamental research in their role as general 'centres of excellence', and the US Department of Defense funds numerous such projects, a good current example being work on GaAs (Gallium Arsenide) devices. On the other hand, the record of the military in identifying appropriate fundamental areas has not always been good. Also, despite occasional claims to the contrary, the ultimate aim of military R & D must be military technology, not the advancement of knowledge!

Personnel: Excessive demand by military projects for skilled personnel can have a negative effect on the supply of staff for companies in the commercial field. This is certainly behind the concern being voiced by many in the American electronics field about the influence of the SDI ('Star Wars') project on the availability of scientific and technical staff for commercial companies, already in short supply. Certain areas of electronics and information technology already make very heavy demands on the supply of qualified scientists, engineers and technicians, so the problem is particularly acute in these areas. Conversely, the complaint has also been heard from time to time that government laboratories tend to lose highly trained staff to more lucrative employment in the private sector, so the flow of personnel can take place in both directions.

Funding: This is a particularly complex matter. To begin with, the general distribution of R & D funding is necessarily affected by government policies and traditional procedures. The concentration of UK public R & D funding in the electronics and IT fields on military projects has had a great influence on the type of companies benefiting, and on the way such companies organise their own R & D investment. However, the precise 'destination' of such apparently military funding is not always clear, since companies may use such monies to purchase equipment or develop facilities which can be used on a much wider range of projects. Defence spending can therefore affect non-military areas in quite unexpected and unrecorded ways. Furthermore, apparent national policies on R & D funding need close scrutiny, as the way they are formulated or justified is naturally determined as much by doctrinal and political as by technological considerations.

Organisational structures: Excessively close links between suppliers and a single purchaser (the converse of a monopoly, sometimes known as a monopsony) can cause problems. Over-dependence of commercial companies on government contracts can result in R & D, marketing, and management structures which are ill-suited to other types of activity. On the other hand, large government contracts may sometimes impose methods of working which are actually more efficient than those which were formerly used. Involvement with procurement contracts does not necessarily foster inefficiency.

Examples of successful spin-off

The following examples reflect some of the ways in which military R & D *has* been exploited commercially.

1   A company that has become highly successful in systems for manipulating television images developed its first product by combining its experience in military displays with work it had been doing on frame buffers. (Frame buffers are large memories needed to synchronize television pictures from two sources). The military work not only gave them an understanding of the technology and manufacturing requirements of their new product, but, as indicated above, the military environment had insisted upon a satisfactory organization of their production facility. This organization has helped the company cope with rapid expansion, and the production of the many versions of their product which have evolved with the rapid changes in computer technology.

2   A small company in Malvern produces commercial software. Most of this software is produced by part-timers working out of normal office hours. The defence Royal Signals and Radar Establishment (RSRE) is based in Malvern and provides many people conversant with programming languages who are willing to earn extra money. Effectively RSRE is providing the training which is the basis of the small company's technical expertise.

3   It is not uncommon to find small companies established as a result of the personal frustrations of an individual working in a large company. (The silicon valley phenomenon owed much to this sort of cross-fertilization.) For example, a large company may stop development on a low-value product because it cannot justify high overheads. An entrepreneurial individual may then leave the large company to set up a small concern with low overheads to manufacture the specialized low volume product. There are many examples where it is military need which has nurtured such small companies.

At this point, though, it is as well to stop and ask *why* there should be such an emphasis on spin-off from military R & D. After all, why not let the defence industry get on with making the weapons needed to defend the country adequately, and let others get on with basic research or making commercial products? If military and commercial goals coincide, or can be harmonized, then by all means encourage interaction, but otherwise why should spin-off be so important?

Some of the difficulties arise from what we shall term 'doctrine' and how this affects industrial activity. What exactly constitutes 'defending the country adequately' is a moot point, and depends on doctrinal and political decisions. Such decisions in their turn affect the defence industries both directly and indirectly. In the case of the British electronics industry, some of these influences have already been noted. The point we wish to make here is simply that the spin-off issue is not merely a question of technology, but also a matter of dogma and policy. The very nature of much of British electronics has been determined by the sector's historical role in defence technology, a role brought about largely by the perceptions of successive governments of Britain's strategic defence requirements. Such doctrinal and political issues must form part of any debate on the current shortcomings of the British electronics industry: technological matters alone are but a part of the overall problem.

A further problem is the fundamental change in the nature of defence policy and defence spending since the last war, again related to doctrinal assumptions over this period. As a former Deputy Controller of Aircraft at the MoD puts it:

> Defence today seems to be near the culmination of a long sequence of trends which started with the birth of industry and which were foreseen in broad measure by Clausewitz. His vision [was] that war would become more violent under the influence of industrialization, so that it might begin to defeat its own ends . . . . Now in the nuclear age we see Clausewitz come into his own: our weapons are capable of destroying civilisation, making all out war unusable as a deliberate instrument of policy and directing defence planning to war prevention . . .
>
> [I]n the nuclear age there must be almost instant readiness; everything has to be already mobilized, including research and development, even though we are nominally at peace. In all past experience we have relied on mobilisation in war; wars have lasted long enough for the creation of great citizen armies and for hectic expansion of arms production to make good peacetime neglect. Now we have a seemingly endless confrontation in which continuous improvement and replacement takes place in a hothouse climate of technology. (Downey, 1986, p. 10)

[. . .] Downey goes on to highlight the 'hyperinflation' of defence costs which has resulted from this military technology environment, asserting that Britain will soon 'have to choose which to keep – our nuclear deterrent, our army in the Rhine or our role in the Atlantic'.

This quotation is interesting from two major points of view. First, it highlights the way that the technological and what we have called the *doctrinal* aspects of the problem are interrelated. For example, the effects of this defence 'hyperinflation' can only properly be discussed in the context of the doctrinal assumptions being made about Britain's defence role: clearly, a defence policy based on a nuclear strategy and the willingness to fight a high-technology, large-scale, war has quite different implications for defence costs from a policy which specifically eschews a nuclear or world role. Secondly, it is particularly interesting that senior military personnel are now beginning to consider this technological 'hothouse' of military developments to be problematic. For many years after the end of the Second War it was customary to see in high defence spending the driving force of technological advance. Rather than viewing continuous military R & D effort as a disadvantage, many observers attributed America's post-war success to precisely such spending, and similar arguments were (and still are) advanced elsewhere:

> . . . defense spending has been making a substantial contribution to technological developments of great importance to our economy. (Weidenbaum, 1974 quotation from De Grasse, 1983, p. 35)

> . . . our research suggests that [military expenditures] are beneficial in the long term to the civilian economy, since much of the additional spending

promotes domestic production in our most capital and technology intensive sectors. (Brown, 1980 quotation from De Grasse, 1983, p. 77)

Now, on the other hand, there is a growing body of opinion which opposes such an assessment. The reasons for this include:

—the lack of commercial applications for devices developed for military purposes
—the incompatibility of organizational structures in commercial and military projects
—the poor record of innovation in military R & D
—concentration of military effort on fields not relevant to civil development
—the (partially) inevitable secrecy which surrounds military R & D

Certain economists even maintain that there is a significant, negative correlation between defence spending and general economic performance (Smith and Georgiou, 1983). Such purely econometric research does not necessarily point to any specific mechanisms for this effect, and although various explanations have been advanced, most observers would agree on the need for further investigation of this field. Until there are more – and to some extent more convincing – research results available in this extremely complex area it would be prudent to heed a recent American report which, in evaluating the technological benefits of the Apollo programme and the proposed SDI project, concluded:

> It would be hasty to assume a specific government project will either help or hinder private sector technological growth . . . Unless the supporters of a specific project can demonstrate how it will help we should assume that the effect is at best neutral. (Council on Economic Priorities, 1985)

> It is not only the technological spin-off of defence spending which is being called into question. The usefulness of defence expenditure in creating and sustaining employment – again a traditional argument in support of high defence spending – is also being challenged. (De Grasse, 1983; Smith and Smith, 1983; Dunne and Smith, 1984)

2   The Maddock Report

The 1983 Maddock Report examined some of these problems in the specific context of the UK electronics industry. The report is unfortunately couched in rather vague terms (specific companies and projects, for example, are not identified). However, it is worth looking in some detail at this report, which received considerable publicity at the time. Maddock identified four types of companies within the UK electronics industry: Type A companies are research–development–design–production companies which have been concerned almost wholly with defence equipment for many decades (initially war years followed by subsequent expansion). Their whole stance is governed by the requirements of their single dominant customer – the Ministry of Defence (MoD) – and much of their own decision making is subsidiary to that of the MoD. In type B companies the civil and defence work is done side by side in the same design offices, laboratories and workshops, These companies do not feel that the two kinds of activities are so different. The only examples identified during Maddock's study were the specialist software houses that could move with ease between defence and civil work. Type C companies are those which have developed very advanced and unique technologies for application primarily in the civil field and have then undertaken, very successfully, the application of some of this technology into the defence area.

The fourth type of company (D) operates almost wholly in the civil field, developing and marketing a range of relatively unique products, some of which are subsequently sold to the MoD. They felt very strongly that the armed forces should make very much greater use of the standard 'civil' products (Maddock, 1983, pp. 3-6).

Maddock's conclusions for technology transfer were not, at first sight, encouraging:

> It has to be faced that the likelihood of type A companies making a major contribution in the civil areas (other than aerospace) is vanishingly small, and even strong measures by the government are unlikely to have more than marginal effect. Type B companies are more likely to generate civil business but, as already stated, there are very few such companies (or divisions of companies) and their market perception is largely beamed onto large, high complexity, capital projects. Type C companies are far more likely to make effective commercial use of any new technological skills they develop or which are made available to them since the bulk of the enterprise lies in the civil area. Type D companies by definition are aimed at civil markets, but because they exist outside the main defence orbit, they are likely to have only limited access to the frontier technologies or have minimal opportunity to cultivate a new technique which would be of benefit in the civil field but also provide an important defence resource. (Maddock, 1983, pp. 10-11)

Maddock made a number of recommendations, primarily aimed at making defence based technology available to his C and D type companies. These included the establishment of technology brokers to facilitate information exchange and technology transfer; the reintroduction of industrial applications units at government laboratories; the drawing up of directories of funding sources and technology development staff; the launching of an awareness campaign aimed at non-electronics companies which might benefit from new technology; and the creation of local liaison groups between defence laboratories and local industry. Further recommendations were made, encouraging the MoD to use commercially available products where possible, and to attempt to diminish the prevailing 'vertical integration' of the larger companies by making greater use of specialist sub-contractors.

Just as telling – but much less widely quoted – were Maddock's conclusions on general prospects for the British electronics industry:

> The purpose of this study was to examine whether by some changes in practices and attitudes the undoubtedly high defence technology can be used as a device for reversing the decline of the civil electronics industry – an industry which is becoming central to all engineering and service industries. Whilst there are certain actions that can be taken, . . . it would be naive to promise that these would have anything more than a marginal effect. (Maddock, 1983, pp.8-9)

Although outside his strict terms of reference, Maddock offered general proposals for the industry in an appendix, where he called for what would be effectively a national industrial strategy for electronics, using public funds to create market pull in non-defence as well as defence areas.

In its response to the Maddock Report, published as an appendix to the report itself, the MoD accepted many of the problems identified and listed its own recent attempts to remedy matters. The Ministry claimed that commercial items were already being bought wherever possible, and noted that various attempts had been made to encourage spin-off in the recent past. It was also noted, quite rightly, that 'the primary purpose of MoD procurement, which includes R & D, is of course to provide the equipment needed by HM forces to fulfil their NATO and national security roles' (Maddock, 1983, comment by MOD, p. 21).

If such expenditure could also further civil and commercial ends, so much the better, but this could not be seen as a primary aim of defence spending. Furthermore, the most valuable form of spin-off (in purely economic terms) from defence R & D was seen as export sales.

3 Developments since Maddock

The Maddock Report received wide publicity in the financial and technical press, Sir Icuan's remarks on his 'type A' companies being particularly seized upon. Whether as a direct result of the report or not, a number of changes have subsequently taken place in the defence procurement field. Competitive tendering has been introduced, and the number of 'cost plus' contracts (criticized particularly severely by many commentators) has decreased. (A 'cost plus' contract is one in which the customer agrees to pay all costs plus a certain percentage in addition, representing the agreed profit. In contrast, a fixed price contract requires the supplier to build in the profit element and manage costs in line with the agreed quotation.) However, there is little sign yet of any real opening up of the procurement market to smaller subcontractors as recommended in the Report. In fact, many smaller companies involved in defence electronics have been hit particularly hard by level funding and now cuts in the defence budget; often they appear to find it hard to diversify out of the defence field, partly at least because of lack of experience of commercial markets and requirements.

One recent initiative in the area of 'spin-off' has been the establishment of Defence Technology Enterprises, a company whose aim is to commercialize British defence technologies by actively seeking out techniques and developments ripe for commercial exploitation at government research establishments. In this way, it is hoped to promote the flow of information and ideas between commercial and military sectors, perhaps by arranging secondments of Ministry scientists to commercial companies as well as simply by identifying commercial possibilities. Defence Technology Enterprises now (July 1986) has privileged access to four government defence laboratories: the Royal Armament R & D Establishment, the RSRE at Malvern, the Royal Aircraft Establishment (RAE) at Farnborough, and the Admiralty Research Establishment.

While such efforts are indeed likely to further the civil exploitation of defence technology, the most disconcerting problems remain. A growing number of observers are now questioning the appropriateness of high defence R & D expenditure in the UK. For a detailed discussion see Kaldor *et al.* (1986), Gummett *et al.* (1986) and Rudge (1986). In fact, the attribution of Britain's technological failure to this alone seems to be in danger of becoming the new orthodoxy! It is important not to over-simplify matters, however. First, a major redirection of defence R & D resources could only be made in the context of major changes in defence doctrine, as noted before. Secondly, although the distribution of public and private R & D finance is certainly significant, there is little evidence to suggest that technological innovation can be directly encouraged simply by increasing non-military or non-public funding. Unfortunately for the electronics industry, Maddock's proposals concerning the raising of the 'civil technological plateau', and the possibility of harnessing public spending to provide appropriate market pull, seem very far from the present government's economic policies – as indeed does any strategic plan for British electronics.

What, then, can we learn from the complex question of the civil exploitation of defence electronics? There is certainly much to be done to improve the flow of information within British electronics, and between the electronics sector and other areas of industry. The way British electronics has become so closely involved with the defence industry has hindered, rather than encouraged, such information flow in the past. Efforts to remedy this are therefore to be welcomed, but it should be recognised that these alone will not result in any radical improvement in the fortunes of British electronics. Indeed, we would maintain that an overemphasis on the civil exploitation of defence electronics is counterproductive for the following reasons:

1   By looking only at technology transfer it encourages neglect of the overall situation, where the effects of defence spending on the economy, employment, etc. are still not well understood. Consequently relatively unimportant examples of civil exploitation of defence technology are accorded a significance which they do not warrant in the global context.

2   The spin-off debate diverts attention from the need to re-examine fundamental defence doctrine if any proper appreciation is to be gained of the complex relationship between the British electronics industry and defence.

3   It diverts attention from the pressing need for a strategic plan for British electronics and information technology, almost certainly involving much greater international co-operation than has been achieved so far in any of the IT/electronics programmes (Alvey, Esprit, Eureka).

4   Conclusions

Defence expenditure is intended to enhance or maintain the security of a nation and its population. Industry provides goods for consumption and for trade. Some of those goods are intended for military application and some military activities are directed towards defending and possibly extending the industrial base of a country. The industries and defences of a nation are interrelated. The dependence of the military on technology focuses increasingly on electronics even in some of the more unconventional doctrines. The interrelationship between electronics and defence requires, particularly in countries that have a strong commitment to defence and aspirations for their electronics industries, the intertwining of defence and industrial policy if those policies are to be realistic. Advances in electronics and anticipated advances have been crucial to the formulation of defence policies in recent years and the fortunes of the British electronics industry, perhaps more than the electronics industry of any other country, has become more dependent on defence.

There will always be questions about the adequacy of defence expenditure and as part of the justification for more expenditure there will always be attempts to show that defence expenditure offers benefits in addition to those of national security – the spin-off arguments. There may be spin-offs from any activity but that is not the justification for the activity, it is merely a lucky bonus. If the activity consistently yields spin-offs of significant proportions from which other sectors obtain substantial benefit, then it is time to re-examine the methods of the other sectors as it seems that they are failing to find the solutions to their own problems. Spin-off is not a reason for doing the work: it is an accidental benefit or cost.

Initiatives such as the formation of Defence Technology Enterprises (DTE) which is an enterprise to search for applicable technology in military laboratories may be a useful way of finding and exploiting results but it is yet to be proven cheaper than duplicating the work. Of course, measures that avoid the loss of ideas that could be useful are to be welcomed, but these measures have costs associated with them. Seeking out ideas and seeking a commercial user may incur higher costs and may create greater uncertainties than duplicating development work with a clearly specified goal. By not taking steps to encourage spin-off, opportunities are missed – but there is a cost to finding ideas and matching them to industrial needs. Adding enterprises and regulations may raise the cost of military work and may not bring net benefits to civilian industries.

We should be prepared to explore ways of increasing the transfer of technology between all industries but should recognize that achieving transfers does not necessarily reduce costs and that the net spin-off from military work is not necessarily positive.

The ways in which one sector of the economy can affect another are immensely varied and many factors are beyond the reach of the official statistics and many influences take many years to create returns or impose costs. There is little doubt that expenditure in the US on military electronics has stimulated and funded many of the significant developments in electronics in the past few decades. However, civilian industries have also provided ideas, products and investment which have provided benefits to both civilian and military products. The military and civilian industries have provided different sets of objectives and different criteria for cost so that when developments in one sector slowed, the other sector saw opportunities. Development in one sector may be started and be seen to be fully justified whereas if the development were to be started in another sector it might be considered to be wildly speculative. This does not mean that this is the only way in which speculative developments begin but with strong justification it involves less political risk. Electronic technology has benefited particularly because so many of the significant developments were not commercially feasible on a small scale and major defence programmes have offered alternative justification for investment and have raised sales above the level that is critical to launch the industry. Electronics too is an industry in which the learning curve has incessantly reduced costs and where commercial purchases are out of the question early in the life of a technology but become reasonable once the military sector has created sufficient volume of sales to reduce prices.

Rapid development in the US and Japan in electronics has taken place when there were clear and widely agreed national goals; in the US these goals have often been military; in Japan the goals have been expressed firstly as social goals and then translated into business goals. With wide agreement on goals and firm leadership, it becomes acceptable to the shareholder and to the taxpayer and thus to the politician to engage in speculative investment. The Japanese, US and recent West German experience suggest that clear focal points must be created to push an industry ahead and there must be a solid base for accumulating and transmitting knowledge and know-how.

The UK electronics industry is dominated by the design and production of capital goods which includes military equipment. Companies have been encouraged to accept this role because of the availability of Ministry of Defence funds and in earlier years by the oligopoly in the UK telecommunications industry. In capital goods relatively few systems are ever made and the value of each product is relatively high. Businesses based on the sale of low volume, specialised equipment need well qualified staff and continual research and development. It is clear that businesses have become used to receiving considerable support for R & D from government agencies and, of course, depend on government for the education of specialists, and even in the area of continuing education of those in work the British companies have a poor record.

The electronic defence industry is a cost causer but in R & D and in provision of specialist staff it is not the principal cost bearer. These are the signs of an economically inefficient market. When other sectors of the economy require similar specialisms, there becomes a shortfall in skills and all sectors feel the effect. Worse still, the defence market with its lack of price discrimination can lead the scramble for staff by paying higher salaries. Other sectors competing in international markets cannot necessarily justify the extra cost. Once it has been decided that a piece of equipment is vital to national security, then it must be built at whatever cost or the doctrine that led to its choice must be altered.

In the interests of promoting economic efficiency, industry could be asked to pay for training and R & D. These costs would be passed on to the customer, the government, but at least the attribution of costs would be linked to the goods that incur the costs. Although mechanisms like this are not essential the defence electronics industry takes such a disproportionate share of R & D monies and the nation's scarce skills that sensible policy making needs the information that such measures provide.

Cuts in military expenditure may be what is required for the long-term health of the British electronics industry but this demands a change in military commitment and approach to defence. It requires a new defence doctrine. The cost of defence is related to its goals. Manipulating competition in the market between the industry and the military does not obviously offer a lower cost solution but may be the only politically acceptable way of being seen to be tackling the issues. As with spin-off there is merit in exploring alternative methods of supply but it seems that there is no obvious money saving formula.

In Britain, lack of competitive pressure has produced an economically inefficient electronics sector, dominated by defence and capital goods sales. The symptoms are an overconcentration on the technical and scientific issues, poor entrepreneurial management and relatively slow growth.

The economic inefficiency of the whole complex does not mean that the companies are themselves inefficient within the environment in which they operate. The companies cannot be criticized for making the most of the opportunities that their environment offers.

In bringing about change the question must be tackled of whether companies or the marketplaces in which they operate are to be reformed, but in the end this is a matter of tactics.

To bring about change there is an urgent need to set the debate into a broader context which includes at least all of the aspects discussed here. Only in this context can individual companies or national government begin to develop strategic plans for the development of the British information technology industry.

This paper has shown that there are a number of interlinked and largely unanswered issues:

'What kind of defence strategies do we want?'
'How do we ensure our defence needs are met efficiently?' and
'How do we secure a thriving electronics industry?'

The first question needs exploring in the context of the availability of resources. The second leads to several others that are relevant here:

'Can we employ more electronic technology to reduce the overall cost?' or
'How can electronics best serve defence needs?'
'Are there more efficient ways of organizing supplies from industry?'
'Can we improve the efficiency of the companies?'
'Can we share some of the development costs with industry?'

Securing a thriving electronics industry poses the questions in relation to defence:

'How valuable are arms exports?'
'How much could spin-off be increased from the defence sector?'
'What constraints does heavy involvement in defence impose?'

Following up questions on spin-off come the questions:

'What is the possibility of spin-off from military to civilian industries?'
'How do we promote spin-off from military electronics?'
'Is the cost of promoting spin-off worthwhile?'

There is a tendency in attempting to answer these questions to treat them as separate issues and not recognize the complexities in their relationships. A reductionist approach is not necessarily appropriate. After all these issues need to be viewed from technical, commercial, political, military, ethical, economic and social viewpoints. The answers are not obvious.

Acknowledgment

This paper is based on extracts from a chapter in a forthcoming book: Blunden, M. and Greene, O. (eds) *Defence Policy Making: Theory and Practice*. Oxford: Brassey.

References

Council on Economic Priorities (1985) *SDI: Costs Contracts and Consequences*. Report quoted in *Financial Times*, 13 August, 'Star Wars threat to civilian research'.

De Grasse, R. W. (1983) *Military Expansion, Economic Decline*. Armouk, N.Y.: M. E. Sharpe Inc.

Downey, J. (1986) 'Defence and the Westland Affair', *The Listener*, Vol. 115, No. 2945, 30 January.

Dunne, J. P. and Smith, R. P. (1984) 'The economic consequences of reduced UK military expenditure', *Cambridge Journal of Economics*, 8, pp. 297-310.

Gummett, P. *et al*. (1986) *UK Military R&D*. Oxford: Oxford University Press, Council for Science and Society.

Kaldor, M., Sharp, M. and Walker, W. (1986) 'Industrial Competitiveness and Britain's Defence, *Lloyds Bank Review*, No. 162, October, pp. 31-49.

Maddock, I. (1983) *Civil Exploitation of Defence Technology* (The Maddock Report), Electronics EDC, NEDC.

Rudge, A. (1986) 'Research, development and decline: Britain's industrial enigma', *Electronics and Power*, May, pp. 347-52.

Smith, D. and Smith, R. (1983) *The Economics of Militarism*. London: Pluto Press.

Smith, R. and Georgiou, G. (1983) 'Assessing the effect of military expenditure on OECD economies: a survey', *Arms Control 4*, 1, May, pp. 3-15.

6

Managerial Strategies, New Technology and the Labour Process[1]

John Child

Any consideration of managerial policies towards the labour process must today take account of the new technologies based on microelectronics. The level of investment in new technology is substantial and is forecast to grow rapidly. It is already proving to be a vehicle for significant changes in the organization of work, and therefore in the position of workers within the productive process. Four managerially-initiated developments, facilitated by new technology, are directed towards (i) the virtual elimination of direct labour, (ii) the spread of contracting, (iii) the dissolution of traditional job or skill demarcations, and (iv) the degradation of jobs through deskilling. These initiatives affect the ability of workers to control the conduct of their work through an exercise of discretion and skill, and each one has implications for the position of the workers concerned in the labour market.

New technology can play an important role in these changes to the organization and control of the labour process. The rationales applied to investment in new technology are not necessarily focused primarily on the labour process, but the technology does carry with it a potential for change in that process. The introduction of new technology in ways that change the labour process is therefore looked upon as the unfolding of a managerial strategy. This concept is, however, controversial, and its use here must be clarified before proceeding to the main argument.[. . .]

1 New technology

The term 'new technology' is applied to a wide range of equipment utilizing micro-circuitry and associated software. In some applications, microelectronics data handling capacity is combined with modern communications facilities to provide what has become known as 'information technology'. While there is yet little agreement on the definition of these terms, it is possible to give examples of where new technology is being applied to work processes in manufacturing and services; these are listed in Table 6.1.

Figure 6.1 *Representation of the role of managerial strategy*

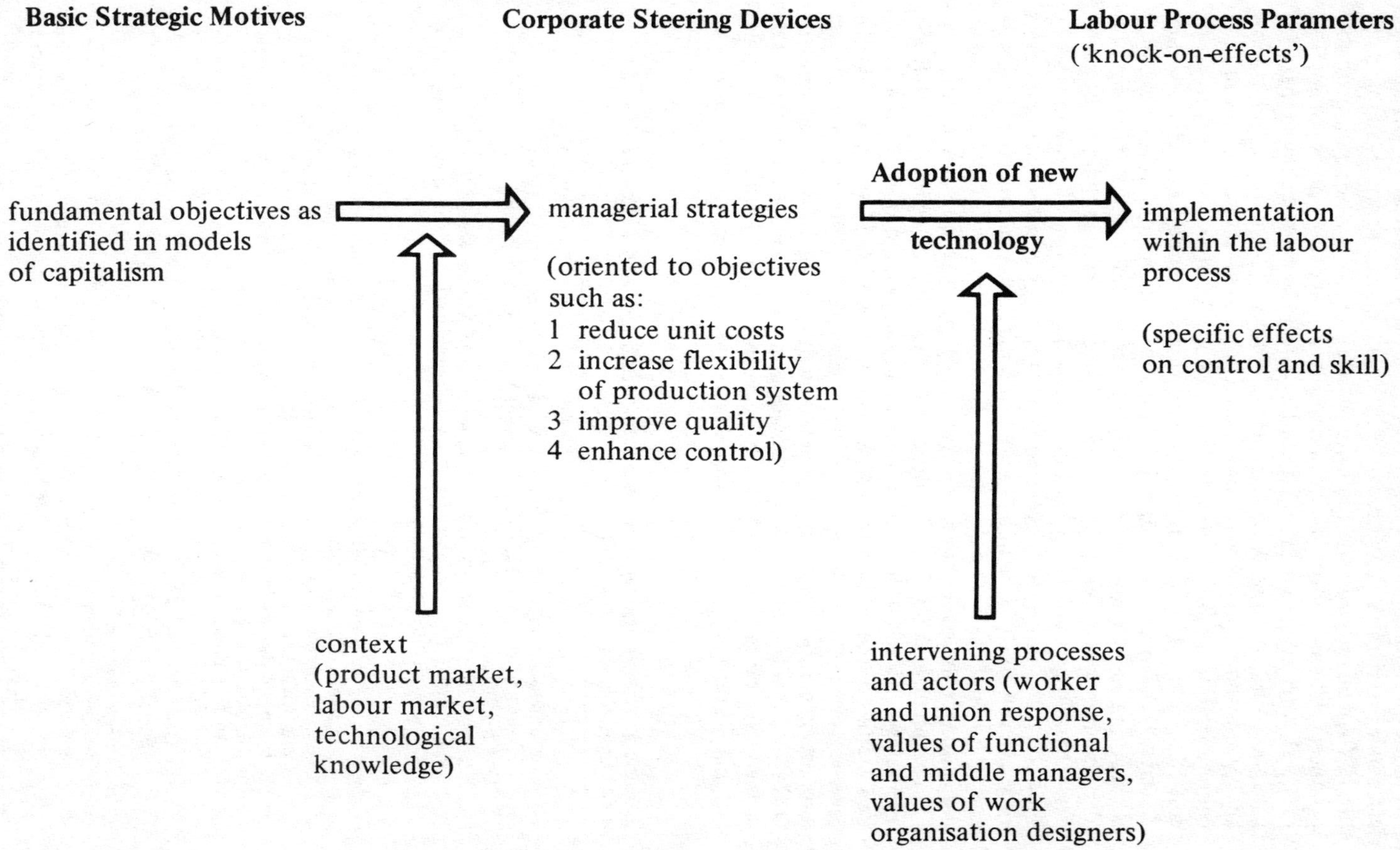

Basic Strategic Motives	Corporate Steering Devices	Labour Process Parameters ('knock-on-effects')

implementation within the labour process

(specific effects on control and skill)

Adoption of new technology

intervening processes and actors (worker and union response, values of functional and middle managers, values of work organisation designers)

managerial strategies

(oriented to objectives such as:

1 reduce unit costs
2 increase flexibility of production system
3 improve quality
4 enhance control)

fundamental objectives as identified in models of capitalism

context (product market, labour market, technological knowledge)

The newness of new technology lies not so much in the application of electronics to data processing, which has been commercially available since the 1950s, but rather in the radically changed nature of the equipment now produced. This has enormously increased the range of its practical applications. Microelectronic technology is distinguished by its (i) compactness, (ii) cheapness, (iii) speed of operation, (iv) reliability, (v) accuracy, and (vi) low energy consumption. When combined with suitable data inputting and communication facilities, the new technology permits information to be collected, collated, stored and accessed with a speed not previously possible.

The real cost of new technology equipment is falling, and its programming is becoming easier (though software costs are not falling in proportion). It is also becoming more versatile. It is not surprising therefore that investment in new technology is already proceeding on an impressive scale, and that this is shortening the innovation cycle both in products and processes. Forecasts vary and obviously have to be treated with particular caution in such a new and changing field. The figures in Table 6.2 do, however, provide an indication of the scale and rate of growth of investment in new technology.

Investment is central to the process of capitalist development, and new technology has today become a significant component of that investment. Few studies of the labour process, however, have yet had an opportunity to take account of this technology, though there has been plenty of speculation about its generation of unemployment and de-skilling. Braverman's analysis (1974) is already dated. The 'automation' he describes is more accurately termed 'Detroit automation', an advanced form of mechanization including automatic transfer which has been applied primarily to motor vehicle mass

Table 6.1 *Examples of new technology applied to processes in manufacturing and services*

Manufacturing
1 Computer-controlled manufacture: CNC machines. robots, flexible manufacturing systems, process plant monitoring and control.
2 Computer-aided design (CAD).
3 Computerized stock control and warehousing: Motor vehicle parts for manufacture and sale of spares. Also examples in service sector: retail store stocks, hospital pharmacies.

Services
4 Financial: automatic cash dispensers/tellers; customers records via VDUs, electronic funds transfer.
5 Medical: computer diagnosis, automated laboratory testing, intensive care monitoring.
6 Retailing and distribution: automated warehousing, stock control, electronic-point-of-sale (EPOS).
7 Libraries: computerized information systems, lending records based on use of bar-coding.
8 Information services: videotext (interactive and one-way systems via modified TV sets and telephone lines).

Office and managerial work
9 Word processing and electronic filing.
10 Communications: electronic mail and facsimile transmission, teleconferencing, networking (local area networks and to homeworkers via microcomputers and telephone lines).

production lines. It is not representative of present-day new technology based on microelectronics. Edwards (1979, p. 122-5) briefly discusses the potential of new technology for extending 'technical control'. He comments that the feedback systems involved 'constitute qualitative advance over Henry Ford's moving line' (p. 125), the older form of technical control which provides the main technological point of reference for Braverman. However, Edwards has little to suggest by way of consequences for the labour process except to say that the new 'technology of production' now becomes the workers' 'immediate oppressor' rather than the supervisor.

Table 6.2 *Examples of investment in new technology and its projected growth*

| Application | Market | Annual sales ($US billion) | |
		1982	1986 predicted
1 CAD/CAM Systems	World	1.15	3.3
2 Robotics	W. Europe	0.17	0.76[a]
			(0.23)[b]
3 Microcomputers	UK	0.56	4.5
4 Total data processing	W. Europe	54.7	151.9
		(1981)	(1987)

Sources: 1 *Financial Times*, 13 December 1982
2[a] *Financial Times*, 16 July 1982
2[b] *Financial Times*, 5 April 1983: revised forecast, 1981 prices
3 *The Times*, 1 March 1983
4 Data International Corporation, 'The Impact of IT', Supplement to Management Today, June 1983

Thompson (1983) provides a carefully considered assessment of the application of new technology based partly on his own research in telecommunications. New technology in his view 'does add to the power of capital to restructure the labour process' (p. 115). Thompson concludes that there is a tendency to use the technology in furtherance of a general trend towards de-skilling. He sees this as an expression of management's motive for change, namely the desire to increase control over the labour process. New technology is also extending de-skilling into the area of office work. Nevertheless, Thompson argues that there is no *technological* inevitability about de-skilling. In so far as de-skilling is underway, it results primarily from competitive market pressures and in many cases predates the introduction of new technology. Examples may also be found of alternative policies, such as 'responsible autonomy' identified by Friedman (1977), while certain new skills are being created as well.

Thompson's analysis is reinforced by the conclusions which Jones (1982a) and Wilkinson (1983) derive from case studies of numerical control technology. Both are critical of 'deterministic and universalistic conceptions of the direction and nature of skill changes' which accompany the introduction of new production technology (Jones, 1982a, p. 181). Jones, for instance, found that firms differed in the forms of skill deployment accompanying the use of numerical control machines. He attributes this variation to differences in product and labour markets, organizational structures and trade union positions. Although cautious about according too much influence to managerial intentions, Jones suggests that one clue as to why he found a variety of skill deployments may lie in evidence that the criteria applied to investment in numerical control equipment did not necessarily include the reduction of labour costs as a determining objective.

Several significant points are suggested by the available research and statistics on new technology. First, it is a major area of investment and one that has important potential for the labour process. New technology therefore links managerial strategy to the labour process, as Figure 6.1 suggested earlier. Second, changes in the labour process accompanying the introduction of new technology can follow a number of possible routes. Third, this choice of possibilities is facilitated by the considerable flexibility offered by new technology, particularly by its software.

This degree of flexibility virtually transforms the application of electronic technology, driven by software, into an aspect of organizational design. Changes to the labour process must for this reason be attributed primarily to non-technological factors, such as managerial strategies formulated in the light of market decisions; established ideological definitions of appropriate structures and working practices can also be expected to play a role. The increasing flexibility of technology renders it far less of a constraint upon, and more of a facilitator of, working practices which emerge from the political processes of management's relations with labour.

Jones presumably had in mind the ability of workers to defend existing working practices when he commented that 'management cannot construct, de novo, the conditions under which labour is to function' (1982a, p. 199). The significance of the introduction of new technology at the present time when the power of organized labour has reached a low ebb is, however, precisely that this gives management considerably more scope than hitherto to use the technology to impose changes upon the labour process. Managers can, and do, justify these changes by reference to competitive pressures and in terms of a need to utilize the technology effectively – in other words, an appeal to the ideology of market-driven technological determinism. In present circumstances, when managerial strategies associated with new technology have teeth, it is particularly important to examine what these strategies are.

2   Managerial strategies and new technology

Evidence from case studies (for example, Buchanan and Boddy, 1983) and surveys (for example, Northcott, Rogers and Zeilinger, 1982) suggests that the following objectives usually feature prominently in managerial intentions when introducing new technology: (i) reducing operating costs and improving efficiency; (ii) increasing flexibility; (iii) raising the quality and consistency of production; (iv) improving control over operations. There is clearly some interdependence between each of these strategic intentions. They are all directed towards enhancing opportunities to create surplus value, and enhancing the organization's ability to absorb the risks of competition.

Improvements in *costs and efficiency* may be secured in several ways relevant to the labour process. New technology may permit reductions in manpower via a substitution for direct labour (as in the automatic spot welding of Austin Metro bodies-in-white: see Francis *et al.*, 1982); or via partial substitution for labour as in word processing (IDS, 1980) and in laboratory automation (Harvey and Child, 1983); or via the more economical allocation of manpower on the basis of superior workflow information such as that provided by electronic-point-of-sale (EPOS) systems in retailing (Cosyns, Loveridge and Child, 1983). New technologies can also reduce costs by permitting improved stock control, the reduction of waste due to operator error, and better plant utilization via computerized scheduling. Advanced manufacturing systems offer a combination of these advantages on the basis of integrating the different elements of design, production, handling, storage and stock control (Lamming and Bessant, 1983). They also offer greatly improved flexibility.

In an industry like engineering, many firms now have to compete on the basis of offering custom-built products produced in smaller batches and often involving complex machining. Achieving *flexibility* in production has therefore become an increasingly important goal. One of the most attractive features offered by new computer controlled technology is the ability to run a range of production items through a single facility with the minimum of cost and delay when changing from one specification to another. A somewhat comparable advantage in flexibility is now being sought in banking with experiments in computerizing customer files and linking these to VDUs used by bank staff. By providing individualized customer profiles, this facility would enable staff to adjust rapidly to the financial circumstances and history of each customer, and on that basis to make decisions rapidly on whether to grant loans or to offer other services. Increased operating flexibility based on new technology is likely to be accompanied by managerial demands for a complementary flexibility in manning and the breaking down of traditional task boundaries, or by attempts to avoid reliance on direct labour altogether.

Improvements in *quality* can be gained from the introduction of highly accurate automated equipment conducting repeatable operations, or from the use of microelectronics for more precise process control. These examples substitute for human intervention. Quality can also be enhanced when electronic assessment complements human judgement, an example being some forms of testing in manufacturing.

The new technology is one of information processing which depends upon the quality of its data inputs. If accurate measurement can be obtained, the ability to communicate information swiftly across distances, and the capacity to apply computational or synthesizing routines when required, clearly enhance the potential for managerial *control*. Senior managers may now no longer have to rely upon operators and middle managers for control data or for their interpretation, if these data can be captured directly at the point of operations. For example, EPOS systems in retailing can, via capturing data through the scanning of bar-coded or magnetically ticketed items, transmit control data on itemized sales, on throughput at each point of sale, and on stocks, directly to store managers and to central buying departments in a company's head office.

New technology is therefore being introduced to advance managerial strategic objectives, and it can be used as a means of facilitating the four types of change in the labour process which were listed at the beginning of the paper. In keeping with the representation in Figure 6.1, these changes are regarded as being in the nature of managerial strategies towards the labour process in so far as they are initiatives which stem originally from corporate objectives and decisions, whether directly and explicitly or not.

It will be evident that each of these managerial strategies effects a reduction in costs through the intensification of labour, whether directly through extending the labour power exerted or indirectly through improving the intrinsic performance of equipment. Moreover, by their very nature as interventions, they each constitute an extension of managerial control. However, the strategies provide different routes towards the increase of efficiency, and the perceived appropriateness of each is presumed to depend on specific circumstances of the kind outlined at the close of this paper. The way in which labour cost reduction is balanced with other objectives also appears to vary with each strategy. Another variable factor is the extent to which proponents have so far come forward publicly, or have been uncovered by researchers, to articulate specific statements of intent towards the labour process in connection with each strategy. Further evidence on managerial intentions is required. Finally, the provisional character of the present fourfold classification needs to be recognized. If found to be useful, it will certainly require considerable elaboration.

2.1 Elimination of direct labour

Abolition of labour has been the dream both of engineers and social visionaries, though from quite different perspectives. The concept of factories without workers has already reached the experimental stage. It is predicted that the wholly automated factory with virtually no direct workers will have become a reality in most advanced industrial countries within five years.

There are two main technological routes to the elimination of direct labour, which though starting from different points in different industries, are becoming more similar. The process industries achieved an integrated flow of production many years ago and have operated with minimal direct labour forces. With increasing market pressures, employers such as chemical producers are turning increasingly to speciality products produced in batches. The ability of manufacturers to make several products and versions of the same product on a batch basis using the same basic plant is becoming particularly important. Computer controls linked to microelectronic sensors and intelligent data gathering instruments are essential to achieving the flexibility and they enable process producers to avoid dependence on human intervention outside the central control room (cf. Williams, 1983).

A second main route to eliminating direct labour in manufacturing is via Flexible Manufacturing Systems (FMS). These are computer-programmed and controlled integrated production systems which bring to discrete item (i.e. non-process) production many of the continuous flow characteristics of process plants. The prospect of achieving greater flexibility in regard to batch changes on the same plant is often cited as a major attraction of FMS. Current interest in FMS is high.[...]

There is evidence of a conscious intention among some managers and engineers to use FMS and process control as a means of extending managerial control over the labour process.[. . .] A line manager, who had led a project team to commission a new highly automated chocolate processing plant controlled by microprocessors, told the writer that 'we had through the commissioning period to decide how much flexibility [discretion] we can give the operator. Our objective was to reduce that to nil if possible.' This plant runs with a total complement of four people concerned with the process per se, only one of whom is an operator/controller who replaces the 23 operators previously required.[. . .]

The labour-elimination strategy can also be found in some parts of the service sector, where it simply manifests the logical conclusion of a widespread trend to shift the labour costs of service provision onto the customer (for instance, self-service in retailing). One example, which is conceptually developed and is already operational in some locations abroad, is 'lobby' banking. This could substitute for branch banks an array of automatic cash transaction machines which have already been developed to perform services such as cash dispensing, cash depositing, crediting of other accounts, balance notification and ordering of statements. Such satellite branches would eliminate the present job of tellers, back office staff and branch managers.

The theoretical implications for labour process analysis of situations where the production process or service provision employs little or no labour are intriguing. Labour is obviously embodied in the plant and processed materials used, but what if it is absent from the workplace as such? This as yet largely hypothetical but prospectively significant case indicates that it is the productive process which is analytically significant as the main source of surplus value, and that labour is not necessarily involved *directly* in that process. The more that this situation comes into being, the more attention will need to be directed to the social relations of exchange, distribution and re-distribution under capitalism rather than simply to the social relations of production in a narrow sense.

Automation has proceeded historically in the train of task simplification and routinization. The archetype of this earlier stage was the degradation of work through deskilling of the kind associated with Taylorism. As the employment of skilled craftsmen in direct production tasks became substituted by the employment of semi-skilled workers, and as the number of alternative employments in the labour market reduced through this process of change, so the market position of the production worker changed. In terms of the classification first developed by Mok (1975) and extended by Loveridge (1983), these jobs had changed from a location in the 'primary external market' to one in the 'secondary internal market'. In the primary external market, the craft jobs provided long-term stable earnings and permitted high levels of discretion – an advantageous 'primary' position founded upon special skills widely marketable in the general labour market 'external' to any one employing organization. In the secondary internal market, the new semi-skilled jobs enjoyed a relatively lower earning capacity with less long-term security (a less advantageous 'secondary' position). These jobs no longer utilised skills derived from specialised craft training but were instead now defined increasingly on the basis of specifications and training prescribed 'internally' by the particular employer. The benefit for the worker of generally sought-after skills commanding high value in the external labour market had gone.

The now emergent stage of direct labour elimination through the means of advanced automation gives rise to a further shift in labour market position for the workers concerned. In so far as they are displaced from regular employment altogether, their location will have shifted to the secondary external segment. They will have been forced onto the general labour market 'external' to the particular employing firm. Their position remains 'secondary' in that the absence of generally marketable skills eliminates the availability of long-term earning security as well as any opportunity to exercise discretion in the performance of tasks if work is secured. The labour market position of production managers displaced by the elimination of direct labour may shift even more dramatically from a relatively privileged primary internal position to one in the external market which will be of secondary standing unless their abilities and experience can still command a premium in the marketplace.

2.2   Contracting

Contracting refers to an arrangement whereby the employer pays for an agreed delimited amount of production or period of labour time, but leaves the organization, manning and sometimes the equipping of the task to the worker or group of workers concerned. It has a long history. An early form of labour management in Britain was the putting-out system in which production was let out to physically dispersed domestic workers by a central employer-merchant. Subcontracting to groups of workers on a central production site became widespread in the nineteenth century (Gospel, 1983). Some putting out persists to the present day in the form of homeworking (Cragg and Dawson, 1981) while subcontracting is still a common arrangement in the building industry.

These historical forms of contracting involved manual workers who were engaged on productive activities which could be performed as discrete tasks or stages. In such cases, the expense of maintaining continuity of employment and a superstructure of control could be avoided, and with it an economic risk when faced with market uncertainties and competitive pressures. There are distinct possibilities that where manufacturing can be carried out in discrete stages, a comparable development could re-emerge with the aid of new information technology. Here a standardization of language for specifying fabrication needs, combined with computer programming which can turn the specifications into production, may eliminate the need to incorporate the separate stages of manufacture within a single location serviced by a unified labour force.

It is noteworthy not only that employers today are displaying increasing interest in contracting arrangements, but that these are now being extended to office and managerial workers located at the core of bureaucracies. Arrangements for working from home while remaining part of a network connected electronically to a central office are clearly motivated by economic considerations, but their achievement relies heavily on new technology (Mandeville, 1983).

Although the problem of controlling the growth of administrative and managerial overheads has been recognized for some time now (cf. Child, 1978), it has not yet been resolved. [. . .] There is a growing interest in the possibility of paying workers to work on their own premises on a contract basis. It has been predicted that fee paying short-term contracts will increasingly come to be substituted for long-term employment within organisations (for example, Handy, 1982).

Williamson (1975) analysed the development of hierarchical working relationships within large bureaucracies in terms of the lower transaction costs, including greater certainty and predictability, which often attended organizational as opposed to market relationships. New information technology, whether for transmission of data, facsimile documents or audio-visual exchange, is beginning to facilitate communication over distances and the precise logging (i.e. measurement) of the transmission. Long-range communication can take place with increasing ease and reducing real cost, and less reliance has therefore to be placed on the close proximity of working that justifies the 'office'. Taking into account as well the burden of wage and salary costs, the balance of transaction cost advantage is thus moving back towards the market relationship in which smaller units and even people working at home are linked electronically and through market contracts to form a whole system of work.

According to a recently reported survey of 255 among the largest 1,000 UK companies, almost two-thirds believe that by 1988 they will be employing executives working from home (Cane, 1983). Already, over 20 per cent of companies with a turnover of more than £500m a year have some executives working from home using personal computers. It is not stated how many of these computers are linked to the corporate office. Rank Xerox has initiated 'networking' arrangements with some of its specialists whereby they now work from their own homes on individualized contracts, and often have Xerox 820 microcomputers linked to the company's head office. The saving to the company is reported to be substantial since it estimates that a manager's or specialist's employment cost approaches three times his or her salary once overheads, secretarial and office services, and administrative back-up are taken into account. Under the 'networking' system, payment is only for a contracted number of days and/or services rendered and not for the non-productive time contained in full-time employment. Under such arrangements, the use of new technology increases the ability to record the networker's output, which further adds to managerial control.

Staff working at home under this kind of arrangement become self-employed contractors, and in fact Xerox encourages them to start up their own businesses or private practices to operate during the time not contracted to the company. In the case of high level specialists able to secure work on their own account, contracting therefore shifts them from the internal to the external labour market while retaining a primary standing. This standing would shift downwards towards a secondary status were the homeworkers not able to attract a market demand for their skills as consultants or private entrepreneurs. They, rather than their erstwhile full-time employer, now bear the risk of providing a secure income flow. They enjoy a greater control over how their work is actually carried out and over their pattern of working time, but the employer enjoys greater control over the conditions for extracting surplus value in that he can now specify the relation between work done and labour cost much more precisely – in addition to enjoying a much reduced overall labour cost.

Another strategic development in this category is already well established.

This consists of contracting out whole areas of work, such as maintenance and services like cleaning and canteens which are regarded as peripheral to the core productive activity, in order again to save bearing the cost of a standing overhead for an activity which can be bought in more cheaply instead. New technology has some relevance to this strategy, particularly with respect to the external contracting of maintenance. Some new equipment has become so sophisticated and complex that its maintenance internally would require the employment of costly highly trained staff. On the other hand, with self-diagnostic systems and greatly improved reliability, the unanticipated need for major attention tends to reduce, and this may make it possible to use an outside contractor on a planned basis. [. . .]

2.3   Polyvalence

The third managerial strategy is frequently adopted in connection with new technology but does not depend on it. This is a strategy of 'polyvalence', in the French sense of the term, denoting a situation in which workers perform, or at least are available to perform, a range of tasks which cut across or extend traditional skill and job boundaries.

Polyvalence may be reached along several different routes. One involves the removal of skill demarcations and is horizontal in nature. In some cases the requirement for specific job skills which once commanded a premium in the external market has disappeared, because of technological change. The jobs concerned are extended to take in other tasks as a result. Lithographic workers in some provincial newspapers provide an example. In other cases, the route will be through the drive by employers to remove demarcation between skills which are still required. The intention here is to reduce employment costs and to increase the flexibility of manpower deployment. The fusion of electronic and mechanical features in the design of new technology is often cited by managers as a rationale for seeking polyvalence of this type among maintenance workers. In the service sector, a similar argument has been pursued in terms of integrating the application of specialist skills to meet the total needs of the customer, once new technology can provide the appropriate information system support. An example is provided shortly from banking, while Heery (1983) describes a development of this kind in local authority 'Neighbourhood Offices'.

A second main route to polyvalence is through enlarging the task competences of the worker in a job requiring relatively limited skills – usually an operative or routine office job. The dimension of this enlargement – how many additional tasks and how much additional responsibility or control – can vary and so correspondingly will the training required. A 'vertical' element of upskilling may be involved in job enlargement, but in other cases tasks requiring little skill are simply added together, and this may even be done in the hope of salving some worker job satisfaction in the wake of de-skilling.

The job definition and routes of possible advancement for the polyvalent worker will in the main be highly specific to the employing organisation, thus locating him or her firmly in the internal labour market. The standing of the polyvalent worker in the internal labour market will depend on the level of the skills which are now combined and on the discretionary content of the job.

Whether or not polyvalence represents advance or regression, upskilling or degradation, will be a question of the route by which the worker has travelled to it.

The polyvalence strategy is often combined with the development of a 'responsible autonomy' type of control (Friedman, 1977). 'Job enrichment' is a case in point, combining an extension of tasks with an increment of autonomy with regard to matters such as checking the quality of completed work. This will often form part of an employment policy which reinforces the internal labour market, through (i) the provision of opportunities to acquire new skills and tasks which are defined in the local organization's own terms, (ii) opportunities to advance at least some way up a grading ladder defined in terms of an organizational scheme of job evaluation, and (iii) emphasis upon long-term employment opportunities, involvement in communications and participation arrangements, corporate ceremonies and events, and other elements designed to build commitment to the corporate objectives defined by management. We are not, of course, very far from the so-called 'Japanese philosophy of management' here, though it is one which has characterised certain Western companies for some time (cf. Ouchi, 1981). It approximates to the more sophisticated form of 'bureaucratic control' identified by Edwards (1979).

As well as offering the employer potential cost advantages by way of flexibility and reduced levels of manning, the polyvalence strategy is also an approach to control over the labour process which may be more effective than blatant and direct controls (as in close supervision) because it emphasizes the consensual and 'positive' side of the employment relationship. This strategy endeavours to tie the worker into the internal labour market of the organization and to render his or her skills specific to that organization. In so far as it succeeds in increasing the dependence of workers on employment in the particular organization and reduces their marketability elsewhere, then the polyvalent strategy enhances management's power in the employment relationship and hence its potential for control. Thus while, in the British situation at least, the initial stages of polyvalence may sometimes be forced through by confrontation with trade unions (though it is more often to be found in non-union situations), the strategy once it has reached a mature stage will tend to develop a more advantageous ground for managerial initiative. It may indeed generate a degree of acquiescence if policies of fostering normative commitment meet with success. It also has to be recalled that the 'responsible autonomy' which tends to complement polyvalence, is a control strategy with its focus typically on output measurement. For instance, the allocation of responsibility to a worker or work group for a more 'complete' set of tasks – what is sometimes called a 'whole task' such as complete assembly of a TV set – can make it easier for management to identify accountability for substandard performance. The application of new microelectronic monitoring devices and information transmission systems facilitates performance measurement, and may thereby make a transition from direct personal supervision of the labour process to a responsible autonomy format that is much more acceptable to management. In effect, new technology can substitute supervision at a distance for supervision in the workplace.

Polyvalence as a strategy is not necessarily pursued in connection with new technology – it may, for instance, take the form of a general managerial drive against craft or custom-and-practice demarcation and against multi-union-ism. However, it can be associated with new technology in several ways: (i) as a policy to maintain the use of workers' capabilities when these would otherwise be underutilised because new technology takes over from the use of skills; (ii) in circumstances where new technology is introduced to enhance the organization's capability of competing – either on the basis of quick response and small job quantities, where flexibility in manning is therefore at a premium, or on the basis of introducing new technology to enhance the quality of service provided by staff whose range of tasks is thereby extended; and (iii) in cases where the new information processing capabilities accompanying plant investment permit polyvalence to a greater degree than before.

Wilkinson (1983) provides an example of the polyvalence strategy in a situation in which new technology might otherwise have resulted in de-skilling. This was a firm manufacturing lenses and spectacles in which job rotation was introduced as a means of preserving the intrinsic content and interest of jobs concerned with lens preparation where the introduction of new computer-programmed machinery had reduced the skill and judgemental component of individual tasks. This policy of job rotation was supported by the careful selection of new recruits to ensure a certain level of competence and considerable attention was given to training. These measures in turn provided possibilities for future promotion to supervisory jobs. A craft-oriented management in this firm had adapted its policies on job design to the introduction of new technology so as in some degree to offset the reduction of skills, but also in a manner which tied the definition of those skills and opportunities for personal advancement more closely to the firm's internal labour market.

Banking provides an example of the second way in which polyvalence is associated with new technology. In one of the largest clearing banks, new technology is currently being considered as a means of enhancing the capacity of staff located behind desks in the lobbies of branches to offer a superior level of advisory service to customers. The idea would be to equip each desk with a VDU unit linked to a file containing customer details. It is argued that immediate file access of this kind would not only facilitate updating, but more significantly it would permit the member of staff to take on a marketing function by suggesting in the light of the customer information how the bank could be of service in terms of arranging insurance, providing a loan and so forth. It would also provide the staff member with data relevant to a judgement *not* to offer certain services – such as a further loan. The bank is already developing the concept of 'personal bankers' to deal with all non-cash transaction services to customers coming into bank branches; this new job is located at a grade above that of counter tellers, and it is claimed that the exercise of additional skills (including interpersonal ones) that it requires will provide a basis for further future promotion into posts such as back-office supervisor. If new technology is introduced in the manner described, then this is likely to enhance the polyvalence of the 'personal banker' role. The definition of this new job and the skills it requires is specific to the bank in question, though in the banking industry barriers already exist to the ready movement of workers from one bank to another through the external labour market. What should be noted with this example is that the new technology involved could just as readily be used to *reduce* the skill and control of the bank worker in dealings with the customer, by means of incorporating programmed decision hierarchies of a standardized form which serve as instructions to the worker over responses to the customer, given the latter's computerized profile. In the case of banks, such decisions are indisputably the direct product of managerial strategy: they are taken centrally, in detail, and with very little employee or union participation (Child *et al.*, 1984). [. . .]

2.4   Degradation of jobs

A central argument in Braverman's book (1974) is that the conflict of classes around economic interest promotes a continual search by the capitalist for ways to control and cheapen the production process. While it may be his dream to eliminate the dependence on labour altogether, his desire for control and cost reduction are seen in the meantime to motivate a long-term trend towards the degradation of existing jobs.

The main features of this strategy are the fragmentation of labour into narrowly constituted jobs, with de-skilling and use of direct control methods either through close supervision or structuring by technology. Of all the developments discussed in this paper, the degradation of jobs can be the most confidently identified as a managerial strategy – it has a long history, has been widely discussed and practised, and for many years found a place in managerial, engineering and even personnel literature (though never without its critics). It was pupil to F.W. Taylor's main theme: that skill, knowledge and hence control should be separated from the worker. Work study techniques were developed to operationalize this maxim, while the moving conveyor technology closely associated with Henry Ford added a 'technical control' over the pace of work and the physical location of the worker (Edwards, 1979).

Managers are able today to use new technology in an attempt to avoid reliance on the skills and judgement of workers, and to regulate their performance more precisely. While this may be perceived by managers and engineers as a stage towards automation, a degradation strategy often has more effect on the intrinsic quality of jobs rather than on their quantity. It permits cost reduction through a substitution of less qualified workers, a minimization of training and a closer managerial definition of performance standards. These changes reduce worker control over the labour process and facilitate an intensification of work, but degradation will nevertheless probably involve fewer reductions in absolute manpower than polyvalence and certainly fewer than full automation.

Many examples of the pursuit of job degradation alongside the introduction of new technology are now recorded in the literature. Those concerning the use of numerical control have borne out Noble's (1979) contention that some managements have made a conscious choice to employ new technological possibilities for the purpose of job degradation even when there was an availability of alternative technologies or alternative modes of work structuring which could be used effectively with the technology (for example, Jones, 1982b; Wilkinson, 1983). Another relevant example is newspaper production where new technology has been introduced in ways that have degraded and in some cases eliminated traditional skills. This has generated defensive measures by alarmed craft unions which appear to have poor prospects of long-term success (Cockburn, 1983; Gennard and Dunn, 1983). Degradation has also accompanied the introduction of new technology into areas of routine office work, such as local government treasurer's departments (Crompton and Reid, 1982). However, a trend towards job degradation was already underway in office work well before the introduction of electronic technology, with the use of an advanced division of labour and close supervision within large open-plan offices (for example, de Kadt, 1979).

Policies of job degradation are even evident in areas of service provision where in the past the quality of the service has been associated with staff discretion concerning the appropriate response to individual customers' needs and covering, if necessary, a wide range of transactions (advice, purchases, services). Two instances, in retailing and banking respectively, may be illustrated from studies undertaken by the writer and his colleagues.

The major introduction of new technology within retailing consists of electronic-point-of-sale (EPOS) systems, which are fronted by electronic cash registers incorporating devices to scan bar-coded individual sales items. The cash registers are linked to a retail company's computer which will (in an advanced application) contain the prices to be applied to each item of sale – 'automatic price look-up'. With the exception of relatively few accounting and systems staff (who may be located at a head office rather than in local stores), the way EPOS has generally been applied so far is to reinforce a work degradation strategy. [. . .]

Also because EPOS systems make readily available much more precise information on customer flows, they enable management to direct the deployment of staff more closely with regard to hours of working and job allocation within the store. There is a consequent intensification of the check-out operator's work. An interesting feature of EPOS is that it is also being used in a way that degrades jobs of higher standing within the organization. The information it provides on sales profiles and stock levels permits routine programming (such as automatic re-order routines) to be applied to some buying decisions for which management had previously to depend upon the judgement of buyers. In a similar way, the new information now reduces the dependency of store general managers upon the assessment of conditions and trends by departmental or section managers. The latter's role then tends to be reduced to that of a supervisor and in supermarkets there may be very few section staff left to supervise now that EPOS can eliminate the need to price-label individual items or to inspect the stock level of shelves visually. (Elimination of item price-labelling, of course, reduces the *level* of staffing as well.)

In the new or refurbished branches of one of Britain's largest banks, the traditional job of teller has been divided into routine and less routine components. While a relatively small number of staff now concentrate on dealing with non-routine customer requirements in a role that has actually been upgraded through taking on additional 'marketing' functions, the larger number of lobby staff now occupy jobs which have been degraded. They are required to specialize only in the handling of small cash transactions (and not even those involving large amounts of coin) and on customer balance enquiries. This policy has been developed by the bank's central management in order to speed up routine transactions for the customer and at the same time to intensify the work of the counter teller. It has been assisted by the introduction of new technology in the form of keyboard operated automatic electronic cash dispensers, in conjunction with a very old technology of pneumatic tubes to transmit cash deposited rapidly to a secure area.

The implications of job degradation for the labour market position of the workers concerned were summarized when discussing the elimination of direct labour through automation, for which degradation can be the forerunner. The application of techniques such as work study and clerical work measurement to the narrowing and deskilling of jobs is typically formalized in job descriptions and gradings which are particular to the employing organization. They serve to locate the worker more firmly within the organization's internal labour market, and along a historical path towards an increasingly secondary position. The worker's power to negotiate favourable terms and conditions as an individual is vitiated both by de-skilling itself (the decline towards secondary status) and by the particularization of his or her skills away from substantive definitions or norms of experience which are recognized and command general value on the open external labour market. It is not surprising that workers who experience degradation often come to regard collective action as the only means of defending their position and securing a tolerable livelihood.

2.5   Discussion

Four managerial strategies have been identified to which the introduction of new technology can be allied. Each reflects objectives relating to the pursuit of capital accumulation under conditions of market competition, and represents in different forms an intensification of labour. All have definable implications for the labour process and for the labour market position of the workers concerned. When pursued severally by the management of a particular organization, these strategies increase the segmentation of its labour force into different skill and status categories as well as increasing the pool of labour in the external labour market. Both these results weaken the capacity of workers to mount an organized resistance against management and its use of new technology, or even to formulate common policies on the subject. The internal and external labour market consequences of managerial strategies towards the labour process will therefore tend to reinforce management's ability to pursue those strategies, unless wider contextual factors change significantly. [...]

An extremely complex framework would be required for a full analysis of variations in the managerial strategies pursued towards the labour process and in the success with which they are implemented or resisted. It is possible only to suggest a bare outline here, which is approached along two planes or dimensions. First, as the previous discussion began to indicate, there are several levels of relevant contextual analytical unit: the mega socio-economic system, the nation or society, the industry or sector, the enterprise or organization. Second, there are conceptually distinct influences, including government policy, institutional and cultural features, product and labour market conditions, organizational and task variables.

It is accepted that the capitalist labour process will embody capitalistic objectives expressed in modern enterprises through management as the agent of capital. This implies a contrast with labour processes and modes of organization in non-capitalist mega systems: in principle with socialism but in practice with what Thompson has labelled 'state collectivism' (1983, p. 223n). While there is a common reliance on hierarchical work organization and the managerial function in both mega systems, the formal status of the worker in the production system is different as are the official organs which express that formal position. Managerial policies connected with the use of new technology are prima facie expected to reflect this fundamental difference.

Within the capitalist system, a divergence is apparent between countries in features that influence managerial strategies and the organization of the labour process. Sorge et al. (1983) illustrate this clearly through comparing British and West German companies in the extent to which the organization of computer numerical control usage is designed to build upon workers' existing skills rather than to substitute for these. Though other factors such as size of company are also found to be relevant, Sorge and his colleagues conclude that the tradition of craft reflected in the scale and quality of present-day German vocational training helps to account for the greater tendency in the German firms to rely on workers on the spot to control and edit machine programmes as opposed to confining this to specialist programmers – in other words a polyvalent rather than a degradation policy. This tradition of craft and practical industrial knowledge is strongly represented in most German line management, and is likely to encourage a polyvalent strategy. [. . .]

The analysis of variety in managerial strategies has to be refined further, to more specific locations within a nation's system of productive relations. Littler (1983) cites Britain as the country most removed from what he calls the monopoly capitalism model of employment and labour relations incorporating a marked development of internal labour markets. At the same time, as he admits, within that one country, internal labour markets developed unevenly between different sectors. British banks and large chemical companies had, for example, developed internal labour markets at an early period, while these remained absent for a long time in other sectors such as textiles. [. . .]

Differentiated employment policies will be evident even at the level of a single plant, such that particularly valued groups may be upgraded and encouraged to acquire new skills (polyvalence) while others are possibly degraded, eliminated or placed on limited contracts. [. . .]

The second analytical dimension relevant to managerial strategies brings in the substantive factors which are likely to promote variety in labour process organization. The major factors to emerge from available research and discussion are government policy, institutions, culture, product and labour market conditions, organization and task.

The first three of these factors are predominantly national in scope. The importance of *government policy* illustrated by the conclusion that legislation provides the most significant single stimulus to industrial democracy in the European countries (IDE, 1981). [. . .]

Culture is the third factor which is primarily identifiable at the national level. While its ontology and role is subject to considerable debate, the thesis has been strongly argued that cultural values such as those concerning the equality of individual worth within society and interpersonal trust will influence the strategies adopted by management: thus a low evaluation of workers' individual worth and trustfulness will encourage job degradation (cf. Hofstede, 1980).

Market conditions can be both general and specific. Ramsey (1977) and others have pointed to the way that managerial strategies are adjusted to general business cycle conditions. In periods of recession and weakened labour power, it is suggested that strategies of labour elimination and degradation are likely to predominate, and that management's ability to enforce any chosen strategy will be greater. Conversely, the ability of workers to resist managerial strategies and to impose their chosen occupational definition of the labour process will be greater in periods of market buoyancy and labour shortage. [...]

Organizational and task factors are specific to the particular unit of production. Among *organizational factors*, company traditions can exert an important influence. They frequently have their origins in the ideology of an entrepreneurial founder who set out both a strategic perspective on the task of the organization and a philosophy on the form of the labour process to accomplish it. 'Fordism' as a labour process to accomplish the strategy of opening up the latent mass motor car market is simply the best known example out of very many. In this way, some companies have developed a mass production culture which encourages a trend towards job degradation, while others have maintained a bespoke tradition to which retention of craft skills and even polyvalence is more naturally related. Size of organization tends to be associated with this particular strategic choice, with mass producers usually being larger. A close relationship between larger size and greater specialization has been found in many studies conducted in a wide range of countries and organizational types (cf. Child, 1973; Hickson *et al.*, 1979). [...]

There is some consensus among organizational theorists that the most significant *task dimensions* for an understanding of how work is organised are those relating to uncertainty and complexity (cf. Perrow, 1970; Van de Ven and Ferry, 1980). The number of exceptions encountered in performing the task and its general variability, a lack of clarity about what is required and about cause-effect relationships are all factors contributing to uncertainty. Complexity is increased by factors such as the amount of relevant information to be absorbed in carrying out the task, the number of steps involved, and the number of contributions required from different sources. A third relevant dimension is the cost of making an error, whether this falls primarily on property or on the person.

An analysis of the introduction of new technology into medicine, banking and retailing conducted by the writer and colleagues (Child *et al.*, 1984) concluded that task uncertainty and the cost of error were particularly significant for enabling service providers to preserve the integrity of their jobs. New technologies will normally have a superiority in receiving, storing and providing rapid access to complex data, so long as these are in a structured form. Moreover, tasks involving uncertainty and risk require the exercise of judgement: the best way of carrying them out is not transparent. This 'indeterminacy' has considerable ideological potential for the defence of the worker's control over the labour process, as professional workers in particular have demonstrated (Jamous and Peloille, 1970). In short, the greater the uncertainty and risk in tasks to be performed, the less likely are strategies of labour elimination of job degradation to be adopted. Since an organization will normally contain a range of tasks with different degrees of uncertainty and risk, this is another factor encouraging a diversity of management strategies towards the labour process within the firm.

Each of the four managerial strategies is likely to be pursued under different circumstances and in relation to different categories of workers. Within the purely British context, relevant product market, labour market, task and organizational influences may tentatively be identified, drawing from the framework just set out.

The *elimination of direct labour* through automation entails considerable investment in new equipment. Leaving aside process production where the properties of the materials are a major consideration, this strategy is most appealing to a management whose firm competes on the basis of embodying complex machining in products manufactured in small batches and subject to variability in specification. Investment of this order is also more likely in a recessionary period but when market opportunities are apparent and an upturn in demand is expected. In so far as FMS developments have so far involved new facilities, the relevance of labour market characteristics has not been clear. However, labour elimination strategies are more likely to be pursued and to succeed in existing establishments when the negotiating position of workers is weakened by unemployment, especially if severance terms are generous or alternative employment is offered elsewhere within the company or locality. Labour elimination would appear to suit tasks of which the performance dimensions are well understood, but which are complex and where precision is required. It is, finally, the strategy most likely to find favour in an organization with a strong professional engineering (as opposed to a craft) culture.

Contracting is a means of reducing the risk incurred in serving product markets which display unstable or seasonal patterns of demand. it commits the employer to maintaining a portion of his employment costs for a limited period only. The spread of contracting is likely to be facilitated by slack labour markets, in which a sufficient number of people come forward who are prepared to work on limited contracts and themselves bear the risk of providing a long-term income flow. Contracting is also more practical where there is a technical possibility of segmenting distinct tasks or stages in production, which can constitute a specific contracted obligation, Finally, the organization with high overheads and whose management has a strong (probably traditional) sense of a 'core' organizational competence, is the more likely to favour contracting.

It may be recalled that *polyvalence* takes the two forms of (i) removal of demarcations and (ii) job enlargement. Product market conditions in which quality of product or service is a significant competitive factor are likely to encourage both forms. An important impetus to removing demarcations may come from competitive pressures bearing on production costs, while job enlargement policies have been more common in buoyant product market conditions. The labour market factor is also relevant here. The removal of demarcation is likely to be seen as a threat to job control and will therefore be more readily introduced when organized worker opposition is weak. In contrast, job enlargement has typically been introduced in tight labour markets as an attempt to reduce high levels of absenteeism and labour turnover. The type of task conducive to a polyvalent strategy is one in which the use of worker discretion and judgement is believed to be functional, and one which permits flexibility of physical movement, of time budgeting and possibly of sequencing. The type of organization more likely to contain polyvalent strategies will have small work units (plants, departments or offices), a craft or professional tradition, and an emphasis on the training and development of workers. It may well have inherited a paternalistic tradition.

A *job degradation* strategy is likely to be stimulated by competitive pressures in product markets, but where the basis of that competition is keenly priced standardized production. Slack labour markets, with a pool of readily available compliant cheap labour from the 'secondary external' sector, are also conducive to the adoption and successful imposition of this strategy. Favourable task characteristics include repeated standard routine operations, the methods for which can be readily defined and performance assessed without undue difficulty. The type of organization in which this strategy will tend to be found is large and without a strong craft or professional tradition. It may well have a history of autocratic management which maintained a considerable social distance from the workforce, and did not enqourage opportunities for workers to gain advancement within the company.

These propositions suggest that the use of new technology to advance particular managerial strategies can usefully be understood in terms of contextual factors of a market, task and organizational nature within a particular country. Governmental, institutional and cultural factors come into account when broader cross-national comparisons are attempted. The analysis presented here implies that a study of job redesign within the labour process needs to be sensitive to specific historical and contemporary features which shape the patterns of its variation around the course of capitalist development.

Note

1 I am grateful to Edward Heery, Stephen Wood, colleagues in the Work Organisation Research Centre, and participants at the Conference on the Organisation and Control of the Labour Process held at Owens Park Manchester in March 1983 for commenting on an earlier draft of this chapter. It draws in part on research funded by the Economic and Social Research Council.

References

Braverman, H. (1974) *Labor and Monopoly Capital: The Degradation of Work in the Twentieth Century*. New York: Monthly Review Press.

Buchanan, D.A. and Boddy, D. (1983) *Organizations in the Computer Age*. Aldershot: Gower.

Cane, A. (1983) 'More expected to work from home', *Financial Times*, 1 September.

Child, J. (1973) 'Predicting and understanding organization structure', *Administrative Science Quarterly*, 18, 168-85.

Child, J. (1978) 'The "non-productive" component within the productive sector: a problem of management control', in M. Fores and I. Glover (eds), *Manufacturing and Management*, London: HMSO.

Child, J., Loveridge, R., Harvey, J. and Spencer, A. (1984) 'Microelectronics and the quality of employment in services', in P. Marstrand (ed.), *New*

Technology and the Future of Work, published for the British Association by Frances Pinter.

Cockburn, C. (1983) *Brothers: Male Dominance and Technical Change.* London: Pluto Press.

Cosyns, J., Loveridge, R. and Child, J. (1983) *New Technology in Retail Distribution – The Implications at Enterprise Level*, Report to the EEC, University of Aston Management Centre.

Cragg, A. and Dawson, T. (1981) 'Qualitative research among homeworkers'. London: Department of Employment Research Paper, No. 21, May.

Crompton, R. and Reid, S. (1982) 'The deskilling of clerical work' in S. Wood (ed.), *The Degradation of Work*. London: Hutchinson.

de Kadt, M. (1979) 'Insurance: a clerical work factory' in A. Zimbalist (ed.), *Case Studies on the Labor Process*. New York: Monthly Review Press.

Edwards, R. (1979) *Contested Terrain*, London: Heinemann.

Friedman, A.I., (1977) *Industry and Labour*. London: Macmillan.

Gennard, J. and Dunn, S. (1983) 'The impact of new technology on the structure and organization of craft unions in the printing industry', *British Journal of Industrial Relations*, XXI, 17-32.

Gospel, H.F. (1983) 'Managerial structures and strategies: an introduction', in H.F. Gospel and C.F. Littler (eds), *Managerial Strategies and Industrial Relations*, London: Heinemann.

Handy, C. (1982) 'Where management is leading', *Management Today*, December, 50-53, 114.

Harvey, J. and Child, J. (1983) 'Green Hospital, Woodall, Biochemistry Laboratory: a case study', University of Aston.

Heery, E. (1983) 'Polyvalence and new technology'. unpublished working paper, Department of Sociology, North East London Polytechnic.

Hickson, D.J., McMillan, C.J., Azumi, K. and Horvath, D. (1979) 'Grounds for comparative organization theory: quicksands or hard core?' in C.J. Lammers and D.J. Hickson (eds), *Organizations Alike and Unlike*. London: Routledge and Kegan Paul.

Hofstede, G. (1980) *Culture's Consequences: National Differences In Thinking and Organizing*. Beverly Hills, Calif.: Sage.

IDE International Research Group (1981) *Industrial Democracy in Europe*, Oxford: Oxford University Press.

Incomes Data Services (IDS) (1980) *Changing Technology*, Study No. 22, London.

Jamous, H. and Peloille, B. (1970) 'Changes in the French University-Hospital System', in J.A. Jackson (ed.): *Professions and Professionalism*, Cambridge: Cambridge University Press.

Jones, B. (1982a) 'Destruction or redistribution of engineering skills? the case of numerical control' in Stephen Wood (ed.), *The Degradation of Work*. London: Hutchinson.

Jones, B. (1982b) 'Technical, organizational, and political constraints on system redesign for machinist programming of NC machine tools', paper for IFIP Conference on 'System Design for the Users', Italy, September.

Lamming, R. and Bessant, J. (1983) 'Some management implications of advanced manufacturing technology', unpublished paper, Department of Business Studies, Brighton Polytechnic.

Littler, C.R. (1983) 'A comparative analysis of managerial structures and strategies', in H.F. Gospel and C.R. Littler (eds), *Managerial Strategies and Industrial Relations*. London: Heinemann.

Loveridge, R. (1983) 'Labour market segmentation and the firm' in J. Edwards *et al.*, *Manpower Strategy and Techniques in an Organizational Context*. Chichester: Wiley.

Mandeville, T. (1983) 'The spatial effects of information technology', *Futures*, February, 65-72.

Maurice, M., Sorge, A. and Warner, M. (1980) 'Societal differences in organizing manufacturing units: a comparison of France, West Germany and Great Britain', *Organizational Studies*, 1, 59-86.

Mok, A.L. (1975) 'Is er een Dubbele Arbeidsmarkt in Nederland?' in *Werkloosheid, Aard, Omvang, Structurele Oorzakenen Beleidsalternatieven*. The Hague: Martinus Nishoff.

Noble, D.F. (1979) 'Social choice in machine design: the case of automatically controlled machine tools', in A. Zimbalist (ed.), *Case Studies on the Labor Process*. New York: Monthly Review Press.

Northcott, J., Rogers, P. with Zeilinger, A. (1982) *Microelectronics in Industry: Survey Statistics*, London: Policy Studies Institute.

Ouchi, W. (1981) *Theory Z: How American Business Can Meet the Japanese Challenge*. Reading, Mass.: Addison-Wesley.

Perrow, C. (1970) *Organizational Analysis: A Sociological View*. London: Tavistock.

Purcell, J. (1983) 'The management of industrial relations in the modern corporation: agenda for research', *British Journal of Industrial Relations*, XXI, 1-16.

Ramsey, H. (1977) 'Cycles of control: workers participation in sociological and historical perspective', *Sociology*, 11, 481-506.

Sorge, A., Hartmann, G., Warner, M. and Nicholas, I. (1983) *Microelectronics and Manpower in Manufacturing*. Aldershot: Gower.

Thompson, P. (1983) *The Nature of Work*. London: Macmillan.

Van de Ven, A.H. and Ferry, D.F. (1980) *Measuring and Assessing Organizations*. New York: Wiley.

Wilkinson, B. 91983) *The Shopfloor Politics of New Technology*. London: Heinemann.

Williams, E. (1983) 'Process control boom near', *Financial Times*, 16 May.

Williamson, O.E (1975) *Markets and Hierarchies*, New York: Free Press.

7

New Technology and Bank Work: Banking on IT as an 'Organizational Technology'

Stephen Smith and David Wield

City institutions represent the apex of a complex division of labour tasks: millions of physical operations performed by thousands of people throughout the UK. It is this 'technical division of labour' which we will concentrate on, and more particularly the organization of work in the branch networks of the London clearing banks.

The division of labour in banking is inherently difficult to manage. Efficiencies to be gained from the centralization and specialization of labour-tasks may conflict with the 'service' nature of much of the banks' business. This conflict is expressed in the recent history of new technology and work reorganization at the branch level.

In the recent past, some banks have pursued information technology as an 'organizational technology' which might overturn the classical patterns of bank branch work organization. This departure from established assumptions has not always been well received by bank workers. Men and women, managers and non-managers, senior and junior staffs have each been affected in different and sometimes negative ways by the new thinking.

It is even suggested that management strategies may have led to some 'proletarianization' of a workforce usually renowned for its conservatism. [...] New technology has certainly contributed to moderate and steady increases in the efficiency of bank workers over a long period. However, recent radical management strategy towards technical change has not markedly increased productivity but has instead generated some new problems in place of those they were intended to solve. This has led at least two banks towards a new and more conservative approach to new technology.

1 Orthodox branch work organization

The classical model of bank work involved customers and staff in face-to-face trust relations. Banking was thus far from an exclusively impersonal set of accounting calculations and ledger entries. It was, and to a declining extent, still is, based on intensive and often long-standing personal relations. In the *Protestant Ethic and the Spirit of Capitalism*, Max Weber hints that banks may indeed be among the very last businesses to adopt a thoroughly modern rational-bureaucratic form of organization (Weber, 1930). This paper will present some reasons why this is likely to be the case.

Under the classical pattern of bank work organization, the recruitment, pay, training and career assumptions which applied to bank staff were above all directed at maintaining a financially secure, dutiful, deferential and therefore trustworthy workforce. In addition, a presumption in favour of wide-ranging apprenticeships in banking created operational advantages at the clerical and at the higher, 'appointed', grades of work and was designed to result in rounded, 'generalist' and therefore flexible bankers for ultimate promotion to corporate management.

Later on we will show that there is considerable evidence that the banks have sought to dismantle this structure of bank work and to replace it with a more intensive or 'Tayloristic' division of labour. In doing so they seem certain to undermine their traditional personnel objectives. Indeed they have already done so.

The traditional bank branch created a particular form of control over work and bank workers. The established ideal in banking was that every branch manager was theoretically capable of performing most if not all branch operations, on the basis of his training and practical experience. A branch manager might be a lending manager, personnel manager, training manager and operations manager. In theory, promotion was open to anyone who could demonstrate the necessary 'aptitude' and 'dedication' (Bunyan and Youdale, 1981). The apprenticeship was long and comprehensive. It began with employment as a 'junior' at 15 or 16 years of age and might in theory at least end in a general managership at corporate HQ. These assumptions are represented in the statement that some recruits joined believing they carried the proverbial 'chief general manager's baton in their knapsacks'. The career paths of senior managers show that this representation of career planning stands up to examination and that managers received their management education within the system.

The dominant principle for promotion was that one would be nominated for career steps to jobs one could not yet do (the opposite of Taylorian specialization, which regards this as wasteful). The newly promoted would learn the job by the example of somebody who had already mastered it, and who would eventually be moved on in turn to a task which he was not yet competent to perform. Over time this knowledge would be entrusted to the next generation of employees. The ethos of the banking apprenticeship was paternal-autocratic (Rix *et al*, 1979). Employees were held in trust and received a career in return for deference to the bank's code of ethics. Indeed the research has shown that banks remain prepared to help employees through periods of illness or where there are difficult domestic considerations, by altering their workload to suit. On the other hand, the banks may expect staffs to implement changes with little advance warning on the assumption that 'the bank knows best'. In principle, nonconformity was devalued. Wide experience and knowledge as a 'general practitioner' in banking might qualify a manager for senior management after a career spanning some thirty-five or forty years. Clearly, this picture is somewhat over-drawn but it is a reasonable indication of how 'old school' bankers were promoted; authority and confidence to manage came with age, experience, generalist skills and a particular outlook. The prerequisite 'passport to success' was, and to an extent still is, the examinations leading to recognition by the Institute of Bankers (IOB). We consider possible changes to this system later.

The generalist principle was evident at the clerical level where people have been trained to do a comparatively wide range of tasks. This brought immediate operational advantages, and the principle has not been completely eliminated.

Because the banking day involves considerable qualitative and quantitative variations in inputs and outputs, staff flexibility is advantageous if a branch is to operate efficiently. For example, an enquiry clerk might be expected to be able to cashier, under some circumstances to 'input' account changes on a terminal, to encode cheques, to move around the branch doing a small number of different operations at different times of the day and to be prepared to cover for colleagues in emergencies. This is how the 'traditional' branch meets its peak loads. There is a certain cameraderie and collective pressure among clerks to work well and not to create difficulties for others to deal with later, though in a crisis employees will help each other out. There is reciprocity. The smaller the branch the greater the interdependence of people and tasks. A clear majority of clerks interviewed expressed a preference for working in smaller traditional branches over larger branches where they had experience of both.

Within the traditional branch, day-to-day managerial control rests with the branch accountant, while ultimate control rests with the manager. The accountant's title is misleading, for in fact he or she is closer to the roles of production, personnel and training superintendent rolled together. The accountant has a considerable say in the allocation of work, in the deployment of staff and in arranging for training. A successful accountant must carry a great deal of knowledge about the branch staff. This is part factual and part intangible. We estimate that an accountant in a large branch probably carries several hundred, perhaps thousands of such mental rules in addition to formal procedural rules. After 'generalist' training accountants may operate these rules quite fluently and carry far more implicit knowledge than they may consciously realize.

The actual balance of power and working relationship between the branch manager and accountant varies between branches according to personalities, despite the presumption in favour of conformism inherent in the organizational structure. This means that branches may vary according to the 'atmosphere' set by this working relationship. Comparable branches thus vary considerably on financial and operational performance. The performance of the same branch might change radically with a change of manager and accountant and their skills are fundamental to effective performance. A good lending manager may raise branch profitability as much as 500 per cent or better.

The term apprenticeship is used quite deliberately in order to suggest parallels between banking and crafts normally associated with manufacturing industry. 'Old school' managers have often referred to this system as 'coming up the hard way'. They identify themselves as 'Bankers' – their own term – rather than as 'Professional Managers'. The emphasis was on gaining new skills through experience.

But as technology was introduced, new design and organizational values were incorporated into bank work. These threaten to overturn the orthodoxy at the first stage: clerical work.

2   Taylorization

The traditional structure is only one of a number of ways through which managers seek effective control over work. An alternative is to break jobs down into smaller, technically interdependent parts. This lowers the discretion, necessary skills and autonomy of individual workers and is believed to be more efficient than craft forms (Taylor, 1967; Braverman, 1974).

Here we argue that although this 'Taylorist' management strategy is now evident in banking, it remains incomplete. This is because it has thrown up new and unexpected problems of its own. Indeed, it is by no means clear that the productivity gains which were envisaged from a more intensive division of labour are materializing.

Partly on the basis of the design values of largely US technology suppliers, corporate managements in banking have overseen considerable changes in bank work and organization. An extreme and widely quoted statement of supplier values was presented by Franco de Benedetti, managing director of Olivetti at a *Financial Times* conference in March 1979. He anticipates that new technology will lead to a new form of work control which would amount to an industrial revolution for white collar workers.

> The Taylorism of the first factories . . . enabled the labour force to be controlled and was the necessary prerequisite to the subsequent mechanisation and automation of the production processes. In this way, Taylorised industries were able to win competition over the putting out system . . . information technology is basically a technology of co-ordination and control of the labour force, the white collar workers, which Taylorian organisation does not cover . . .
>
> However, EDP (Electronic Data Processing) seems to be one of the most important tools with which company management institutes policies directly concerning the work process conditioned by complex economic and social factors. In this sense EDP is in fact an organisational technology, and like the organisation of labour, has a dual function as a productive force and a control tool for capital. (cited in Downing, 1981)

Similarly, Docherty (1978) observed that within the branch increased automation converted tellers who were in effect mini-bankers into 'automatons'.

Advantages have also been sought from further managerial specialization. In keeping with most clearing banks, one recently announced:

> For some time, we have been moving away from the concept of a generalist banker and have now decided that we must provide a greater degree of specialisation to serve our personal and corporate customers. (Press Release)

Such a process is not new but appears to have accelerated during the 1970s.

As we explained in the last chapter, the primary application of new technology in banking has so far been the *automation of the branch accounting system*. Branch ledgers have been progressively replaced by main-frame files: men's italic book entries by women's keyboard entries. Indeed, business growth and information control could not have been handled without new technology. While the accounting principles have remained the same, the social organization of the accounting process has changed in important ways, particularly with the feminization of the workforce. The direction of change points towards Taylorism, although as we shall see later, the banks are far from convinced that this is the best approach. Furthermore, while banks clearly seek productivity gains, the use of technology as a form of control is far from most managers' minds (see Taylor, 1984, pp. 280-1).

There has been progressive specialization and several tiers of entry have replaced common entrance at 15 or 16. The career structure has become horizontally and vertically segmented; men and women tend to do different jobs, often physically segregated within a branch. What were once stages in a long career have tended to become more or less permanently staffed by one segment of the labour force, and what were a series of more or less coherent clerical processes have been progressively broken down into detailed stages.

A number of banks have taken this division of labour to its logical conclusion and piloted American style Hub and Satellite banking, where specialist tasks are geographically and hierarchically defined. At the hub branch a full range of services are provided and this is where a management team of specialist lenders, administrative and training managers may be found. The processing of remittances may be undertaken in this building, or in a separate data processing office. Payments handling is usually done by women on a semi-automated basis, sometimes working part-time or in shifts. This layout has, at least until recently, been articulated by US suppliers of new technology as the best fix to rising costs (for example, at recent *Financial Times* banking and new technology conferences, and in interviews).

Standing order clerks and many 'appointed' grades are also grouped centrally in this local network, as is typing/word processing. The hub and DP offices are linked to satellite or service branches, which offer a narrower range of services directed at the personal customer and which therefore house only a fraction of the range of bank jobs. Many satellite branches have no managers and the banks have achieved this partly by non-replacement of a post-war age cohort of generalist or 'general practitioner' branch managers. Instead, central managers nominally cover a number of satellite branches each. In most clearing banks the lines between the branches largely represent van-runs for voucher and other collections and deliveries, relief staff cover and journeys by the management team who oversee the network. A separate corporate branch may be established for purely business custom and may have no counter service (see Figure 7.1).

This form of reorganization has been successful on the lending-side, provided that the network is not too geographically dispersed, nor its corporate customers too conservative. It is not ideally suited to rural areas. Specialized lending managers are almost unanimously pleased with reorganization because it enables them to concentrate on marketing the bank's services. This is seen as rewarding work. The younger lending specialists clearly welcomed not having to perform the wider administrative functions which a generalist branch manager would deal with. In some networks administrative managers have no lending responsibilities at all while in others they do have limited lending duties.

Figure 7.1 *Hub and satellite banking*

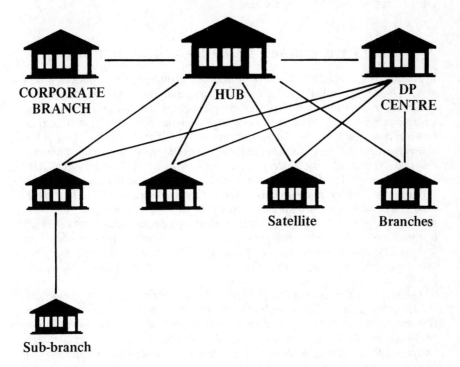

CORPORATE
BRANCH   HUB   DP
                                                 CENTRE

Satellite   Branches

Sub-branch

However, reorganization in this form has brought a series of new problems. The management, administrative and co-ordination input is increased with specialization despite reductions in branch managers. Banks which have piloted hub and satellite banking have found that there are few if any clerical staff savings – clerical staffing seems to rise by degrees and appointed or intermediate staffing also seems to increase by as much as 32 per cent in one bank (EFILWC, 1984, p.95). These changes can be a little more than proportionate to the increase in business which banks have been enjoying. In other words, specialization may slightly reduce labour productivity. It quite definitely *does not 'revolutionize' clerical work performance*. Hub and satellite banking has also accentuated the need for a qualitatively different management style of supervision which old school managers may find difficult. But probably the most immediate reason for the disappointment over productivity is that specialization tends to reduce staff flexibility. The qualitative and quantitative variations in the 'banking day' are inconsistent with Taylorism which works best on continuous inputs and outputs, for example, as occurs on an assembly line. A Tayloristic new technology strategy is bound to create some important new difficulties given the nature of the business which clearing banks undertake, the range of products to be serviced and the face-to-face nature of much service delivery. Many new messengers jobs are created in the network and considerable van mileages may be run up. These are a quantifiable symptom of the new control difficulties of hub and satellite systems, but other real, if less quantifiable, disadvantages from reorganization may be as decisive.

3 Qualitative change in bank work organization

Specialization highlights differences between groups of employees in a new way. Young 'specialist' graduate managers, and older GP managers are conscious of profound differences of outlook which separate them. The graduates have intimated that they may feel uncomfortable in a branch environment and that older bank workers find it difficult to 'place' them in the status hierarchy. One old school manager complained of new school managers that 'you can't just inject people with thirty years' experience'. Old schoolers are inclined to argue that they can understand balance sheets in a rapid, intuitive way, and can better understand the branch staff milieu. This, they claim, only comes with experience. On the other hand, new schoolers suspect that such GP 'intuition' represents benign prejudice rather than strict business sense. The new managers seem more inclined to treat branches as industrial systems rather than as a particular or special form or organization. GPs regard this as a regrettable offence against a revered way of working life. [...]

There is also a hiatus between women who predominantly work as cashiers, standing order clerks, personal bankers (upgraded enquiry clerks) and 'mech' (machine)-room operators, and men on the accelerated career programme. Men appear to be put through these grades more quickly, particularly through the mech rooms, probably as a gesture towards the old notion of a banking apprenticeship. We have thus found men allocated for no more than several months as part of their 'man management training' to mech rooms run

Table 7.1   *Percentage of men and women working in the banks, national*

Year	% women	% men
1959	40.5	59.5
1965	47.6	52.4
1970	53.0	47.0
1975	(54.5)	(45.5)
1979	(55.5)	(44.5)
1984	(57.1)	(42.9)

Notes: Figures in brackets count part-timers as ½. This data only available from 1975.
Source: Palmer, 1983.

by women. There is an obvious association between the historical automation of clerical work in banking and the recruitment of women.

The overall proportion of women to men has steadily risen (Table 7.1), though not so rapidly in London (Table 7.2). Table 7.2 also shows that female part-time working in London declined between 1974 and 1981.

The proportion of women to men appears to be higher in the satellite branches than in hub branches, while in the mass processing centres, women are in the majority by far.

Table 7.2   *Employment composition in banks, Greater London*

Year	Total women	Total men	Total part-time women	% women	% of women working p.t.	% part-time women out of total bank employment
1974	57,992	62,044	10,975	48.3	18.9	9.14
1981	66,024	69,233	7,921	48.8	12.0	5.9

Source: Department of Employment.

Staff morale in DP is quite variable. However, there were numerous complaints that women staff who joined as bank workers find themselves limited to repetitive 'factory work' as dedicated machine operators. Several complained that, 'This isn't banking, it's factory work'. The changing morale of staff and the weakening of certain incentives to work hard – collective pressure to finish and go home, reciprocity, the satisfaction of seeing a task through to completion, the promise of a career in return for conscientious work – may have contributed to some 'proletarianization' of staff in these areas (see also Crompton and Jones, 1984). Two groups of Taylorized clerks in the research complained of boredom from the sameness of their work. Three groups of interviewees were in a surprisingly volatile mood.

In some branches, men and women seem to have clearly accepted the division of labour between them. Both men and women thus responded to questions on this issue by pointing to the different social expectations held by men and women. And it was certainly true that a majority of younger women interviewed emphasized that bank employment was not the central feature of their lives and that marriage and child-care were valued more highly than 'getting ahead'. Some found male competitiveness and ambition to be distasteful, or 'OK for them but not for me', while certain women were ready to assume that 'career women' in the bank had otherwise failed in their domestic lives. However, in other branches there was an undercurrent of tension, especially among women of around 30 years old and above whose values had shifted with their experience both in banking and in the home. Here earlier objectives – marriage, child-care – had proved unsatisfactory; for example, those who had divorced or were childless. They felt that they could have achieved more in banking. In the most closely studied branch networks, trade union membership was slightly higher among older compared with younger women.

4   Management and workforce styles: negotiating consent for new systems

All clearing banks have progressed some ways towards factory-like work at most levels or stages in the production of standardized services. This has dictated the need on the bank's part to develop factory management styles and has necessarily altered workforce images of the situation. This is particularly evident in the banks' central clearing where work conditions resemble batch processing in manufacture. It has enabled banks to cope with a long history of cheque growth and new centralized services. As one moves closer to the branches, however, the logic for this pattern of organization looks progressively weaker.

The essence of the difficulty is that branches are called upon to conduct two rather different types of work which cannot easily be separated for practical purposes: meeting customers (with different needs) and processing large quantities of information. Given the lags and leads in the banking day referred to above, there is a good case for fitting these two spheres into the one branch workforce, in order to gain maximum utilization of people, machines, skills and time.

Clearly, hub and satellite banking is a radical attempt to divorce the two types of work with partial automation. As we have suggested, this strategy has failed to prove itself conclusively. But only in the crudest sense is the productivity of bank work set by the machines themselves. It must also be realized that neither are even the formal organizational structures directly linked to performance. The same organization with the same machines may produce one set of outcomes in one place which will not be reproduced elsewhere and this is admittedly true of traditional 'free standing' branches, of networked branches and of factory-like processing units. [...]

An intensive division of labour can be made to work under certain conditions. The key here is whether or not both men and women, managers and non-managers broadly accept or reject a view of their work drawn more or less in 'factory' terms. There is no guarantee of this happening. [...]

5   Training

With the intensification of the division of labour and the tendency to place many more women at machines than men, a double problem had emerged around the question of bank education and training.

The belief that women had 'nimble fingers' and were therefore better suited to machine work came up with striking regularity. Because keyboard skills take time to acquire, and because women spend longer at machines, this belief became self-reinforcing. The stereotype is coming under strain because a growing percentage of women are seeking Institute recognition and staying at work longer. Further, when few promotions are on offer, staff perceive an added incentive to take their examinations. It is unfortunate that a more egalitarian view of women by banks has coincided with employment stagnation.

The IOB qualification means that women have increasingly won what theoretically might have functioned as a 'passport to success' under the old orthodoxy. [...]

At a time of employment stagnation, promotion opportunities are necessarily limited. But increasingly formal career ceilings have been placed across the paths of employees comparable to the civil service.

There have been two responses to these developments. First, the banks have sought to limit day release provision for IOB courses. To date this has not significantly reduced the record number of candidates registered as students (self-tuition and evening classes remain options).

Secondly, specialization appears at least partly to be having an impact on the *structure* of the Institute's syllabus and examinations. Probably because the IOB's role as a 'passport' contradicts the growing horizontal and vertical segmentation of the labour force, the Institute is placed in a difficult position.

A compromise is being sought which might channel students either to an upgraded form of banking qualification or to a new diploma in financial sector services work, possibly beyond banking as such.

This development could have further effects on the gender and career structure of banking employment and might conceivably underscore the separation of women's and men's work in the industry as well as in related financial service industries.

Much remains to be decided, not least whether the existing membership of the Institute of Bankers will be prepared to vote through such changes. Old schoolers might be expected to resist them.

These few examples show that technical and organizational change raises questions far beyond the machines and that new technology of itself does not bring clear and self evident advantages. The Olivetti claim that information technology is a Tayloristic '"organizational technology" ... which lends itself to the co-ordination and control of the labour force' seems to have proved premature in the case of banking. Should specialization result in workforce dissatisfaction, particularly at the clerical level, then IT may instead be in the process of generating entirely new control problems for the banks. We have some evidence that this has indeed happened and that the loss of career prospects and work satisfaction has caused clerks to become less 'duty-bound' by their employment. Bankers have certainly referred to 'motivation' problems among non-career staff, for example at the 1982 Cambridge Seminar on *The Banks and Technology in the 1980s*.

However, as we will now explain, information technology does not have to take a Tayloristic path. There is a more conservative alternative.

6 Towards a more conservative view of new technology in banking

Recently, observers have detected a sense of disappointment and surprise among senior bankers over new technology. A recent report (Touche Ross, 1985) has placed the blame for this on the banks themselves and in particular on the 'old culture' of the banks. At least one software supplier has made similar comments (Arthur, 1985). [...] Tayloristic forms of design, embodied in some systems show a lack of fit with branch banking and that problems then result from *organizational* change around the kit. IT as an 'organization-al technology' has proved inappropriate, and if bankers are to blame, then it is for accepting suppliers' productivity claims and design-values. [. . .]

We will list some of the limits of new technology as both product and process innovations. But we will close by explaining how the current shift of thinking provides an opportunity for a paradoxically more conservative, yet more imaginative organization of bank work and technology. There are signs that this is happening.

It is now realized that the interaction of inputs and outputs at branch level is extremely complex, and not capable of at-a-stroke technology fixes. According to one clearer, even the most important process innovations envisaged in the next five to ten years 'may not produce as much as one whole staff or equivalent time saving per branch!' Far from 'wiping out' clerical staff, one further 'revolutionary' innovation will save an estimated five person-hours per branch per month.

Technical and organizational changes have brought other surprises. Two major clearing banks have found that the most operationally efficient branch is the 'traditional' 15 person branch and that reorganization 'hasn't produced any staff savings really'.

One experience with a prominent innovation has underlined the inadequcy of Taylorian assumptions about efficiency – the 'Automated Teller Machine' (ATM). To the American suppliers who coined the term, the terminal was primarily a process innovation, literally an *automated teller*. Obtaining cash by customer self service at a machine was thought equivalent to between one-third and one human cashier, a calculation initially accepted by the UK clearing banks.

The problem was that this was a very rough approximation greatly affected by considerations apart from the nominal 'efficiency' of the machines. With hindsight the notion of the human equivalence of an ATM is misleading, particularly in a European context where, despite the advance of specialization, 'cashiering' has not been sufficiently split up to allow for one-for-one machine replacements of human operations. The two are not compar-able. Cashiers perform many operations which machines cannot conveniently reproduce yet which must still be performed for most customers. The assessment of ATMs as a process innovation is complicated because custom-ers use ATMs in a quite unanticipated way. The typical cash withdrawal at an ATM was surprisingly small. This pattern simply has no equivalence with customer behaviour at the cashier position which involves fewer visits for larger amounts and other queries besides. (Counter transactions continue to rise despite ATM usage.) Here IT has made a difference but not necessar-ily the one that was anticipated. Certainly useful, but again not 'revolution-ary'.

However, the suppliers did not rest their efficiency arguments there. They have attempted to persuade European banks that the ATM should form a more sophisticated 'self service banking terminal'. Sited in the wall, the lobby or at a remote site, customers might transfer funds across their accounts, initiate payments, set up standing orders, all without the intervention of bank staff (or in supplier terminology without a 'warm body').

The clearers are hesitant and although many innovations are operational, including 'home banking' terminals, uptake appears to be restricted to a narrow segment of the customer profile. Another 'substantial' innovation saved more in postal charges than it did in staff costs.

7 Discussion and conclusions

Our research has led to two conclusions. First, the productivity gains which were sought through a more intensive division of labour in the branch network have not materialized. In this form, information technology has not lived up to the claims made for it. Secondly, a better understanding of bank work organizations is causing the banks to think again about new technology, and to evolve a new, yet paradoxically more conservative view of technical change.

In the light of both these findings, many forecasts of the employment effects of new technology in banking are beginning to look unrealistic.

Attempts to increase productivity by specializing clerical work have been compromised by the loss of operational flexibility which this has created. In some areas this loss of flexibility has been compounded by a reduction in staff morale, though in others the changeover to a new regime at work was accomplished more successfully. Yet there has been no 'revolution' in labour productivity. Moreover, the more carefully one looks at the branch networks of the major clearers the less easy it is to see where technically-induced job-loss might occur. This leads us on to a different view of what the role of information technology might be.

Our conclusions that the overall figures for banking employment may stagnate but not decline over the next eight to ten years broadly fit in with Rajan (1984), but not with most other studies known to us which posit more or less 'substantial' to 'massive' labour reductions. For example, Shaw and Coulbeck (1983), Game and Pringle (1984), BIFU (1980) and Hewlett (1985).

The reasons for these different estimates are almost certainly methodological. Rajan's study was distinguished by reporting senior management estimates of job-loss in a number of service industries. However, the mechanism of the relationship or what he terms the 'mediating factors' between technology and employment change is not properly explored.

The higher job-loss forecasts found in other studies are clearly linked with a method which estimates the theoretical capabilities of innovations on a machine-by-machine basis. (Suppliers may be forgiven for thinking of change in this way.) It seems to us extremely unlikely that this method of forecasting will prove accurate. The approach probably guarantees that overestimates will be produced. This method merely establishes the absolutely worst case conceivable.

The other major weakness of the machine-by-machine method is that it seriously underestimates the nature, complexity and particularity of technical change as it affects the *quality* of employment. It is most unwise to isolate 'the new technology' from changes in career, work, organizational structure and management. These issues are additional to the question of how customers will react to new systems.

However, new technology need not primarily be thought of in terms of labour productivity and the fragmentation of tasks as it most often is.

In order to develop an alternative to the strategy of work specialization, it is necessary to make a shift in emphasis around some basic assumptions. Instead of assuming that the banking day can be remade in order to fit the (theoretical) advantage of a more intensive division of labour, one may begin with the traditional branch as it stands and what it is supposed to do.

Although the banks have reduced the 'service' content of many of the services they provide, the *raison d'être* of a bank branch is customer contact. Yet, historically, new technology has not really been directed at enhancing this function, but has instead been concentrated on the branch accounting system: and on the back office. The information produced for accounting purposes is relatively opaque and a number of older managers and many back office clerks have complained that they have lost contact with the customer in the meantime.

However, recent proposed developments would establish a transparent 'information' system operating separately to the opaque 'data' generated by the automated accounting system. Personnel would be able to ask the system sensible questions on the nature and spread of customer accounts in order, for example, to get to know about their accountholders and devise marketing strategies. 'It's back to the old days!' said one supplier. Jobs could then be constructed around 'service' and information. There are no technical reasons why, for example, personal bankers (enhanced enquiry clerks who are usually women) should not be given access to any such system and be allowed to develop 'banking' skills further, thus demonstrating old style 'commitment', 'aptitude' and 'dedication'. This might even lead to a new 'appointed' job status for successful personal bankers, involving not simply selling but also marketing financial services. They would become 'bankers' in the old sense.

This policy of using new technology to upgrade the marketing skills of bank workers would be compatible with a number of recent developments in branch work organization. Several steps have been taken which promise to recover the traditional control skills of the clerks (clerical work having been broken up over a period of several decades).

For example, the trend is now against separate local processing centres which represented the ultimate in task fragmentation. New open-plan branch layouts are a physical recognition that cashier and 'mech' operations are best shared by several employees. Here there are few specifically back office clerks as such, and efficiency gains have resulted. This widening of clerical duties has recovered much of the cameraderie and spirit of mutual helpfulness (and mutual coercion) among clerks. For clerks at least, the notion of knowing each others' jobs and seeing work through a reasonable number of steps is becoming re-established. We have seen just how well this can work in a branch that was very short staffed through sickness and leave yet which was coping well with the intensive peak loads of the week. Staff found satisfaction in meeting the challenge, though men admitted some reluctance at using the terminals.

Even within the hub and satellite pattern which formally centralizes the management function, clerks may find themselves enjoying more rather than less autonomy.

Some satellite branches from which the manager has been removed, are left in charge of grade four clerks – often women. It is quite clear that their work involves management responsibility. The problem is that these skills are not actually recognized or rewarded as management skills – especially as these clerks spend much time cashiering and machining alongside more junior clerks (wherein lies the secret of their authority and success). Although the organization chart may indicate a certain centralization of control, this may paradoxically leave clerical workers in a more autonomous position than before the removal of the manager.

In recognition of this change there was considerable debate in one bank as to what the senior clerk in managerless branches ought to be called. Part of the difficulty in finding a form of words involved deciding whether or not the job involved 'management'. In effect, the definition of management compared with operational skills was being negotiated.

Indeed, we have been struck by the degree to which technology, work organization and the roles of men and women in banking are subject to tacit negotiation. This contradicts the conventional wisdom on technical change in a number of ways. For example, there is a mythology that technical change carries a coherent logic which organizations simply must pursue and which then have an 'impact' on the workforce. Certainly technology in banking *has* been followed *as if* it did possess a correct logic, notably a logic of efficiency through an increased division of labour. But if technology had this simplistic quality then it would surely not have presented the banks with the difficult issues which have arisen. As we have explained, neither is a more conservative approach to bank work organization and new technology guaranteed of success. But given the context it seems less of a risk than the radical strategy of specialization.

A 'traditional' approach *may* succeed where a 'factory' approach has not and vice versa. Much depends on the managers and the non-managers concerned, on the balance of new and old schools, and on the perceptions of men and women. To this may be added the character of the local labour-market, the degree of unionization, regional labour and household traditions and the nature of the local demand for bank services.

The future involves choices both for management and the trade unions.

Within management there is a struggle of ideas between those who believe in the advantages of task specialization and those who do not. This debate is far from being settled.

The trade unions in the industry also appear to be cross-cut by competing caucuses, though on the surface the issues seem clear cut. Trade unions are understandably concerned, primarily with job security and pay in relation to new technology, and seek to link them in 'new technology agreements' (BIFU, 1980). The union approach is to negotiate a 'share in the benefits' of new technology in terms of a shorter working week, earlier retirement and improved pay. Unions also seek consultation in advance of the implementation of new technology in order that negotiations can be made meaningful. In the absence of such agreements, trade unions are inclined to fear job-loss.

Here we would make two points:

First, it would appear that the unions' fears over job-loss are exaggerated. As the employers have discovered, what a machine implies in theory is not at all the same as what a machine may mean when placed within the structure of an organization.

Secondly, the mix of traditional and rationalized branches presents the trade unions with different sets of members working in very different circumstances. Because new technology does not therefore affect workers in anything like the same way there are some difficulties in identifying a common set of worker interests. There are differences of interest and perception between men and women, between those who have joined the union because they have become 'proletarianized' and those who have joined because they do not wish to become proletarianized, and who seek to retain staff status; between 'job' people and 'career' people and between managers and non-managers.

Each of these issues ultimately express themselves in terms of technical change and the way staff are allocated to tasks. These decisions have important consequences for the well-being, security and work satisfaction of staff. However, despite the different circumstances of bank workers in the branch network, the majority clearly valued customer contact, flexible task sharing, group cameraderie, trust and skill.

This means that there is a happy coincidence between staff values, efficiency and the conservative approach to new technology and clerical work organization in branches. Our proposal that both unions and employers should embrace some old school, or banker values might even seem bizarre. Yet we conclude that trade unions, employers and suppliers should co-operate to develop model technology design values which articulate what is at heart a conservative concept of banking.

Many permutations exist, and an ideal technical and organizational form will never be found. It is an elusive chimera. Our broad conclusion remains that a stronger case can be made for the traditional form than for the factory form of branch organization. Indeed, as Weber seems to argue, it may prove irrational to 'rationalize' bank work.

References

Arthur, C. (1985) 'Bankers begin to doubt technology', *Computer Weekly*, 961, 2 May.

BIFU (Banking Insurance and Finance Union) (1980) *Microtechnology a Programme for Action*.

BIFU (1983a) *Microelectronics Briefing No. 1*, BIFU Research, January.

BIFU (1983b) *Microelectronics Briefing No. 2*, BIFU Research, April.

Braverman, H. (1974) *Labor and Monopoly Capital, the Degradation of work in the twentieth century*. New York: The Monthly Review Press.

Bunyan, D. and Youdale, R. (1981) *Report of a case study on the impact of New Technology on Women and Trade Union Organisation in Banking*. Bristol: Bristol Resource Centre.

Child, J. (1984) 'New Technology and the service class', paper to the *Annual Conference of the British Sociological Association*, Bradford, April.

Child, J., Loveridge, R., Harvey, J. and Spencer, A. (1984) 'Microelectronics and the quality of employment in services' in Marstrand, P. (ed.) *New Technology and the Future of Work and Skills*. London: Frances Pinter.

Crompton, R. and Jones, G. (1984) *White Collar Proletariat?* London and Basingstoke: Macmillan.

Docherty, P. (1978) *Automation of the Service Industries*, IFAC Round Table.

Downing, H. (1981) *Developments in Secretarial Labour: resistance, office automation and the transformation of patriarchal relations of control*,

PhD Dissertation, University of Birmingham.

EFILWC (European Foundation for the Improvement of Living and Working Conditions) (1984) *Technological Developments in Banking and Insurance: The Impact on Customers and Employees*. United Kingdom, Dublin.

Game, A. and Pringle, R. (1984) *Gender at Work*, London: Pluto Press.

Goulder A.W. (1954a) *Wildcat Strike*, Yellow Springs, Ohio: Antioch Press.

Goulder, A.W. (1954b) *Patterns of Industrial Bureaucracy*. New York: Free Press of Glencoe.

Hewlett, N. (1985) 'New Technology and Banking Employment in the EEC', *Futures 17*, 1, February.

Lowe, J. (1979) 'Staff Representation in Banking', *Industrial Relations Journal*, 3, 195, March.

Marshall, J.N. and Bachtler, J.F. (1984) 'Spatial perspectives on technological changes in the banking sector of the United Kingdom', *Environment and Planning*, 16.

Palmer, L.S. (1983) *Technical Change and Employment in Banking*, Brighton, Sussex University Dissertation.

Rajan, A. (1984) *New Technology and Employment in the UK Financial Services Sector; past impact and future prospects*, Institute for Manpower Studies.

Read, C.N. (1983) 'Information Technology in Banking', *Long Range Planning*, 16 August.

Rix, A., Keates, L. and Rees, T. (1979) *Employee Attitudes to Representation in Barclays Bank*, University College of Wales, Cardiff.

Shaw, E.R. and Coulbeck, N.S. (1983) *UK Retail Banking Prospects in the Competitive 1980s*. Loughborough: Staniland Hall Associates.

Smith, S.L. and Wilkinson, B. (1984) 'From Old School Hunches to Departmental Lunches', *Sociological Review*, 32, 1, February.

Spybey, T. (1984) 'Traditional and Professional Frames of Meaning for Managers', *Sociology*, 18, 4, November.

Taylor, A. (1983) *New Technology in Banking, Insurance and Finance*, Research Report 59, London Borough of Hammersmith and Fulham.

Taylor, A., Coppin, P. and Wealthy, P. (1984) *The Impact of New Technology on Local Employment*. Aldershot: Gower.

Taylor, F.W. [1967 (1911)] *The Principles of Scientific Management*. New York: W.W. Norton.

Touche Ross (1985) *The Impact of Technology on Banking*. London: Touche Ross and Co.

Weber, M. [1976 (1930)] *The Protestant Ethic and the Spirit of Capitalism*, trans. Parsons, T., Giddens, A. (ed.). London: George Allen and Unwin.

Wilkinson, B. and Smith, S.L. (1983) 'Management Strategies for technical change', *Science and Public Policy*, 10, 2, April.

8

Telecommunication: Policy Directions for the Technology and Information Services

William H. Melody

1 Introduction

On 24 May 1844, Samuel Morse sent the first telegraph message, 'What hath God wrought!', between Washington, D.C. and Baltimore, Maryland. Morse undoubtedly would be astounded to see the technological advances in electronic information processing and transmission that have taken place in less than 150 years. Indeed, many writers seem to attribute these developments to 'God', inviting individuals and societies to submit themselves to technological determinism. Although Western societies have so institutionalized computer and communication technologies that they are becoming ever more dependent on these technologies, there are wide areas for policy choice that will significantly influence the direction and speed of technological changes, the institutional arrangements for managing and controlling them, the type of product and service applications, and the characteristics of the information content that is generated and transmitted using these technologies. This has always been the case. But for the future the stakes for society are much higher than they have been in the past. [...]

Until relatively recent times, the term 'information technology' tended to be associated narrowly with the computer industry and data processing. More established forms of information technology associated with print, film, mail, telephone/telegraph, speech and language were neither new nor undergoing path-breaking changes. Radio and television provided broadcasting, not interactive information exchange. Communication generally was viewed as a separate function from data or information processing.

In this discrete, compartmentalized world, dramatic technical advances in microelectronics and related computer hardware and software were promoted in a government-supported market environment. Many national governments (particularly the US through its military and space programmes) provided large subsidies for R & D and experimental service applications, and stimulated a large market through government purchases of the industries' products and services. Restrictive government regulations toward the computing industries were few, and were related primarily to selective limitations on sales of technologically advanced equipment to 'unfriendly' nations, and periodic concerns about IBM market dominance. The computing industries operated in an extremely dynamic market characterized by continuous technological improvement and market expansion.

In the 1960s, the computing industry realized that the constraints of stand-alone data processing were becoming unnecessarily limiting. Continuing reductions in the unit costs of data storage, processing, and retrieval pushed back the intensive margin of the data processing market. But access to data processing from a distance through telecommunication connections, i.e. teleprocessing or telematics, could push back the extensive geographic boundary of the market and open vast new market opportunities. The convergence of computing and telecommunication technologies and the integration of computing and telecommunication functions so as to provide information networks have been underway for almost two decades (OECD, 1973, 1975).

The direction and pace of these developments have been influenced primarily by government policies in the telecommunication sector, not by technological developments in the computing industries. The telecommunication sector historically has been subject to monopolization and direct control by national governments. Traditional practice has been to prohibit the interconnection to the telecommunication network of terminal devices (even basic telephones, let alone sophisticated computers) that were not owned and controlled by the telecommunication monopoly. Telecommunication has been one of the most protected, insulated and monopolized industries in the economies of virtually all nations. International agencies in the field have tended to operate as a cartel of national monopolies, establishing policies to prevent or limit encroachment into the domain of the telecommunication monopolies.

The traditional policies and practices of telecommunication monopolies have been called into question in most Western countries. It began in the USA in the late 1960s, and gradually spread north to Canada and across the oceans to Japan and Western Europe. But the speed of policy changes has been extremely slow. The USA is still wrestling with most fundamental policy issues that were raised initially almost two decades ago. Canada, the UK, and Japan have just begun lengthy processes for re-evaluating a wide range of regulatory and tariff restrictions that now limit the application of information technologies and services. Some countries have yet to begin this reassessment. With the exception of OECD, which has no direct power to effect policy changes, international agencies have been slow to recognize the evolving policy issues, and often seemingly incapable of addressing them on any terms other than eleventh-hour, *ad hoc*, incremental adjustments.

It is perhaps ironic that, in the name of 'deregulation', more regulatory activity has been generated than ever existed in the so-called 'regulation' era. Under monopoly conditions there need not be a lot of regulatory activity. Most decisions taken by the monopoly supplier are not challenged or challengeable. Controversial issues are negotiated quietly among a few dominant interests, or resolved by the direction of government authority. But under deregulation, there is a mixture of monopoly, oligopoly, and competitive markets, many sensitive issues to resolve at the margin between competition and monopoly markets, and more affected parties with interests to be considered and the financial backing to warrant vigorous advocacy. In the USA and Canada, the telecommunication regulatory agencies are busier than ever attempting to address telecommunication policy issues. When the UK privatized – some say 'deregulated' – telecommunication, it became necessary to create a regulatory commission, OFTEL, when none was previously necessary (Wigglesworth, 1985). International regulatory agencies, such as the International Telecommunications Union (ITU) and the International Radio Consultative Committee (CCIR) are virtually overwhelmed with policy and regulatory problems. Under 'deregulation', regulation is more important than it ever has been.

This paper is a review of the major areas of government policy that are influencing now, and will continue to influence, the pace and direction of application of telecommunication technologies and services into the 1990s. Although these policy issues derive primarily from a reassessment of historic policies in telecommunication, it is clear that telecommunication is becoming the centre-piece of national industrial policies, that it carries significant implications for historic social and cultural policies, and that it brings to the forefront important policy issues relating to information as a tradeable commodity. In each of these areas there are related important policy issues to be addressed. But their effects will depend to a significant degree on the telecommunication infrastructure and the policies that guide its development and application.

2   The evolution of computer/telecommunication issues

Perhaps the initial recognition of evolving computer telecommunication policy issues and problems came from the US Federal Communications Commission (FCC) when it announced in 1966 a formal 'Inquiry into the Regulatory and Policy Problems presented by the Interdependence of Computer and Telecommunications Services and Facilities' (FCC, 1966). In 1971, OECD established a 'Panel on Policy Issues of Computer Telecommunications Interaction' that began a study of the problems from an international perspective (OECD, 1973). Canada established a task force to address these issues in the same year (Department of Communications, Canada, 1972). Other nations established task forces to address these issues throughout the 1970s. Yet, as we approach the late 1980s, no country or international agency has developed a clear set of policy guidelines. In the USA, the FCC is snarled in the midst of assessing its third 'Computer Inquiry', with no apparent end in sight.

The integration of computing and telecommunication has quite different consequences for these two enormous industries. The computing and data processing industries become (1) suppliers of equipment to be used by the telecommunication industry, or in conjunction with telecommunication systems and services, (2) high-volume users of advanced digital data telecommunication systems and services, and (3) suppliers of information services provided over telecommunication networks. The future of these industries for telematic services is totally dependent upon the efficient supply of high-quality telecommunication facilities and services. In essence, the data processing of the past must become teleprocessing for the future, and efficient telecommunication networks must provide the infrastructure over which the services can be supplied.

The dependence of the computing industries upon the building block of telecommunication for developing their new services is so significant that it prompted the US FCC to conclude in its first 'Computer Inquiry' that '... data processing cannot survive, much less develop further, except through reliance upon and use of communication facilities and services' (FCC, 1972). This unique dependence upon telecommunication systems and services for the future development of data-processing and information services explains the concern expressed by the computing industry and potential users of teleprocessing services about the adequacy and efficiency of the telecommunication system for data communication services. For them, the most significant constraints and problems are not computer issues, but rather telecommunication issues.

In contrast, the telecommunication system does not have a similar dependence on the computing industry for its continued growth and development. The existing telecommunication system was designed for the efficient transmission of voice telephone services. Voice demand has continued to grow at quite high rates (10 to 15 per cent per annum in most Western countries, and even higher for international traffic), requiring the continuing investment of large amounts of capital by the telecommunication entities in order to maintain sufficient capacity for voice demand alone. In fact, for a variety of reasons, the telecommunication systems of many countries historically have been unable to keep pace with the growing demand for standard voice telephone service. [...]

The problem is magnified by predictions that future demand for data communication is likely to grow at extremely rapid rates. Although data communication presently represents less than 10 per cent of all traffic on telecommunication systems, its current annual growth rate is in the neighbourhood of 40 to 50 per cent. Moreover, even this growth rate is constrained not by the limits of the utility of data communication to users but by the technical and regulatory restrictions associated with the telecommunication services being supplied. Despite expectations of continuing high growth rates in voice communication, some telecommunication forecasts predict that, *if* telecommunication systems are responsive to the needs and requirements for data communication, there will be more data communication than voice communication on the telecommunication network, at some time during the 1990s.

In contrast to standard voice communication, data communication demands are enormously diversified. Applications reflecting data communication demands range from services that require only a small portion of a traditional 4 kHz voice communication channel to those that require enormous broadband capacities; from services that require connections of only a few seconds at a time to those that require almost continuous interconnection; from services that require very high quality transmission standards to those that can be adapted readily to the inherited voice communication system. For data communication, the service characteristics are quite different from voice, both in its technical and in its economic parameters.

The existing telecommunication system has been designed to meet the technical standards for voice communication. It employs the analogue transmission method using signals that are exact reproductions of the pattern of sound waves being transmitted. But this restricts the speed with which digital data signals can be transmitted. In addition, signal distortions that do not significantly affect the quality of voice communication create errors in data transmission. The human ear is a much better filter of extraneous noise than a computer. For many years, a major thrust of research and development in the industry has been a search for new techniques that will improve error performance in data communication. [. . .]

Telephone companies and administrations now are converting their signal standards from analogue to digital and upgrading the telecommunication system to the standards of digital computing. Progress has been most rapid for the long-distance transmission function, and digital terminals are widely available. The conversions of local switching and loops are more costly and are being implemented more slowly. POTS (the plain old telephone system) is in the process of being converted to an ISDN (integrated services digital network), a sophisticated multi-purpose network used to provide a wide variety of communication and information services. This conversion process will continue at least until the end of the century, and raises important policy issues with respect to the specific technical standards that will be adopted for ISDN, the financing of the very substantial investments required to convert from analogue voice to digital data communication standards, the limits of the telecommunication monopoly and the restrictions that it places on users of the system, and the structure of rates for the range of data, voice and other services that will be provided over the future fully digitalized telecommunication system.

3   The changing role of the market

The provision of telecommunication services in all countries is made under conditions where the allocation of economic resources and the provision of services are determined by a mix of market forces and governmental administrative decisions. In this sense, there is a commonality across all countries, whether the provision of telecommunication services is by a government administrative agency, an independent government corporation, or a private corporation subject to government regulation. In each case, decisions taken with respect to the technology, the allocation of resources, the type and distribution of services provided, and the tariff conditions establishing the terms and conditions of service have reflected, in part, market forces and, in part, government policy direction reflecting the consideration of non-market or extra-market political, social, industrial and cultural concerns. The particular mix of market and administrative factors influencing the decisions has varied from country to country and from time to time in the same country. But, in every country, both market and non-market influences have been significant. The non-market influences generally are exercised through a series of regulations that constrain or direct the behaviour of the telecommunication monopoly in its relations with customers, potential competitors, suppliers and/or investors. These regulations may restrict the discretion of management (for example, by not allowing profit-maximizing rates), but they may also enhance managerial discretion (for example, by protecting its monopoly markets).

The policy changes that have taken place in the USA to date, and the policy issues that are under consideration in most Western countries, reflect changes in the mix of market and non-market forces in the industry. They do not reflect a wholesale shift from a condition where industry decisions were based totally on administrative decisions reflecting political and social criteria to a condition where they will be based totally on market criteria reflecting only economic considerations. The government-administered and publicly owned telecommunication systems always have been heavily influenced by market conditions. Indeed, the most fundamental social policy objective has been the widespread supply of efficient telephone services within the constraints of limited resources. And the privately owned, primarily market-driven companies, such as AT&T and Bell Canada, have been constrained and directed by government regulatory decisions attempting to impose very similar economic, political, and social objectives to those adopted by the government-administered systems.

The changes in the role of the market that are taking place in telecommunications are not founded upon ideological shifts and a new found faith in the free market, even in the USA. Nor are they a directly determined response to the new technologies. Rather, the inherited monopoly institutions (public or private) have been unable to adapt to changing economic, political, and social conditions, of which changing technology is only a part.

The monopolies have been unable to absorb or accommodate the new technologies satisfactorily. For users who understand the potential opportunities of the new technologies, such as the computing industry, the growing magnitude of the potential benefits being foregone has led to mounting pressure for change. Also the new technologies proved to be a vehicle for exposing the inefficiencies and deficiencies of the inherited monopoly arrangements for achieving the traditional economic and social objective of efficient universal service. If the telecommunication monopolies are not providing service as efficiently as could be done, are not satisfying social and public services effectively, and are not responding adequately to the opportunities provided by the new technologies, is there any good reason to prevent others from entering the industry? These are issues that the new technologies helped expose for a more intensive examination than has taken place heretofore.

Under the inherited monopoly structure, telecommunication has been presumed to be a natural monopoly, i.e. an industry characterized by economies of scale and scope of such magnitude as to foreclose the possibility of effective competition and to require monopoly for maximum economic efficiency (Melody, 1975). Because of its natural superior efficiency, the natural monopoly also could perform social functions by providing universal service and charging uniform prices based upon average costs and without regard to the variations in costs of serving individual customers. In this manner, both the objectives of economic efficiency and universal service could be satisfied. In some countries, attempts to implement these policy objectives were by means of government regulation of private telecommunication companies. In other countries, direct public ownership was the institutional mechanism for attempting to implement these same objectives.

But the natural monopoly conditions are based upon assumptions about the characteristics of the economic production function, which in turn is determined by the underlying technology. If the technology changes, the production function will change. Economies of scale under the new technologies might be much less significant than they were under the old, and the inherited monopoly no longer justified as 'natural' (Melody, 1975).

Changing technologies in the telecommunication industry have helped focus attention both on the actual performance of the inherited monopoly structure, and on the validity of the previously unquestioned policies founded on the assumption of natural monopoly. They have permitted serious questions to be raised with respect to the adaptability of the established monopolies to the new opportunities for supplying traditional services, as well as new markets, such as computer communication. As evidence has begun to accumulate that perhaps other companies can supply many telecommunication markets more efficiently than the established monopolies, a question as to whether they are efficient in supplying traditional telecommunication services is brought to the forefront. The claimed universal service and social cross-subsidy benefits are beginning to be examined more closely to assess precisely how significant they are, where they are being realized, and what classes of users are providing the subsidies. Also, the blanket restrictions placed by the monopoly carriers on the activities of others have come under serious scrutiny for the first time, as to whether they really protect economic and social benefits in the public interest or simply the privileged position of the monopoly at the expense of opportunities for others that are compatible with national economic and social goals.

The policy changes that have taken place to date, even in the USA, have arisen from a very gradual and painstaking assessment of experience under the inherited monopoly structure. This assessment has been pushed along by new constellations of both industrial and general consumer interests in response to concerns that the inherited monopoly structure is not serving their respective needs as well as it could, and is not likely to be able to reap the full benefits made possible by the new technologies for either group.

There is a common perception that the USA abandoned public service principles associated with the provision of telecommunication services in favour of free-market conditions because of pressure from big business and an ideological shift to the right. In fact, the so-called ideological shift associated with the Reagan years came more than a decade after the process of institutional adjustment had been underway. Moreover, telecommunication carriers in all countries always have been particularly responsive to the special needs and interests of big business. Historically, this has been especially so in the USA. Ironically, the policy shift to allow an increased role for competition in telecommunication was not a response to big business, but rather a response to new and smaller businesses attempting to exploit the technology in order to compete with big business. It was opposed by the largest company in the history of the world, AT&T, every step of the way with every weapon at its command.

In the USA, the policy makers only grudgingly and gradually gave in to the forces for change. The long and tortuous experience of the last two decades demonstrates that, with a few significant exceptions, the policy makers attempted to support the interests of the established monopoly as much as possible, and to delay the adjustment process substantially. It will be interesting to see how government policy makers in other countries will respond to these same issues raised in different national contexts. Preliminary indications are that the adjustment process may be even slower in other countries than it has been in the USA, although certainly a lot less noisy and public.

Policy issues are being raised in many different areas involving technical, economic, social and even cultural considerations. The issues are being, or will be, addressed in an environment heavily influenced by national and international political economic considerations, and reflecting a variety of administrative and market policy options. Unfortunately, this constellation of policy issues is not likely to be evaluated in a systematic manner as an integrated set of policies. To a certain extent, there are likely to be inconsistencies among some policies, making them counterproductive. Nevertheless, they will establish the ground upon which national and international markets in a great many industries will operate in future, creating advantages for some and disadvantages for others. The source of the so-called efficiencies of the international market 'winners' of the future is more likely to be found in the underlying labyrinth of negotiated policies, regulations and administrative rules relating to telecommunication and information than in 'superior skill, industry and foresight' as idealized in the theory of perfect competition. Let us now turn to the major areas for telecommunication policy determination.

4   The radio spectrum

The fundamental technical building block for many telecommunication technologies is the radio spectrum. All mobile communication, landline microwave and satellite transmission systems (which carry the great majority of long-distance telecommunication traffic), as well as over-the-air broadcasting, employ the radio spectrum. The radio spectrum always has been allocated by government-administered decisions, both at the national and international levels. Different frequency bands within the spectrum have varying technical and economic efficiencies for applications to particular types of communication. Once bands of radio frequencies are allocated to classes of use, telecommunication facilities are designed with technical specifications that are conditioned greatly by the radio frequencies that have been allocated. These in turn significantly influence the cost of the equipment and, ultimately, the services provided with that equipment.

As frequencies are assigned to specific users, the capacity of the frequency band will be used up, creating congestion. Potential new users may be assigned frequencies in less desirable frequency bands, or refused frequency assignments altogether. Perhaps the most common rule applied in allocating radio frequencies has been the 'first-come, first-served' rule. The cost to users of obtaining frequency assignments has been the nominal cost of processing applications. The spectrum has not been allocated by market criteria, although the administrative rules adopted have been influenced by developments in related telecommunication equipment and service markets (Levin, 1971).

As use of the radio spectrum has increased over time, congestion has increased. Because of the nominal cost of acquiring radio frequencies, efficient use of assigned frequencies has not been encouraged, and the stockpiling of unused radio frequencies has been common. This has led to pressures to reform the existing system of spectrum allocation. One method of reform is to improve the administrative methods for spectrum allocation and assignment. Another is to attempt to introduce economic market conditions into the process of spectrum allocation and assignment. This can be done by auctioning frequencies to the highest bidder, permitting the resale of spectrum licences and attempting to use the price system as a means of improving efficiency in the allocation and assignment of the radio spectrum resource. The USA already has taken limited steps in this direction in an attempt to privatize certain aspects of the process. Canada and the UK are considering modifications to their existing administrative rules to reflect market criteria (Melody and Smythe, 1985). But it is important to note that, even in circumstances where the role of the market and market criteria are maximized, there must remain a major component of administrative management to the spectrum allocation and assignment process. Market criteria can play a more influential role in the administration of the radio spectrum than they do at present. But it is a very limited role (Melody, 1980a). [...]

Over the foreseeable future, both national and international agencies will be engaged in a continuous process of adapting the administrative rules for spectrum allocation and assignment to changing circumstances, including an explosive growth in the demand for frequency assignments. The changes in the administrative rules will have significant effects on the characteristics of national and international markets for equipment and services, and the nature of the competition that develops.

5   Technical design standards

Decisions taken with respect to the technical design standards of new technologies seldom are determined by unfettered competitive market forces. When new technologies are in the formative stages of the innovation process, the design standards generally are established by administrative decisions, sometimes taken by national or international government agencies and sometimes taken by dominant corporations or industry groups. These technical design decisions then become essential ground rules that condition directly the nature of competition in the equipment supply market, and indirectly in the service markets that use the equipment. When the design standard decisions are taken, some firms, and sometimes nations, are favoured at the expense of others. The relative competitiveness of firms and nations is often determined by the technical standards decisions taken at the outset of market development, even before the equipment market is recognized as being significant.

For about the next quarter century, telecommunication systems will be in the midst of conversion from analogue voice standards to digital computer standards. The new integrated services digital network (ISDN) could be established at a number of different levels of technical sophistication (Rutkowski, 1985). There are now at least nine levels in the hierarchy of open systems interconnection (OSI) protocol layers, ranging from simple physical connection to sophisticated programmed-access applications. If the common public network of the future is established at a modest level of sophistication, then the more sophisticated users will require expensive upgrading and conditioning equipment, or separate networks or systems. But if the technical standards for the entire network reflect the most sophisticated uses, then the super highway network will cost substantially more, and the vast majority of the costs will be common integrated network costs.

The technical standards that are selected will influence not only the equipment market but also the services supplied over the telecommunication system. And this in turn will have significant implications for users of different services. The most sophisticated ISDN system, built to 'Rolls Royce' standards, certainly will be capable of providing local voice telephone service. Yet, if one were constructing an efficient local voice telephone service, a much lower-cost and lower-quality system would be built. A major policy question raised by the technical design standards decision is, will the charges for local voice telephone service reflect the costs of the much simpler and cheaper system that would fully satisfy local voice communication needs, or do residential users get to pay 'Rolls Royce' prices because their only option is to obtain service on the more sophisticated system. The ISDN technical design standard selected will have a significant influence on the answer to this question, and thereby affect the price and availability of local telephone service. [. . .]

The basic decision with respect to technical design standards establishes fundamental ground rules that influence the operation of the market that can develop on the building block of the technical design standards selected. But in virtually every case, market decisions reflecting relative competitive market efficiency play no significant role in the selection of the technical design standards. These are administrative decisions taken by government authority or by dominant industrial interest. In essence, the technical design standards establish a system of handicapping in the evolving future markets for telecommunication equipment and services, not only among firms within specific industries, but also including potential new entrants. Technical standards can be used to promote competition or restrict it. Those fundamental, essentially administrative decisions with respect to technical design standards that are taken within the next decade will influence the role that the market actually does play in the future.

6 Interconnection

The terms and conditions for interconnection to national telecommunication systems have a decisive influence upon the structure of markets in the equipment industries, as well as the telecommunication and information service industries. Historically, the telecommunication monopolies have applied virtually exclusive restrictions against the interconnection of equipment that they did not own and control. Suppliers of telecommunication equipment could not sell to end-users, but only to the monopoly carrier. But the monopolies purchased virtually all their equipment from manufacturing subsidiaries or nationally favoured suppliers in a rigid vertically integrated structure.

In its tariff, AT&T defined 'foreign attachments' as equipment, on subscriber premises, that it did not own. Interconnection was prohibited. The interconnection of alternative transmission systems to the national telecommunication systems was restricted to licensed and approved monopoly telecommunication carriers in other geographical areas or other countries. Independent systems that were seen as potentially competitive were denied interconnection. Even such specialized systems as those of the railways, along their rights of way, were allowed interconnection only for emergency purposes.

Efficient interconnection is crucial to the effective implementation of virtually all public policies permitting competitive opportunities in telecommunication. Interconnection has been at issue since the earliest days of telephony, and restrictions have played a key role in building the heavily monopolized structure in national telecommunication service markets and the highly concentrated oligopoly equipment markets. Although often presented as an issue of technical harm or compatibility, the real issue surrounding interconnection always has been economic. To be sure, there are technical issues, but they can be, and always have been, quickly resolved when there has been an economic incentive to do so. Telecommunication interconnection is far less complex than interconnection in the computer field, and it carries no serious concern for safety as does electricity. The national monopoly carriers in countries around the world are interconnected in a global system despite an enormously wide range of equipment standards, technical incompatibilities, and variations in service quality. Nevertheless, interconnection restrictions have been the policy foundation for maintaining the all-inclusive telecommunication monopoly over end-to-end service and monopoly over the telecommunication equipment market (Melody, 1972).

Issues of national defence occasionally are raised as a reason for prohibiting interconnection. But it is soon recognized that these are not technical issues, but rather issues of planning and co-ordination. Defence telecommunication planning always has encompassed far more than the national public telecommunication system, including specialized high-security military systems and interconnection to international systems and systems in other countries. The primary concern for defence interconnection to the national public telecommunication system is for redundancy and alternative routing. In fact, maximum, rather than minimum, interconnection to the national public system may better serve national defence interests.

The greater concern of the telecommunication monopolies has been the loss of a portion of 'their' market. If competitors are allowed to enter a market, the market share of the established monopoly will have to decline below the previous level of 100 per cent. But the monopolies argue that, inasmuch as they are engaged in implementing the social policy of universal service with uniform pricing for basic telephone service, they must earn high profits in their business and luxury services in order to finance this social policy by means of internal cross-subsidies. Therefore, the apparent attractiveness of market entry in any telecommunication market simply reflects, and indeed is evidence of, the social policy at work. Any entry into any market can provide only private gain at the expense of social loss. [...]

7   Telecommunication facilities competition

The demand for new telecommunication facility systems derives from the opening of opportunities in more competitive equipment markets. The flexibility with respect to how the telecommunication network can be used is enhanced by the options that the terminal equipment can provide. But for some services, alternative transmission and/or switching systems are desired. Over the next decade, most national government policy makers will have to face up to a serious challenge to the justification for maintaining a national monopoly on long-distance transmission services.

The proposed interconnection of competitive long-distance transmission systems to the national monopoly system raises policy issues similar to those raised by terminal interconnection, but generally in a context of licensing new telecommunication facilities and services. If the licences are granted by the policy authority, interconnection must be provided for the licensed services.

Here also the US experience shows a gradual, sometimes grudging accommodation of regulatory policy to changing circumstances over a long period of time. [...]

For other countries, the economic and social dimensions of competition in long-distance transmission services may be more difficult to assess both because their national circumstances and national markets are very different from those of the USA and because of a severe lack of evidence in respect either of economic efficiency or of the performance of social policy by the national telecommunication monopoly. Certainly the social cross-subsidy claims will be made by the national monopolies. But one would think that in countries where the so-called 'universal service' policies of a national telecommunication monopoly leave 30 to 60 per cent of the population without residential telephone service, and where village telephone booths are installed only where they are profitable, policy makers ought to be considering the viability of alternative arrangements. The new telecommunication technologies make it possible to do so.

The evolving characteristics of competition in long-distance communication will be governed by national licensing policies. These in turn will influence significantly the nature of competition in related equipment markets as well as telecommunication-based value-added network services (VANS) and information markets. [...]

8   Conclusion

Some of the major areas in which administrative decisions relating to telecommunication policy will guide the development of telecommunication technologies and services over the next decade and beyond have been reviewed. It is apparent that, despite a definite shift toward an increased role for market forces, the primary influence upon future developments will not be the 'invisible hand' of the competitive market, but rather the more visible hands of those crafting administrative policy decisions. By providing the infrastructure for a plethora of electronic information services, telecommunication policies will have a major influence on the characteristics of information content services that are developed.

It must be noted, however, that there is a wide variety of additional policy considerations that will affect the characteristics of information markets. Military policy will continue to provide the primary force directing research and development, as well as purchasing the most sophisticated applications of it. Industrial policy in many countries now focuses heavily on the information and communication sector as an engine for macro-economic growth. Cultural policies relating to mass media production and distribution will constrain and direct market influences in these industries. Legislation relating to intellectual property and personal privacy, as well as government policies in respect of access to national statistical and data archives as raw material for value-added information services, will have a major influence upon the development of markets in tradeable information. Social policies relating to education and training, as well as the role of public libraries, will help define the scope and limitation of private and public information markets.

The move in many countries to privatize and deregulate the telecommunication sector in recent years has served to expose to public view and debate the superstructure of administrative policies and regulations that lie beneath the market competition that exists on the surface. Competition is not a substitute for policy and regulation. It is a tool of policy that, under some circumstances, can facilitate the achievement of the objectives both of economic efficiency and universal telephone service; under other circumstances it can promote efficiency at the expense of social policy; under still other circumstances it can promote neither. It is the task of policy research and analysis to examine the circumstances and determine the appropriate role of competition.

In the past the role of market forces generally has not been an integral part of policy analysis. Too often the market was viewed simply as a direct substitute for regulation, and perhaps a competitor to policy makers! This grossly overstates the power of both. There always will be a major role for both administrative policy guidance and market forces. The historic policies and practices of national telecommunication monopolies clearly have been superseded by events. An increased role for market forces is inevitable, and an increased role for active competition in some markets and services probably is desirable. But this is not the end of policy direction and regulation. It is a shift in the balance between administrative regulation and market forces. Hopefully, it is the end of passive policy-making consisting of little more than a superficial acceptance of the status quo and simplistic self-serving justifications for the continuation of special privileges. It is the beginning of a more thorough and explicit analysis of policy alternatives and their implications, and of active policy implementation in a dynamic market and technological environment. For the future, the institutionalization of ongoing in-depth research on the implications of policy alternatives, and of informed policy analysis, selection and implementation, will be the most important enabling 'technologies' in the telecommunication and information sectors.

References

Brooks, J. (1975). *Telephone: the First Hundred Years*. New York: Harper and Row.

Department of Communications, Canada (1972) *Branching Out*. Report of the Canadian Computer Communications Task Force. Ottawa: Department of Communications.

Federal Communications Commission (FCC) (1939) *Investigation of the Telephone Industry in the US*, 76th Cong., 1st sess., House Document No. 340. Washington D.C.: US Government Printing Office.

FCC (1959) In the matter of allocation of frequencies in the bands above 890 Mc. *Report and Order*, 27 FCC 359.

FCC (1962) American Telephone and Telegraph Company. Regulations relating to connection of telephone company facilities of customers. Docket No. 12940. *Memorandum, Opinion and Order*.

FCC (1966) Report of the Telephone and Telegraph Committee of the FCC; in the matter of the domestic telegraph investigation. Docket No. 14650.

FCC (1969) Application of MCI, Incorporated for construction permits to establish new facilities. Docket No. 10509.

FCC (1969) *Carterfone Corp*. 13 FCC 2d 420. See related decisions at 14 FCC 2d 571; 15 FCC 2d 605; 18 FCC 2d 871; 19 FCC 2d 1068.

FCC (1971) *Computer I*. CC Docket No. 16979. 29 FCC 2d 870. 906.

FCC *Notice of Inquiry*. FCC 10 November 1966; *Memorandum Opinion and Order*, FCC 28 March 1972; 29 FCC 2d 870 (1972).

FCC *Telpak Rates and Charges*. FCC Reports, Vol. 37, 111 (1964). See related FCC Docket 18128, 61 FCC 2d 587 (1976).

FCC *Computer II*. Tentative Decision and Further Notice of Inquiry and Rule Making, Docket No. 20828 (1979); *Final Decision* (1980).

FCC (1981) *The Future of Digital Technology in the Private Radio Services*. Policy Division, Private Radio Bureau, Washington, D.C.

FCC (1985) In the matter of MTS and WATS market structure and Public Notice No. 3206 seeking data, information and studies relating to bypass of the public switched network. CC Docket No. 78-72.

FCC (1985) In the matter of Tel-Optik Limited and Submarine Lightwave Cable Company. FCC Docket 85-99, *Memorandum, Opinion, and Order*.

FCC (1985) In the matter of establishment of satellite systems providing international communications. CC Docket 84-1299, *Report and Order*.

Ferguson, M. (ed.) (1986) *New Communication Technologies and the Public Interest: Comparative Perspectives on Policy and Research* (Sage Communications in Society Series.) London: Sage Publications.

Gabel, R. (1967) *Development of Separations Principles in the Telephone Industry*. Graduate School of Business Administration. Michigan State University, East Lansing, Mich.

Gerbner, G., Gross, L. and Melody, W.H. (eds) (1973) *Communications Technology and Social Policy*. New York: Wiley.

Irwin, M.R. (1971) *The Telecommunications Industry: Integration vs. Competition*. New York: Praeger.

Irwin, M.R. (1984) *Telecommunications America: Markets without Boundaries*. Westport, Conn.: Quorum Books.

Levin, H.J. (1971) *The Invisible Resource: Use and Regulation of the Radio*

Spectrum. Baltimore, Md.: Johns Hopkins University Press.

Mathison, S. and Walker, P. (1970) *Computers and Telecommunications: Issues in Public Policy*. Englewood Cliffs, N.J.: Prentice-Hall.

Melody, W.H. (1975) 'Relations between public policy issues and economies of scale', *IEEE Transactions on Systems, Man and Cybernetics*, January.

Melody, W.H. (1980a) 'Radio spectrum allocation: role of the market', *American Economic Review*, May.

Melody, W.H. (1980b) 'Competition and subsidies as instruments of social policy in telecommunications' in *Energy and Communications in Transition* (ed. H.M. Trebing). East Lansing, Mich.: Institute for Public Utilities. Michigan State University.

Melody, W.H. and Smythe, D.W. (1985) *Factors Affecting the Canadian and US Spectrum Management Processes: a Preliminary Evaluation*, Report to Canadian Department of Communications, Contract No. 36100-4-4259, Ottawa.

National Academy of Sciences, Computer Science and Engineering Board (1970) *Report on Technical Analyses of Common Carrier/user Interconnection*. Washington D.C.: National Academy of Sciences.

OECD (1973) *Computers and Telecommunications: Economic, Technical and Organisational Issues*. (*OECD Informatics Series*, No. 3) Paris: OECD.

OECD (1975) *Applications of Computer/Telecommunications Systems*. (*OECD Informatics Series*. No. 8.) Paris: OECD.

Rutkowski, A.M. (1985) *Integrated Services Digital Networks*. Dedham, Mass.: Artech House, Inc.

Wigglesworth, W.R.B. (1985) Deregulation of telecommunications in the UK, *Le Bulletin de l'Idate* (21), November 30-40.

US District Court for District of Columbia (1983) *US V. AT&T*, Civil Action No. 82-0192.

US General Accounting Office (1982) 'Can the Federal Communications Commission successfully implement its computer II decision?'

PART III
Some Critical Issues for the Information Age: Control and Power

Introduction to Part III

We are all familiar with the adage: 'knowledge is power'. Never has it been more true than in contemporary society as a result of developments in information technology. Microelectronic systems are making radical changes in the way data is processed, stored and transmitted, and control of those systems is the key to power. Some of the most critical social issues in relation to information technology are concerned with unequal access to IT resources, both within society and between societies. Within our own society, the agencies of the state and rich commercial enterprises are accused of exploiting the possibilities of expensive information technologies so as to increase their own power. Internationally, the gap in wealth and power between the developed countries and the developing countries is said to be widening as the unequal distribution of IT resources exacerbates other resource inequalities.

Are these negative consequences inevitable? Some of those who write about information technology, or who are involved in promoting its adoption, prefer to stress the potential benefits. They point out that computerization of government agencies could increase the efficiency of the welfare state and provide information about threats to the security of its citizens. Similarly, with respect to the promotion of IT in industry and commerce, it is claimed that everyone will benefit from the creation of wealth or the improved efficiency of services, even though the benefits may be spread unevenly, nationally and internationally. In the developing countries it is hoped that information technology might make up for some of their shortages of other resources, provided they can get it from the multinational enterprises on the right terms.

There is no shortage of promoters of information technology, ranging from politicians to salesmen, and including technologists and scientists who are excited by the intellectual challenges. The writings of social scientists have a different purpose, which is neither to promote nor to retard the spread of information technology. Their task is to analyse the trends, including the social and ideological trends involved in information technology, and to examine the social issues that are raised.

Among the most contentious social issues concerning information technology and power are those of surveillance and control of individuals by the state, and the threat to privacy presented by commercial databanks containing confidential information that may be acquired or accessed without the subject's knowledge or consent. Some people may fail to see any threat from the development of massive and interlinked databanks, on the grounds that they themselves have 'nothing to hide', but this is unrealistic in the light of the many documented cases of innocent people suffering because the information about them was incorrect, incompetently handled, or unfairly used for a purpose other than that for which it was provided. The dangers of unregulated databanks and information trafficking range from the harassment resulting from being on unwanted mailing lists through to the denial of employment, promotion or credit, and even the denial of people's fundamental civil rights such as that of being free to express their opinions or express their needs. It is in the light of these threats that Duncan Campbell and Steve Connor, in 'Surveillance, Computers and Privacy', discuss the politics of information privacy and the loopholes in the law relating to it.

The theme of the threat and the promise of information technology, particularly as it relates to education, is taken up from a different angle by Robins and Webster in 'Dangers of Information Technology and Responsibilities of Education'. This paper is written from the standpoint of educators in the humanities and social studies who have experienced the strong pressures to switch resources to information technology, often at the expense of other scarce resources such as library books. They raise questions about some of the ideological assumptions of 'IT awareness' initiatives, and they urge us to use our critical faculties to develop a 'social awareness' about the social context and consequences of developments in information technology. The message that information technology can have socially negative consequences, or that it is not 'neutral', is a difficult one to get across and risks being condemned as 'Luddite'. However, Robins and Webster would respond that the truly enlightened Luddite is not opposed to machinery as such, but wishes to protest against pressures to adopt it without any consideration of social consequences and of the costs and benefits to different interests. They provide a forceful argument for taking seriously the need for education in information technology to include responsibility for the cultivation of an analytical and critical social awareness.

Analysis of information technology within an international context reveals a widening gap between the developed nations of the northern hemisphere and the less developed societies that are mainly to be found in the southern hemisphere. Bessant's 'Information Technology and the North-South Divide' charts this trend. He shows that, although IT has something to offer to developing countries, the rate of development is likely to be far slower there than in the North because the limiting factors are present to a higher degree – shortage of skills, capital, technology and equipment, lack of an infrastructure to support and maintain sophisticated equipment, insufficient managerial experience. Bessant also points out that IT can be an inappropriate technology, making demands on already scarce resources, and requiring a level of technological sophistication which can only be supported by increasing technological dependence on the North. The threat to the industrialization process in the southern hemisphere is now growing, as the more advanced application of IT in the North allows it to regain a comparative advantage in traditionally labour intensive sectors, such as textiles and foundries. The problem is further complicated by the growing concentration of knowledge-intensity in the North and the increasing difficulty of access to this information by developing countries. Multinational corporations, with their headquarters in the developed countries, seem likely to lock the South into an ever more dependent relationship on the North.

Finally, the social implications of information technology can be analysed in political science terms with respect to the application of computers and computer models in policy-making. Are they neutral devices that operate to increase organizational efficiency and rational decision-making? Or do they have a tendency to service other purposes and interests, such as that of increasing the power of technocrats or established elites? Some observers have adopted a partisan perspective, seeing models as tools or propaganda and persuasion for special interests in the policy process, and they often cite the example of President Reagan's Director of the Office of Management and Budget, David Stockman, who admitted to having manipulated models of the economy so as to legitimate 'Reaganomics'. Dutton, in 'Decision-making in the Information Age: Computer Models and Public Policy', examines some of these alternatives in the light of empirical studies and favours a 'consensual perspective'. According to this perspective, models are primarily tools for negotiation, bargaining, and interactive decision-making among the representatives of conflicting interests and opinions in the policy process.

9

Surveillance, Computers and Privacy

Duncan Campbell and Steve Connor

1 The politics of information privacy

British public opinion has long avowed concern for personal privacy – and, in particular, its protection from encroachment by centralized systems of surveillance and supervision, such as data processing machinery. Electronic computers – impersonal, mechanical, often incomprehensible and certainly quite unlovable – are consequently a centrepiece of popular demonology.

But public interest in privacy is matched and more than countered by official lack of interest. The key problem about computers and databanks is the nature of administration. The power of computers to convert fiction to totalitarian fact is in the hands of the administrators – administrators who should be accountable to both electors and elected, but seldom are, though official possession of personal information can confer the opportunity to govern in detail the lives and actions of masses.

For that reason, we concentrate primarily in this account on official databanks and on the handling of information by public agencies and organizations. From welfare to health, from taxation to policing, it is government agencies who are the collectors, distributors and users of the most sensitive of personal information. It is these agencies who have at their disposal, also, the most exclusive and effective means of social control. The record shows that society has been best protected from autocratic excesses not by the altruism or honesty of administrators but by their incompetence.

A similar conclusion was reached in 1978 by the government's own Data Protection Committee, which spent over two years examining in depth the threats which computers might pose to personal privacy. The committee's chair, Sir Norman Lindop, recalls:[1]

> We did not fear that Orwell's *1984* was just around the corner, but we did feel that some pretty frightening developments could come about quite quickly and without most people being aware of what was happening.

'In the view of most of us who have looked at the subject in some detail,' Lindop has added, 'the greatest threat, if threat there be, does not come from the private sector, from the entrepreneurial sector, it comes from the public sector.'[2]

Years before the scale of personal data on official computer had reached its present level, public concern on the issue was clear. In 1971, a Royal Commission on Privacy examined public attitudes to the subject through a wide-ranging national opinion survey. They found that 'protecting people's privacy' was the social issue rated most important throughout the population. They also discovered that, among a wide range of potential threats to privacy outlined in their survey, none attracted more public concern, fear or hostility than the putative creation of a central computer, the collation of all personal data and files in a national databank.

Every group polled regarded such a databank as the most disturbing example of intrusion on privacy that the Royal Commission's survey team could cite – more disturbing, for example, than unsolicited sex manuals in the mail, spying neighbours or breaches of personal privacy by the news media. All but 7 per cent of the population considered the establishment of an open official databank a serious breach of privacy; and 90 per cent of the population wished the creation of a central computer to be prohibited by law. But – regardless of popular fears or the warnings of the Lindop committee that such a central computer should not come about by stealth – it is now in the process of creation.

Many extensive works have been written about the meaning of privacy. It is a social and political idea, which needs legal form to have effect and to be enforced. In fact, it is extraordinarily difficult to define privacy, particularly in relation to the handling of information. The type of personal information which the subject may desire the right to control will vary from country to country, and across age, class, sex, race and other barriers. Personality, temperament and culture each plays a role. Whether the handling of personal information affects privacy depends much less on the information itself than on *who* may have and use that information, which items of information are correlated, and what use is to be made of the information.

In Britain, the age of a woman is usually held to be particularly sensitive. It is not so in other European societies. Details of personal taxation and financial affairs, the secrecy of which is revered in the United Kingdom, are openly accessible to any enquirer in Sweden. Details of personal (and corporate) land and house ownership are wholly secret in England and Wales, but wholly public in Scotland. And so on. Some types of data are universally regarded as sensitive – information stored about personal health, sexual life and religious belief comes in this category. But the sensitivity with which information about criminal convictions is regarded can depend entirely on the individual's situation – on, for example, which social groupings he or she belongs to, or on a temporary concern such as facing an employment interview. Some male youths may wear convictions like a badge of pride, or regard them as a mere nuisance and think nothing of discussing them or having them known; while middle-class women may regard a single shoplifting conviction as an unending source of stress and shame.

'Data protection' is something of a misnomer, although we are stuck with it. In the 1984 Data Protection Act, data is given (otherwise inaccurately) to mean machine-readable information such as that stored on magnetic or paper tape, magnetic discs, and so on; while 'information' is human-readable, i.e. sheets of paper. The distinction between the two is anyway eroding, as optical character recognition (OCR) equipment has given computers the facility to read most ordinary printed text (such as this page) as efficiently as most humans. It is not the data, however, that needs to be protected, other than in the orthodox sense of security; it is the use to which it may be put that needs to be controlled.

'Information privacy' is often thought to be a more meaningful term. A useful definition which we would endorse is 'the claim of individuals, groups and institutions to determine for themselves when, how and what information about them is communicated to others'.

Britain's data protection laws were finally enacted not through the good intentions of government, but in consequence of the European Convention on Human Rights, which came into force in 1953, under the auspices of the Council of Europe (embracing 21 non-Soviet bloc European states). Although, throughout history, human societies and civilizations have adopted legal codes requiring respect for the rights and liberties of the citizen, the idea of an internationally enforceable human rights code is relatively modern. Since the Second World War there has developed a body of international law – and accompanying regulatory and enforcement institutions – concerned with human rights. The British government, it may be noted in passing, has had more cases brought against it in the European Court of Human Rights than any other member of the Council of Europe. The British government's attitude in respect of human rights, as the following account amply illustrates, has been both dilatory and negligent.

The starting point for recent human rights legislation is the 1948 United Nations Universal Declaration on Human Rights, which called for 'respect for human rights and fundamental freedoms for all, without distinction as to race, sex or religion'. Regional treaties on human rights – such as the European Convention – then followed. Article 8 of the European Convention deals with the right to privacy, and it is this article that has ultimately led to the British data protection law:

1   Everyone has the right to respect for his private and family life, his home and correspondence.

2   There shall be no interference by a public authority with the exercise of this right except such as in accordance with the law and is necessary in a democratic society in the interests of national security, public safety or the economic well-being of the country, for the prevention of disorder or crime, for the protection of health or morals, or for the protection of the rights and freedom of others.

When the Data Protection Act finally comes into effect, late in 1987, it will have been over 20 years since the issue was first raised in Britain as a matter of serious parliamentary and public concern. In the interim, legislation has been postponed, delayed and sidestepped via a bewildering collection of standard Whitehall dodges – one departmental committee report, one Royal Commission, two draft bills, three Private Members' bills (dismantled), three White Papers, four conveniently disruptive general elections, and official 'consultation' exercises almost beyond number. The two decades of non-legislation on privacy are as impressive a textbook achievement of Whitehall delaying tactics as one might hope not to find.

Privacy, in legislative terms, is a Home Office matter. With a few honourable exceptions, no one senior in the Home Office, be they civil servants or ministers – of either party – has ever given a damn about personal privacy. The process of giving British citizens the right to privacy began by accident, as an attempt to head off an MP's private bill on the legal 'Right to Privacy'. It has only now been enshrined in law because British international trading interests in information technology might otherwise have been damaged.

During the two decades of inaction, the Home Office first excluded all government activities from being considered as threats to privacy. Forced to broaden the issue, they ruled that Home Office interests, which in fact pose the major threat to privacy – police, immigration and national-security activities – should be wholly exempt from scrutiny. Finally driven to the point of near legislation, they nominated a Home Office official as a suitable protector of privacy against the abuse of personal information. Dragged by Parliament and public opinion far enough to give the Data Protection Registrar some measure of independence, they robustly fought to ensure that the Registrar had few duties, no powers to speak of and a staff as small as conceivable. To acknowledge that a little useful protection for privacy may yet have come from this process is not to minimize the determined and forthright avoidance of the issue successively displayed by Home Secretaries James Callaghan, Reginald Maudling, Merlyn Rees, William Whitelaw and Leon Brittan. [. . .]

The bill was published in December 1982. It set out the data protection principles, which are listed in Table 9.1 (below). The purpose of the bill was to

Table 9.1   *The data protection principles*

1	The information to be contained in personal data shall be obtained, and personal data shall be processed, fairly and lawfully.
2	Personal data shall be held only for one or more specified and lawful purposes.
3	Personal data held for any purpose or purposes shall not be used or disclosed in any manner incompatible with that purpose or those purposes.
4	Personal data held for any purpose shall be adequate, relevant and not excessive in relation to that purpose or those purposes.
5	Personal data shall be accurate and, where necessary, kept up to date.
6	Personal data held for any purpose or purposes shall not be kept for longer than is necessary for that purpose or those purposes.

7	An individual shall be entitled –
	(a) at reasonable intervals and without undue delay or expense–
	  (i) to be informed by any data user whether he holds personal data of which that individual is the subject; and
	  (ii) to access to any such data held by a data user; and
	(b) where appropriate, to have such data corrected or erased.

8*	Appropriate security measures shall be taken against unauthorized access to, or alteration, disclosure or destruction of, personal data and against accidental loss or destruction of personal data.

*Applies only to computer bureaux.

do the 'minimum necessary' to enable Britain to ratify the European data protection convention. Manual records were excluded, but computerized records of almost every description had to be registered; failure to register was to be a criminal offence. The Registrar was nevertheless given few formal powers and duties. The bill had failed to make the statute book when a general election was called in 1983. Before that time, the government had estimated that registration would take at least two years, meaning that a new Act could not take effect until 1985.

Despite the collapse of the 1982 Data Protection Bill because of the election, the argument was over. A new bill, presented quickly by the returning government in June 1983, was described as 'simplified'. Computer information held solely for payroll and accounting purposes was excluded. In a move to further weaken the bill – which the Home Office were pleased to describe as 'easing the Registrar's workload [and enabling] him to devote more of his resources to the general oversight of data protection' – the Registrar lost powers to enter premises to check on the conduct of databank operators. The new bill required him to apply to a circuit judge for this purpose.

The bill faced renewed, fierce and well-deserved criticism, particularly from such powerful professional lobbies as the British Medical Association (BMA). The BMA described it as 'a load of holes joined together'. The major features criticized were the total exclusion of manual records, the vaguely drafted definitions and terms of reference, and above all the numerous and very widespread exemptions. It was rather doubtful, according to both the National Council of Civil Liberties and Conservative Lawyers, that the bill even achieved its objective of enabling Britain to ratify the European Convention. The vagueness of its terms created considerable doubt as to how the bill would apply to computer applications such as word processing systems. The weak position of the Registrar was attacked, and there was renewed pressure for an independent authority, as Lindop had recommended. But if there was one thing the Home Office would not do, it was to accept any part of any of Lindop's suggestions. Because of this hostility, all reference to codes of practice was excluded.

During examination in the House of Commons, the exemption provisions continued to attract the greatest criticism. The Home Secretary proposed to grant to himself, rather than the Registrar, powers to create special regulations for data on religious belief, political opinions, physical or mental health, or sexual life. He would take further powers to determine the extent of subject access to health and social work records. And in one small but sweeping section, the Home Secretary was granted power to exempt from subject access any material the disclosure of which was already restricted or prohibited by an existing enactment. Since all information handled by the government is prohibited from unauthorized disclosure under the Official Secrets Acts, this section (Section 34 (2)), allows the complete exclusion of the whole or any part of any government databank from subject access, if the department does not wish to authorize disclosure. For such access to be obtained regulations would have to be drafted and laid before Parliament. But in the last resort, the government can rule – and might yet decree – that despite the Act there should be no subject access to any of its databanks.

As the bill was debated, the Home Office refused to give way on these provisions. Ministers also refused to appoint an advisory committee to help the Registrar – even though a suggestion to this effect had been made in their own 1982 White Paper. The White Paper had given a cautious endorsement to the codes of practice proposals, but this too was now rejected; it was, after all, a Lindop heresy. The government was forced to drop a proposal which would have wholly exempted from subject access all personal data held for the 'control of immigration'. Such a provision was completely contrary to the letter, as well as the spirit, of the European Convention. There was no permission under the Convention to 'derogate' (make exclusions) in respect of immigration records when they did not involve crime, taxation or national security.

A more remarkable example of the unfitness of the Home Office to supervise data protection would be hard to find. The sole department concerned in the control of immigration had sought *carte blanche* to continue to gather personal information on possible unlawful immigrants secretly from other departments and public agencies. The move was intended to protect the system whereby the Home Office encouraged local offices of other departments, particularly those concerned with health and social security, to provide details of their clients, for immigration checks. Naturally, the victims of this process were usually Asian or West Indian blacks, many of whom, although not subject to immigration control, were nonetheless checked and harassed. Critics pointed out that this exemption was unnecessary to deal with criminal offences concerned with illegal immigration. But for the sake of Home Office convenience and prejudice, the bill lumped persons subject to immigration control together with criminals.

The Home Office argued that immigration fell within the meaning of 'protecting the rights and freedoms of others', which they evidently took to mean their right and freedom to keep other people out of the country. But the immigration exemption was dropped after four months' debate. Had the Home Office succeeded in its self-interested intentions, the bill would have failed even to achieve its primary (commercial) objective – the ratification of the European Convention. Another major concession for the privacy of patients' records was won by the BMA and the powerful medical lobby. An independent agreement was reached between the DHSS, the Association of Chief Police Officers and the BMA that medical data should not be disclosed except by a doctor, and only in extreme circumstances without the consent of the patient. The increasingly tortuous Act was again modified to allow the Secretary of State to exempt some categories of data from the exemptions to the non-disclosure provisions. In plain English, this meant that health information could not normally be passed to police, tax or security authorities without the disclosure being admitted.

Finally, the Home Office introduced amendments requiring the Registrar to investigate (non-trivial) complaints brought to attention (he had previously been given no duty to do this), and to promote the adoption of codes of practice. During its final reading in June 1984, the Labour Party chose to support the bill.

The Data Protection Act received the Royal Assent in July 1984. Mr Eric Howe, the Deputy Director of the National Computing Centre in Manchester and chair of the National Computer Users' Forum, was selected as the first Data Protection Registrar, at a salary of £35,000 a year – equivalent to a Deputy Secretary in the civil service. It took less than a year for him to discover that the Home Office's concept of fewer than 20 staff and a diminishing workload was an hilarious underestimate. In August 1985, the Registry was given an establishment of nearly 50 staff, with a starting budget of £1.2 million. There might be over half a million register entries, many times the number originally estimated before the bill became law. Complaints about the alleged misuse of computer data started arriving during 1985 – even though the Act would not take effect for another two years.

Some public servants made an auspiciously early start with the Act, seeking its aid in situations it did not and was never intended to cover. Even before the bill was passed – after years of fighting it – some Whitehall officials started using its terms as an excuse for *more* secrecy, in order to withhold public records from disclosure.[3] By the beginning of 1985, voluntary advice agencies began reporting that officials in many public services – gas, electricity, and local authorities – were citing the Act in refusing to disclose personal data to advice agency workers who were acting on behalf of their clients. This new attention to personal privacy would have been commendable, were it not that the new law – even if the information *is* held on computer, and the Act *were* in force – does not restrict the authorized transfer of data in these situations; and that the officials' real intent, perhaps, was to protect their own privacy at work from the public and their representatives.

Offices for the Data Protection Registry were established in 1985 in Wilmslow, Cheshire. The two-year transitional period for the Act to take effect began with the opening of registration of data users in November 1985. The initial registration period ended on 11 May 1986. It is now an offence to operate a databank holding personal information unless you have registered, and are acting in accordance with the data protection principles of your register entry. Each user has to pay £22 for a three-year registration period. The register, itself stored on computer by the Datasolve bureau, at a cost of about £2.5 million, will be published via libraries or Viewdata (Prestel) services.

The subject access provisions, finally granting individuals the right to check and correct personal information held on computer (subject, of course, to the numerous exemptions), take effect on 11 November 1987. For better or worse, the Home Office's long battle against privacy legislation ended with the 1984 Act. But the war was far from over.

Most people now know that computers store personal medical information, tax and financial details, social security and employment records, police criminal records and other intelligence. But very few outside the departments directly concerned are aware that several very large government computer complexes are being expanded and interconnected, which will result in the linkage of important but hitherto distinct record systems. Linkages between different computer databanks already exist – but so far they have been partial. Computer systems such as those run by the police or MI5 now have both the technological potential and the legal authority to extract personal information from all other official databanks.

Orwell's fictional design for the year 1984 was not completed on time or to its original specification. But many key elements of technocratic autocracy are available today. Government departments and agencies now hold one and a half *billion* personal computer records. By the year 2000, public sector databanks will probably store more than 600 gigabytes (about one hundred thousand million words) of personal information, accessible from a hundred thousand computer terminals; no one will be excluded. Every day, a new government office is computerized. Central government will remain the largest holder and processor of personal information for the foreseeable future, followed closely by other public agencies such as the police service.

For the individual, there is a balance of advantage and risk. Much information is held for the ostensible benefit of the person named on a computer record (the data subject), for example to provide appropriate health care or to grant correct welfare benefits. But many databanks are concerned almost entirely with information of which the holding is at worst to the disadvantage of the individual concerned and at best intended to strengthen the hand of authority. These databanks include the information files of the police and security services. The terms of the Data Protection Act were largely designed by the Home Office, which sponsors or controls those same agencies. The most sensitive personal data are often held by agencies which are the least regulated.

Successive governments have found it difficult to grasp or tolerate the idea that citizens might need independent protection and some statutory rights for their defence against the authorities. Opposition to libertarian measures guaranteeing *individual* rights still remains entrenched in the Home Office. [...]

2   Loopholes in the law

The Data Protection Act received the Royal Assent in July 1984, but there remains a lengthy period – until November 1987 – before many of its provisions can be enforced. The two-year timescale for the introduction of the Act began in November 1985, with a six-month period for the registration of users of personal data on computer. From 11 May 1986, the operation of an unregistered databank became an offence; and compensation became available for some victims of inaccurate data. After November 1987, people who are the subject of computer data files will, finally, have a general right to see and challenge information which is held about them.

But the new Act is plagued with deficiencies and uncertainties, reflecting the uneasy compromise sought by the government between the concerns of official, institutional and commercial information processors and those of interest groups who place a higher value on personal privacy. In the legislation, the balance has almost always been drawn in favour of the information processors. Some of the Act's most informed critics, including former members of the Lindop committee, do not believe that the Act can survive much longer than two years before its many faults become glaringly obvious, and make clear a need for re-legislation.

Since the Act was passed, concern about data protection has been high amongst data users, on whom the burdens of registration, ensuring compliance with the data protection principles (see Table 9.1), and eventually of providing subject access, now fall. Public criticism has to some extent been muted by the impression that personal privacy has at last won some formal legal protection; and by the need to wait and see how the Act works in practice. But although some valuable protection has been provided (especially where the private sector is concerned), the new law will not necessarily curtail some of the most dangerous practices of the information-gatherers and information-swappers.

The power of sophisticated surveillance technology is changing qualitatively as well as quantitatively every few years. As public administration comes increasingly to rely on automatic data processing, as electronics continue to penetrate more and more areas of daily life, the information pool that the malign or merely curious may tap is growing. It is unlikely that either the Act or the Registrar will require any review of the privacy aspects of the central computer plans of the DHSS and the Inland Revenue – or of any other central databank plan still held in the dark recesses of the Central Computing and Telecommunications Agency.

To these regulatory problems may be added those presented by the new potential surveillance tools: scanners, character readers, vast text retrieval databanks, identity-card and passport monitors, telephone-call logging equipment, and much more – tools which would create grave enough difficulties for a law which had actually been designed to protect personal privacy. But the Data Protection Act was designed minimally to comply with the intentions of the European Convention on Data Protection, lest British business suffer from a prohibition on international electronic information processing.

Some – probably the vast majority – of data users will nonetheless meet their obligations under the 1984 Act. But for those who are not ready or willing to do this, the Act is replete with loopholes through which abuses of personal data may escape:

> It does not cover manual records, allowing information users to protect their most damaging data by retaining them or transferring them to paper.

> Information once held on a computer databank need not be disclosed to the data subject if it is later processed only on paper.

> Even if data users do not transfer their sensitive data to paper, they can evade the Act by processing it in a fashion contrived to avoid referring to individuals in their main records.

Sir Norman Lindop has christened such activities *extrusion* – the process of moving personal data onto manual records, or otherwise altering it radically, in order to evade data protection law. Other problems posed by the Act concern its weakness so far as regulation or enforcement is concerned:

> There is no duty of supervision or inspection placed on the Registrar after data users have registered; violations of the Act will only be detected, in almost all cases, if the data subject happens to stumble across evidence of abuse (although the Registrar intends to 'monitor' the working of the Register).

> In consequence, data subjects have no chance of ensuring that damaging or unlawful processes are stopped before they cause actual harm; the harm must necessarily occur first.

> Data subjects have no right to have inaccurate data changed or removed.

The Registrar can issue an 'enforcement notice', but such data may still remain if the user records the subject's claim that the data is inaccurate alongside the data. Data subjects may, with difficulty, apply for a court order – but a court is not obliged to order that erroneous data be corrected.

The Act does not allow government departments to be prosecuted for any offence, although private users are liable to criminal prosecution and penalties.

The Act provides no safeguard against a data subject being forced to obtain access to sensitive personal data about themselves, and then pass it on to a third party (such as an interviewee being asked by a potential employer to produce a copy of their criminal record).

Further problems may arise from the special exemptions for some data users, allowing them to hold data secretly or obtain it from third parties:

There are powers to make widespread exemptions from subject access for information about physical or mental health, or records concerned with social work – for which statutory regulations have yet to be written.

The Act grants ministers absolute power to exempt 'national security' databanks even from registration; other databanks are fully registered but partly or wholly exempt from subject access.

Information exempt from access for a purpose such as the 'prevention and detection of crime', the 'apprehension or prosecution of offenders' or the 'assessment or collection of any tax or duty', as well as for 'national security'. will not be inspected or supervised by the Registrar.

Information gathered by or for these databanks need not be obtained or processed 'fairly or lawfully', as normally required by the Act.

The Act could become a tappers' charter for the exempt agencies, who could conceivably use the Data Protection Register itself as a guide to gathering further personal information.

All these pitfalls were pointed out to the government as the legislation went through Parliament, but the Home Office paid little attention.

So far as the exclusion of manual records from the Act is concerned, the government has circumvented the normal meaning of the terms of the European Convention by exempting from subject access 'mixed' records (i.e. those handled partly by computer, partly on paper). Article 2 of the convention requires ratifying states to legislate to control information processed by 'operations ... carried out in whole *or in part* by automated means' (our emphasis). In contrast, the Data Protection Act speaks only of 'information ... processed by equipment operated automatically'. Thus information of the most sensitive type, obtained or held in breach of the data protection principles, or even of the law, indexed but not 'held' on computer, need never be disclosed to the subject and therefore cannot be challenged. [...]

The new law leaves many key issues yet to be defined. After so many years of study and struggle, there had been public hopes for an Act that would be a powerful tool for privacy, one that would give the public an understanding that information privacy rights existed, and could effectively be enforced. These hopes have been dashed. But the Act does create a new climate, promoting the education of data users about their responsibilities, and we may be grateful for that. Perhaps, too, a battle lost by the Home Office after a 20-year struggle is *ipso facto* worth celebrating.

Registrar Howe has said that 'what the Act means will ultimately be defined by the courts; case law will define it'.[4] Sadly, this is all too true. Recent British legislative history has seen comparable major civil rights initiatives – on race relations and equal opportunities – picked apart, watered down, and all but annulled by the indifference of administrators and the conservatism of lawyers and judges. The Acts which created regulatory bodies such as the Equal Opportunities Commission and the Commission for Racial Equality left them without vital powers, and hemmed them about with 'safeguards' to curb their real effectiveness (on civil liberties grounds, it was occasionally claimed). The data protection situation is little different.

In many respects, the Data Protection Act is woolly, ambiguous and formless. The Act's supervisory body, the Data Protection Registry, is small, weak, burdened with some excessive regulation, constrained from entering the few real danger areas, and bereft of necessary powers of investigation, inspection and surveillance. Were the Registrar and Registry now to disappear in a sea of paper, never to be seen or heard of again in Whitehall, the mandarins might well exchange thin, reserved smiles over a morning's sherry, and reflect quietly that data protection was less of an impediment to efficient public administration than first they had feared. This is how the British establishment had always seen off and neutralized irritating civil rights reforms, they would later recall in their memoirs.

Notes

1 *Guardian*, 21 February 1980.
2 *Data Protection – Perspectives on Information Privacy*, 1983, Continuing Education Unit, University of Leicester.
3 *Guardian*, 1 July 1983.
4 *Informatics*, July 1985.

10

Dangers of Information Technology and Responsibilities of Education[1]

Kevin Robins and Frank Webster

1 Introduction

It is well known that the concern for an injection of Information Technology (IT) into education stems from government's commitment to revitalize the economy by restructuring industry so that it can more effectively compete against other nations, thereby resulting in increased market share which will – presumes the theory – generate more domestic employment. A central element of this strategy is that technology and technically proficient personnel are supplied to effect the necessary restructuring.

Every citizen, certainly every school-leaver or college graduate, at least aspires to be part of the economy; *ipso facto* everyone has a role to play in the restructuring process. Therefore, though the recovery will be led by computer scientists and electronic engineers, everyone with or wanting a stake in the nation must get involved in this 'second industrial revolution' heralded by the advent of computer-communications technologies. From this analysis it follows that the problem of recession, depression, crisis, collapse, call it what you will, has a technical, i.e. uncontentious, solution: new technology is the key to prosperity and education, the locksmith charged with producing at speed the requisite quality and quantity.

Pressure on education to play its part has been intense and expressed negatively and positively. Negatively there has been a wave of accusations that education, holding to an unworldly elitism and anti-business ethos, has been ill-serving 'industry' for generations and that it ought to change.[2]

An upshot is that finance is increasingly coming into education explicitly tied to corporate goals – witness the spate of 'science parks' opening on and around campuses in the eighties,[3] the insistence of Alvey that the £200 million committed by government to develop fifth generation computers should be spent in consortium with industry[4] and a recent ACARD (Advisory Committee for Applied Research and Development) report urging academic-industrial collaboration.[5] Positively there have been generous resources made available for IT programmes in schools and further and higher education.

Lectureships in computing are flowingly available; funds for purchase of hardware and software pour into primary and secondary schools from the Microelectronics Education Programme; 'industry' is falling over itself to invest in the establishment of an 'institute of information technology'.[6] Funds have been taken from the arts, humanities and social sciences and 'steered' towards the 'more relevant' science and technology courses; badly cut institutions have rushed out into the 'real world' to make good lost resources by winning contracts for science and technology consultancy (Salford University is the premier example); higher education, despite massive cuts, has continued to increase its investment in IT often at the expense of spending on library books (university and polytechnic libraries bought 30 per cent fewer books in 1981-82 than in 1978-79)[7] and because no one will be allowed to shelter from the technological gale all disciplines and subject areas within the jurisdiction of the CNAA are instructed to incorporate IT in their teaching.[8] Policy has also been bipartisan: it is as well to remember that it was Prime Minister Callaghan who initiated a 'Great Debate' on education's shortcomings as regards 'industry' back in October 1976 though the severity and speed of adaptation and reform are doubtless greater nowadays.[9]

Less direct, but nonetheless influential, pressure has come from what might be called the moral climate now prevailing. It is said that we are set to enter a 'post-industrial society', an 'information age'; that we are on the brink of an 'information technology revolution' that will change all of our lives, our leisure, work, learning and entertainment. In 1982 a massive propaganda campaign – *Information Technology Year* – backed by substantial government cash went by road and rail to transport the populace into its electronic future.

A recurrent theme of this comment and pressure has been that in the Information Society the computer/IT *illiterate* (a highly resonant and threatening metaphor: to be illiterate in this day and age!) will be severely disadvantaged, particularly as regards employment. The jobs of the future, we are assured – and this seems to follow from all the talk of restructuring the economy by equipping with the most advanced technologies – will only go to the IT aware. This vocational prediction has been, we suspect, an especially powerful mobilizer of educationalists. With unemployment high and a widespread feeling that it will remain so in the foreseeable future, teachers readily feel anxious that their charges will be less employable if they fail to acquire the requisite skills.

They have responded to the call. Today there is scarcely a school in the country without its micro and a quota of teachers that has undergone a course in computer awareness. Already the changes are formalized, the Associated Examining Board, for instance, announcing new forms of assessment for school-leavers which measure 'basic skills of use to employers', prominent amongst which is a 'computer awareness test . . . to enable young people to see the computer in its contemporary context, to develop a positive attitude towards using computers and to be able to use the computer'.[10]

In addition, educationalists are told that, since we are entering an Information Society, then we must get involved with IT because it increases the efficacy of teaching and research. Article after article has told us how machines can help learning by accessing the very best specialists at the touch of a button while still able to proceed at a pace decided upon by the needs and abilities of the individual pupil; how a few keys on a terminal give us entry to data networks that mine rich bases in California, Paris and Dusseldorf, thereby improving the quality of information simultaneously with saving hours of tedium in searching digests and footnotes in library stacks. The message is that for anyone with professional pride IT is irresistible.

Finally, we are told that we must be tutored in IT, not to be expert programmers, but so that we may be comfortable in a 'computer-rich society'. This is the argument which has it that if we want to belong in the new era, if we do not want our children to feel we are an embarrassment to them (recall that powerful slogan from *IT'82*: 'Is your seven-year-old better equipped to run an office than you are?'), then we must keep up-to-date with the 'IT Revolution'. Have you thought what it will be like, what an anachronism you will appear in the eyes of your children, if you are using a manual typewriter or – God forbid – a Bic biro in 1990? This premonition comes in a stronger version which has it that 'IT awareness' is essential not only to fit into an Information Society where one will be able to drive and manoeuvre along the highways of the information grid, but also so that we might have some *control* over our destinies which, if we remain ignorant of the new technologies, will be decided upon by 'experts'. In the name of democracy itself we are urged to make ourselves familiar with computer-communications.

We believe that the reasoning behind these developments is spurious and that examination of historical and contemporary evidence shows it to be so. We also think that the capitulation of intellectuals to such reasoning is depressing and debilitating. Since we have discussed this elsewhere[11] we shall underplay the intellectual betrayal and concentrate our remarks on considera-tion of evidence which undermines the insistence that educationalists must make shift to learn and teach IT skills.

2   Preliminaries

But first two preliminary points. One is that there is something profoundly distasteful about all the rhetoric concerning 'progress' upwards and onwards into a super-rich electronic wonderland when so many people on this planet are suffering intensely not for lack of IT, but because they are deprived of things in superabundance in the Western part of the world and of things that could be made good by use of existent technologies, knowledge and resources. [. . .]

Our second preliminary point refers specifically to Britain and to assertions that education in computer-communications technologies will be a passport to high tech jobs. We consider in a moment the question of the relation between advanced technology and skills, but at the outset it must be stated forcefully that this hype that IT education has a vocational spin-off has the unfortunate (but politically useful) effect of blaming the unemployed for their unemployment. It cannot be said too often that unemployment is structural because of a slump in the advanced capitalist economies, that in Britain the number of job vacancies, officially put at about 150,000 in 1984 – leaving aside the regional, age, gender, remunerative and skill variables – is massively outweighed by the official estimates of well over 3 million workless. The unemployed can scarcely be blamed for their plight. Nonetheless, the talk, heard from employers, politicians and even some teachers, about education in IT being an investment in a job helps shift the blame for unemployment away from structural issues back to the personal, to the 'what-do-you-expect-studying-divinity?' kind of argument. This is a classic case of 'blaming the victim'.

It can also raise false hopes amongst those most concerned to get a job. For instance, when Lord Young spoke recently to the Society of Education Officers he was reported as saying that 'Too many (school-leavers) were emerging from 11 years of compulsory education without a single qualification that employers would accept' (and Lord Young added, for good measure, that 'too often they (school-leavers) were de-motivated and lacked the personal qualities required').[12] But does anyone seriously think that, even if all the young emerged with IT skills, there are three million plus vacancies in computer science and electronic engineering? Can it really be mooted that the recession is caused by a mischannelling of talents in the schools?

The figures speak for themselves. In 1980 the Electronic Computers Sector Working Party of the National Economic Development Corporation found a shortage of 25,000 people with computer-related skills (of whom about 16,000 were programmers and analysts);[13] four years later the Information Technology Skills Shortage Committee of the Department of Trade and Industry reported a shortfall of 1,500 IT graduates (chiefly computing, physics and electronic engineering) that could rise to 5,000 by 1988; more recently a House of Lords Select Committee has concluded that by 1990 Britain might be short of up to 10,000 personnel qualified in computer technology.[14] These are undoubtedly serious shortages, but even the uppermost estimate would find work for less than 1 per cent of the present officially unemployed (and half of one per cent of the truly unemployed).[15] How hollow this must seem to those unfortunates stuck in the Giro Cities where unemployment is upwards of 40 per cent!

It would be risible were it not the case that one of the largest public examination boards has just introduced a 'computer awareness' course designed to impart 'skills of use to employers' and that there is so much evidence that the unemployed are blamed and blame themselves for their demise.[16]

3   High technology equals high skill?

Connected to the assertion that our pupils and students should develop skills in IT to work and live in an 'information-rich' environment is the assumption that computer-communications technologies demand high skills. This unproblematical notion is supported by the connection IT has with white-collar (information) work, which smacks of the 'professional'. It borrows too from the image of computers and computer work as recondite. Thus it follows that thorough education in IT is crucial, and to this teachers have a knee-jerk reaction: 'Of course we'll train our charges appropriately; of course we'll equip them with the requisite skills for survival and success in a post-industrial society.'

One might respond to this by asking of educationalists where is the evidence of the connections between enhancement of skill and technological innovation? This is pertinent since historical and sociological evidence leads one to a different interpretation from that which perceives IT as one more step along the road to a professionalized 'post-industrial' era. Indeed, the history of technological change, from at least the late nineteenth through the twentieth centuries, is of a process which has resulted in minimal skill requirements of most workers and arguably has systematically deskilled them.[17]

The lack of skills in our workforce originates not from the inabilities of the populace, but from the fact that modern industry requires little of its operatives, and advanced technologies, in their conception, design and application, are the major cause of this. It has been argued that, starting in the early years of this century when large-scale business led to the breakdown of personal supervision, modern management began to initiate new strategies to ensure control of its charges. The major figure in this was F.W. Taylor, the godfather of Scientific Management, who argued that the key to effective management was meticulous observation of the labour process and careful planning of how best it could be carried out from the company's point of view. This was, as contemporary management guru Peter Drucker recognizes, the *real* information revolution,[18] since it saw that knowledge of work and management's monopolization of that knowledge was the prerequisite for increased productivity. From this knowledge, management has gone on to develop techniques – first organizational, later technological – which have always presumed that the worker is a liability to the labour process, hence techniques were developed which made management less dependent on their employees by reducing skill (allowing for control by the line, easy replacement of workers with rudimentary skills, etc.) or keeping skill requirements to an absolute minimum. Always management has pioneered techniques and technologies which have regarded the worker either with distrust or at the least indifference. Seldom have techniques or technologies been developed that enhance work and the upshot has been the allocation of demeaning 'low-trust' roles to the bulk of workers.[19] The priority of management has been to increase productivity and/or to reduce costs and in this regard labour has been seen as a problem. A major way of overcoming that problem has been to put the skills required in the labour process into advanced technologies which reduce the mental contribution, the thinking role, of employees to a minimum. One has but to consider the Fordist factory and the philosophy and practice of Henry Ford himself ('one of the most thorough practitioners of Scientific Management, though he had never heard Taylor's name')[20] to conjure a picture of the 'skills' advanced technological production has required of workers.

And IT, as it is being constituted today, stands in the same tradition of technological domination and deskilling. This is the only way in which one can appreciate the language of Russell Heddon, president of Cross and Trecker Corporation, when he observes that computer-controlled machine tools are simply 'taking more of the skill off the shop floor and putting it into the computer'[21] or the evidence gathered by Barry Wilkinson on the introduction of microelectronic technologies into West Midlands engineering factories[22] which suggests that the 'ideal worker is essentially mediocre, working steadily at an average pace, accepting meekly the dictates of the technology'.[23]

There is one advance! By a nice irony 'The men who applied Taylor to the workers are now themselves Taylorized'[24] as IT, finding application in white-collar work, is initiating the era of Taylorism/Fordism in the office. To be sure, the adoption of IT in some offices may increase the skills of some workers, especially where many are made redundant, but if we look at what are far and away the major applications of IT in the 'factory office'[25] today we can in no way sustain the fiction that these require high-level skills. In banks, building societies, estate agencies, travel agencies, insurance brokers and offices generally the machinery incorporates much of the skilled work (it calculates interest rates, recalls accounts, spells, even counts notes, determines routes and individual costs, etc.) and the employees (significantly, very frequently women rather than the 'men who applied Taylor') – who without doubt have the dexterity learned in a few hours that might impress a casual observer who is awed by computerized machines – require no advanced skills. It has even been demonstrated that the short history of computing itself, frequently portrayed as being a skill attainable by the super-intelligent, has witnessed, with the application of Taylorist precepts, routinization and deskilling by such procedures as increased division of labour, standardized languages, structured programming, user-friendly packages, and the extensive recourse to data dictionaries:[26] the bulk of the work is divided between programmers and operators (the latter overwhelmingly females) who frequently 'complain of boredom, lack of interest, and the loss of self-esteem'.[27]

This returns us to education and the recent enthusiasm for training people in IT so they will be up to the high skills of the jobs of the future. And it raises the question of whether the current workforce is not, in fact, *overeducated* for the work that it does. The evidence, which is substantial, is indicative of precisely this.[28] It shows that for work of all kinds education has virtually no direct pay-off, that the bulk of work requires few highly-developed skills and that those that are needed are usually taught on the job. Certainly there has been an inflation of credentials – in some parts of the country today kids need five O levels *and* luck to get an apprenticeship – but there is no evidence to suggest that these are prerequisites of, or even related to, the work that people do. The frantic effort of the school system to teach children skills 'of use to employers' is defined by the fact that – if only there was work to get – for the most part they do not need what education offers or even what it hopes to offer in the future.

4   Coping, being powerless and having control in an Information Society

The point made earlier that high technology typically demands low skill for operatives leads one to ask why we need instruction in IT. There is certainly a good deal of apprehension about computer-communications in our society, a feeling that mastery of them is exceedingly arduous, but once we do use them – and this increasingly so almost in spite of ourselves – we find them characteristically 'user-friendly', so much so that to use most we need to know nothing whatsoever about computers. Since we can learn, usually in a few minutes and rarely in more than a few hours, how to operate viewdata and teletext systems, electronic banking facilities, television games, word processors and even personal computers and since we need no training at all to use computerized technologies in motor cars, washing machines or telephones, why should we need to receive formal instruction when, in the course of time and depending on choices and circumstances, we could take aboard the requisite skills?

It might be suggested that we will not be able to *cope* with the 'computer-rich' society of the future if we do not get instruction right away, so perhaps we ought to be grateful that our local authorities are willing to pay to make us competent. But in reply, and still worried that we might be frittering away public funds, we really must observe that already there are hosts of computers and computer-communications technologies in use in society – in government, in airlines, in factories, in tax offices, in banks, in insurance businesses, even in educational institutions – and we need to know nothing about these in order to cope with life. Moreover, knowing about the technical features of these machines would make no practical difference to our lives at all. How many could tell us how telephones work? How many could explain the theory of relativity and its relevance to nuclear power? And yet few of us feel that this makes us unable to cope, makes us functionally 'illiterate'. Few of us feel pressure to be 'electricity literate', 'radio literate', 'telephone literate', 'nuclear literate' . . . why is it so different with computer-communications?

It may be argued that, in our personal lives at the least, in the 'electronic cottage' towards which we are all rocketing, without technical knowledge, without 'computer literacy', we will be *powerless*; that an understanding of computers is crucial so we can have genuine power over the machine, particularly if it starts going wrong. Yet the retort here has to be that there are lots of machines – 'user-friendly' machines – that we use today without technical knowledge. If the car breaks down, the dishwasher conks out or the phone stops functioning we call a repair person. Surely no one would argue that this sort of reliance on the fitter or service engineer makes us powerless, makes us unable to cope with a society dedicated to using advanced technologies. We do not deny that sudden breakdowns are frustrating and infuriating, but we do claim that we are quite able to cope, we are not powerless, if we must resort to employment of repair people.

It may be argued further that without technical knowledge of IT we will lack *control* over those who do possess it; that to be powerless when faced by technology is to be in the control of the 'experts'. This is an especially common justification, one which taps a deep sense of insecurity and suspicion, the argument that with knowledge of IT we could constrain those people who might otherwise exploit us or abuse their expertise. There are two major difficulties with this sort of reasoning.

The first is that we are *already* living in a technologically advanced society without ever having been asked if we wanted it that way. Since the public has never been consulted about whether or not it would accept or reject the 'IT Revolution', what grounds have we for believing that IT training, education in this latest technology, will change things? Douglas Noble puts the point well:

The truth is that our society is already shaped primarily by the designs of the few and the momentum of technology, and it makes no sense to suggest that a minimal understanding of computers will empower an already technologically impotent citizenry. Computer literacy does not provide the public with tools for wrestling control of these technologies from the hands of corporate decision-makers. In fact, it is much more likely that a focus on minimal technical competence ... will lead to a sort of pseudocontrol, a false sense that one has power simply because one can make a computer do a little something. Real control of the direction the new technology will take involves political understanding, not trivial technical understanding, and it must focus on decisions which affect the design and use of large systems, not on the ability to create catchy little BASIC programs.[29]

The second objection is to the implicit theory of technocracy in the proposition that knowledge of advanced machines is where power in society lies. While this idea has a long history in social analysis, it has to be said firmly that the claim that technocrats rule and will in the future is intellectually discredited chiefly because if confuses indispensability with power.[30] As Max Weber observed many years ago, 'If "indispensability" were decisive, then where slave labour prevailed and where freemen usually abhor work as a dishonour, the "indispensable" slaves ought to have held the positions of power.'[31] Education in the technicalities of IT will not give the public control over the technologists because they do not have power in the first place.

The evidence is overwhelming that the resources of power lie with inherited advantage and privileged (usually non-technical) education. As an instance we can look at profiles of leaders of the British IT industry, at our flagship high tech concerns, GEC, ICL, Ferranti, Plessey, Rank Xerox, Cable and Wireless and Thorn-EMI, where above all one might expect to find technological experts playing a critical role. And what does one find? Lord Weinstock, head of GEC, is a statistician who took his degree at the London School of Economics and had the good fortune to marry the boss's daughter (Sir Michael Sobell was the previous chairman of GEC) while in his mid-twenties and his chairperson is the farmer and politican James Prior (Charterhouse, Estate Management at Cambridge University) who succeeded an aristocrat, soldier and diplomat, Lord Carrington (Eton, Sandhurst) to the post; the chairperson of Ferranti is one Sebastian de Ferranti, coincidentally the son of the previous head and direct descendant of the company's founder, who has no higher education but was well schooled at Ampleforth and in the Dragoon Guards; Hamish Orr-Ewing, chairman of Rank Xerox, also has no degree, but no doubt being of a distinguished Scottish family, plus attendance at Eton followed by service in the Black Watch regiment, helped him on his way; Sir Ernest Harrison of Racal-Decca is a chartered accountant; Sir John Clark who leads Plessey studied electronics for a few months in the USA after Harrow and Cambridge University, but who would doubt that his parentage – Sir Allen and Lady Clark – did not help his career along (Sir Allen was owner and founder of Plessey)?; Eric Sharpe, chairman and chief executive of Cable and Wireless has got nothing less than a BSc (Econ) from the London School of Economics, an institution that has never been known to house any technological discipline; Sir Michael Edwardes, chairman of ICL until it was bought out last year by STC, is a South African who graduated in law from Rhodes University....The only technologist we can find who recently headed a major IT corporation in the UK is Peter Laister of Thorn-EMI who got his degree from Manchester University College of Technology, surely the exception that proves the rule. It is our view that the 'IT Revolution' can only be adequately understood by scrutiny of the priorities and concerns of these corporate decision-makers, these people who determine the allocation of Research and Development funds, targeting of this market rather than that one, employment of these graduates rather than those. But IT education, as it is, systematically ignores such questions.

5   IT education as myth

Roland Barthes in his classic study of mythology makes the point that 'Myth does not deny things, on the contrary, its function is to talk about them; simply, it purifies them, it makes them innocent, it gives them a natural and eternal justification, it gives them a clarity which is not that of an explanation but that of a statement of fact'.[32] We believe that IT education, as currently constituted, functions in the creation of a technological myth. This can be better understood by looking at a proposed short course offered in a department of social studies as a polytechnic's 'IT initiative':

1   Introduction to the machine. Operating systems. How to use floppy disks, setting up machine, copies of material, Basic.

2   Introduction to Word-Processing. How to enter, format, save and print material.

3   Introduction to a Spreadsheet – forecasting departmental finances, planning spending, capital and revenue calculations and predictions. Staff hour calculations.

4   Introduction to a data base. Filing and references. The storage and retrieval of large quantities of data.

All this is very practical, hands-on, training, with a tangibility that is indisputably real and insistent. At the end of such a course students will be able to *do* something with the new technologies. But what this, posing as education which will equip people for an 'information society', represses and mystifies is what the 'IT Revolution' is much more significantly about. It tells us nothing about major shapers and users of computer-communications such as the military which accounts for the majority of satellites currently in orbit round the earth and the appetite of which for Command, Control, Communications and Intelligence systems is a constant stimulant of new technologies from research centres in industry and higher education institutions.

'IT awareness' tells us nothing of the role or significance of transnational corporations in the development and deployment of IT and in the evolution of communications policies, though the growth of computer-communications networks and the principles of their operation have been decisively shaped by the expansion of these massive corporations within North America, Japan and Europe, and out across the globe where a few thousand transnationals, 60 per cent of which are US owned and based, account for the majority of trade.

It tells us nothing about the vexing question of transnational data flows, of the threats such developments can pose for national sovereignty: remote-sensing satellites, owned and controlled by rich Western nations, survey land masses and oceans across the globe in minute detail; picking up data on crop conditions, mineral locations, fish concentrations and the like; satellite television stations, again the monopoly of the West, can transmit programmes around the world without recourse to national governments; electronic information about economic, social, political and strategic affairs moves around the world at the behest of corporations and countries affluent enough to afford the requisite technology (that are in no way answerable to observed and analysed nations) or of the decade-long debate conducted on this issue by members of UNESCO anxious for a 'new world information order' (resisted by the United States and Britain in the name of the 'free flow of information').[33]

It tells us nothing of the emergence of a 'new international division of labour' shaped by increasingly centralized corporate concerns in which information generation, processing, transmission and dissemination play vital parts;[34] nothing about the trend, facilitated by IT, for modern corporations to combine centralized control with decentralized (dispersed) production.[35] And it tells us nothing at all about the integral relations between technological change, politics, economic strategy and industrial relations – yet the 1984-85 conflict between the NUM and the NCB and government, or between Rupert Murdoch and the printing unions (and preceding struggles concerning telephone engineers and printers in 1983 and 1984), revolved around the politics of technological innovation.

It tells us nothing about the trend towards adoption of increasingly integrated police computer systems, local, regional and national, which are inaccessible to public scrutiny and which pose fundamental questions for civil liberties. It makes no mention of the ease with which telephone tapping and telephone metering will be conducted in an era of computerized exchanges though in media, politics and trade unions the question and attendant dangers regularly emerge.[36]

It tells us nothing about the 'information factories' constructed by the likes of Reuters, Datastream, Telerate, Dun and Bradstreet, ITT and Dow Jones; nothing about why these on-line services, mainly financial but also political and economic, are booming; nothing about the significance of developments which, boasts Citicorp give 'your company . . . information. In seconds [on] . . . current money market rates. Up-to-the minute foreign exchange summaries and exposure analyses. Cash availability analyses. And more . . . in over 33 countries . . . through our own private financial telecommunications network'.[37] Nothing about the significance of money-market on-line services, like those offered by Reuters to four hundred or so brokers and bankers able to afford the £1,250 initial subscription plus £600 per month. It tells us nothing about electronic funds transfer systems such as SWIFT (Society for Worldwide Inter-Bank Financial Telecommunications) which has about 1,000 member banks and credit card companies in 40 countries and handles some 250,000 transactions per day for a membership fee of several thousand pounds; nothing about its character, its meaning or its significance.

It tells us nothing about the likes of TRW, a high tech Californian conglomerate, a single division of which makes it America's biggest credit information agency that, with 'the largest single commercial concentration of computers in the world' and its own nationwide communications network, processes 250,000 credit reports per day and holds files on 86 million customers.[38] Nor does it tell us of the emulation of such practices in Britain as cable accounts, credit services and customer profiles are developed, and retailers like Marks and Spencer introduce electronic shopping with the expectation of between two and three million customers by 1990 providing the company with 'invaluable feedback and data concerning individual customers, their needs and their purchasing power' (*Observer*, 25 November 1984).

It tells us nothing about the inexorable rise of quintessentially 'information age' companies, such as Saatchi and Saatchi, enthusiasts of all the new technologies because of the 'opportunities' they offer to systematically monitor patterns of behaviour, precisely amass and analyse social data, and then manufacture and disseminate 'information' at the behest of their paymasters. And it tells us nothing of the role these forces play in shaping new forms of IT — cable, satellite, video, etc. - to suit commercial operations (sponsorship, advertising, subscription) as they launch simultaneously a sustained assault on information made available as a public service. It tells us nothing of the significance of the struggle in Britain to retain public service broadcasting in face of threats from new communications technologies; nothing of the meaning of the *Making a Business of Information*[39] ethic that is resulting in major changes in information access and transmission in telecommunications (the privatization of British Telecom), government publications (the price of HMSO materials to bring them into line with marketability, the charging of commercial rates for central statistical office material, the diminished regularity of census investigations), and public libraries (the decline of the service as funding is cut, upshots of which are fewer materials, charges for loans of records and tapes, book or pamphlet requests and the like).

It tells us nothing of the information inequalities, endemic in our society, that are exacerbated and exaggerated by the application of ability to pay criteria in development of new technologies, nothing of the types of information restricted to the corporate and state sectors that can afford the multi-million dollar hardware and software, the expensive on-line connections, the thousand dollar subscription fees to international data networks; nothing of the garbage information supplied to the 'general public' (a revealing term from market research in IT, used to distinguish the commercially unattractive areas from the lucrative 'office' and 'military' avenues where the bulk of spending is located) via enhanced television – the round of movies, sex and sport 'on the cable', the intensified diet of 'entertainment', the mindless 'video games' like Frogger and Herpes.

It tells us nothing of the creation of a new kind of information, 'transactional information', generated every time we use electronic terminals, not just in the home, but also on the phone, in banks, shops and restaurants. A consequence is that it becomes increasingly possible to 'pinpoint the location of an individual at a particular moment, indicate his daily patterns of work and sleep, and even suggest his state of mind'. The value of this constant stream of information, when aggregated, is nowhere estimated in 'IT awareness' classes. But with it, with the emergence of the electronic grid via the phone system, electronic funds transfer and cable systems, the individual becomes constantly and routinely subject to monitor and study. In these ways IT can constitute an indispensable 'tool to burrow into the psyches of unsuspecting customers'[40] and citizens. But this is nowhere considered by those who would equip us for life in an 'Information Society'.

6   Social science and 'post-industrial society'

These absences – and there are many more in 'IT awareness' courses – lead us to ask an old but vital question: what is and should education be for? At the moment the vocational and training dimensions are receiving heavy emphasis, but a more important and fundamental aim is to know and make known the world in which we live. To pursue that aim is to ask questions about the 'Information Society' and technological change that are unanswerable so long as the 'IT Revolution' is conceived merely as something to which we must 'adjust' and 'adapt' through crash courses in 'computer literacy'. And to try to fulfil that aim is a matter of discipline and scholarship of vastly more importance than these narrowly technical skills. Quite simply it is to say that someone who knows a computer or an integrated circuit is not an economist, historian, political scientist or sociologist and that these disciplines have major contributions to make in understanding and explaining the world, the world of which IT is a part, the world in which we find ourselves being harried by a technological juggernaut. And these disciplines ask, where they are true to themselves and their traditions, what conditions and circumstances have led to such a concern with the 'IT Revolution' that we must make shift to learn its tricks, what processes and principles are behind the current rhetoric, pressure and haste. There is a role here, we believe, for the *critical* disciplines of sociology, political theory, history, cultural studies, to demystify the ideology of the 'IT Revolution'. Under critical scrutiny many of the assumptions behind the post-industrial/information society myth begin to crumble. It is imperative that educational institutions – at all levels – do not sacrifice humanities and social sciences to subsidize science and technology. [. . .]

7   The 'neutrality' of IT

We want finally to examine the popular claim that IT is a neutral tool which can be used for good or ill. This is to call to mind a common response to technology in our society, the view that a car can be used either for ferrying people to hospital or for robbing banks, a computer for sinister surveillance or for making information more widely available. It follows from this that there can be no harm in adopting IT *per se* and therefore that there is nothing wrong with governmental, business and managerial recommendations that we pursue 'IT initiatives' since all they call for is familiarization with technologies which we are then *free to choose* either positively or negatively. From this premise much of what we have written above can be incorporated as 'perhaps useful for discussion', but secondary to the task of coming to grips with this inert *thing* which is IT.

We hope that we have managed to suggest something of a critique of this already in arguing that the thrust of 'IT awareness' courses, intentionally or not, is to make the public accept change quiescently; that it is, in the words of Douglas Noble, 'propaganda which parades as public enlightenment . . . to create a populace that can comfortably accept the prospect of a computerized world'.[41] We hope to have also made the case for a need to analyse change, the reasons for change and for adoption of any particular changes, with a sceptical and discipline-based eye by historians, social scientists and the like.

The presumption that technology is neutral – and thereby that it is in crucial ways asocial – is anathema to everything the social sciences and humanities stand for. It unavoidably makes them secondary, as disciplines, to science and technology because it relegates their role to study of the effects of technological innovations which are presumed to be the major motor of change. It is nonetheless a widely held perception, apparent in a range of comment from *Tomorrow's World*, through Alvin Toffler, to university vice-chancellors. Technology is seen as a *deus ex machina*, a phenomenon that has been developed outside of the social world yet which arrives in society with such consequence that society, more or less rapidly adjusting and always responding to technology, can be defined by that technology – The Railway Age, The Nuclear Society, The Cybernetic Society. In turn, this perception of technology (it has mysteriously emerged from an extraterrestrial domain – Silicon Valley, Bell Labs, the brain of Clive Sinclair . . .) and the effects of this technology (it will revolutionize life as we know it) result in incomprehension (even when, perhaps because, it is explained in simplified and sweet technical terms) and awe (the gee-whiz and reverential tones characteristic of *Horizon*).[42] Of course such a formulation could and occasionally does lead to hostility – not everyone will welcome an invasion by alien forces – so we are quickly assured that this technology which is set to change the world is benign and beneficient unless abused. Margaret Thatcher got it just right when she said recently that 'Information Technology is friendly; it offers a helping hand; it should be embraced. We should think of it more like *ET* than IT'.[43]

It is at this point that we encounter an astonishing paradox as regards technology, IT included. This is that it is at once presented as an asocial, neutral and amoral force which can be manipulated at will and yet it is simultaneously unstoppable: it is at once something we are free to choose to use as we like, since it is uncontaminated by values or beliefs, and yet it is something to which we must *inevitably adjust*. As regards computer/communications technologies, we are free to choose anything save whether to accept or reject the technologies themselves.

There are several responses humanities and social sciences may make to this conception of (information) technology. Numerous studies have shown that the image of technologists as neutral decipherers of the book of knowledge is misconceived. Far from being pure 'scientific' pursuers of 'truth', unmotivated testers of dispassionately designed experiments, insistently unbiased intellects methodically and exactly representing the physical world and all the rest the sterotype would have us believe, laboratory work is fitted into this acceptable paradigm only after it has reached its conclusion; during the process of research many social factors intervene (researchers' evaluations of one another's standing, shortages of funds, lunches, breakdowns of machines, etc.) which are excised after the discovery of a new fact, product or process when it is assigned a clearly logical, impersonal and 'natural' status.[44] Another critique of this conception of 'technology-as-asocial-yet-of-massive-social-significance' centres on the philosophical critique of instrumental/technocratic reasoning (as an ideology that disguises interests, motives and power in the language of 'science', 'progress' and 'modernization') a formidable assault launched many years ago by Max Horkheimer and Theodor Adorno, revived in the sixties by Herbert Marcuse, and more recently restated by Jürgen Habermas and Michel Foucault.[45] Also of importance is the life's work of Lewis Mumford that has been dedicated to the proposition that technology is not what determines social relationships, but rather that the 'dominant human trait . . . is [the] capacity for conscious, purposeful self-identification, self-transformation, and ultimately for self-understanding,'[46] something which easily gets lost sight of amidst the 'megamachine' where 'electronic entropy'[47] prevails. A cognate attack comes from Jaques Ellul's influential polemic against 'the technological society' wherein 'technique' comes to serve as an end in itself, achieves the status of 'technolatory' and thereby creates 'the universal concentration camp we live in'[48] where there seems to be little if any choice as to how we live our lives. None of these thinkers, and we hasten to say this because the philistines so readily leap to the defence of their pristine image of 'technological advance', suggests that particular scientific findings – the melting-point of ice or the boiling point of water, laws of motion, etc. – are simply outcomes of social forces. They are not so crass as to endorse such reductionism. What they do reject, however, is the assumption that scientific/ technological discovery is divorced from the social world. Instead they suggest that the social – values, feelings, beliefs, morals – is ever present and its contribution to analysis is not to be introduced as a mere afterthought.

This becomes clearer when we move to a third form of assault on the conventional wisdom, to empirical and historical studies of technological innovation, which demonstrate that the technological imperative (change comes primarily from technology which itself emanates from an asocial realm) is mistaken and that, on the contrary, technological innovation, adaption and effects are all social processes, that technology is an integral part of society from start to finish. These studies show – to borrow Lévi-Strauss's useful metaphor – that the presentation of technology as raw is wrong: it is always cooked.[49]

The social is present in technology from the point of origination to the point of application and social analysis is therefore warranted throughout. It is in this sense, in the sense that the social is intrusive into technological development all along the line, that it cannot be regarded as neutral.

8   Conclusion

From all sides the advice is to adjust to the new circumstances, to become 'IT aware', to help 'secure greater acceptance of new technologies by developing their positive aspects, and minimizing their negative aspects, from an enhanced understanding of the cultural and organizational determinants of public attitudes'.[50]

In our view, however, the reasoning behind 'IT awareness' initiatives is intellectually and educationally phoney. It is certainly effective and it has easily wrong-footed those people who feel insecure when faced with advanced technology and self-confident philistines. But because we are being railroaded in the name of an 'IT Revolution' is neither reason to lose our critical faculties nor reason to abandon our disciplinary bases. The primary role of intellectuals and educationalists is to understand and explain the world in which we find ourselves and from which we have emerged. It is neither to sell the world to the upcoming generation nor to manufacture products suitable for a society which is not in the first place thoroughly scrutinized, though this is what 'IT awareness' courses and pressure for their introduction are fundamentally about. If intellectuals and educationalists stand true to themselves and their disciplines, if they can regain confidence sufficient to reaffirm their responsibilities, they will surely refuse to fall prostrate in front of the technological deity.

Notes

1 A first draft this paper was presented on February 18th, 1985 at a History Seminar at Oxford Polytechnic. A version was published by Oxford Polytechnic's Faculty of Modern Studies, Occasional Papers No. 2. Arguments developed here are expanded in a forthcoming book, *Education and Technology* (Macmillan) and in K. Robins and F. Webster, 'Technology and Education: progress or control?', *Critical Social Policy*, 15, Spring 1986, pp. 36-61; 'Higher Education, High Tech, High Rhetoric' in T. Solomonides and L. Levidow (eds) (1985) *Compulsive Technology: Computers as Culture*. London: Free Association Books.

2 See Weiner, M. (1981) *English Culture and the Decline of the Industrial Spirit, 1850-1980*. Cambridge: Cambridge University Press.

3 See Bullock, M. (1983) *Academic Enterprise, Industrial Innovation, and the Development of High Technology Financing in the United States*. London: Brand Brothers and Co.

4 Department of Industry (September 1982) *A Programme for Advanced Information Technology: The Report of the Alvey Committee*. London: HMSO.

5 ACARD (June 1983) *Improving Research Links between Higher Education and Industry*. London: HMSO.

6 *Guardian*, 1 November 1984.

7 Technological Robin Hood in action *Library Association Record* 86(7/6) June/July 1984, p.255.

8 *CNAA Information Technology – Cover Paper*. Paper CASS/83/5. Agenda Item No. 8. 21 December, 1982; cf. DES (Department of Education and Science) (March 1979) *Microelectronics in Education: A Development Programme for Schools and Colleges*. London: HMSO.

9 A useful overview is Kogan, M. and D. (1983) *The Attack on Higher Education*. London: Kogan Page.

10 *The Times*, 12 February 1985.

11 Robins, K. and Webster, F. (1985) 'Intellectual Self-Mutilation' *Universities Quarterly* 39(2), pp. 97-104.

12 *Guardian*, 26 January 1985.

13 NEDC (1980) *Computer manpower in the '80s: the supply and demand for computer related manpower to 1985*, Electronic Computers Sector Working Paper, NEDO.

14 IT Skills Shortages Committee. First Report. *The Human Factor – The Supply Side Problem*. Department of Trade and Industry (1984); House of Lords Select Committee on Science and Technology (1985) *Education and Training for New Technologies*. London: HMSO; cf. Waddilove, K.

'Let the micros rot!' *Guardian*, 19 February 1985.

15 We are aware of course that there is a school of thought that has it that a cadre of IT specialists, provided their endeavours create the growth the economy hungers for, can generate employment for the mass of the workless. But accepting this on its own terms is no argument for generalized IT training.

16 See *inter alia* Economist Intelligence Unit *Coping with Unemployment: The Effects on the Unemployed Themselves*. Economist Intelligence Unit, December 1982. Jahoda, M. (1982) *Employment and Unemployment: A Social-Psychological Analysis*. Cambridge: Cambridge University Press; Seabrook, J. (1982) *Unemployment*. London: Quartet; European Economic Community (1977) *The Perception of Poverty in Europe*. Brussels: EEC. de Boer, C. (1983) 'The Polls: Attitudes towards Unemployment', *Public Opinion Quarterly*, 47(4), pp. 432-41.

17 The classic statement of this thesis is made by Braverman, H. (1974) *Labor and Monopoly Capital: The Degradation of Work in the Twentieth Century*. New York: Monthly Review Press; cf. Shaiken, H. (1985) *Work Transformed: Automation and Labour in the Computer Age*. New York: Holt, Rinehart and Winston.

18 Drucker, P.F. (1969) *The Age of Discontinuity*, p. 254. London Heinemann.

19 cf. Fox, A. (1974) *Beyond Contract: Work, Power and Trust Relations*. London: Faber and Faber: Edwards, R. (1979) *Contested Terrain: the transformation of the workplace in the twentieth century*. London: Heinemann.

20 Drucker, P.F. (1955) *The Practice of Management*, p. 252. London: Heinemann.

21 Quoted in *Business Week*, 3 August 1981, p. 63.

22 Wilkinson, B. (1983) *The Shopfloor Politics of New Technology*, London: Heinemann.

23 Blackburn, R.M. and Mann, M., op.cit., p. 187.

24 Kumar, K. (1978) *Prophecy and Progress*. London: Penguin.

25 The phrase is from Mills, C.W. (1953) *White-Collar: The American Middle Classes*. New York: Oxford University Press.

26 See Kraft, P. (1977) *Programmers and Managers: The Routinization of Computer Programming in the United States*. New York: Springer-Verlag; Harris, M. (1985) 'Invasion of the Tape-Apes', *New Society* 7 March, pp. 364-6.

27 Greenbaum, J. (1979) *In the Name of Efficiency: Management Theory and Shopfloor Practice in Data-Processing Work*, p.163. Philadelphia: Temple University Press.

28 See Berg, I. (1970) *Education and Jobs: The Great Training Robbery*. New York: Praeger; Collins, R. (1979) *The Credential Society*. New York: Academic Press; Burns, V. (1983) 'The Social and Political Consequences of Overeducation', *American Sociological Review* 48(4), pp. 454-67; Dore, R. (1976) *The Diploma Disease*. London: Allen and Unwin; Rumberger, R.W. (1981) *Overeducation in the US Labor Market*. New York: Praeger.

29 Noble, Douglas (1984) 'The Underside of Computer Literacy', *Raritan Review*, 3 Spring, p. 55.

30 See Giddens, A. (1973) *The Class Structure of the Advanced Societies*, pp. 262-3. London: Hutchinson.
31 Gerth, H.H. and Mills, C.W. (1967) *From Max Weber: Essays in Sociology*, p. 232. London: Routledge and Kegan Paul.
32 Barthes, R. (1973) *Mythologies*, p. 143. London: Paladin.
33 See *Many Voices, One World* (1980). Report by the International Commission for the Study of Communication Problems. Paris: UNESCO.
34 See Frobel, F., Heinrichs, J. and Kreye, O. (1980) *The New International Division of Labour: Structural unemployment in industrialised countries and industrialisation in developing countries*. Cambridge: Cambridge University Press.
35 See Murray, F. (1983) 'The Decentralisation of Production – the decline of the mass-collective worker?', *Capital and Class* (19) Spring, pp. 74-99; cf. Webster, F. and Robins, K. (1986) *Information Technology: A Luddite Analysis*, Part Three Norwood, New Jersey: Ablex.
36 See *inter alia* Campbell, D. and Connor, S. (1986) *On the Record: Surveillance, Computers and Privacy*. London: Michael Joseph; Leigh, D. (1980) *The Frontiers of Secrecy: Closed Government in Britain*. London: Junction Books; Manwaring-White, S. (1983) *The Policing Revolution: Police Technology, Democracy and Liberty in Britain*. Brighton: Harvester Press; Campbell, D. (1980) 'Society under Surveillance' in P. Hain (ed.) *Policing the Police*, Vol. 2, pp. 63-150. London: Calder; Burnham, D. (1983) *The Rise of the Computer State*. London: Weidenfeld and Nicolson; Ackroyd, C. *et al.* (1981) *The Technology of Political Control*. Harmondsworth: Penguin; Davies, N. and Black, I. (1984) 'Techniques for eavesdropping on the public', *Guardian*, 18 April, p. 6.
37 Citicorp Advertisement in *Financial Times*, 17 January 1985.
38 Burnham, D. op.cit., p. 44; cf. Snoddy, R. and Hall, W. (1983) 'The rise and rise of the "information factories"', *Financial Times*, 13 April.
39 Information Technology Advisory Panel (1983) *Making a Business of Information*, Cabinet Office, HMSO, September.
40 Burnham, D. op.cit., pp. 56, 242. See also Robins, K. and Webster, F. (1987) 'Cybernetic Capitalism', in Mosco, V. and Wasko, J. (eds) *The Political Economy of Information*. Madison: University of Wisconsin Press.
41 Noble, Douglas op.cit., pp. 60-1.
42 See Gardner, C. and Young, R. (1981) 'Science on TV: A Critique' in Bennett, T. *et al.* (eds) *Popular Television and Film*, pp. 171-93 British Film Institute in association with Open University Press; Robins, K. and Webster, F. (1985) Today's Television and Tomorrow's World in Masterman, L. (ed.) *Television Mythologies*, pp. 110-13. London: Comedia.
43 Thatcher, M., *Speech at the Opening Ceremony of IT '82 Conference*. Press Office, 10 Downing Street, 8 December 1982.
44 See Mulkay, M. (1979) *Science and the Sociology of Knowledge*. London: Allen and Unwin; Yearley, S. (1984) *Science and Sociological Practice*. Milton Keynes: Open University Press; Latour, B. and Woolgar, S. (1979) *Laboratory Life: The Social Construction of Scientific Facts*. Beverly Hills: Sage; Knorr-Cetina, K.D. and Mulkay, M. (eds) (1983) *Science*

Observed: Perspectives on the Social Study of Science. Beverly Hills: Sage.

45 See *inter alia* Horkheimer, M. (1974) *Eclipse of Reason.* New York: Seabury Press; Horkheimer, M. and Adorno, T.W. (1973) *Dialectic of Enlightenment.* London: Allen Lane; Marcuse, H. (1964) *One-Dimensional Man.* London: Routledge and Kegan Paul; Barthes, R. (1973) *Mythologies.* London: Paladin; Foucault, M. (1979) *Discipline and Punish: The Birth of the Prison.* Harmondsworth: Penguin; Habermas, J. (1984) *The Theory of Communicative Action, Vol. 1: Reason and the Rationalization of Society*, esp. Part 4. London: Heinemann.

46 Mumford, L. (1967) *The Myth of the Machine: Technics and Human Development*, p. 10. London: Secker and Warburg.

47 Mumford, L. (1971) *The Myth of the Machine: The Pentagon of Power*, p. 293. London: Secker and Warburg.

48 Ellul, J. (1965) *The Technological Society*, p. 397. New York: Knopf.

49 See Winner, L. (1980) 'Do Artifacts Have Politics?', *Daedalus* 109(1), pp. 121-36 and his books (1977) *Autonomous Technology: Technics-out-of-Control as a Theme in Political Thought.* Cambridge MA: MIT Press, (1986) *The Whale and the Reactor: A Search for Limits in an Age of High Technology.* Chicago: University of Chicago Press.

50 These words are from the Dept. of Trade and Industry's brief to the Economic and Social Research Council as quoted in *Times Higher Education Supplement*, 26 August 1983.

11

Information Technology and the North–South Divide

John Bessant

As we have seen, information technology is likely to make radical changes to the way data is processed, stored and transmitted. The basis for these changes is the use of microelectronics, and the application of this technology in products, manufacturing processes and service sector activities. For the purposes of discussing the international implications of IT, it will be useful to take a broad definition, which includes both the technology itself and its applications in these fields.

The implications of this technological change at a national level are considerable: on the positive side, early and widespread *adoption* of IT might be expected to substantially improve the competitiveness of a country. This is certainly the position of the UK, which has invested large sums of public money since 1978 in various schemes aimed at promoting development and use of IT. Similar ventures can be found in most developed countries – see Bessant (1982a) and Schwartz (1981).

The justification for this can be seen in statements such as the following from the UK Department of Industry (1978): 'If British firms do not seize the opportunities which microelectronics offers, the effects will not fall on them alone: inevitably Britain's capability as an exporting nation will also be affected. Therefore, the UK cannot afford to let its manufacturing industries miss the microelectronics boat.' Or, as the Minister for Information Technology, Kenneth Baker, put it more bluntly, 'the choice for UK firms today is stark – automate or liquidate!'

Similar statements of policy can be found in other developed countries, always quoting the same arguments regarding international competitiveness and the need to be an early entrant into the field.

The argument is given further emphasis if we consider the *production* of information technology. Market sizes here are very large. In 1986 this was estimated to be worth around $485bn, growing at the rate of about 20 per cent per year and expected to be worth $1000bn by 1990. If anything, this growth is likely to accelerate – fuelled partly by the need of producers to achieve economies of scale and thus penetration of new markets. Clearly, early entry into such a large and lucrative field will be a primary goal of developed economies, and this is reflected in considerable state support for IT-producing industries – via grants, procurement, subsidy and other policies.

Discussion and policy-making have not been solely confined to *promotion* of IT: there has also been considerable concern expressed about unwanted negative side-effects, the most serious being employment displacement. It is not proposed to discuss this complex issue here (but see Evans, 1980; Bessant *et al.*, 1981; Forester, 1985; Burns, 1981; Jenkins and Sherman, 1979). However, it is important to note that the response by most policy-makers in the developed world has been to see the employment and adverse social consequences of adopting IT as being preferable to those arising from the declining international competitiveness likely to result from non-adoption.

Such considerations place any discussion of IT in a global context, and the aim of this chapter is to explore some of the issues involved and the likely implications of IT for North-South relations.

1   The North– South divide[1]

Without going into detail of the immensely complex pattern of world development, it will be useful to go over some relevant issues before looking at the implications of IT. 'Developing countries' is an umbrella term covering a wide variety of nations differing in size, population, resource endowment and, particularly, the ability to participate in and benefit from the world economic system. For the majority of these, there are immense problems associated with factors like:

- acute material deprivation,
- highly unequal income distribution,
- substantial unemployment, underemployment or employment at very marginal rates of productivity.

To some extent it is possible to classify these countries into groups associated with their level of industrial development: an analysis of this kind reveals a basic split between very poorly developed nations, newly industrializing countries (NIC), and resource-exporting countries. In this context, it becomes clear that access to technology and the ability to use it become factors of increasing importance – particularly for the industrializing group of countries like India, China, Korea, Taiwan and the Latin American nations. Most commentators (for example, Jacobsson, 1981; Cole and Chichilnisky, 1980) are agreed that in principle the NICs have the relevant economic strength and technological capability to adapt reasonably well to shifts in the world economy. However, this is still a relatively small 'club' for, as Hoffman and Rush (1980) point out, only 12 NICs account for nearly 80 per cent of total manufactured exports from the Third World (based on World Bank data). For the more recently industrializing countries the position is less secure.

Hitherto there has been some growth in world markets for these countries, particularly in sectors where they are able to exploit comparative advantages, for example in textiles, garments and footwear, iron castings, plastics moulding and so on. These advantages lie mainly in the area of lower costs for unskilled labour and it is a characteristic of development sectors like these that the industrial processes involved are largely traditional and based on craft/manual skills, with relatively low capital intensity. Given the current recessionary pressure on countries in the developed North and the associated problems of unemployment and low growth, it is likely that some form of economic counter-attack will take place. The most obvious solution is the use of protectionist policies – an issue much discussed in the textile and garments field. However, this is illustrative of a more general defence mechanism operated by the North when its own markets and industries are threatened.

The question of technological relationships across the North–South divide is again complex, but in essence is characterized by inadequate transfer of technology. Leaving aside questions of how appropriate modern technology might be for developing countries, the pattern has been for the export of technology and capital goods from the North with very little passing in the reverse direction. This reflects a concentration of knowledge and information in the North – and growing difficulties for the South to gain access to such information. Additionally, such items of technology that are bought by the South from the North are often sold as packages with little direct transfer of technology: after-sales service and maintenance is carried out by the supplier. Although this is a broad oversimplification (see Kaplinsky, 1979; and Jacobsson, 1979 for a thorough treatment), it is clear that the trend has been to foster a dependent relationship between North and South – again, because this helps to create and preserve markets.

Strategies of developing countries will clearly be concerned with the need to reduce this dependence and to try and participate more fully in export markets in a growing number of industrial sectors. How far they are able to achieve this depends largely on their internal resources, and their ability to finance development. Thus, foreign exchange earned in markets where they possess a comparative advantage is of considerable importance. The balance is fragile, and it is a question of some significance to ask what the effect of IT – clearly with radical implications for the developed North – is likely to be on the development of the South.

1.1   The rise of knowledge-intensive economics

IT clearly illustrates a change that has been going for some time amongst developed countries which might be defined as a shift towards 'knowledge-intensity'. The long-term developments in most industrial sectors have been towards high levels of capital intensity and growing convergence and concentration of processes and industries: with this has come an increasing dependence on knowledge. As Rada (1980) puts it, electronics is becoming the heavy industry of the future and will be an essential sector in the development of 'knowledge-intensive' economics. Whereas such knowledge-intensity used to be confined to 'high-technology' industries like nuclear energy, aerospace, etc. it is increasingly coming to include 'traditional' industries – textiles, food processing, etc.

The effect of this is to shift the economic emphasis to the design and development stage within manufacturing processes and products. In turn this makes the production and control of knowledge an increasingly important economic commodity – and one which the North with its highly developed science and technology infrastructure is in a strong position to exploit. The extent of the disparity between North and South can be seen in a comparison of research and development (R & D) expenditure. OECD figures for 1973 indicate that developing countries only had 13 per cent of all researchers, and spent only 3 per cent of the worldwide total R & D budget of around $100 billion.

One of the major implications of this trend towards 'knowledge intensification' is that comparative advantages will become increasingly man-made rather than dependent on geographical or historical position. Since the resources to develop and support knowledge-intensive industries lie almost exclusively in the developed world, and developing countires are not likely, in the short term, to be able to create and support the necessary infrastructure, there is likely to be a two-fold effect on world trade. First, those comparative advantages which developing countries have been able to secure on the basis of low labour or materials costs are likely to be eroded, because of the considerable productivity and quality increases made possible through extensive automation based on IT. Hoffman and Rush (1980) discuss the example of textiles and garments in some detail, and suggest that the potential threat posed by IT is quite considerable, given the high labour intensity of these operations and the emergence of suitable automation technology. Another example might be drawn from the foundry sector, where novel processes such as the Disamatic, from Denmark, can produce high quality castings of uniform consistency at rates of up to 700 per hour. Such equipment is expensive – around £3 million – but its microprocessor-controlled functions mean that it requires only a small team of operators and maintenance staff. The productivity and quality increases and labour cost reduction make it an effective competitor to labour-intensive methods used in developing countries.

Another feature of this shift in technology which has wider implications is the convergence and concentration of both products and processes. The key concept here is one of 'embodiment': that is, all the relevant skills, knowledge, components and so on are becoming packaged into a 'black box'. Familiar examples in products include the digital watch, various electronic consumer goods and, not surprisingly, computers and calculators. To this list might be added industrial examples, like computer-controlled machine tools. However, the shift is not simply one of component substitution but also process integration. Thus, on the foundry machine mentioned above, a substantial portion of the casting process – from moulding, through melting and pouring, to knock out and sand recovery – has been automated. All the relevant skills and instructions have been embodied in the microprocessor controller. Similar examples can be found in most manufacturing sectors (see Bessant, 1982b).

In the short term, it might be argued that technology of this kind could be beneficially applied in developing countries, since it offers a way of coping with shortages of skills, sophisticated components and a suitable support infrastructure. However, this does not take account of the implicit problem of technological dependence: the essence of embodied technology is that the requisite knowledge rests with the supplier.

The fact that operations carried out by 'black boxes' are invisible and require specialist support and maintenance means that there will be minimal technology transfer or opportunity for 'unbundling' – breaking the package down into elements more suitable for assimilation by developing countries. Perhaps most significantly, control is retained by the supplier, and the opportunities for imitation by developing countries are reduced. Given the massive investment being made by the North in IT, it is clear that protecting markets in this way is an important consideration.

Overall then it appears that IT and the rise of other convergent knowledge-intensive technologies pose significant threats to the South. This is a matter of some urgency, since the process has already begun with a growing concentration of control over the production and application of IT in the North. Clearly, it is important that the South act quickly to redress this imbalance. However, the available options are limited and the entry barriers high – as the following indicates.

1.2   The production of IT

The development of the microelectronics industry from the invention of the transistor has been well-charted (see, for example, Braun and MacDonald, 1978 and Mackintosh, 1980). It is significant to note that its evolution has been characterized by:

- close and often synergistic involvement of user industries, with constant and highly specified demands, joint ventures, etc.
- government support, via procurement, direct and indirect R & D funding, etc.
- high mobility of qualified personnel, leading to high rates of technology transfer between universities, technical establishments and companies.
- competitive pressures forcing a continuous investment in new plant, facilities and R & D.

In terms of the structure of the industry, the changes have been dramatic, most of the discontinuity arising from the inability of many firms to appreciate the full complications of the technical changes taking place. Examination of the 'league table' of the top ten firms in electronics reveals that many of the giants of the 1950s had completely disappeared by 1975, to be replaced by small innovative firms like Fairchild and Texas Instruments (Mackintosh, 1980).

Tables (a) and (b) indicate that although the USA has dominated the electronics industry, in recent years it has been under increasing pressure from Japanese competition. Despite a number of attempts to bring what many see as a price war under control, the US industry is increasingly being forced to move into more specialist high technology manufacture at the expense of the high volume products, such as the 256K RAM chip, production of which is almost entirely dominated by Japanese firms. For different reasons, the European industry, while strengthening its position, is mainly able to do so by virtue of specialist products, captive domestic markets and second-sourcing policies pursued by US and Japanese firms.

That said, it seems unlikely that there are significant entry possibilities for developing countries amongst the characteristic barriers to entry in microelectronics are:

- *capital costs:*   to support specialist equipment, high levels of expertise and large plants exploiting economies of scale requires considerable capital investment, often running into hundreds of millions of dollars. For example, the UK INMOS facility has so far cost £75 million in loan guarantees, whilst the Matra-Harris-Intel plant in France is expected to cost over $100 million.

Table 11.1 *World manufacture of microelectronics*

(a)   *Worldwide market shares of semiconductor producers (%)*

Country	1980	1983	1985
USA	64	44	38
Japan	25	31	35
Europe	8	19	21
Others	1	6	6

(b)   *World sales by semiconductor companies*

Company	1985 $m
Nippon Electric	1950
Texas Instruments	1815
Hitachi	1750
Motorola	1650
Toshiba	1370
Fujitsu	950
Intel	900
National Semiconductor	890
Matsushita	870
Philips	850

Total 1985 world market size around $22bn

- *R & D intensity and shortages of high-grade skills:* the knowledge-based nature of the industry requires considerable investment in R & D to retain a competitive edge. Estimates suggest that US manufacturers spend between 5 and 10 per cent of turnover on R & D; in 1978 this figure was about $420 million for the industry. The skills problem has two components: first, there is a shortage of first rate design and development engineers; secondly, there is high mobility amongst this group which leads to high levels of technology transfer but reinforces the need for more knowledge-intensity to keep pace – something of a vicious circle. It should also be noted that this transfer of personnel and technology takes place within a closed and concentrated community. There is little evidence to suggest that widespread diffusion of knowledge outside Silicon Valley or its equivalents has taken place.
- *labour costs:* the stage in the production process which is labour intensive at present is the assembly of chips: traditionally these costs have been kept low by using labour in developing countries, principally in the Far East. However, given the growing trend towards increasing automation in assembly and testing which will provide higher quality and labour saving, this picture may change, with a relocation in the developed North with all manufacturing and assembly operations in single plants.
- *economies of scale:* Rada (1980) makes an important point regarding the relationship between prices, costs and production volume. He suggests

that costs reduce by up to 30 per cent with a doubling of output volume; this, given the highly competitive nature of the industry, tends to encourage large plants, and attempts to secure economies of scale through industrial concentration and global diffusion.

The effect of these entry barriers is to restrict the production of microelectronics to a small number of firms within the advanced economies. New entrants require some kind of external support – government backing, technology sharing, joint ventures or whatever – and this usually involves some kind of strategic justification beyond that of simple market economics. Two common arguments used in this connection are that it is important to secure the supply of microelectronics by having an indigenous capability and that there will be valuable technology transfer involved.

The pattern for other IT production sectors is broadly similar, with the same entry barriers, technological intensity and industrial concentration. Significantly, the field is dominated by firms involved in all aspects of IT, indicating considerable integration. (Tables 11.2 and 11.3 give the major suppliers of telecommunications and computers). There seems little doubt that the growth in IT production will expand, with considerable acceleration during the next 10 years. While there may be major technological changes on the horizon (for example, the development of VLSI technology or, in the longer term, fifth generation computers), it seems likely that the IT industry will continue to be dominated by a small and highly concentrated group of large multinational corporations. These will be located almost entirely in the US, in Europe and Japan. Given the nature of the entry barriers, there seems very little likelihood that developing countries can compete in the *production* of IT. Indeed, it can be argued that the existing pattern is one which actively militates against developing country participation. Location of operations in developing countries conveys a number of other advantages which have been exploited by IT Producers without significant benefit to the host countries.

Table 11.2 *Leading telecommunications suppliers*

World's 10 top telecommunications firms

Company	Nationality	1983 sales $bn
AT&T	USA	11.16
ITT	USA	4.86
Siemens	W.Germany	4.49
Ericsson	Sweden	3.16
Alcatel-Thomson	France	2.74
Northern Telecom	Canada	2.66
NEC	Japan	2.41
GTE	USA	2.38
Motorola	USA	2.31
IBM	USA	1.73

Source: Arthur D. Little.

Beyond the financial – low labour costs, preferential and low tax arrangements, etc. – there are other factors like abundance of suitable labour, stability of industrial relations, minimal constraining legislation and so on which influence location policy. In addition the nature of IT *application* within large multinational organizations means that it is possible to operate production plants in developing countries without needing a large on-site managerial infrastructure or to rely on local services. Such operational independence of the host country has two effects: it minimizes transfer of technology or other benefits, and it facilitates rapid relocation. Charting the pattern of IT production location in the Far East over the past 15 years reveals many examples of such rapid change.

Table 11.3 *Leading computer suppliers*

World's 10 top computer firms

Company	Nationality	1984 sales $bn
IBM	USA	44.3
Digital	USA	6.2
Burroughs	USA	4.5
Control Data	USA	3.7
NCR	USA	3.7
Fujitsu	Japan	3.5
Sperry	USA	3.4
Hewlett-Packard	USA	3.4
NEC	Japan	2.8
Siemens	W. Germany	2.8

Source: Datamation.

1.3   Application of IT

Let us now consider the *application* of IT and the prospects for the participation of developing countries. In principle, the highly competitive nature of IT production might be expected to lead to widespread availability of suitable equipment, but this is only true in certain sectors. Within manufacting industry, rates of diffusion in both product and process applications have been relatively slow – certainly not matching those which might have been expected from the 'miracle chips' in 'the microelectronics revolution'. The reasons for this are complex, but include the following factors:

THE ECONOMIC CONTEXT
The decline in the world economy has effectively put a brake on capital investment and this has slowed the adoption and application of IT.

Northcott *et al.* (1984; 1985) have attempted to monitor the diffusion of microelectronics in products and processes and even now, some 10 years after the technology first became prominent, only half of the factories in the UK are making use of microelectronics in their processes and less than a third in their products. Similar figures emerge for France and West Germany; significantly, economic factors are the most commonly mentioned barrier to adoption.

SHORTAGES OF SUITABLE MANPOWER
In these and other surveys the second most common barrier to the successful adoption of microelectronics is the shortage of suitably skilled manpower at all levels but particularly in electronics and applications engineering, systems analysis and technician support.

SHORTAGES OF SUITABLE TECHNOLOGY
Despite the growth in production of IT-based equipment, there are problems in certain technological areas. One of the biggest has been the transducer problem where an inadequate understanding of relevant control variables, and lack of availability or high cost of sensors and actuators have become growth-limiting factors. Another problem has been the lack of off-the-shelf systems for many applications: the supply field varies enormously, so that computer-controlled (CNC) machine tools or programmable logic controllers are well represented, whilst other industries are unable to buy ready-made equipment incorporating IT.

DEVELOPMENT AND SYSTEM COSTS
The biggest component of system costs is software, often accounting for up to 80 per cent of total costs. This – the analysis, design and development, programming, testing and so on – is notoriously hard to control or standardize. Since it relies on scarce, highly-skilled manpower and is still very labour-intensive, it is an expensive component in any system. Attempts have been made to improve this position through a variety of options – simpler languages, modular programming and so on – but the major software block still remains in many cases.

For industrial systems, it is also important to note that, despite significant falls in the price of electronic components, the overall costs of automated equipment are still high. This is for two main reasons: unlike consumer products, the sales volumes are likely to be small, and so development costs must be distributed over a smaller range, and in any case the proportion of total costs represented by control systems is often only 10–20 per cent. Certainly, there is potential for capital saving, for example in replacing several fixed-purpose machines with a flexible one, but at £10–50,000 for a CNC machine tool or a robot, IT-based automation is not necessarily cheap.

LACK OF EFFECTIVE PROJECT MANAGEMENT
One of the features of IT is the need to involve specialists who will often have to be drawn from outside the organization. Coupled with the novelty of the technology itself, this raises problems of project management. Research suggests that the quality of this is a major determinant of project success particularly in those cases involving major manufacturing systems (such as flexible manufacturing systems or CAD/CAM) rather than stand-alone items of equipment (see Bessant, 1982b; Bessant and Haywood, 1986).

LACK OF INFORMATION
Despite extensive publicity and promotion of IT, it still appears that there are problems associated with knowledge about the technology. As a recent UK government report put it: 'there is a high general level of awareness of the contribution advanced technologies can make to improve manufacturing efficiency . . . by contrast with competitors, however, the actual take-up by

industry remains sluggish . . . potential users have, as yet, insufficient knowledge and understanding of the specific applications of the new technologies in their own sectors' (NEDO, 1981).

COMPATIBILITY ISSUES

The 'fitting-in' of any innovation in an organization involves a number of areas of difficulty. This is especially true of the wider implications of IT (see Bessant and Dickson, 1982 for a detailed discussion). Important factors include the attitudes of management and workforce, the impact on formal and informal industrial relations, changes in work organization, availability of suitable skills and support, and so on.

In the service sector the problem is broadly similar, although the rate of change is considerably faster. This appears to be due to a number of factors including:

- low cost opportunities for the automation of discrete tasks – for example, word processors, cash dispensers – which are attractive even to smaller numbers of users;
- greater standardization of tasks in this sector, such that the production of packaged low cost software becomes possible;
- most applications are based around standard computers rather than being designed from scratch: flexibility is embodied in the software. This standardization again reduces prices;
- the potential market size has attracted major manufacturers and thus introduced sophisticated marketing and distribution arrangements: the resulting high degree of competition has tended to keep prices low.

Clearly, this set of factors represents temporary conditions only. With such enormous *potential* application – any task involving information is amenable to some use of IT — it can only be a matter of time before problems associated with diffusion are solved. What is significant in our North–South discussion is that the *rate* of change is likely to be far slower in the South because the rate-limiting factors are present to a much greater degree. Shortages of skills, capital, technology and equipment, lack of a developed infrastructure to support and maintain sophisticated equipment, lack of management experience and a wide range of other problems are present, which are likely to make the application of IT difficult. Even the relatively technologically sophisticated newly industrializing countries face structural problems which militate against their successful use of IT.

Thus for many reasons, developing countries face a dilemma in terms of their response to IT applications. On the one hand it can be seen as an inappropriate technology, making demands on already scarce resources, detracting from other socially important development priorities, providing a level of technological sophistication which can only be supported with difficulty, increasing technological dependence on the North – and so on. On the other hand, the threat to the industrialization process, which has been based on the exploitation of comparative advantage, is now growing. As we have already seen, IT makes it possible for the North to regain a comparative advantage even in traditionally labour-intensive sectors like textiles and foundries – and the North is strongly placed to consolidate this position, through its extensive knowledge/technology base. The problem is further complicated by the growing concentration of knowledge-intensity in the North and the increasing difficulty of access to this information by developing countries.

2   The options for the South

On a more positive note, there are opportunities within the application – and even, in some cases, the production – of IT. First, there is the possible development and expansion of domestic markets and those between developing countries – as part of a planned development strategy. This sort of approach might be well suited to a region like Latin America. Secondly, there is some scope for acquiring and developing software expertise, particularly for non-standard packages to suit a local environment. Thirdly, there are considerable market niches to be filled at least in the short term – where local knowledge can contribute a competitive advantage. Maxwell (1982) describes an excellent example of this concerning computer systems in Argentina.

Fourthly, there is the option of using IT-based equipment to cope with skill shortages as a short-term measure rather than as one which encourages long-term technological dependence. This would require considerable resource commitment in the field of training suitable manpower and, in the longer term, a do-it-yourself design and manufacturing strategy to produce IT-based equipment locally. Policies which mobilize scarce expert resources to tackle particular industrial problems have already been successfully tried in some developing countries.

Fifthly, there is the development of service sector applications, and it is here that many commentators see the most potential for developing countries. Given the complex and local nature of many service sector tasks, the relatively high growth potential, the use of standardized equipment, and so on, there are possibilities for competitive home-grown solutions: again, Maxwell gives an interesting Argentine example.

Whatever the threats or opportunities, it is clear that developing countries need to make their response to IT quickly, whilst they still have room to manoeuvre. Morehouse (1981) sums up the position of the developing countries succinctly with three propositions:

1   To rely on access to microelectronic technology on terms and conditions decided by those in the North who now control the technology and are determining the future of its development is a prescription for disaster for the Third World.
2   Developing countries must, therefore, gain access to this technology on their own terms and shape its further development and application to meet their own economic, social and political requirements.
3   Such access is possible only if developing countries mount a determined, aggressive campaign working individually and collectively. But that campaign, if it is to be successful, must go beyond slogans and rhetoric to the formulation of hard-headed and detailed strategies and their determined implementation through sustained application of substantial human and financial resources.

However, the practical problems facing countries which attempt to implement such strategies are considerable. This has meant that efforts have so far largely been confined to the newly industrializing countries. Particular examples which illustrate this can be found in India, Brazil and Korea. The first point to be noted is that these all have achieved a relatively high level of industrialization and can draw upon a significant pool of technological manpower. They share the common strategic objective of achieving a high degree of self-sufficiency and technological independence and have used broadly similar policies to reach this. The case of Korea is interesting, since it is indicative of the problems developing countries experience in gaining access to technology. Korea has often been used as an illustration of the ways in which developing countries can industrialize and compete in world markets – but it has recently been encountering problems of exclusion from important new technological areas. To combat this, a number of agencies were set up in fields like electronics and industrial automation. The aim was to train and acquire expertise such that Korea could pursue a do-it-yourself policy. Such a programme has met with some success in electronics where the two firms of Hyundai and Samsung had a capacity in 1985 for producing between them 10 million 256K RAM chips/month, and in engineering, where a South Korean designed and built CNC machine tool has been available since 1983. However, Morehouse (1982) reports that 'at least one part of the Korean initiative – placing Korean engineers in US industry to gain relevant experience through industrial internships in electronics – has been meeting with considerable resistance in Silicon Valley'.

In Brazil, industrial growth prior to the debt crisis had been spectacular and electronics has been particularly important, growing at a rate of 12 per cent per annum; in 1977, exports reached a peak of around $433 million. The problem is that the bulk of the 'leading edge' industry is foreign-owned and the national industry has, in fact, declined. Consequently – and it is still the subject of much debate because of other social priorities – the government has sought to develop a strong national capability and has introduced an 'informatics strategy' loosely modelled upon that of France. The minister of communications expressed the problem thus:

> Technological evolution shifted the most significant part of the equipment manufacture to the design and production of components, mainly integrated circuits. The high costs of R & D in this field have caused concentration of the production of most complex components in the hands of a restricted number of suppliers, who distribute them on a world-wide scale. Brazil is convinced of the necessity of being one of these few manufacturers. (Quoted in Rada, 1981.)

This policy was pursued very actively, with the commitment of considerable resources and met with technological success in several fields – notably the establishment of a viable minicomputer industry (Tigre, 1984). However, three problems remain which threaten Brazilian development along these lines: the serious debt crisis and its impact on the economy, the difficulty of preserving access to advanced technology know-how (or of funding the necessary R & D to develop this internally) and the high social costs associated with diverting major resources away from areas like housing and welfare and into informatics. Much will depend on how far Brazilian informatics-based products can penetrate world markets in an industry which has been almost entirely dominated by the developed countries of the North.

One other option is to develop national and 'developing country' markets for IT and components in particular, and there are signs that this is the likely future direction for Brazil. This strategy is similar to that used in India, but it has to be stressed that such an option implies a considerable technological lag. That is, the state of both component manufacturing technology and the diffusion of IT-based equipment within these markets is lower than that in the technologically advanced North. Therefore, the successful development of such markets requires considerable protective legislation via tariff barriers, constraints on foreign ownership and so on.

Bhargava (1982) discusses the role played by the Electronics Commission and the Department of Electronics in taking the Indian industry from 'entertainment electronics' in the 1960s to a more structured and defined industry with R & D, exports and production priorities clearly outlined, and with considerable private sector involvement. The industry has been successful both in technological terms (domestic capability exists for the production of medium-scale integrated circuits and since 1985 8 bit VLSI microprocessors have been manufactured under a joint venture arrangement using European and US technology) and in market terms. The growth prospects for the next five years are put at around 20 per cent per annum, with up to 40 per cent in computers. As a strategy, India has tried to develop indigenous capability through R & D (unlike most developing countries, they have a high population of graduate-level personnel to draw on) and also through the use of foreign technology bound by technology transfer agreements. All of these examples share the following strategic points – it can be argued that these represent guidelines for policy development elsewhere in the South.

- long-term planning and strategic commitment;
- commitment of resources to R & D and to building up an infrastructure;
- making use of various sources of technological – foreign and indigenous (at least in the short term);
- making use of overseas training and experience opportunities for indigenous personnel;
- acquisition (where possible) of technology licences, use of technology agreements, joint ventures and other access strategies.

The above examples confirm that it is possible to develop IT policies within some developing countries, and that some formula based on a mixture of indigenous industry/technology promotion and the use (with technology transfer) of outside expertise and technology is the most likely prescription for success. Nevertheless, the question of control of outside technology and the terms and conditions under which it is transferred is something we must now examine more closely. In particular, it is time to consider the role of the multinational corporations.

3 The role of multinational corporations

The global economy is increasingly coming to include a new group of 'pseudonations' with considerable influence – the multinational corporations (MNCs). Although this might seem an exaggerated claim, it is a sobering thought to realize that the 20 largest MNCs have gross sales greater than the GNPs of the majority of member states of the United Nations, and the world's largest MNC, Exxon, had gross income in 1980 larger than the GNPs of all but the five largest developing country economies and the three largest Soviet Bloc economies.

It is of particular significance to note the businesses in which MNCs operate since these give an even stronger sense of why they are so economically (and, many suggest, politically) influential. Oil and other energy resources, food and commodities, motor vehicles, electrical goods – and information technology. The presence of major manufacturers like IBM in computers, or General Electric in integrated circuits, is in itself a source of some concern regarding concentration of industrial control. However, many commentators point to the growing patterns of integration and involvement in IT of all the major MNCs. Certainly the evidence for this is convincing. Consider the following examples:

- IBM is the world's largest producer of microelectronics for use in its products. It is the world's leading computer supplier and has major interests in satellites and telecommunications technology, backed by extensive R & D.
- General Motors has begun to make its own integrated circuits for use in its products and processes. It has extensive interests in all fields of industrial automation, especially in CAD/CAM and robotics and, using the software skills of its recent acquisition – the giant software firm EDS — developed the Manufacturing Automation Protocol, the de facto standard for interconnection of all forms of factory automation equipment throughout the developed world.
- AT & T are the world's largest telecommunications manufacturer and also have interests in manufacture of semiconductors and computers.
- ITT, the third largest telecommunications supplier, is also a major integrated circuit manufacturer, and has interests in office automation, computers and electronic consumer goods.
- NCR are one of the largest integrated circuit manufacturers and also have extensive computer and service sector automation interests – particularly in banking and retailing.
- General Electric have a declared intention of 'becoming number one in automation by 1990' (*Engineering Today*, 14.4.81). To this end, they have established manufacturing facilities for microelectronics, have acquired robotics and CAD technology (they are now dominant in the latter), have placed considerable emphasis on automation software and on relevant computer/communications systems and so on.
- Siemens, Philips and GEC are three of the major European multinationals. All have interests in the manufacture of integrated circuits, in telecommunications equipment, in industrial control systems, in robotics and automation systems development, in CAD/CAM, in office and other service sector automation, and in various sizes of computers.
- most of the major oil companies have some measure of involvement in IT. For example, Exxon owns Zilog, the integrated circuit manufacturer, and has extensive interests in office automation.

The above examples provide a clear indication of trends within the developed world towards concentration of control amongst a small group of MNCs. These MNCs are confined to the OECD countries, and principally the US, Japan and some European states. Given that this process is taking place, what are its likely implications for developing countries?

First, the economies of scale and high investment needed in the production of IT demand world-wide markets. This is likely to put pressures upon any country trying to develop an internal industry. Some commentators have suggested that MNC strategy will be to seek to invest in plants overseas in order to avoid protectionist legislation. (This is, as mentioned, the pattern in Brazil.)

Secondly, and related to this, the position of technological dependence is likely to worsen, with a growing gap between producers and users of IT — to the extent that internal 'catching up' becomes increasingly unlikely.

The ability to pay for sophisticated imports of technology depends to a large extent on the success of the South in penetrating Northern markets, yet these are likely to be lost by diminishing comparative advantage as the North takes up IT. Consequently, a third implication is that MNCs will increasingly put pressure on Northern governments to adjust their foreign aid polic- ies – via transfer payments, etc. – to provide facilities for MNC exports to developing countries. Morehouse (1982) suggests that this is likely to lock the South into 'an abjectly dependent relationship on the North as they struggle with increasing difficulty to earn enough foreign currency to service their huge external debt'.

Overall, the implications of MNC strategies for developing countries appear essentially negative, and may well have an adverse effect on their capability for self-development of industrial resources. Significantly, there is another way in which IT is likely to have an adverse effect on developing countries, and that is through its application within MNCs. The use of sophisticated information networks, satellite links, data-bases, and other IT equipment, will enable world-wide communication of high quality and integrity. This is likely to enhance the ability of MNCs to operate and control their activities more effectively, and will thus reinforce their strong position. These benefits would also be of considerable value to developing countries because they would enable better participation in the world economy and a more effective use of scarce managerial resources.

The case of banking is illustrative of this. Most world banking is now linked into the SWIFT system. This system has been in operation since 1977 after research by 240 of the largest European and North American banks. The system enables member banks to transmit between themselves international payments, statements and other transactions associated with international banking. The use of the network is more convenient and reliable than past methods of communication (mail, telex and cable), and enables the banks to offer a better service to customers. Over 500 banks in 15 countries are currently connected to the system. Japan operates a similar (ZENGIN) system which covers all internal banking and has some international links.

Clearly, for developing countries to operate successfully in the global context, they too will need a banking and financial sector linked into such a network. They are likely to be operating at a considerable disadvantage relative to the more developed economies if they do not participate. However, gaining access to such a network carries with it several problems, mainly how to pay for it and who controls it. It will inevitably mean importing hardware and software resources, which will have the effect of reinforcing the position of technological dependence.

There is no doubt that developing countries could benefit significantly from an expansion of their information sector in other fields. Internally, the value of good communications in achieving national stability, improved planning, more efficient use of scarce resources, and so on, is considerable – as shown by the high priority given to this issue by the more advanced industrializing countries. (The Arab oil states, for example, currently represent a major proportion of total world investment in modern telecommunications systems.) However, the costs and technological dependence associated with the provision of such services limit the chances for developing countries to achieve rapid progress in this field.

Beyond this, there is the growing problem of the control and concentration of resources in the hands of multinational organizations. An analysis of databases confirms the general picture which is beginning to emerge for information technology. In 1977, the bulk of the world's data-bases were held by Lockheed and the System Development Corporation: these accounted for 75 per cent of the European and 60 per cent of the US market for searches (*New Scientist*, 11.1.79). This is disturbing, because there is little doubt that the use of data-bases as sources of information is increasing dramatically. Developing countries will require access to this kind of information in order to be able to compete effectively, but the resources are essentially concentrated and controlled by the developed North. The question must inevitably be raised about how free that access will be when the Northern nations', and particularly the MNCs', interests are threatened.

This is only one example: estimates indicate that MNC's share of world R & D is around 30 per cent – equivalent to about $45 billion. On this basis, it is clear that access to and use of information technology will be increasingly controlled by these organizations, since they already have such a high degree of control over its development and production.

This 'lightning tour' around the North–South issues raised by the emergence of IT has not dealt in detail with the problems of individual countries. Nevertheless, it has given a general overview of the emerging trends and their likely implications. The options open to developing countries seem limited: as far as participating on a world-wide basis is concerned, the cards appear to be very heavily stacked against them. Rada (1981) estimates that the 'information capacity' gap – measured in terms of demand for usage of computers and telecommunications systems – between North and South is likely to double by 1990, and sees this as the inevitable basis for a widening of the North–South divide.

Where options do exist, they are in the form of niches – chinks in the Northern armour which might be exploited, at least in the short term. In any event, the responses required are political and will require in particular a dedication and commitment to long-term goals – and may incur social costs elsewhere. The appropriateness of IT for developing countries has only been mentioned briefly, but it seems clear that there is an urgent need to revise conventional wisdom on this subject. Certainly the idea of developing countries operating self-contained labour-intensive economies is attractive – but the threat from IT (and its successors in other technological fields) needs to be recognized and acted upon before a permanent and widening North-South gap becomes established.

Morehouse (1981) uses the image of 'letting the genie out of the bottle' in a discussion of the implications of IT for development. It seems that the problem for the South is that there is no chance of rebottling that genie: the only alternative is to try to cope with it on relatively advantageous terms. With so much of the control over IT in the developed North and in the hands of the multinational corporations, the prospects do not look good.

Note

1 The terms North and South were introduced in the Brandt Report to draw attention to the fact that the rich developed nations are to be found predominantly in the North, whereas the Third World of poor developing nations is predominantly in the South.

References

Bessant, J. *et al.* (1981) *The Impact of Microelectronics: A Review of the Literature.* London: Frances Pinter.

Bessant, J. (1982a) 'Microelectronics and information technology; an overview of the European experience', Proceedings of the First Latin American Seminar on Microelectronics, FLASCO, Buenos Aires.

Bessant, J. (1982b) *Microprocessors in Production Processes.* London: Policy Studies Institute.

Bessant, J. and Dickson, K. (1982) *Issues in the Adoption of Microelectronics.* London: Frances Pinter.

Bessant, J. and Haywood, W. (1986) *The Introduction of Flexible Manufacturing Systems as an Example of Computer-integrated Manufacturing,* Occasional Paper 1, Innovation Research Group, Brighton Business School.

Bhargava, P. (1982) *Microprocessors for the Indian Environment,* Paper presented at Microelectronics and Development Seminar, Buenos Aires, 1982, op. cit.

Braun, E. and Macdonald, S. (1978) *Revolution in Miniature.* Cambridge: Cambridge University Press.

Burns, A. (1981) *The Microchip: Appropriate or Inappropriate Technology?* Chichester: Ellis Horwood.

Cole, S. and Chichilnisky, G. (1980) *Technology, Domestic Distribution and North-South Relations.* New York: UNITAR Report.

DOI (1978) *Microelectronics – the new technology.* London: Department of Industry.

Evans, J. (1980) *The Impact of Microelectronics in W. Europe,* European Trade Union Institute.

Forester, T. (ed.) (1980) *The Microelectronics Revolution.* Oxford: Basil Blackwell.

Forester, T. (ed.) (1985) *The Information Technology Revolution.* Oxford: Basil Blackwell.

Hoffman, K. and Rush, H. (1980) 'Microelectronics – The New Development Challenge', *Futures*, August.

Jacobsson, S. (1979) *Microelectronics, Technical Change and Employment in Less Developed Countries*. University of Lund, Sweden: Research Policy Institute.

Jacobsson, S. (1981) *The Use and Production of NC Machine Tools in Argentina*. University of Lund, Sweden: Research Policy Institute.

Jenkins, C. and Sherman, B. (1979) *The Collapse of Work*. London: Eyre Methuen.

Kaplinsky, R. (1979) *The Impact of Microelectronics Technology on LDC Exports of Manufacture to DCs*. University of Sussex: Institute of Development Studies.

Mackintosh, I. (1980) 'Micros – the coming world war', in Forester, T. (1980) op.cit.

Maxwell, P. (1982) 'Specialisation decisions in electronics production – lessons from the experience of two Argentine firms' in Sigurdson, J. (ed.) (forthcoming), *Technological Trends and Challenges to the Third World*. London: Frances Pinter.

Morehouse, W. (1981) 'Letting the genie out of the bottle? The microelectronic revolution and North-South relations in the 1980s' in Szyliowics, J. (ed.) *Technology and International Affairs*. New York: Praeger.

Morehouse, W. (1982) 'Technological intelligence and other strategies for enlarging developing country access to microelectronics technology', draft paper for FLASCO seminar on Microelectronics and Development, Buenos Aires, December 1982.

NEDO (1981) 'Memorandum to Director-General', National Economic Development Office, April 1981.

Northcott, J. (1984) *Microelectronics in British Industry – The Pattern of Change*. London: Policy Studies Institute.

Northcott, J. *et al.* (1985) *Microelectronics Adoption in the UK, West Germany and France*, London: Policy Studies Institute.

Rada, J. (1980) *The Impact of Microelectronics*. Geneva: ILO.

Rada, J. (quoted in) (1981) 'The impact of microelectronics and information technology with case studies in Latin America'. Paris: UNESCO Report.

Schwarz, M. (1981) 'Governmental responsibility for technology-microelectronics in W. Europe', *Microprocessing and Microprogramming*, 8, pp. 67-82.

Tigre, P. (1984) *The Brazilian Computer Industry*, London: Frances Pinter.

12

Decision-making in the Information Age: Computer Models and Public Policy

William H. Dutton

1 The problematic role of information technology

1.1 Decision-making in the information age

Two rather paradoxical themes are increasingly prevalent in discussions of the role of information technology in decision-making. On the one hand, we are said to be in the midst of a new age in which information is the primary resource, and information technology – computers, telecommunications, and management science technique – is the primary means for mining and refining this resource. This information age has been labelled as the era of 'C⁴I²', representing 'command, control, communications, computing/information and intelligence' (Kahn, 1982). These characterizations leave no doubt that most observers champion the information age as a new frontier that offers great benefits. In fact, there is mounting pressure to develop the national resources to compete in the international marketplace, not only as a strategy for developing growth industries, but also as a means for improving decision-making and productivity in the public and private sectors (Dizard, 1982; Forrester, 1981; Nora and Minc, 1981; Oettinger, 1971).

However, it is in the midst of this era that there is growing concern over the complexity and political character of decision-making that strains our capacities to create, disseminate and effectively use information technology (Ackoff, 1967; Benjamin, 1982; Danziger *et al.*, 1982; Kling, 1980; Mowshow-itz, 1977). One basis of this concern is that problems are perceived to be increasingly complex and less capable of being fully comprehended. There are grave doubts about the ability of experts to understand and predict the behavior of social and economic systems of today. For example, one account of discussions at SRI International in Menlo Park, California, indicated that the growing complexity and incomprehensibility of social systems became a general theme of discussions at this think tank. The reporter illustrated this theme by noting that someone 'recalled a comment by Reagan's Budget Director, David Stockman, that no one really understands what is going on in the economy' (Moritz, 1981, p. 65). In the absence of such an understanding, the value of many tools of the information age is quite problematic.

The second basis of skepticism is the fundamentally political character of decision-making in democratic societies. As Heinz Eulau (1970, p. 194) suggests, 'a highly accurate, reliable and complete information system is not *ipso facto* conductive to rational decision-making.' Such beliefs have been supported by a variety of empirical analyses of the role of computers and automated information systems in public sector decision-making (Brewer, 1973, 1981; Kraemer *et al.*, 1981; Laudon, 1974; Moss, 1980). A recent study of computing in local government reflects the thrust of research on the politics of information technology in finding that computing is selectively adopted and utilized in ways that serve 'the interests of those who control' the organization, thereby tending to reinforce 'the prevailing interests and values of the organization' (Danziger *et al.*, 1982, p. 231).

1.2   Computer models in the information age

Among the many components of this new age, computer models are one that clearly reflects these paradoxical trends. On the one hand, computer models are an especially promising information technology, for they can be used to simulate and forecast the outcomes of alternative operational, management, and planning decisions. By computing answers to a variety of 'what if' questions, models are presumed to be valuable tools for policy and management analysis. Certainly this has been an argument of those promoting the use of computer models and those identifying computer models as important to the array of technologies driving the information society (Khan, 1982; Kraemer, 1973; Oettinger, 1971; Simon, 1960). This promise, along with the increasing complexity of modern society, the growing availability of models and model builders, and the rise of politicians and managers who understand how to use and manage new information technologies, is creating a supply and demand for computer models. There is little doubt that models are becoming an increasingly visible and potent part of the American political landscape (Ascher, 1978; Frantzich, 1982).

On the other hand, these promising expectations are not well borne out by empirical research. Studies of the use of computer models indicate that they often fall short of serving the rational-analytical functions commonly attributed to them (Brewer, 1973; Dutton and Kraemer, 1985; Greenberger *et al.*, 1976; Kraemer *et al.*, 1981). This is manifested time and again in the unveiling of new computer-based modeling techniques designed to forecast everything from the economy to the weather, without their analytical basis being either clear or documented, in many cases. For example, the forecasting of political crises is said to be within the range of current technique. Models aimed at forecasting crises have long been sponsored by the Department of Defense, as well as firms with international financial interests (Zientara, 1979). Yet capabilities for predicting political crises remain poor, becoming an obvious shortcoming after failures to anticipate the Iranian crisis.

Closer to home, *Time* magazine ('The forecast is for accuracy', 1982, p. 72) describes a $16 million 'supercomputer' built by Control Data for the Suitland weather center that 'is expected to double the accuracy of the weather service's daily forecasts'. The same article quotes the National Weather Service Director, Richard Hallgren, who claims (not necessarily referring to the supercomputer): 'The larger the computer, the better the forecast . . . . As the computer gets bigger, we can get more of the mathematics and physics of the atmosphere into our models.' Such arguments are echoes of debates over models in other areas of application. And there are similar counter arguments. One forecaster wondered whether computers will 'actually improve forecasts or give bad forecasts more frequently' ('The forecast is for accuracy', 1982, p. 72).

In short, new forecasting and modeling techniques are being called to the service of an increasing variety of tasks for which we appear to have little increased understanding. In fact, some have documented cases in which models are likely to misinform users due to faulty theoretical and statistical assumptions (Freedman, 1981). In this regard, Joseph Weizenbaum has long argued that many automated information systems approach what Russell Ackoff called 'misinformation systems' (Ackoff, 1967). They fail to inform because they are based on invalid theories and assumptions. We might write computer programs for calculating a person's horoscope, but, as Weizenbaum suggests, if 'astrology is nonsense, then computerized astrology is just as surely nonsense' (Weizenbaum, 1976, p. 35).

Even when models are believed to provide valid information, such information is not necessarily utilized to inform policy decisions (Brewer, 1973; Dutton and Kraemer, 1980). Several studies suggest that models are often used to serve more partisan-political than rational-analytical functions (Dutton et al., 1980; Frantzich, 1982; Greenberger et al., 1976). And, even when used, the information from computer models is only one of many decision inputs to the policy process. Such empirical observations make positive views of the new information age far more problematic than assumed by those who believe that the utilization of new information technology will improve the decision-making process and its outcomes in the governance of democratic societies. [. . .]

The central theme that emerges from this review is that computer models are likely to alter the decision-making process by changing the language, subjects and process of political negotiation and bargaining. While computer models are only one of several influences in the policy-making process, they influence public policy-making processes at the margins and, thereby, shape policy outcomes. This is largely because computer models shape the analytic framework of policy debate, the criteria for choice, the extent to which decisions will be binding on the participants, and the range of alternatives that are the subject of negotiation and compromise. Once accepted and institutionalized as part of the policy process, modeling can change the way in which policy debates are carried out, and thereby fundamentally change the nature of policy-making and policy outcomes in the longer run (Dutton and Kraemer, 1985). In these ways, the study of computer models in the policy process not only provides an important perspective on the assumptions behind the information technology push, but also an important perspective on the effects of information technology on the content and process of elite communication, a process that shapes decision-making outcomes and the policy process more generally.

2   Perspectives on the role of models

How are computer models expected to affect decision-making and the public policy process? The dominant expectations regarding the role of models in the policy process vary widely, but they can be summarized by a few competing perspectives (Danziger *et al.*, 1982; Dutton and Kraemer, 1983). The primary proponents of modeling – the optimists – hold a very 'rational perspective'. The rationalist views models as tools for scientific management and policy analysis that provide new and better information to assist in the policy-making process (Kahn, 1982; Pinkus and Dixson, 1981).

Those who hold the rational perspective view models as almost revolutionary in their impacts. Models are expected to change the way in which policies are formulated and chosen. Politics will be conducted in new ways as new people, the modelers and the policy analysts, will be more central to the provision of expert (objective) guidance. New people and new techniques, therefore, will become more prominent to politics and policy making in the information society.

Some critics of modeling – the pessimists – also tend to be rationalists, but disappointed rationalists. This group is concerned with the scientific validity of models and will, therefore, criticize models and modelers that use invalid data or violate accepted theoretical or statistical assumptions in the construction of the model. In this category stand such mathematicians and statisticians as David Freedman, who has provided an excellent statistical critique of important econometric models (Freedman, 1981). Still, such critics tend to hold a rational perspective in the sense that they believe models can be valid analytical tools if they withstand certain tests of internal validity.

Other critics hold a 'partisan perspective' (i.e. Frantzich, 1982; Lupo *et al.*, 1971). They view models as tools for propaganda and persuasion rather than information. To the partisan critics, models are adopted to legitimate choices that have already been made, and, therefore, models might simply provide new tools to support the policy initiatives of the dominant coalition of interests within an organization or society. Political commentators and journalists, who hold a more partisan perspective, are not surprised by the partisan use of models by public officials and interest groups. Political manipulation of information is regarded as only a new twist to a routine of partisan deception. To those who hold a partisan perspective, models are not revolutionary in their impacts at all. They are merely 'old wine in new bottles' (Gaffney, 1978). Politics, in the sense of personal power and influence taking precedence over the rational weighing of the merits of an argument, continues as usual. Politicians will continue to control the policy-making process. Experts will continue to serve and advise the 'Prince', but as experts with new tools (Benveniste, 1977). Large-scale computer models might replace hand calculators, just as hand calculators have replaced slide rulers. While revolutionizing the analytical process, such changes in techniques are not expected to have demonstrable effects on decision-making processes. Politicians and analysts have simply updated their techniques to respond to the language and technology of a new era.

Still other critics hold a more 'technocratic perspective'. They view models as tools of the high priests of the emerging information society – the information elite, which in this case are the modelers. Modelers use information technology to baffle, impress, and promote their positions, defeat their opponents, and seal their position as authorities on the issue at hand (Danziger, 1979a, b; Downs, 1967; Greenberger et al., 1976). To those who hold a technocratic perspective, models are powerful and potentially revolutionary in their impacts. Technocrats are expected to gain political power by authority of their expertise. Models are viewed from this perspective with a skeptical eye as complicated representations of a modeler's personal theory and biases.

Finally, this author and Kenneth Kraemer have suggested that empirical research on modeling supports a more 'consensual perspective' (Dutton and Kraemer, 1983; 1985). A consensual perspective views models as tools of negotiation, bargaining, and interactive decision-making. Modelers tend to mediate conflicts and uncertainty over the current state of affairs, policy options, and outcomes by using models to define the rules and structure for debate and compromise. Modeling is viewed as a political process, but one that might be functional for resolving conflict and achieving consensus. From this perspective, modeling could have important, albeit marginal, impacts on the decision-making process and its outcomes by changing the language and resources necessary to effectively participate in the policy process.

These four alternative perspectives are neither well defined nor are they traditional perspectives within the modeling literature. Rather, they have been developed as a conceptual device for integrating and simplifying a diverse literature within which such perspectives are normally implicit assumptions or positions of the researcher. They are labeled the rational, technocratic, partisan, and consensual perspectives on modeling to capture their dominant theme. Yet, as ideal types, they tend to capture two major debates within the literature on the role of models in policy making. These debates concern *who controls* the modeling process and *whose interests are served* by the process.

Debate on the locus of control over modeling is particularly controversial. Some scholars argue that technical experts – modelers – control this process (Greenberger et al., 1976) by dominating day-to-day decisions and technical actions. Other scholars indicate that political elites – politicans and bureaucrats – control the modeling process because they dominate the most critical features of model adoption and utilization (Brewer, 1973). Debate also turns on the interests served by modeling. The proponents of modeling generally perceive the process to be nonpartisan in the sense that it provides 'objective' information that is not biased to serve any particular special interest. Critics of modeling most often suggest that models serve partisan interests – the self-interests of particular individuals or groups in the policy process.

Both of these dimensions, locus of control and interests served, are in actuality continua rather than clear dichotomies. For example, politicians, bureaucrats, and technocrats all share some control over models in the policy process; yet the relative control of each of these actors is likely to vary such that one or the other of these categories is more descriptive of a particular distribution of control. Similarly, the degree to which the partisan interests of politicians, bureaucrats, and technocrats are served is likely to vary on a broad continuum. But in any particular case, and over many cases, a *dominant* pattern can be discerned.

It is the intersection of these two dimensions of 'control' and 'interests served' that identifies the four perspectives on the modeling process. Both the rational and technocratic perspective view experts to be in control of the modeling process. However, rationalists view their control to be neutral and nonpartisan, for they are guided by a scientific process and an apolitical objectivity. In contrast, technocrats view expert control as likely to be used in ways that maintain and enhance the role and preferences of the experts in decision-making. Similarly, both the partisan and consensual perspectives view politicians and bureaucrats to have more control over the modeling process. However, partisan critics view their control to be biased toward a few special interests, while consensual critics view their control to be relatively more pluralistic and therefore more likely to serve a broader array of public interests.

These basic interests served by the results of modeling are termed model 'impacts'. This concept refers both to the specific array of benefits and costs that result from model use and to the distribution of benefits and costs among actors and groups. These impacts might involve unintended as well as intended effects. Therefore, it is important to discern the pattern of impacts implied by alternative perspectives on the modeling process.

These dominant and conflicting expectations are especially apparent in the popular rhetoric of modeling. Visionaries of the new information society believe that models are information resources, taking a rational perspective. They see models being used to improve decision-making and thereby the productivity of organizations and society. To such visionaries, models are a benign force for coping with the complexity of modern society. They are solutions to information overload and the incomprehensibility of complex systems. At the same time, there are critics of the new information technology who expound a more technocratic, partisan, or consensual perspective on the modeling process. Here, these alternative perspectives will be systematically related to one another and the literature, by comparing their respective assumptions regarding the dynamics of the model implementation process and the role or impacts of models in the policy process.

Most critics of rational perspectives on modeling argue that the use and impact of models is likely to be a function of the nature of the modeling (implementation) process. Policy modeling is viewed as a dynamic, multi-stage, social and organizational process, involving three broad phases: introduction, adaptation and incorporation (Dutton and Kraemer, 1985; Kraemer, 1981; Kraemer et al., 1982; Yin, 1981; Yin and Quick, 1979). 'Introduction' refers to the period during which the model is considered for adoption. Some early pilot testing may occur on a small-scale basis, and the results of this testing may bring about a decision to adopt the model. 'Adaptation' refers to the period during which broader support for the model is developed, plans are made for instructing and training relevant users, model use begins as widely as resources permit, and the results of use are monitored. 'Incorporation' refers to the period in which the use of the model no longer appears as a new innovation per se but becomes a part of the routine of the organization.

These stages are not distinct, nor do they bear a simple relationship to one another. However, each stage has distinctive characteristics, and each stage occurs sequentially over time. Moreover, each stage might be differentially

Table 12.1 *Four perspectives of modeling*

Alternative Perspectives	Rationale for model adoption	Dynamics of Implementation		Key impacts of modeling
		Critical relations between modelers and other participants	*Most critical phase of the modeling process*	
Rational: Models are tools of 'scientific' management and policy analysis	Adopted to 'inform' policy choices of public officials	Modelers are independent and free to exercise professional judgement	*Incorporation:* Ongoing use of models for analysis	Provide objective information about the implications of policy alternatives
Technocratic: Models are tools of expert persuasion	Promoted to further the position of modelers and other information elites	Modelers promoted or discredited by politicians	*Incorporation:* Ongoing use of models for analysis	Explicate the rationale of a policy argument
Partisan: Models are tools of propaganda and persuasion	Adopted to legitimate choices made by dominant political elites	Modelers lack independence, assuring support for the dominant coalition	*Introduction:* Adoption of models that reinforce dominant interests of political elites	Provide support for a policy initiative
Consensual: Models are tools of interactive decision-making, negotiation, and bargaining	Adopted in the belief that modeling will somehow serve multiple and shifting interests of different contestants	Modelers consult broadly, anticipating reactions of various groups and interests in a broadly participative process	*Adaptation:* Mutual adjustments of models to take account of competing beliefs	Provide a process for resolving conflict and achieving consensus

Adapted from Dutton and Kraemer (1983. Table 3).

related to the use and impact of policy models. Table 12.1 summarizes various dimensions of the modeling process and its impacts, on which the four perspectives can be compared and contrasted. [. . .]

3   Politics in the information age

[. . .] For the most part, the modeling literature has been written from one of three alternative perspectives. Generally, modeling experts, decision science academics, and the advocates of modeling techniques describe modeling from a rational perspective. The textbooks, the professional societies, and the trade magazines speak from this viewpoint in prescribing the appropriate role of modelers and models. While the rational perspective is the most common *prescription* and is sometimes descriptive of reality, it deviates from most empirical accounts of the modeling process. Both journalistic and academic studies of the actual implementation and use of models have given rise to the technocratic and partisan perspectives as more accurate descriptions of the process, especially in highly unstructured, nonroutine, and more consequential policy decisions (Brewer, 1973; Frantzich, 1982; Greenberger *et al.*, 1976; Kling, 1980).

These behavioral accounts suggest that the introduction of computers, communications, command, control, information, and intelligence-oriented technologies into the policy making process is unlikely to alter its fundamentally political character. At times, models have been used as partisan tools, whether to legitimate exclusionary fiscal zoning policies, or to provide support to particular governmental programs or policies. In other cases, models have been used to delay decision by shelving an issue for more study. But, in many cases, models have been useful in resolving conflicts among groups with different opinions, interests, and beliefs about policy impacts, and, thereby, tend to serve a relatively more pluralistic array of interests than portrayed in more partisan perspectives on the modeling process.

The policy making process in the information society is likely to remain highly political rather than rational because the new information technologies will not fundamentally alter differences of opinion, beliefs, and values over public policy. Problems that move into the public sphere often involve conflict. Public issues and choices are often poorly structured. Public policy issues normally involve controversy and uncertainty over the consequences of alternatives. However, politics in the information age might be fundamentally different from politics of earlier eras. New people and new techniques might supplant older ones. It seems that those who know and understand the new information technologies will increasingly be involved in the political process, especially as the use of information technologies in the policy process will become routine, if that is not already the case.

This trend does not necessarily empower the technocrats of the information age. The modelers, analysts, and technical experts are seldom powerful actors on their own, and are seldom successful unless they are unusual individuals (Greenberger *et al.*, 1976), tied to powerful individuals, or skilled mediators who can use modeling as a tool for negotiation and bargaining.

One of the most critical problems that this trend poses for a pluralistic society is the increased importance that this technological change places on the organization and political resources of groups and interests in the society. Groups and interests that cannot marshall the resources and expertise to effectively participate in the process of defining reality, forecasting the consequences of alternative policies, and defining alternative policies, are unlikely to be well served by the new politics of the information age. If such is the case, we will be left with a pluralistic political process for the haves that will accentuate inequalities between the haves and have nots of the information age.

References

Ackoff, R. L. (1967) 'Management misinformation systems', *Management Science 14* (No. 4), B-147-B-156.

Ascher, W. (1978) *Forecasting: An Appraisal for Policy Makers and Planners*. Baltimore, Maryland: Johns Hopkins University Press.

Benjamin, G. (ed.) (1982) *The Communications Revolution in Politics*. New York: Academy of Political Science.

Benveniste, G. (1977) *The Politics of Expertise*, 2nd ed. San Francisco, California: Boyd & Fraser.

Brewer, G. D. (1973) *Politicians, Bureaucrats and the Consultant: A Critique of Urban Problem Solving*. New York: Basic Books.

Brewer, G. D. (1981) 'Where the twain meet: Reconciling science and politics in analysis', *Policy Sciences 13*. pp. 269-79.

Danziger, J. N. (1979a) 'The use of automated information in local government', *American Behavioral Scientist 22*, pp. 363-92.

Danziger, J. N. (1979b) 'The skill bureaucracy and interorganizational control', *Sociology of Work and Occupations 6*, pp. 204-26.

Danziger, J. N., Dutton, W. H., Kling. R. and Kraemer, K. L. (1982) *Computers and Politics*. New York: Columbia University Press.

Dizard, W. (1982) *The Coming Information Age*. New York: Longman.

Downs, A. (1967) 'A realistic look at the final payoffs of urban data systems', *Public Administration Review 27*, pp. 204-10.

Dutton, W. H. and Hollis, M. S. (1980) 'Fiscal impact budgeting systems' in K. L. Kraemer and J. L. King (eds) *Computers in Local Government Urban and Regional Planning*. Pennsauken, New Jersey: Auerbach.

Dutton, W. H. and Kraemer, K. L. (1980) 'Automation bias', *Society 17* (No. 2). pp. 36-41.

Dutton, W. H. and Kraemer, K. L. (1983) 'The politics of modeling', *Systems, Objectives, Solutions 3*, forthcoming.

Dutton, W. H. and Kraemer, K. L. (1985) *Modeling as Negotiating*. Norwood, New Jersey: Ablex Publishing Corp.

Eulau, H. (1970) 'Some potential effects of the information utility on political decision-makers and the role of the representative' in H. Sackman and N. Nie (eds) *The Information Utility and Social Choice*, pp. 187-99. Montvale, New Jersey: AFIPS Press.

'The forecast is for accuracy' (1982) *Time* (2 Aug.) p. 72.

Forrester, T. (1981) *The Microelectronics Revolution*. Cambridge, Massachusetts: MIT Press.

Frantzich, S. E. (1982) *Computers in Congress: The Politics of Information*. Beverly Hills, California: Sage.

Freedman, D. (1981) 'Some pitfalls in large econometric models: A case study', *Journal of Business of the University of Chicago 54*. pp. 479-500.

Gaffney, M. (1978) 'Fiscal impact analysis' in W. H. Dutton, M. Hollis and K. L. Kraemer *Fiscal Impact Budgeting Systems*. Proposal to the National Science Foundation, pp. 134-49. Irvine, California: Public Policy Research Organization.

Greenberger, M., Crenson, M. A. and Crissey, B. L. (1976) *Models in the Policy Process*. New York: Russell Sage Foundation.

Kahn, H. (1982) *The Coming Boom*. New York: Simon and Schuster.

Kling, R. (1980) 'Social analyses of computing', *Computing Surveys 12*. pp. 61-110.

Kraemer, K. L. (1973) *Policy Analysis in Local Government*. Washington, D.C.: International City Management Association.

Kraemer, K. L. (1981) 'The politics of model implementation', *Systems, Objectives, Solutions I*. pp. 161-78.

Kraemer, K. L., Dickhoven, S., Fallows, S. E. and King, J. L. (1982). *Computers, Planning Models, and Policymaking: The Implementation of High Technology in Federal Agencies*. Irvine, California: Public Policy Research Organization, University of California.

Kraemer, K. L., Dutton, W. H., and Northrop, A. (1981) *The Management of Information Systems*. New York: Columbia University Press.

Laudon, K. C. (1974) *Computers and Bureaucratic Reform*. New York: Wiley.

Lupo, A., Colcord, F. and Fowler, E. P. (1971) *Rites of Way: The Politics of Transportation in Boston and the US City*. Boston, Massachusetts: Little Brown.

Moritz, M. (1981) 'A dip into a think tank', *Time* (30 Nov.), p. 65.

Moss, M. (1980) *Telecommunications and Productivity*. Reading, Massachusetts: Addison-Wesley.

Mowshowitz, A. (1977) *Computers and the Mechanization of Judgement*. Paper delivered at the National Symposium for Philosophy and Computer Technology. SUNY at Albany, New York.

Nora, S. and Minc, A. (1981) *The Computerization of Society*. Cambridge, Massachusetts: MIT Press.

Oettinger, A. (1971) 'Communications in the national decision-making process', in M. Greenberger (ed.) *Computers, Communications, and the Public Interest*, pp. 73-91. Baltimore, Maryland: Johns Hopkins University Press.

Pinkus, C. E., and Dixson, A. (1981) *Solving Local Government Problems*. London: George Allen & Unwin.

Simon, H. A. (1960) *The New Science of Management Decision*. New York: Harper & Row.

Weizenbaum, J. (1976) *Computer Power and Human Reason*. San Francisco, California: W. H. Freeman.

Yin, R. K. (1981) 'Life histories of innovations: How new practices become routinized', *Public Administration Review 41*. pp. 21-8.

Yin, R. K. and Quick, S. K. (1979) *Routinization 1: Thinking About Routinization*. Santa Monica, California: The Rand Corporation. (Mimeo.)

Zientara, M. (1979) 'Technique aids forecasting of political crises', *Computerworld* (4 June), p. 30.

PART IV
*Some Critical Issues for the Information
Age: Access and Participation*

Introduction to Part IV

This part complements the last, still in one sense concerned with questions of power and control, but this time considering them more from the 'bottom-up' viewpoint, from the end of the *users* or potential users. Here too there are crucial issues: who will have access to the new information technologies? Will some groups or countries inevitably lose out? How far will employees be allowed to participate in the introduction of new technologies? Will modern IT lead to greater personal participation in society or to some being increasingly shut out from the work and leisure of the 'new information age'? The papers here cannot cover all these issues and certainly provide no quick answers, but they do highlight a number of differing questions and areas which need to be considered.

The first, Neville Jayaweera's 'Third World Perspective', reminds us of the global context of these issues. He disputes the idea that 'development' is essentially constituted and determined by technology and GNP (gross national product) or that the technological media – whether television, radio or, by now, satellites – are by themselves enough to bring about improvements in people's lives in developing countries. Instead, in the context of a critique of earlier 'development' theories, he looks at how satellites have actually affected people's lives. One result, for example, has been a yet greater concentration of power within capital cities with less and less participation and contact from those in the villages where, as Jayaweera points out, 80 per cent of the population of the Third World live. Similarly communication satellites are likely to set up greater international centralization, with Third World countries increasingly dependent on the culture and economy of the world leaders. And though new technologies such as satellites can bring benefits, they 'cannot provide the solutions to problems which are primarily political, economic and sociological . . . if satellites are used as an alternative to painful structural reforms, they are more likely to consolidate and perpetuate those conditions which produced the problems' (below, p. 207). He concludes that the key issues lie not in the technology as such but in questions about inequalities among different nations and groups in their access to the benefits from new technologies. What is ultimately needed to bring about equitable access and participation is democratic accountability rather than private profit – so that the benefits of technology can 'be put at the service of *all* of the human race'.

Miles and Gershuny take a national – rather than global – perspective, but they too see the issues as more than just technical. They provide a critical assessment of what is, or might be, meant by that well-known term, 'the information society', and discuss its wider implications for people's lives. As they see it, various scenarios are possible, and need urgent policy debate. Will increasing unemployment lead to certain individuals and groups no longer being able to participate fully economically with at best, only unskilled jobs, at worst none? Or will this be compensated for by new kinds of work, perhaps more acceptable jobs in different sectors of the economy? Will new information technology bring about a dualistic economy, increasing inequalities of access to its benefits, or increase new forms of social participation in work and leisure? Will decision-making become more, or less, centralized in business organizations and in the social services? How can informatics be distributed or designed so as to encourage equitable participation? The authors point to the importance of considering such questions before systems are developed and installed, and thus to the need for informed public debate on these and similar issues.

The final paper moves away from the national and international levels of the earlier papers to a more detailed analysis of how information technology is likely to develop at the grass roots: in people's homes and local communities. This is taken from a more general consideration of 'IT Futures' and includes a brief critique of the pros and cons of various kinds of forecasting and of the problems of isolating cause and effect in complex change processes like that of IT in the household: the 'chicken-and-egg dilemma'. Nevertheless, despite these intractable difficulties, the authors point to various likely developments of IT in homes and communities, for, though some of the utopian predictions about technological wonders are unlikely to be fulfilled, there are real possibilities for wider applications of home-based IT, particularly given present trends towards increasing cheapness, reliability and effectiveness. One possible result may be that people can take more personal responsibility for their own well-being, through direct access to computer-delivered information and services on, say, health, employment, educational or leisure questions. There may also be opportunities for greater participatory democracy or new social movements and community services. But as the authors point out, social innovations can take one of several directions, and could lead equally to greater isolation and divisiveness. Which will come about is dependent partly on people's individual choices within the context of their homes and communities, partly on technological developments, partly on governmental policy decisions. The issues of access and participation at the household and community level essentially resemble those in national and global contexts; 'the challenge is to find socially useful and gainful applications of IT, while limiting and redressing any further disadvantages that might accrue to the already disadvantaged' (below, p. 242).

13

Communication Satellites: a Third World Perspective

Neville D. Jayaweera

Science and technology can be borrowed, imported and adapted from abroad. But ultimately creativity from within is the only answer. For development, essentially, is not a matter of technology or GNP, but the growth of a new consciousness, the movement of the human mind, the uplifting of the human spirit, the infusion of human confidence. – Everett Kleinjans[1] (President, East-West Center, Honolulu, 1975).

We may accept this quotation as a useful jumping-off ground for our discussion, not because we can all share Kleinjans' understanding of what development is 'essentially' about, but because his rejection of science, technology and GNP as constituting the essential determinants of development, is by itself important. It is important firstly because it is a formal admission of the failure of a particular development cum communication ideology, i.e. the 'modernization' pattern, that emanated from the United States in the 50s and the 60s and holds sway in many developing countries to this day. Secondly, because it comes from the head of an institution which, since its inception by an Act of Congress in 1960, has been virtually the bastion of that ideology, at least in its communication aspect.

Let me dwell a moment on the circumstances that led Kleinjans to make this pronouncement.

In 1964 a conference was held in the East-West Center in Honolulu which was intended to develop a global consensus on the role of communication in development. To this end were brought together the purveyors of 'development' and 'communication' wisdom conventional at that time – Max Millikan and Harry Oshima *et al.* on development theory, and Daniel Lerner and Wilbur Schramm *et al.* on communication theory.

The consensus achieved at this consultation was published in 1965 with a Foreword from President Lyndon Johnson.[2] Reduced to its most simplistic expression, it reads something like this: Developing countries remain underdeveloped because of their 'traditional' ways. If they are to 'develop', that is, to become like Western industrial societies, their 'traditional' habits of thinking and behaving have to be changed drastically. This can be achieved most quickly through mass communication. Therefore if 'development' or 'modernization' is to be achieved, heavy investments have to be undertaken in the development of mass communication systems, principally radio. If only developing countries could be persuaded to invest in efficient delivery systems, then, notwithstanding the content of the message, the very presence of the mass medium would be adequate to set in motion those socio-economic processes that would ultimately 'modernize' their societies.

During the decade that followed, both the 'modernization' concept and 'development communication' concept received wide acceptance within the Third World. Massive investments in mass media infrastructure were willingly undertaken. Transmitters, transistor radios and TV sets multiplied many times over. For instance, between 1963 and 1973 the number of radio receivers increased by 300 per cent in Africa, by 450 per cent in Asia and by 250 per cent in Latin America.[3] However, out of this injection of 'communication' into the system, 'development and modernization' did not result in proportion to expectations. For instance, if we take two key indicators of economic growth, namely increases in per capita food production and increases in the share of world trade over the same period, it will be found that the developing countries recorded negative or negligible growth rates and that communication correlated to development in an inverse ratio.[4] Granted that not even the most die-hard modernization addict would claim precise correlations between mass media variables and development, although Daniel Lerner tried to do precisely that, the general picture that emerged after a decade was that mass media delivery systems did not necessarily generate the kind of development that was sought.

What *did* emerge was the realization that 'development' was a more complex phenomenon than could be compassed within a very few simple variables like foreign aid, capital investment, management, communication, productivity, etc. and that it required a far wider and deeper strategy of social and political engineering than had been imagined earlier.

The initiative taken by the East-West Center, Wilbur Scramm and others in 1975 to summon another conference in Honolulu, of almost the same theoreticians who met there in 1964, to map out a strategy for communication and development, was largely a response to the same set of facts that prompted the UN to launch the Second Development Decade – the failure of the development paradigm of the 60s. The modernization theorists were meeting to ask 'what went wrong?' And this is the confession they made: 'the past decade did not produce the enhanced quality of life that we had hoped for ten years ago. Even the impressive gains of GNP in many Third World countries evaporated when restated in per capita terms, for these economic gains were largely swallowed up by greater increases in population. In several poor countries around the world, the quality of life today is, if anything, down'.[5] The pronouncement from Kleinjans in his opening address to the group, quoted at the beginning of this paper, had already set the tone for the discussion that followed.

1   Relevance of satellites to the development-communication debate

I have taken some time going over the development pattern formalized at the East-West Center in 1964 and abandoned by its very proponents a decade later, because it seems to me that, another decade later, on the threshold of 1984, we are witnessing a return to the same pattern. But the tools and the prophets of the 80s are different. In the 60s the tools were radio and TV. In the 80s they will be satellites. In the 60s the prophets came from the behavioural sciences – economics, sociology, etc. In the 80s the prophets are technologists and engineers. But basically the argument is the same: 'Development is something that can be stimulated and engendered through mass communication. The more penetrating, the more widespread, the more efficient the delivery system, the more easily the ultimate development goals can be realized'. One senses the same retreat from complexity that characterized development-communication thinking in the 60s.

At this point it will be useful if we state objectively what specific Third World needs the advocates of communication satellites believe the new technology will be able to satisfy. The following are the principal needs that satellites, by virtue of their special characteristics, are said to be able to meet more cost-effectively than existing terrestrial systems.[6]

National integration. Many Third World countries, either by reason of their immensity and geographical dispersal like India and Indonesia, or by reason of their heterogenous social composition or because of natural barriers like vast expanses of forests, deserts or mountains, have yet to be integrated into a single polity. The construction of roads and railways, the laying of telephone lines, and the construction of transmitting stations will take a long time and consume meagre capital resources. Meanwhile, domestic distribution satellites can perform this function much more cost-effectively.

Administrative effectiveness. As a corollary to the above, administrative integration and effectiveness is hampered. The bureaucracy tends towards concentration and higher effectiveness in the metropolis, and declines outwards.

Education, both formal and non-formal including teacher training. The shortage of schools, teachers, equipment and buildings is chronic in most Third World countries. Satellites have the capacity to multiply these meagre resources at a fraction of their terrestrial costs.

Agricultural extension. As in the area of education, effective agricultural extension work is hampered by the lack of trained extension workers, the lack of transport, the inability to have as many demonstration plots as are needed, etc. All this can be overcome through satellites.

Family planning programmes. It is claimed by many development economists that the greatest single impediment to development in the Third World is population growth which every year either outstrips or at least equals economic growth. Family planning is therefore seen by them to constitute the centrepiece of any long-term economic strategy. But the crucial question underlying all family planning programmes is the one concerning communication. It is claimed that satellites are the answer.

Medical and health care services. What has been said of educational, agricultural and family planning extension is equally true of medical and health care. The same infrastructural and personnel inadequacies frustrate the delivery of adequate diagnostic and curative services from the metropolis, where professional skills are concentrated, to the outlying provinces where they are grossly inadequate or totally absent. Such skills as are available can be multiplied and dispersed through a domestic distribution satellite. Additionally, by linking to a global satellite network like the Intelsat system, the limited professional staff concentrated in a Third World capital city can have instantaneous access to the most sophisticated and skilled consultative services available in any major medical centre, disposing of the need to transfer patients over vast distances and enabling a constant upgrading of skills at the periphery.

Isolation from marketing information, both national and international. A modern economy must be able to offer the most up-to-date data, instantaneously and on call, both to suppliers and customers, abroad and at home. The speed of modern international commerce has rendered telegraph and all narrow-band telephonic communication using shortwave frequencies, including telex, almost as obsolete as surface mail. Unless entrepreneurs, banks and firms have access to data banks and facsimile services through computers linked to satellites, the international market will collapse. On a much smaller scale, this would be equally true of the domestic market.

Region-specific cultural programming. One of the major shortcomings of nearly all Third World radio and TV networks is that they are mostly centrally controlled and put out blanket programmes often ignoring cultural diversity within the national community. The solution to this consists of providing as many regional radio and TV channels as there are cultural groupings. Quite clearly this would be impossible through terrestrial systems, because of the costs involved. But with the arrival of direct broadcast and multi-beam high gain satellites each cultural and linguistic group can be serviced through just one satellite, without the aid even of a ground station or a terrestrial network.

Political and social pluralism. Of the approximately 110 Third World countries recognized by the UN as being Less Developed Countries, except perhaps six among them, the rest have autocratic governments (either of the left or of the right), controlled economies (either capitalist or socialist) and closed societies. It is claimed that communication satellites will seriously erode the power and durability of such systems. Once a national telephone network is linked to an international direct-dialling network through a satellite, the barriers to communication are breached forever and the official censor stands to lose his job. Similarly, through access to outside material beamed from direct broadcast satellites, any closed society must begin to breathe again.

Participation as a development tool. Most Third World societies are highly hierarchical. Planning and decision-making are centralized and remote from the people. There are neither political nor societal mechanisms that enable the largest possible community to participate in either the political or the production process. This is one of the reasons given to account for low productivity in these societies. Normally, securing participation in broad societal processes is a highly complicated enterprise in social engineering. But technologists see in communication satellites the final answer. What is unique in the new generation of satellites is that they enable interactive communication. As far back as ATS 1 which was launched in 1966 and later became PEACESAT, interactive communication on an audio frequency was possible. But now interactive video communication is possible and within the next decade the wristwatch interactive receiving-transmitting terminal could be a reality.[7] So the utopia of participation which has challenged and perplexed ideologists, social scientists and politicians down the ages is now said to be instantly realizable by means of the communication satellite.

Natural disasters.   Many Third World countries are notoriously prone to natural disasters such as cyclones, typhoons, tornadoes, tidal waves, floods, droughts, earthquakes and famines. When disaster strikes, the capacity to organize relief on an adequate scale depends on the efficiency of the local telephone and transport systems. The availability of the communication satellite alters all that. Not only can relief be summoned speedily but the extent and severity of the disaster can be communicated in all its starkness to the whole world, thereby enabling the mobilization of maximum support. Additionally and more importantly, the onset of some of the disasters, such as a typhoon, a tidal wave or even a famine, can be sensed by satellites and predicted well ahead of the event so that there is maximum preparedness when the disaster actually strikes.

I have stated the case for communication satellites in the Third World at its strongest and in the categories in which it is generally seen by technologists, in order to mount a comprehensive critique of it later in this paper. But before doing so, it will help to remind ourselves that currently, establishment and technological thinking is heavily in favour of using communication satellites in a development support role in the Third World. This articulation comes mostly from technologists. Perhaps somewhat surprisingly, but significantly, the prophet of radio and mass communication in the 60s, Wilbur Schramm, argues the case for communication satellites with greater caution than he showed when he pleaded the cause of radio two decades earlier. He says, 'the almost miraculous development of the communication satellite, and its spectacular capacity for delivering information over vast areas have over-leaped anything any planner, two decades ago, felt he needed to be concerned with. We are living and shall continue to live for some years in the shadow of those remarkable years, 1945, 1946 and 1947, the years of the satellite, the transistor and the computer . . . . This is to the credit of our technology. But we have by no means thought through the related questions of how and whether . . . we must ask these questions both about the satellite and what it carries, how, when and whether to use satellites, and how, when and whether to use television in connection with it, for the purpose we have in mind.'[8]

2   Communication satellite usage in the Third World

The first communication satellites to be used for experiments in a development support role were ATS 1 and ATS 3. They were launched by the USA in 1966 and 1967 respectively and were used for interactive voice communication by the University of South Pacific, in Alaska for health care delivery to remote areas and by PEACESAT for international conferencing. Then came ATS 6, a more powerful satellite, capable of carrying video channels and a larger volume of communication traffic, but not interactive. This satellite was used in India in 1975-76 for the SITE experiment, which to this day has been the single largest attempt to deliver development programming via a satellite.[9]

The first Third World country to own a satellite for domestic communication purposes was Indonesia – Palapa 1, inaugurated in 1976. Palapa is tied to a terrestrial microwave system covering the whole republic. The first Arab satellite is expected to be launched by the end of 1984, mainly for intra-regional telephony. It is claimed that ARABSAT will contribute to the development of the educational and social welfare of the Arab states. The University of the West Indies, after experimenting with ATS 3 and ATS 6 in 1978 is now seeking the collaboration of AID for investigating the feasibility of having a satellite system for educational purposes in the Caribbean. A similar project is being planned for the Philippines. In addition there are several Third World countries who are already making use of transponder facilities leased from the Intelsat system, such as Algeria, Nigeria, Brazil and Peru, for their domestic communication and development needs. Domestic satellite systems are also planned for Chile, Nigeria and Zaire.

This is merely an inventory of the better known instances of Third World satellite usage. Unfortunately, except in the case of the SITE experiment in India, none of these instances has been competently researched by persons devoid of vested interests in their perpetuation. At least, if they have been researched, their findings have not been circulated too widely. The literature widely available concerning them has been put out mostly by suppliers of equipment and by commercial interests.

However, SITE is a notable exception. This was an experiment for using a communication satellite for delivering and generating development over the vast rural sector of the subcontinent of India. It had been planned almost ten years before it was carried out, by an interdisciplinary group of technologists, broadcasters, development economists, anthropologists, agronomists and administrators. The experiment was accompanied by an intensive and highly sophisticated monitoring exercise undertaken by a research unit lodged in the project itself. This built-in evaluation unit has placed before us a vast volume of research findings.[10] However, it is almost impossible to express within the scope of a limited article like this anything more than a distillation of this mass of data. Let me try to sketch out the broad outlines of the picture that emerged.

The objectives of SITE, reduced to their most basic terms, were:[11] the improvement of primary school education; facilitating teacher training; the diffusion of improved agricultural practices; the extension of health, hygiene and nutrition; the extension of family planning; and national integration. These objectives were to be promoted during the period of 1 August 1975 to 31 July 1976 in 2,330 villages scattered over 20 districts and six states of India, by linking thousands of community TV sets to the ATS 6 communication satellite. On the completion of the experiment, the evaluators found:

1　In respect of primary school education – that children and teachers responded to TV attentively, that very little gains were registered in science, social studies and mother tongue, that children did not learn from the content of science education programmes, but that the 'general under-standing and information seeking behaviour of the children had changed'.[12] Also, very importantly, that 'there were no significant differ-ences between SITE and non-SITE groups'.[13]

2　In respect of teacher training – that the majority of the teachers felt that the training had been useful, that TV was preferable to radio and that there were significant gains in the understanding of science subjects.

3 In respect of improved agricultural practices – that 'no appreciable gains were observed', but that TV viewing did lead to changes in behaviour.

4 In respect of health extension, nutrition and family planning – that females gained more than men in health innovations and family planning but TV viewing 'did not increase the adoption or use of family planning methods'.

5 In respect of national integration – that 'continuous exposure to community TV viewing served to break down social barriers unthinkable earlier'.

The SITE project was beset with many problems. None of the stated objectives was realized fully. But non-achievement should not be attributed to the failure of the satellite as a delivery system. For the most part, non-achievement was logistical. The supporting services, both human and technological, never seemed to mesh. Despite the minuteness of the planning, and the long period of time over which preparations had been made, the project suffered from constraints which had little to do with the adequacy or inadequacy of the technology that was to be tested. The vastness of the country, the uneven quality of the administrative and other supporting services, the sheer paucity of simple maintenance facilities, the problems presented by having to produce programmes in different languages, all took their toll. Also, the experiment itself lasted only one year, hardly enough time in which even to get an experiment of such a magnitude under way. Therefore, while valuable experience was gained, one cannot conclude, on the basis of the evidence alone, that the experiment was either a success or a failure.

So we are left with little empirical evidence with which to validate the communication satellite as the catalytic development tool that technologists claim it to be. On the other hand, there is no lack of pessimism in respect of these claims, although such pessimism is not the expression either of empirical research or of rigorous theoretical thinking.

3 A theoretical approach

In the absence of hard evidence, we are compelled to fall back on theoretical thinking. We need to have both a theory of technology and a theory of development.

Arthur Clarke and several other technologists claim that technology is 'neutral' – 'like all technologies, the ability to communicate is neutral'.[14] Technologists rarely define the word 'neutral'. But if by neutral they mean that technology does not predispose those who use it to the acceptance of values, attitudes and lifestyles of the societies of which they are an organized expression or product, they are going contrary to the evidence of history. We must, however, draw a distinction between mere 'inventions' and 'technology'. Gunpowder and the printing press were 'invented' in China and brought across to Europe where they then served to lay the foundations of European expansion and global power. But Europe did not succumb to Chinese culture by adopting their inventions! Neither did Europe absorb Arab culture by taking over the mariner's compass which was 'invented' by the Arabs.

On the other hand, these 'inventions' were not organized expressions of the productive structures of medieval Chinese or Arab societies. An 'invention' is translated into 'technology' only when it is used in an organized way to extend the productive capacities of a particular society. But in order for this to happen, there must be within that society a particular meeting of economic, social and political circumstances which automatically guarantee its exploitation and conversion into an instrument of economic and social power. In medieval China those conditions were not available, but in Renaissance Europe, they were. It is the export and use of such 'inventions', i.e. technology, which have either been incorporated into the productive structures of a society, or are expressions thereof, that transmit culture.

Let us try to understand the communication satellite within this frame. Arthur Clarke may be said to have 'invented' the communication satellite in 1945. But for over a decade no one took notice of it. It was only when the rapidly expanding production machine in the advanced industrial societies began to exert pressure on existing communication systems necessitating massive investments in underground cables, etc. for instantaneous and voluminous commercial transactions, and when the whole Western capitalist system came under serious threat from the rival communist system, that attention was turned to Arthur Clarke's invention. That invention has now been integrated into the production process and is to be used in turn to transform and expand it.

It is in that sense that technology is not neutral. It comes in a socio-economic-cultural-political package. By its very inner dynamic it seeks to integrate its users into the larger system of which it is the expression and the tool.

That leads us to a consideration of a theory of development. As we saw at the beginning of this paper, by the start of the 70s, the development concept fashionable in the 50s and the 60s had come to be abandoned. Development had been understood to mean 'being like' the advanced industrial societies, i.e. acquisitive, affluent, consumerist and measuring progress in terms of the quantity of goods produced, possessed and consumed.

Two questions are involved here. First, a moral one as to whether life so lived is 'development' (but let us not delay by discussing that question). Secondly, a question of economics and politics. Granted that there has been for nearly 300 hundred years a global economic structure that is described as the 'international division of labour' (IDL) whereby two-thirds of the world supply cheap labour and cheap raw materials to the other third, which in turn processes and manufactures and exports them back to the two-thirds at enormous profit, and granted that the one-third would never willingly yield or modify this unequal relationship, was it ever possible that the poor countries could catch up with or be like the rich countries?

The communication theorists of the 50s and the 60s sought to support this development concept with a communication strategy. Radio and TV were to be used as substitutes for re-ordering economic structures, both global and domestic. It was easier to generate demand by using radio and TV and thereby to widen the markets for the metropolitan producing countries than to undertake painful political, social and economic restructuring. It was naively assumed that people could be motivated to learn, produce and consume by exposing them to mass media. The lack of motivation was interpreted in psychological terms as being due to a lack of psychic mobility which, it was said, could be supplied by radio and TV. The possibility that the lack of motivation could also be a product of oppressive structures and that the mere removal of such structures could be the best stimulus to production was not highly considered.

The 70s were characterized by an increasingly strident demand for economic and social restructuring, both internationally and within the domestic sector. On the international plane there were demands for a 'new international division of labour' (NIDL), for a 'new international development strategy' (NIDS), for a 'new international economic order ' (NIEO) and for a 'new international information order' (NIIO). All these slogans represent demands for major global structural changes. The domestic sector has been characterized by an even greater agitation. There have been demands for land reforms, for redistribution of incomes and for greater participation and more democracy, often accompanied by insurrections, liberation struggles and even disorganized and meaningless violence often described as 'terrorism'. The international and the domestic expressions are not separate entities. They are expressions of the same reality, of an unjust and iniquitous global system. Both internationally and within the domestic sector, these strident manifestations have been met with increasing obstinacy and repression on the part of the dominant interests.

This then is the broad frame within which we have to consider the arrival of the communication satellite as the new development tool.

4   Relevance of the communication satellite for the Third World – reconsidered

From the foregoing theoretical discussion we noted that technology is inextricably linked to a given economic base and that the global economic system is characterized by great inequalities both in respect of the distribution of power within it and in respect of access to benefits from it. Given such a situation, the use of communication satellites can only result in an enormous strengthening of the power of the dominant interests, and in the consolidation and perpetuation of existing structures, both internationally and within domestic situtations. Far from enabling 'development' as understood in the 70s and 80s, they are likely to return the global economic system to the disparities of the 50s and 60s. That is to say, contrary to claims concerning their potential for enabling interaction and participation they are more likely to strengthen the structures of which they are the product.

Let us now re-examine within this theoretical frame the eleven claims made on behalf of communication satellites as set out earlier in this article.

National integration.   One has to remember that the lack of national integration can be a symptom of something far more complex than is suggested by territorial vastness or the incidence of forests, mountains and deserts. Very often the lack of integration points to the need for more autonomy for the constituent national entities. Such entities have often been lumped together for colonial expediency and lack an inherent *raison d'être*. In such situations satellites can be used either as instruments of coercion or as a substitute for more human forms of achieving integration.

Administrative effectiveness.   Bureaucratic concentration in the metropolis, which is largely responsible for administrative ineffectiveness in the Third World, is likely to be aggravated through a communication satellite. Officers will be able to work from the capital city, using telephones linked to the satellite, interactive radio systems, computers and other satellite-based gadgetry. But that would only give a spurious impression of efficiency whereas in fact the administrator will become less and less involved directly with the people in the villages. Eighty per cent of the population of the Third World live in the villages. What administrators need most is a face-to-face encounter with those people and not an electronic interface.

Education.   This slogan has been used consistently, and with unerring success, to justify the introduction of TV into the Third World. TV is recommended to the Third World not for entertainment, or for commerce, but for education! For over two decades experiments have been conducted for determining the adequacy of TV as a vehicle for education. Particular instances are American Samoa, the French Niger and SITE. But in none of these have we been told unequivocally that TV is the best vehicle, or even an adequate vehicle. On the contrary there is considerable evidence to show that education is best delivered in a face-to-face situation.

Agricultural extension.   The problem of agricultural extension in Third World countries is more than a question of access to knowledge and demonstration. It is primarily a question of land tenure, the lack of credit, exploitation by landlord and middleman, the lack of irrigation facilities, the high cost of inputs, etc. Most of these are structural and political questions. Reliance on satellites to deliver the right information presupposes that what hampers farm output and productivity is merely the lack of information. This is a grossly inadequate and naïve understanding of the nature of agricultural production in poor countries.

Family planning.   The considerations that apply to education apply here too. Additionally, this argument presupposes that population growth is really the principal constraint on development in the Third World. It is sometimes argued that preoccupation with family planning is itself a search for an escape route out of the untidy business of undertaking structural changes. Satellites will perhaps help broaden and pave this escape route.

Medical and health care.   The fundamental issues of medical and health care in the Third World are not related to lack of communication but have to do with lack of clean drinking water and of protein and vitamins. They are not diagnostic but stem directly from poverty.

Isolation from marketing information.   This is a disability peculiar to big entrepreneurs and multi-national corporations based in Third World metropolitan centres and not a need among small-holding subsistence farmers and village co-operatives who constitute the bulk of the rural sector. The solution to the latter's need for fair prices is not likely to be provided by instantaneous satellite communication.

Region-specific cultural programming.   Far from providing a stimulus to local cultures, satellites are likely to obliterate them completely. The needs of local programming and cultural renewal cannot be met by having more powerful transmission facilities but by providing appropriate programming. Even existing terrestrial TV with only a single channel cannot be supplied with enough programmes to fill available airtime. How much less can several channels be supplied? This would necessitate filling the increased channel time with alien and cheap programme material which would be disastrous for local cultures.

Political and social pluralism.   Far from eroding the power of autocracies, satellites are likely to consolidate them beyond the capacity of even organized mass movements to challenge. Pluralism is ultimately a matter of political consciousness and not a question of technology. In the hands of centralized and autocratic governments, satellites can function as powerfully as the military and the police.

Participation.   Like pluralism, participation is a product of political consciousness, of the pressure of organized and motivated people on the structures of power. It can never be contrived, least by recourse to technological devices.

Natural disasters.   This again is less a matter of information than a matter of basic infrastructural and resource inadequacy. What does a community on a seacoast town in an average Third World country do even if adequately warned of an impending cyclone? Their houses are so fragile that nothing they can do can save them. And where are the people to evacuate to? In what? And once disaster has struck, satellites cannot supply resources that the society never had. In any case, advance warning is already available through existing weather satellites without Third World countries having to have their own.

5   Misconceptions and misjudgements

The Third World's current preoccupation with satellites tends to repeat the cardinal error of communication strategies of the 50s: the assumption that the cognitive element (access to information and knowledge) is fundamental to the development process. This may be true of certain cultures and societies, particularly of Western industrial societies, where the cognitive element has been for centuries the dominant factor. The development communication pattern of the 50s universalized this limited truth. Today, dazzled by the awesome information-delivery capacity of the satellite, there is a visible return to this assumption.

The return to the cognitive is fundamentally an unwillingness to see the problems of Third World poverty in structural terms. The breakdown of the development-communication pattern at the close of the 60s saw the communication theorists of the behavioural school yield centre place to the structuralists – Schiller, Halloran, *et al.*[15] During the 70s we saw a growing tendency, particularly in Britain and Europe, to perceive communication problems in structural terms. But the onset of satellite communication is doing to communication thinking what the eruption of radio and TV did to communication theory in the 50s. Apparently the hope is that this marvellous new tool will make it unnecessary to undertake the structural changes that the Third World has been agitating for.

The communication satellite is likely to do for the industrial-military complex in the 1980s what the steamship, the railways and the telegraph did for the colonial empires in the 1880s, but more efficiently and more irrevocably. It will help bind the periphery to the centre in a more durable way than was possible then. Dependency will be aggravated and domination strengthened.

There is likely to be a willing acquiescence on the part of Third World leaders, political and technological, to this new subservience. While the local leadership deepens its subservience to foreign interests, its stranglehold over its own rural sector will be strengthened. So there will come into existence a strong symbolic relationship between the industrial-military complex working abroad and the domestic leadership working locally.

Not only will the satellite increase the economic stranglehold of the industrial-military complex over the rest of the world, but it will simultaneously provide a platform for a resurgence of global cultural domination. With the arrival of direct broadcast satellites and the multi-beam high-gain satellites capable of sending as many as 40 programmes directly into one's TV set, bypassing all terrestrial control systems, the stage is now set, at least technologically, for the obliteration of the cultures of poor societies. This will be brought about largely through the inability of poor societies to produce quality programmes for filling up the enormous amount of airtime that will result from placing a satellite in orbit. In the absence of local programmes, national networks will have no option but to buy cheap and inferior productions from the foreign salesman who will be already at the door.

The goals and objectives of both the NIEO and the NIIO are likely to be severely impaired. Both these global strategies call for major structural rearrangements. The satellite is likely to offer a technological alternative to such painful surgery.

At the root of this malaise is a defective understanding of the nature, causes, and mechanisms of Third World poverty. Basically, the error lies in assuming that Third World poverty is caused primarily by lack of communication, and that its alleviation can be engineered by supplying an enormous volume of information to the widest possible community. Communication is indeed a factor in development, but the causes of poverty are mostly structural, both national and international. A massive injection of communication into an unequal structural relationship will mostly help to consolidate and deepen that inequality rather than alleviate it.

6 Technology and development

Having painted this somewhat pessimistic (or optimistic – depending on one's allegiances) picture about the possible consequences of communication satellites for the Third World, I feel the need to refute some misconceptions that might arise concerning my perception of the relationship of technology to development.

While technology is never neutral, 'progress' and 'development', in whatever way we may interpret them (except in the purely spiritual) are also never possible without it! It is the organized use of tools for overcoming the constraints of nature that has propelled the human race from the earliest times. The axe and the bow and arrow were the technologies of the hunting phase. The plough enabled the human race to settle down and develop an organized community life, culture, philosophy and religion. The stirrup, the wheel and the sail gave isolated communities mobility, extended their horizons and welded them into societies and nations. Similarly – the printing press, gun-powder, the mariner's compass, the steam engine, the spinning jenny, the internal combustion engine, etc. down to the nuclear reactor and the silicon chip – it was technology that brought about the most fundamental changes in the way human beings related to their environment, even to the extent of eroding and transforming fundamental religious values and beliefs. No social organization or power in history has yet thwarted, for any considerable length of time, the march of technology.

Conversely, there has been no technology that has not had negative consequences. The primitive axe must have been used for killing the cave man next door as well as to fell the over-hanging tree for fuel. A Roman Emperor is said to have prohibited the use of water power to turn wheels to grind corn on the ground that it would keep the slaves idle! Motor cars cause a great deal of environmental pollution. The jet engine has resulted in the loss of thousands of lives. Every year hundreds of people die of electrocution. Similarly, the communication satellite will bring in its wake its own negative results. But in none of these instances would anyone suggest the obliteration of the technology in question because of its negative consequences.

The thrust of this paper is not that we should reject communication satellites, and much less that we should wage war against technology. I have argued that the assumptions underlying the proposal to use communication satellites in the Third World are wrong, that satellites cannot provide the solutions to problems which are primarily political, economic and sociological and that if satellites are used as an alternative to painful structural reforms, they are more likely to consolidate and perpetuate those conditions which produced the problems.

Technology should be put at the service of *all* of the human race. But in history technology has been used mostly by the dominant powers for extending and perpetuating their domination. Communication satellites have an important role to play, more important perhaps than the steam engine in the industrial revolution. But we must ensure that the societal, economic and political mechanisms to guarantee that the new technology will not deepen global inequalities are also simultaneously in place.

Whenever in history a dramatic development in technology was not matched by a corresponding rearrangement in power relationships, it ceased to be a liberating force and was transformed into an instrument of oppression. The more powerful the technology and the more pervasive its capacity for influencing individual lives and for transforming the character of whole cultures and societies, the greater the need for social control and democratic accountability. We cannot afford to leave the direction and application of such technologies in the hands of entities whose social and moral accountability is constrained by the needs of private profit. Throughout history, it has been the failure to match technological progress with social accountability that has aggravated inequalities, deepened oppression and produced enormous social violence.

Notes

1 Everett Kleinjans, President, East-West Center, Honolulu – from his introductory address to the Conference on 'Communication and Change in Developing Countries' held in Honolulu in January 1975, quoted in foreword to *Communication*

and Change – the Last Ten Years and the Next edited by Wilbur Schramm and Daniel Lerner, The University Press of Hawaii.

2 *Communication and Change in Developing Countries*, edited by Daniel Lerner and Wilbur Schramm, East-West Center Press, 1965.

3 Figures quoted from p. 12, 'Data on Communication Systems' in *Communication and Change in the Last Ten Years*, edited by Wilbur Schramm and Daniel Lerner.

4 See FAO *Monthly Bulletin of Agricultural Economics and Statistics* March 1974, p. 2 and UN *Yearbook on International Trade Statistics 1973*.

5 Preface to paper by economist Harry Oshima, p. 15 in *Communication and Change – the Last Ten Years and the Next*, edited by Wilbur Schramm and Daniel Lerner.

6 See 'Satellites for Rural Development: The Era of Experimental Satellites' by Anna Casey-Stahmer, in *Journal of Communication*, Vol. 29, No. 4, p. 138.

7 'New Communication Technologies and the Developing World' by Arthur Clarke, p. 14, address delivered to opening session of IPDC Council meeting, Paris, June 1981.

8 'Some questions about television satellites' by Wilbur Schramm in *Satellite Communications and Christian Mission*, p. 45, published by IMMI, Kristiansand, Norway, 1979.

9 *Television Comes to Village – an evaluation of SITE* by Binod Agrawal, published by ISRO, Bangalore 1978.

10 See *Satellite Instructional Television Experiment*, Binod Agrawal, published by ISRO, October 1978. Also *SITE Social Evaluation: Results, Experiences and Implications*, Binod Agrawal, published by ISRO, 1981. The *Journal of Communication*, Vol. 29, No. 4, also has a section devoted to summaries of some of the research findings. Bella Mody writes a competent piece *Lessons from the Indian Satellite Experiment* in the Educational Broadcasting International of September 1978, pp. 117-20. K. E. Eapen has also written fairly extensively on this subject, see his 'Social Impacts of Television on Indian Villages: Two Case Studies', published in *Institutional Exploration in Communication Technology*, Honolulu, East-West Center, 1978. Also his 'The Cultural Component of SITE' in the *Journal of Communication*, Vol. 29, No. 4, pp. 106-13. For the planning stage of SITE read Yash Pal 'Some Experiences in Preparing for a Satellite Television Experiment for Rural India' in *Proceedings of the Royal Society London*, 1975, pp. 437-45. The most comprehensive interdisciplinary overview of the SITE proposal, written before the experiment was completed and setting out its planning history and conceptual range, is Unesco publication No. 78 on Mass Communication titled: 'Planning for Satellite Broadcasting' by Romesh Chander and Kiran Karuik.

11 See *SITE Social Evaluation*, Binod Agrawal, summary published by ISRO, 1981.

12 Ibid.

13 See 'Impact of SITE on Primary School Children' by Srehalata Shukla in *Journal of Communication*, Vol. 29, No. 4, p. 104.

14 *New Communication Technologies and the Development World*, Arthur Clarke, 1981, p. 10.

15 Herbert Schiller, *Mass Communication and the American Empire*, 1969; *The Mind Managers*, 1973; *Communication and Cultural Domination*, 1976; James Halloran, *Mass Media and Society*, 1974.

14

The Social Economics of Information Technology

Ian Miles and Jonathan Gershuny[1]

1 'Information society': a second coming of post-industrial society?

1.1 From post-industrial society to the information economy

According to a widely accepted view of economic development, the economy can best be seen as consisting of three main sectors: agriculture and other primary production, industries such as construction and (especially) manufacturing, and a tertiary or 'residual' sector producing services. Economic development is then viewed as a progressive shift in the focus of activity, first from the primary to the secondary sector, and then from the secondary to the tertiary.

Post-war developments seem at first sight to demonstrate the usefulness of this view. Agricultural employment declined rapidly with the introduction of mechanized, fertilizer-intensive and factory-farming methods. And service employment grew more rapidly than manufacturing, so that by the 1960s economists were talking of the 'service economy': more than 50 per cent of all workers were employed in the service sector in the 1970s for the European Economic Community (EEC) as a whole. If we include workers from white-collar and other service-type jobs in the primary and secondary sectors, the dominance of such 'non-production' work is overwhelming.

The idea of a march of workers from primary through secondary to tertiary employment was taken to mean that there was little reason to be alarmed by the prospect of automation in manufacturing industry. The service industries would soak up surplus employment, it seemed – although close inspection of the data would have revealed that rather little of the growth in tertiary employment represented a migration of employees from the secondary sector into these industries of the future.

The implications of this process for social development more generally were elaborated in terms of certain assumptions about changes in social values. The progression through the economic sectors was attributed to shifts in consumer demand resulting from affluence and social equality. As people's basic needs were satisfied, the role of foodstuffs in their expenditure declined relative to that of manufactures (Engels' Law). And as they became satiated with material abundance, their desires for intangibles such as health and education grew in prominence. This hierarchy of values explains the march through the three economic sectors, and in turn has other social consequences that justified an intellectual shift from service *economy* to post-industrial *society*. 'Post-industrialism' became a dominant diagnosis of the present, and prognosis for the future, of the Western world.[2]

Social and economic developments were seen to be mutually reinforcing. As people's attitudes shifted away from a concern with the bare necessities of life, there would be a growth in demand for political participation, for care of the environment and for weaker members of society. These concerns, rather than the traditional issues of management of the economy, entered the political agenda in the late 1960s and early 1970s – what Inglehart called the 'silent revolution'. Furthermore, with the growth of white-collar and knowledge-intensive work, increasing power would be vested in scientific and technical workers, in people whose work depends upon their intellectual or interpersonal abilities, rather than in the owners of capital or other traditional bearers of power. Emerging as a dominant force in post-industrial society is a *new service class* of 'knowledge workers', with the values, skills and resources appropriate for the new agenda of political and economic development.

Thus there would be a shift toward greater social planning, and a subordination of business interests to values of meritocracy and welfare. The existence of some stresses and strains was conceded – such as the conflict between libertarian and personal-growth values and those of preserving high culture and maintaining media standards – but the general expectation was that of an end of ideology. Disagreement over social goals would be reduced to a minimum (especially as East – West conflict subsided with the convergence of both blocs towards post-industrial societies); that over the means to achieve the goals would be transformed into a technical debate in which tools such as technology assessment, social indicators and computer simulation would allow for the fine-tuning of social progress . . .

Despite the traumas of the last decade, the term 'post-industrial society' remains remarkably respectable. Admittedly it tends to be used as a hand-waving description – but, as we shall argue, many of the underlying assumptions of post-industrialism are still commonly reproduced, and enter into the currently fashionable concept: the 'information society'.

The information society literature has moved on in some respects from the post-industrialists. Concern over job loss and de-skilling has become prominent with the industrial application of microelectronics, so the literature is more marked by disagreement over positive and negative consequences of technological and organizational changes than was the case for the post-industrialists. One recent study lists debates over whether informatics leads to: decentralization or increased centralized decision-making, upgrading or de-skilling of work, increased computer literacy or alienation from everyday technology, economic dualism or a more participatory economy, and intensified or debilitated interpersonal relationships. Most authors see one pole to be the logical consequence of current tendencies, rather as post-industrialists saw their future to be a logical consequence of social evolution: but in the economic climate of the 1980s the information society commentators add the imperative for countries to compete to make use of new processes and to produce new products to gain comparative advantages in international trade. Information society (perhaps with concomitant future shock and unemployment) or economic failure (with even more stress and unemployment): this is the implicit choice. But there remain a number of fundamental points where agreement between the 'post-industrial' and the 'information' society schools is strong.

The march through the sectors underpins much information society literature. However, some influential writers have proposed updating the three-sector model. Recognizing that the model loses much of its usefulness when an extremely diverse set of tertiary industries rise to the prominence which they now occupy, these authors suggest adding a fourth sector – the information sector. They similarly describe information occupations – all formal employment that is largely concerned with the production, processing or distribution of information, or with the installation, operation and maintenance of associated physical, electronic and mechanical infrastructure – which have formed an increasing proportion of the labour force (more than a third of all employment in the UK and North America by the 1980s).

Information society, then, rests upon the expansion of economic activities concerned with information flows. This expansion is attributed the centrality that was earlier accorded to the services. New technologies may check the growth of employment in information occupations by enabling increases in labour productivity; but they will also dramatically reduce the costs of information, leading to a considerable growth in demand for existing information services and informatics products, and the development of a host of new ones. Information services are seen as particularly important emerging areas of public demand (manipulated by media moguls according to some critical accounts). Industries too are seen as being forced to become more information-intensive owing to the changing nature of products and markets, and because of the drive for increased productivity. (For example, it is argued that rapid shifts in product design – corresponding to innovation or fashion – require production technologies that can be readily geared to different volumes of production and designs, as in computer-aided design – computer-aided manufacture (CADCAM).)

The debate over the relative rates of job replacement and job generation in information activities, relating closely to public and media concerns about unemployment, has helped raise the concept of information society to greater prominence than that achieved by post-industrial society. But other concerns have also surfaced: fears about the erosion of public service broadcasting (and the standards it has promoted) by cable and satellite services, and fears of surveillance and other forms of insidious social control, in particular. While this means that there is more critical thought about the prospects afforded by informatics, the shared core of assumptions here is suspiciously like that used by the post-industrialists. Is there any essential difference between the information workers, and the older new class of knowledge workers? What is it about information that makes it sufficiently desirable to form a base for a future general expansion? What will consumers be doing with all the information produced by the expanding army of information workers? The literature is rather short on answers to these questions.

1.2   Beneath the trends

Let us look a little more closely at the factors that underpin the growth of the service economy. The tertiary sector includes very diverse types of economic activity, which, as they have grown to be a major areas of employment, appear increasingly incongruous when lumped together. More detailed classifications give a rather different picture of the rise of the service economy.[3]

For one thing, not all tertiary activities have been growing. In the UK, employment in personal services has declined since the last war. Employment in transport and distribution has been declining since the 1960s. In contrast, employment has increased in social services and also in producer services – that is, services sold to firms. Thus the growth in service sector employment in part reflects political choices and changes in industrial structure rather than changes in private demand for services. But has not private demand for services increased – and does this not reflect a shift away from materialist values?

Demand for services has increased with increasing affluence – but so has demand for goods. There is little evidence for services per se having a greater income elasticity than goods. There has been a shift in household expenditure along Engels' Law-like lines, away from basic purchases such as food and shelter and towards education, entertainment, etc. But within these latter categories, there has been a shift in private expenditure *away from services and towards goods*. Thus more money is spent on cars, televisions and washing machines, less on rail, theatre and laundry services. This would mean, other things being equal (which they are not), that service employment would decline relative to that in manufacturing – with the creation of some new service employment, for example in garages, TV studios and domestic equipment repairs. These service the use of manufactured goods by consumers producing their own final services (the shift to domestic production that Toffler suggests in his neologism of 'prosumers'), rather than supplying final services. Just as the producer services are supplying intermediate services to industries, we have here intermediate consumer services. Thus a portion of service sector growth derives from these two types of intermediate service, which appear to be contributing largely to the manufacture and operation of goods.

But service sector employment has grown mainly under the impetus of two other factors. First, increases in labour productivity have been lower in most services than in most other economic sectors. (This is why we suggested above that not all other things were equal.) Similar rates of demand increase across sectors will mean shifts in relative employment to those with lower rates of productivity growth. Second, collectively-provided services have been responsible for a very large share of the growth in tertiary employment. Again, as far as can be established given the problematic accounting methods available here, low productivity growth is involved in the rapid expansion of employment in these sectors.

The view of the service economy provided by this analysis is radically different to that of the post-industrialists. Rather than there being an inherent bias in favour of the purchasing of services with increasing affluence, the growth of services reflects rather complex political and economic trade-offs made by the state, firms and households. In several countries the growth of many skilled occupational categories in the first few post-war decades had much to do with the aerospace industry and the Cold War; and the expansion of social services can be related to the strength of socialist and social-democratic movements in different Western countries. Firms have participated in an increasing division of labour and found it expedient to purchase many of the services that might otherwise have been provided in-house: this choice, shaped by technological change, fiscal policy and employment protection legislation and unionization, has led to the development of new intermediate producer service industries. And while consumers have been more concerned with sophisticated luxury expenditure, the choice about how to make that expenditure has increasingly been weighted toward goods rather than services. This reflects a variety of factors shaping the relative cost and convenience of different modes of provision of final services, and hardly bears out the idea of a growth of post-material attitudes; indeed, the groups most prepared to endorse Inglehart's 'post-bourgeois' values have the highest aspirations for material affluence.

The future of the service economy, then, cannot be as rosy as post-industrialists imagined. The march through the sectors is less a disciplined advance than a scattering of the tribes. There are at least four distinct elements in the service sector (the intermediate producer and consumer service, and the marketed and non-marketed final service, subsectors). Low productivity growth in tertiary sectors may lead to increased limits on public expenditure and increased shifting of consumers to goods rather than services. Or, if the use of new technologies does permit more innovation in tertiary industries, service employment may be restricted through job displacement: unless, that is, new service products can find mass markets.

What does this imply about accounts of information society, which follow the post-industrialists in projecting a march through the sectors, but provide little substantial analysis of the growth of what are quite heterogeneous varieties of activity? Lumping together a variety of 'new' activities under a common heading is a gesture of recognition to the problem, not a step toward solving it. If the tertiary sector is internally diverse, the 'information sector' is equally so. The range of occupations covered under the heading of information workers includes research scientists, typists, broadcasters, telephone operators and television repairers. It can be useful to group together all these jobs as belonging to one industry: the ones we have chosen could all be associated with television, and one could relate their patterns of development together as part of a systems analysis of the industry. But when we consider that there are a host of industries in which these categories of occupation are found, the notion of information occupations begins to look more like a handy slogan ('vanguard of the information age') than a concept of any real explanatory relevance. The Organization for Economic Cooperation and Development (OECD) does list such a range of 'information occupations', and distinguishes between primary information industries (whose purpose is the production of information as a final commodity or benefit), and secondary information industries (which provide information as an input to the production of material commodities); but it fails to reveal the diverse prospects for growth within these categories.

A better understanding of the rise of information-related activities, and the potential transformations that may be associated with the introduction of informatics, really requires an analysis of large-scale processes of social change. But in the first instance, we can take the distinction between information work concerned with production, processing, distribution and infrastructure as a helpful guide to the sorts of activity that might take place in any location. In addition to this we would distinguish between activities that are intermediate inputs to producers, intermediate inputs to consumers, and final inputs to consumers, and between those that are marketed and non-marketed. Within these different types of activities there are information flows, and different applications for informatics. 'Information work' has different meanings within these different sectors. The development of these activities is closely interrelated: by considering the costs and benefits to the different actors involved we may gain some idea of the likely course of social change in the future, the possibilities for use of new technology, and the conflicts and broader consequences that might result.

2   Long-run processes of social change

2.1   The end of the post-war boom

Can our account of the growth of the tertiary sector account for the drastic way in which the predictions of post-industrial theory were undermined by the changes of the 1970s and 1980s?

To a large extent, the end of the post-war boom reflects the erosion of the various structures that formed the post-war political settlement – and the basis for the pattern of growth described above, and the view of the post-industrial future it fostered. The growth of welfare states and the application of Keynesian counter-cyclical measures was part of the post-war political settlement within the West. These arrangements helped regulate demand and provide markets for a wide range of other products, including those central to the boom, and facilitated a large growth in service sector activities. The breakdown of the post-war settlement was related to internal problems of these arrangements as well as to international travails. A view of long-run social change is required to grasp this process.

With the world economic crisis has come renewed interest in the 'long waves of economic life', and researchers have focused on the technical paradigms in manufacturing industry that characterize each of these waves. They argue that long downswings are associated with industries maturing and their technological systems becoming subject to cost-cutting, rationalizing innovation. The upswings are in contrast associated with new products and processes, with new industries and technological systems. Innovations in 'heartland technologies' permit the development of diverse new products and processes, and the development of infrastructure makes possible the diffusion and widespread application of these new technologies. But these researchers have paid little attention to social innovations: changes that people make in their ways of life so as to take advantage of the opportunities offered by new technologies – and to cope with the changed social relationships that are thus created. Whether or not they are 'cycles' with a definite periodicity, long waves should be interpreted in terms of the growth, maturity and stagnation of socio-technical systems, of which technical paradigms form just one, albeit important, part.[4]

The post-war boom involved considerable change in technologies – and in ways of life. The key industrial sectors – consumer durables and automobiles – relied on new methods of mass production and industrial organization (which meant, among other things, the 'tertiarization' of secondary industries), and sold their products to newly affluent populations. Infrastructures – mains electricity, telecommunications and modern road systems – made possible the widespread application of these products, changing their cost and convenience relative to other modes of service provision. New ways of life were developed in which the automobile and telephone, washing machine and television played an important role, and often involving shifts away from the purchase of final services to self-service provision of transport, domestic services, entertainment, etc. And collective provision of social services expanded reflecting changes in the family, the workforce, and in social aspirations.

Women's employment (and part-time working) grew, with the expansion of the services and the greater division of labour, and domestic technology was used to reduce 'their' housework load. While some de-skilling of work was the norm for many traditional occupations and within whole industrial sectors, there was also considerable growth of white-collar posts of various kinds, and the expansion of the services – especially, as noted, non-marketed and producer services – meant the creation of large numbers of professional and semi-professional posts. Employees belonging to these groups became bearers of 'post-bourgeois values', and a major social basis for many of the new social movements of the 1970s and 1980s.

But the growth of state expenditure of the post-war boom fuelled inflationary tendencies. The expansion of employment in the services meant an increasing proportion of national income going to the relatively lagging sectors of the economy – and the new public sector unionism placed obstacles in the way of attempts to keep wages at low levels here. The market was showing signs of maturity and stagnation by the end of the 1960s. No radically new products were emerging, worldwide overproduction was becoming apparent in several sectors – if not actually saturating, markets were no longer as elastic as they had been. Government policies in the UK and many other countries were directed towards shoring up mature and traditional industries rather than stimulating innovation; and these industries were rationalizing rather than developing substantially new products. The post-war boom petered out, with constraints being placed upon public expenditure, with the downturns of business cycles creating increasing unemployment – a general exhaustion of a pattern of growth involving a particular set of products, processes, infrastructure and ways of life. The destabilization of the international economy, and the appearance of a baby boom generation (born in the upswing) on the labour market, set the scene for a long period of economic trauma.

The transformation that we are undergoing, then, involves more than just technical change – although new technologies would form part of any return to long-term growth, if a future growth wave is to resemble past experience. Informatics are clearly central, if for no other reason than that they offer to reduce the bottlenecks in information flow created during the post-war boom. But changes in institutions, infrastructures and ways of life are also required for the opportunities they present to be seized. The design of products and infrastructures has considerable relevance to the ways of life that may evolve, the values and practices that are integral to a new sociotechnical system. But the question is not really about the *impact* of informatics on ways of life, values and culture, but the way in which societies reproduce and adapt themselves, using and reshaping technologies in the process.

2.2   An informatics upswing?

Informatics provides heartland technologies for process innovations: CAD-CAM, rapid information transfer and retrieval, new paradigms of industrial organization. It provides new products: home computers, control devices for household equipment, new telecommunication facilities. It involves new infrastructures: cable and satellite systems. But innovations in people's ways of life would be both precondition and consequence of the widespread adoption of informatics.

The potential uses of new technology extend well beyond the proliferation of video games and television channels, which do not exactly sound like the recipe for renewed economic growth. A new telecommunications infrastructure could permit the development of new services, and the transformation of many existing ones. Changes in entertainment are obvious enough. Distribution and transport could be transformed through teleshopping, improved travel booking and scheduling, telebanking, telework. Education could move more to Open University-type formats, with public information utilities for informal and community education and training. In medicine, in addition to remote diagnosis and monitoring services for chronic disorders, preventative advice and improvement of community care could involve informatics. Even domestic services might be the focus of innovation: pensioners' safety, household security and energy use can be monitored, payments and purchasing could be substantially automated, and so on.

Cable TV and home computers may be dominant at present, but this does not mean that the other innovations are unlikely. Indeed, the advent of improved telecommunications infrastructure is a prerequisite for most of the services outlined above to be effective. The development of an infrastructure for entertainment purposes may precede its use for a much broader range of interactive services – although this may well depend crucially upon appropriate design of the systems.[5]

There are many different ways in which informatics could be developed within our society, with correspondingly varied implications for economic expansion and the details of ways of life. To reduce the rate of diffusion of new technologies in industry would be likely to lead to continued stagnation. To concentrate on improving industrial efficiency by process innovation could lead to considerable improvements in delivery of many existing products – although in practice this seems likely simply to mean labour-saving and cost-cutting change in non-marketed services, and an overall reduction in employment. A combination of product and process innovation, of infrastructural and way-of-life changes is also possible: while this may not be able to restore full employment as understood in the post-war boom, we can outline areas where formal employment might begin to expand.

On the one hand, we can expect to see some jobs created in the manufacture of informatics equipment and the installation of the infrastructure, although neither may be as demanding of labour as some optimists hope. We might see some loss of work in final services, although this *could* be offset by improvements in service quality: for example, increased efficiency of travel services, and the associated tasks of booking and scheduling, might go some way toward reversing the trend away from public transport. Political choices are very important here: again, it is not the potential of the technology, but the application of that potential that is the key issue.

As for intermediate services, contradictory trends would operate in the case of producer services (increased labour productivity through the use of informatics, but also increased need for information services of various kinds), but there may be considerable growth of intermediate consumer services. Consumer uses of informatics like those discussed above often require extensive backup services including, as well as maintenance and related functions, various sorts of information brokerage. And the intermediate consumer services would involve people in the production of software, which we understand to mean more than the material that is purchased (or pirated) to run on computers, to cover information encoded on media for use in informatics hardware more generally. Software production involves the embodiment of applied human skills in information-storage devices for use in the production of services, then; it spans recorded entertainment and expert systems, the writing of video games and that of teletext pages. This means seeing actors in a television studio as producing software (the TV broadcast or video) as an intermediate consumer service, to be used by consumers in their application of their manufactures (TV sets); in contrast the actor on the public stage is providing a final entertainment service (with the aid of a built infrastructure rather than a telecommunications one). (The self-same actor may provide both sorts of service at once, just as one production process in industry may yield two different products simultaneously, or yield one product which can be used both as a capital good and as a consumer item.)

This pattern of introduction and reshaping of informatics might be compatible with social and economic innovation in general, with the establishment of a new sociotechnical system rather than the recuperation of the existing one. The diffusion of domestic equipment and infrastructure might be led by demands for entertainment and further education. But existing services might be transformed: and there could be the emergence of new information and advice services, and the growth of interactive informal use of telematics (to establish like-minded or like-needful groups for car-sharing, pressure groups, romantic liaisons, consumer advice, bartering of child-care or do-it-yourself (DIY) work, personal advice, the sponsorship of performances and cultural events . . .). Some shift away from formal provision of final services to self-service provision might be expected to continue, even to accelerate. The key questions of political choice here relate to the future of collective services: will informatics be used to substitute for existing provisions, or to expand and augment them?

3   Social choice and information societies

We have suggested that distinctive periods of growth and stagnation in the world economy are related to the 'life cycle' of vigour and exhaustion of particular sociotechnical systems, of specific constellations of process and product technology, infrastructure, social organization and ways of life. These constitute different ways of representing and satisfying consumer demands through the political economy. The choice between the different available *modes of provision* of final service functions – i.e. between, on the one hand, purchases of final services, or, on the other, communal- or self-servicing (cars versus public transport, laundry versus washing machine, traditional performance versus information-technology-mediated entertainment etc.) – has become as important as the shifting of priorities from one of these functions to another.

Informatics may well help underpin a wave of innovation, but it has not arrived like the fifth cavalry at the whim of a benevolent scriptwriter. Its emergence is built upon the achievements of the last long upswing, and is a response of technicians and engineers to their perception of the developing problems in that growth paradigm. (This is one of the reasons why our view of informatics is liable to be blinkered, to be framed too much in terms of incremental solutions to pressing problems, such as the costs of clerical work.) A leap in the dark is inevitable in any major process of technological change. Can we avoid stumbling into some of the obstacles which are more likely to be encountered by less innovative strategies? What implications for social organization and political choice are raised by our analysis?

3.1   Employment and industrial organization

It is evident that employment in primary and secondary production is likely to continue its decline. In addition, employment in many of the 'information occupations' of the traditional services is likely to be reduced by the application of informatics, even though some compensation for this labour-saving might be brought about by increased demand due to reduced prices related to innovation in the services. More significantly, informatics could also be used to bring about quality improvements in services – reduced waiting time and delay, more personalized services, resources freed from routine business to deal with priority cases. This might stem or reverse the trend from services to goods in some areas, and also defuse opposition to expenditure on social services (where anger about cuts is attenuated by the perception that costs have risen much more than output). Some producer services may continue to expand, and new consumer services, especially information services and other intermediate consumer services, may undergo rapid growth.

These developments are unlikely to restore the total amount of formal work to a level sufficient to restore full employment as it has been known. Two extreme consequences would be the development of a highly dualistic economy, with regional and class differences sharpened between those with employment, those in insecure work, and the permanently unemployed; and the redistribution of work through reduced lifetime working hours and the expansion of life-long education, community activities, etc. Informatics could be used to support either kind of development – arguments that it inevitably fosters either one, or can magically restore the previous sociotechnical system to its full vigour, should be discounted. The new technology might increase the strains of a dualistic economy: for example, accentuating awareness of the extremes of poverty and wealth that coexist. On the other hand, new security systems, new types of pass and credit card, surveillance and psy-ops methods could be used to bolster up an increasingly repressive social order. Or 'bread and circuses' could be the order of the day: wall-to-wall video games and computer nasties.

Despite ominous portents, there are prospects for more positive changes – not least in the public discussion over information society. One of the problems, however, is the relative paucity of analysis of the interrelations of social and technical innovation. Trade unionists have been pressing for substantial reductions in the working week, and have begun to pay attention to the design of technologies as well as to their introduction into the workplace. But the sorts of innovation required for a new sociotechnical system are more wide-ranging. The point of our analysis is not that anything can happen, but that it is necessary to establish linkages between different sorts of change around which shared interests could be mobilized.

For example, reduced working lifetimes have social implications that could bring together diverse social interests. Women might see this as an element in a strategy to reconstruct the sexual division of labour, since men typically blame their evasion of child-care, etc. upon the requirements of full-time breadwinning. Recurrent training may be necessitated by a rapid pace of technological change, so sectors of management could support changes in this direction, which educationalists would doubtless welcome. Many leisure industries would benefit from a more equitable distribution of leisure time. Education and entertainment – and various forms of meaningful leisure – also offer possibilities for innovative applications of informatics to the delivery of final and intermediate services.

What of the quality, rather than the quantity, of employment? The post-war boom involved the de-skilling of many traditional production activities, with a growth of middle-skill jobs in secondary and tertiary sectors alike. Informatics offers the prospect of subjecting service occupations to a similar 'capital-deepening' and division of labour. The tertiarization of the secondary sector is likely to be complemented by a secondarization of the tertiary sector. Despite some increase in scientific and technical skills, many existing semiprofessional jobs could be substantially deskilled, leading to polarization of the labour force within industries. (This has obvious implications for the prospects for reduced lifetime working hours and retraining discussed above.) Again, this is not an inevitable consequence of the potential of the technology, nor is it necessarily the preferred management strategy. In manufacturing industry, lessons are being learned from Japanese methods of production, where the Taylor/Ford types of assembly-line division of labour are modified so as to give workers more responsibility for a coherent set of tasks (with the eminently non-altruistic goal of reducing costs incurred in bottlenecks and stockpiles). The automation of tasks only means a de-skilling of jobs if the range of tasks covered by a job remains fixed: in this instance conventional demarcation systems may run counter to improving the quality of working life.

There is considerable opportunity for different actors to intervene in the resolution of these contradictory tendencies. Outcomes are liable to be quite different in firms of different sizes and based in different sectors. Legislation over working conditions and training processes may make a difference, as will the organizational culture of firms from different national bases. But on balance, we would expect that the relative autonomy enjoyed by many service workers will be somewhat decreased, with informatics used to introduce more monitoring of operations into areas of activity where control and accountancy has to date remained more formal than substantial.

Another issue of industrial organization concerns the spatial and managerial dimensions of economic restructuring. Informatics can support a wide variety of different combinations of centralized and decentralized information processing and decision-making. The strategy of larger corporations, at least, seems to involve increased centralized monitoring and control of the overall performance of more specialized subunits or branches, with these given more responsibility for their own data processing and specialized decision-making. There may be considerable reduction of the middle ranges of the managerial pyramid, with the functions that are now typically performed by these levels in the head office being partly shifted upward and partly distributed among branches. This would reinforce the occupational trends discussed above.[6]

3.2   Households and lifestyles

Post-industrialists' theories that mass communications would bring about a massification of society, with increased commonality of opinions and practices across different social groups, have proved inaccurate to date. The social developments of the post-war boom supported heterogeneity, although this can be a mutually rewarding 'cultural pluralism' or a destructive 'social fragmentation': recent trends have displayed elements of both processes. Narrowcasting and interactive services might permit these processes to continue apace. The privatization of individual households might be accompanied by a greater segregation of social groups distinguished in lifestyle terms. But the choice of lifestyle, and the access to diverse views and practices, could also be widened.

Lifestyles remain overwhelmingly structured by class and stage in the family/employment life cycle. Thus the evolution of the employment situation – in terms of greater dualism or a decreased emphasis on formal employment in everyday life – would be an important determinant of the evolution and diversity of household consumption patterns. A dualistic labour market may mean a dualistic market more generally: for example, shops, products and discount rates that cater for owners of 'intelligent' credit cards, increased differentiation between luxury and basic goods. Working life is also extremely relevant to the development of lifestyles: and a culturally active society would be more likely to develop were informatics used to upgrade working conditions and skills and reduce weekly hours of employment.

Informatics could be used by an active citizenry to engage in more varied leisure and cultural activities, and to take part in and create new forms of social participation. Indeed, using the technology in this way – by making interactive services available to individuals and communities – might render increased leisure more attractive for many working people. We would see household consumption shifting from services to goods, with people applying informal labour to help produce many of their own final services. In some cases this 'production' would imply little more creativity than that involved in selecting a videotape; but the potential would be there for access to more

educational opportunities, more networking of people with common interests, more use of recreational facilities and development of specialist services.

3.3   Social welfare

The shift toward self-servicing may be expected to continue within areas that
are largely catered for by social services. Many services are likely to remain a
matter of collective organization, and the main issues may surround 'community care' versus central provision. Informatics could be used to improve
community facilities – monitoring the circumstances of pensioners, relating
the need for services to provisions at a local level, supplying access to expert
systems for para-professionals in health and welfare (along the lines of the
computerized benefit claim systems used by some Citizens' Advice Bureaux).

The trend toward community care is deeply ambiguous. It combines
genuine recognition of the problems of impersonal, bureaucratized service
organizations – oriented toward cure rather than prevention, labelling and
institutionalizing their clients, allowing them little autonomy and creating
dependency – with cynical efforts to reduce costs and to shift the burden of
care onto charities and families. And in the background in Britain is the
pressure towards the privatization of (profitable) areas of social service. This
tendency toward a two-tier structure of welfare services is found sufficiently
threatening by most employees in public services to reduce their interest in
innovation: it is difficult constructively to criticize what one is desperately
struggling to defend. By and large, privatization means allowing the relatively
privileged to jump queues and segregate themselves from other social strata.
But valuable experiments in care for the elderly, education, and self-help are
taking place outside of the public services (though often with their financial
support). Furthermore, alongside institutional moves in the direction of
community care are attempts to develop alternative services along the lines of
free schools and self-help health groups. (Social innovators could learn a great
deal from the experience of different countries in these respects: for example,
the extremely original educational experiments of the Folk High Schools in
Denmark.) It would be possible to direct informatics toward advancing and
promoting their methods.

These strategies will interact with the ongoing shift toward self-service
provision. Self-servicing in areas of health and education (and social and
political organization) is bound to grow with the cheapening of informatics.
Public and voluntary services, then, need to capitalize on these developments.
This might mean pressing for community access to informatics facilities (so
that these do not remain the preserve of the more affluent or better educated),
and designing appropriate intermediate services. It might involve improving
the scope and quality of both routine and non-routine service delivery, as part
of a wider strategy of rebuilding social services to cater for the needs of late
industrial society. Just as new technologies, by offering possibilities for
product and process change, simultaneously threaten employment in private
services and offer possibilities for demand expansion through reduced costs
or new facilities, so may public services face a choice of whether merely to
rationalize existing practices, and thus save costs, or to develop new services,
and perhaps gain wider public support for their efforts.

4   Critical issues for information society

We have contrasted a strategy of social innovation with other possible information societies: societies based on protectionism and greater social dualism. But the leap in the dark that we have tried to illuminate is by no means assured of a comfortable landing. Any process of technical change unevenly benefits people at different locations in a structure of social inequality. People may differ in their financial or cognitive abilities to make use of the technology, or to assess how its use by others will impinge upon them. Some inequalities could be amplified. Therefore the reduction of major inequalities should be explicitly incorporated as a goal in the design of information society. Otherwise, poorer communities are liable to receive poorer services, women are likely to be accorded greater burdens of caring, etc. The key issues include:

– the *distribution* of informatics resources. Infrastructural provision is of considerable importance in *regional* development and in the rise and decline of *urban* areas. Given the potential of informatics for making training and information services available, the provision of facilities for *social groups* disadvantaged by restructuring is of considerable importance. This may involve policies of positive discrimination, and adaptation of different media (or their 'programmes') to different social groups.
– the *design* of informatics. How far do the technologies permit interactivity rather than just expand the transmission of information in hierarchical structures? This raises questions for the design of infrastructure: whether the nodes of the cable systems can communicate with each other, rather than act as mere passive receivers of broadcast information as in a root-and-branch system; whether the systems have sufficient channel capacity to carry two-way video signals, and so on. The state and the market are unlikely to promote – or even formulate – the whole range of social innovations here. It will be necessary for a wide range of interest groups to evaluate technical alternatives and affect the process of technical change. Given that choices with long-term consequences are already under way, it is important that debate and analysis of these alternatives be promoted more widely.

Given the eventual importance of these issues for the future quality of life, the *public debate* on these issues is muted to the point of inaudibility. The questions posed above, together with those about the implications for privacy and the possibilities of public surveillance and control, all need to be asked *before* the systems are developed and installed. Firms and telecommunications authorities, in this country and elsewhere, are busily designing and building: where is the debate?

Notes

1 The authors are currently funded by the Joseph Rowntree Memorial Trust, to which we express our gratitude. Rather than provide numerous notes, we cite below only the main texts relevant to our arguments.

2 The main theoretical contribution on post-industrial society is Bell (1974); see also Kahn *et al.* (1976). Probably the best critique of the political assumptions of post-industrialism is Kleinberg (1973). The 'silent revolution' in values is the theme of Inglehart (1977). An early statement of our views concerning the social and psychological approaches of this school is Miles (1975); see also Miles (1980). The information society dichotomies we outline are drawn from Colombo and Lanza-vecchia (1982); for similar perspectives see a related collection, Barry *et al.* (1982). The most influential proponent of an information sector is Porat (1977).

3 Our discussion follows Gershuny and Miles (1983). See also Gershuny (1983) and Gershuny and Miles (1985). The term 'prosumer' is introduced in Toffler (1981), one of the better popular books attempting to explicate information society. The OECD text is an output of its series 'Information Computer Communications Policy' (1981).

4 The most interesting study of long waves is Freeman, Clark and Soete (1982). For the relation between automation and the economic crisis, see Kaplinsky (1984). See also various papers (especially those by Freeman and Coombes) in Martstrand (1984).

5 For a wide-ranging account of potential uses of cable systems, see the CNET/INA volume (1983); also relevant are the collections on information society referred to in note 2, and the popular discussions of Grossbrenner (1983) and Nilles (1982).

6 Our thinking here has been enriched by the work of Carlota Perez Perez: in particular by discussions around her papers in *Futures* (1983) and *World Development* (1985).

References

Barry, U., Bannon, L. and Holst O. (eds) (1982) *Information Technology: Impact on the Way of Life*. Dublin: Tycooly.

Bell, D. (1974) *The Coming of Post-Industrial Society*. New York: Basic Books.

CNET/INA (1983) *Images pour le Cable*; Paris: La Documentation Française. (Centre National d'Etudes des Télécommunications/Institut National de la Communication Audiovisuelle.)

Colombo, J. and Lanzavecchia, G. (1982) 'The Transition to an Information Society' in Bjorn-Andersen, N., Earl, M., Holst, O. and Mumford. E (eds) *Information Society: For Richer, For Poorer*. Amsterdam: North Holland.

Freeman, C., Clark, J., and Soete, L. (1982) *Unemployment and Technical Innovation*. London: Frances Pinter.

Gershuny, J. (1983) *Social Innovation and the Division of Labour*. London: Oxford University Press.

Gershuny, J. and Miles, I. (1983a) *The New Service Economy*. London: Frances Pinter.

Gershuny, J. and Miles, I. (1983b) 'Towards a New Social Economics' in Roberts, B., Finnegan, R. and Gallie, D. (eds) *New Approaches to Economic Life*. Manchester: Manchester University Press. (Published in 1985.)

Grossbrenner, A. (1983) *Personal Computer Communications*. New York: St Martin's Press.

Inglehart, R. (1977) *The Silent Revolution*. Princeton, N.J.: Princeton University Press.

Kahn, H., Brown, W. and Martell, L. (1976) *The Next 200 Years*. New York: Morrow.

Kaplinsky, R. (1984) *Automation*. London: Longman.

Kleinberg, B. (1973) *American Society in the Post-Industrial Age*. Columbus, Ohio: Charles E. Merril.

Martstrand, P. (ed.) (1984) *New Technology and the Future of Work and Skills*. London: Frances Pinter.

Miles, I. (1975) *The Poverty of Predication*. Farnborough, Hants: Saxon House.

Miles, I. (1980) 'Effacing the Political Future', *Futures* (12) 6, pp. 436-52.

Nilles, J. M. (1982) *Exploring the World of the Personal Computer*. Englewood Cliffs, N.J.: Prentice-Hall.

OECD (1981) *Information Activities, Electronics and Telecommunications Technologies*. Vol. 1. Paris: Organization for Economic Cooperation and Development.

Perez Perez, C. (1983) 'Structural Change and Assimilation of New Technologies in the Economic and Social Systems', *Futures*, October: pp. 357-74.

Perez Perez, C. (1985) 'Microelectronics, Long Waves and World Structural Change', *World Development*.

Porat, M. (1977) *The Information Economy*. Office of Technology Special Publication, US Department of Commerce; Washington, D.C.: Government Printing Office.

Toffler, A. (1981) *The Third Wave*. London: Pan.

15

IT Futures in Households and Communities

Ian Miles, John Bessant, Ken Guy and Howard Rush

1 Forecasting approaches in the literature

Broadly, forecasts of the long-term implications of IT can be divided into three groups. The first group, while recognizing that ITs are important, views their development and implications as part of a regular, evolutionary process. To some extent these forecasts have emerged as a counter to the initial excitement and dramatic prognostications (both optimistic and gloom-laden) which followed the first diffusion of microelectronic-based devices. They tend to stress continuity, pointing out that the 'silicon revolution' essentially extends long-established technological trends.

The forecasting methods employed here are really geared to medium-term projections at best, and their views of the development, application and diffusion of new technologies are liable to prove increasingly unreliable as the time horizon recedes. As is well known from the study of complex systems in biology and elsewhere, quite regular trends in a number of components of a system may well add up to substantial and dramatic changes in the overall 'gestalt' to which they contribute. (To take another metaphor, think of the rapid qualitative changes that overtake water when, having had its tempera-ture steadily raised, it reaches boiling point.) Furthermore, many of these authors confine themselves to single issues (such as job losses or gains in a particular sector) and implicitly assume that other factors remain constant. Critics of this approach claim that such assumptions are inappropriate in circumstances where major changes are taking place. These critics, who belong to the other two groups of forecasters, argue that we are indeed currently living in such circumstances. They see the boundaries between activities and the relations between sectors as being thrown into flux, and thus important features of the social structure undergoing profound shifts.

The most stark contrast with this first group of forecasts comes from a second group which argues that the changes associated with IT are truly fundamental, marking a period of epochal transition. The suggestion is that we are moving into an 'information society', a process of transition with implications as great as those attributed to the agricultural and industrial revolutions. By their very nature, such massive and revolutionary changes are difficult to forecast; many far-reaching developments are interconnected. This is reflected in the second group of studies, which cover a broad canvas with extremely broad strokes. They rarely offer concrete visions of the future. To draw an analogy, these forecasters are suggesting that unlike the first group, they have correctly identified current changes as representing a process of metamorphosis. It may be easy enough to extrapolate growth trends and predict that a kitten will grow into something rather like a cat, but it requires a greater leap of imagination – or substantially more subtle analysis – to anticipate that a caterpillar will become a butterfly. While, for the most part, shying away from detailed predictions – especially concerning the rate of change, as opposed to its broad direction – this group envisages a total shift in social values, with information-processing playing an ever more important role: 'information workers' and 'knowledge workers' will become increasingly central social actors, and the ability to deploy knowledge – intelligence – will displace other bases of social power.

The third group falls, in some respects, between the other two. These forecasters acknowledge that the introduction of IT is well-rooted in previous generations of technological innovation. If they talk of an 'information society', it is not presented in such epochal terms as deployed by the second group; instead, they depict current changes as of great significance, but as essentially involving the restructuring of industrial society. Since the industrial revolution new sectors have emerged to stimulate growth; and the process of change has been uneven, with quite distinct 'technological paradigms' characterizing successive stages of industrial society. Many of the 'long wave' theories – which seek to identify and account for cycles of change which span four or five decades – fall into this category. Forecasts in this category predominantly concentrate on changing industrial and organizational structures, and only a few have begun to address wider aspects of social change.

Each of the three approaches has its virtues and limitations [...] The future is bound to be characterized by both continuity and change, and the first group of forecasts is of value in damping the wilder speculations of the others, who sometimes seem to pay too little attention to the inertia of attitudes and institutions. The third group probably succeeds best in simultaneously grasping both poles, but fails to deal with many of the broader concerns of the second group, even if these are handled in an extremely speculative way.[...]

2   IT in households and communities: a complex change process

Many activities currently carried out by households and in communities, or provided by public services, could well be transformed by the application of IT; a large number of forecasts wax eloquent about such transformations. However, there have been relatively few attempts to provide precise forecasts of the rate of change over the long-term (in contrast, say, to estimates of demand for video-recorders and home computers over the short-term of five years or so). In general the publicly available literature reviewed here contained few confident predictions of the long-term pace of change of final demand for IT-related products.

In many respects, the forecasters' uncertainty is completely appropriate, and there are two related reasons for this. First, the change process is extremely complicated: a host of social trends and technological innovations will interact to determine the applications of IT in everyday life. Some trends are unlikely to be influenced by new ways of life made possible by IT (at least, not in the short-term): thus the age distribution of our population over the next few decades is fairly predictable, short of a major calamity. Others may be directly influenced by IT: new telecommunications facilities, for example, may lead to changes in the use of transport and preferences for urban living. And there are many indirect ways in which IT-related changes could shape our ways of life. IT, for example, may facilitate major changes in the ways people work – thus, given that many features of lifestyles are intimately related to income, working hours and occupational status, corresponding changes in attitudes, social relationships and time-use are likely.

Second, many researchers make the case that the change process involves more than the continuation of trends. These researchers argue that we are witnessing the early stages of a process of structural change, in which we are moving into a new phase of development which cannot be grasped simply in terms of present trends. Some well-established trends may indeed reverse, or the way in which trends relate together may be transformed. For example, many forecasters argue that the long-term trend towards increased centralization will be confronted by increased tendencies to decentralize social activities as a result of the diffusion of IT; and others argue that the relationship between consumer demand and market supply of services will be recast by changes in the informal economy and social attitudes. (It is because of this belief that structural change is taking place that terms like the 'information society' and 'post-industrial society' are coined, and popular authors describe current developments as 'the IT revolution' or 'the third wave'.) If we take these arguments seriously, more sophisticated theories of social change will be required for adequate views of options for the long-term future to be developed.

The difficulties of forecasting complicated processes and structural changes have, however, only rarely resulted in more sophisticated analysis. Indeed, they have often been seen as providing something of a licence for wild speculations. Many forecasters seem to have felt little need to constrain their visions by an assessment of practicalities: because there are immense possibilities for change, there is an attitude of 'anything goes'. There has thus been relatively little serious attention to the process of social and technological change that would create an information society. This makes many of the forecasts redolent of science fiction rather than serious social analysis, and there is thus good reason for scepticism about many of them. However, this is neither a reason for discounting the importance of long-term forecasting, nor for completely dismissing all of the forecasts that have been made. Serious and substantive research is quietly proceeding, even if it tends to be drowned out by sensationalism.

While few of the forecasts of IT's implications for lifestyles offer any precise estimates – and, since most of the forecasting effort is North American, this is especially true for the UK – it is evident that there are substantial differences in the degrees of impact which various forecasters see as likely over the next few decades. Some commentators anticipate practically unprecedented changes within the twentieth century. To take extreme, but not unrepresentative examples, there are predictions that by the year 2000 30 per cent of the workforce of industrial countries will be engaged in telework, or that symbiotic 'marriages' between humans and artificial intelligences will be established. Others argue that it is extremely uncommon, short of major disasters, for long-established social trends to change pace and direction as rapidly as these projections imply. Even where the domestic use of IT is concerned, there has been considerable scepticism about whether we are really so close to developing IT-based products that can be cheaply mass-produced, and win consumer acceptance, for the range of applications identified by futurologists.

Looking back at the record of forecasts about IT over the last few decades certainly seems to support this scepticism. While estimates of the technical capabilities of IT have been fairly close to the mark, reviews of the performance of forecasting suggest that there has frequently been a tendency to overestimate the degree and rate of application. But there have been notable exceptions to this: the popularity of home computers and pocket calculators was generally underestimated, while commentators focused more on telecommunications and the use of large-scale computer systems in public libraries and databanks. (Ironically, the diffusion of the microcomputer may now provide the basis for these large-scale applications to have an impact on the domestic market.) Recently, attention has been directed to the problems experienced in selling new cable systems and videotext services to the public in several countries – these have been widely read as meaning that the picture of an emerging information society is at best premature.

There are two reasons for not letting the case rest with the more sceptical view. First is the precipitous drop in price and ascent in power of IT.[...] Applications that were in the past unthinkable (or unthinkably expensive) may soon be well within the reach of the average household. Over the next quarter century, many of the developments anticipated for the 70s and 80s could be more realistic. Second, it is not necessary for the diffusion process to be completed for technological innovation to have had a substantial social and economic impact. Only a fraction of British homes now have home computers, for example, but this has provided the spur for the growth of many small firms, some of them internationally successful; it has led to changes in the composition of the mass media (newspapers carry computer sections, radio and TV broadcast hobbyists' programmes, and railway station bookstalls are full of computer magazines); and it has surely played an important role in reshaping the attitudes of the young and not-so-young toward new technology. [...]

3   Household activities as a focus of change

Classifying the various activities pursued by households into a small number of groups – such as nutrition, personal care (for example, bathing and sleeping), domestic maintenance (for example, household cleaning and security), communications and transport, entertainment, health care, and education – can help to describe past trends in household behaviour, and to outline the potential social and technological innovations that are implied by social forecasts, and the new demands discussed by some forecasters. [. . .] Over the long-term, the ways in which households have carried out these different activities have altered tremendously. This has reflected growing affluence (so that basic goods like foodstuffs have declined as a proportion of household expenditure, while within this category there have been immense changes in the types of food people have bought); technological change (for example, the use of television for entertainment purposes); and government policies (for example, the provision of educational and health services through state agencies). The relative weight of each of these three factors in promoting change is not easy to determine: all three are closely interconnected. But all will remain important determinants of future change.[. . .]

How the trends interact in the future will be a matter of technological possibilities, economic costs and benefits, and government policies. The shift towards, say, the use of motor cars and washing machines reflects such factors: the development of more trouble-free and what is now called 'user-friendly' equipment; a relative cheapening of these goods as against services (which may be limited by the application of IT to previously labour-intensive service tasks); the provision of the infrastructures of mains electricity and motorways; the shortening of the working week; etc. In many of these developments the diffusion of the innovations involved overcoming a chicken-and-egg problem: the new ways of life required both the new products (hardware such as new domestic equipment, and in some cases software, such as TV programmes) and the infrastructure (including not only motorways and the like, but also garages, service stations, convenient cafes and car parks, etc).

Thus not only are the technological innovations necessary. There must also be activities to which they may be applied more cheaply, comprehensively or conveniently than can existing goods or services – and there must be the infrastructure and services which can support their widespread use. The slow take-off of cable systems in the UK, and of pilot interactive services elsewhere, is reminiscent of just such a chicken-and-egg dilemma: the range of services which could motivate large numbers of people to invest in cable facilities are themselves only likely to emerge slowly in the absence of sizeable markets. Scrambling the metaphor a little, while optimistic forecasters have been quick to describe the chicken – the wide range of services that might be provided – their more pessimistic colleagues have stressed the difficulties of breaking the eggshell – triggering the growth process. Much of the divergence among forecasts reflects the degree to which the different researchers have placed their emphasis on technological possibilities or on social constraints.

4   New household goods and services

Most forecasters argue that the 'information society' depends upon the development of markets for new IT-based goods and services. While the possibility of increasing the efficiency and quality of existing industries by the use of such products is widely anticipated, many commentators suggest that what is more important will be their finding applications in households and communities – in other words, satisfying final demand. It is quite possible to set out many of the technical capabilities of IT in applications for final consumers, and we shall shortly turn to this task. But we should first note that it is much harder to assess the rates of diffusion of these applications, especially at a point in time when only what will surely be viewed in the future as crude prototypes have appeared on the market. As we have seen, social and technological innovations necessarily go hand in hand. Some of the proposed applications imply major changes in people's ways of life, rather than small modifications of existing consumption patterns, and this also renders fore-casting problematic. Finally, we have also seen that such social innovations are likely to be heavily influenced by such factors as investments in infra-structure and policies concerning working hours.

These considerations must make us cautious about accepting forecasts that confidently predict the uses that IT will find at the end of this century. Perhaps we are in a position comparable to that of people in the 1930s, caught up in the gloom of the Great Depression and trying to speculate about the implications of the growth of the automobile, radio and chemical industries. It would have been easy to grasp that the products of these industries would have a marked impact on ways of life. However, the types of transport system, broadcasting, and plastic products that have emerged would have been much harder to foresee. Even if there is considerably more speculation about the possible applications of IT than these earlier developments evoked, it is likely that we are too bound up in current ways of life to envisage the social innovations that may lead to the realization of the technological potentials. If long-term forecasting can help us to overcome the inertia of the present, then it will be able to contribute to establishing a climate where social innovations can be fostered, experimented with, and assessed for their contribution to individual and public well-being.

Thus technological wonders are not themselves the key feature of an information society. What is necessary is for people to see that IT can provide them with opportunities to undertake desirable new activities, or to improve upon existing activities, in ways they find convenient and at costs they find reasonable. While the price of telecommunications capabilities is dependent to a considerable extent upon infrastructural policies (although it may be that ingenious ways of amplifying the potential of existing communications systems will be found), the price of home-based computer and other microe-lectronics-based equipment is likely to be so low that many of the powerful applications that the forecasters have envisaged will be potentially available for home users in the near future.

Some specialists argue that forecasts of 'artificial intelligence in every home' understate the problems still to be faced in the development of expert systems, voice recognition and other components of this vision. Electromechanical equipment (such as would be required for home robotics) is likely to remain expensive compared to purely electronic equipment. But even if such factors are important, a wide range of IT hardware, with vastly more power than currently employed by domestic users, should be readily available at relatively low prices. To gain an impression of the scale of change that is feasible, recall that home computers which are now purchased essentially as children's toys have the capabilities of systems that only a few decades ago required rooms full of equipment, specialist operating skills, and a fortune in refrigeration expenses. A few decades prior to that they were science fiction dreams.

But can this hardware be applied to household activities in convenient ways? One way in which our present ways of life may be constraining our views of the future is the tendency (not uncommon among forecasters) to represent the domestic life of an information society as centering on a household computer-communications console that is little more than a large-scale television. While there may well be control centres and entertainment rooms much as these forecasts imply, the household applications of IT are likely to be more pervasive, and perhaps less immediately evident.

In some instances IT can be embodied in existing household equipment, to make 'informed tools'. This is simply an extension of the ongoing sophistication of cookers, washing machines, stereo systems, and the like. It would be possible to integrate household utilities that currently operate in a rather mechanical and independent fashion. For example, various features of the internal environment could be monitored and controlled by a central computer: lighting, central heating, household security and similar functions could be responsive to whether members of the household were at, or on their way, home, asleep or awake, and so on. But integrating systems in this way requires more reorganization of the household than does the addition of a few more gadgets or replacement of an obsolete item with an up-to-date one. In the future, the design of household information may become a craft (like installing central heating or decorating are today), and the 'automated household' is likely to emerge only slowly (except, perhaps, for the very rich and for some institutions) and to be preceded by a period of increased gadgetry. Even then, IT equipment will need to be considerably more convenient before it becomes acceptable: finding room for even a flat-screen VDU in one's kitchen is not always going to be easy!

These examples essentially involve IT in monitoring and controlling the operation of familiar domestic equipment, and enabling household members to 'program' the equipment to carry out tasks in specific ways. The equipment could readily provide information, as well, which would enable the 'programming' to be undertaken in the light of expert knowledge or precise information on current circumstances. The cooker, or the kitchen computer, for example, could be in a position to suggest menus and cooking methods: and these could take into account the goods in the larder (keyed in by the cook rather than directly sensed by the equipment), the available time, and the current prices of foodstuffs of various kinds (if in communication with commercial databases). Environmental control systems would be able to indicate the cost of alternative heating regimes, and the preferred temperatures of other household members. While we have warned against seeing future household IT applications in terms of computers and visual displays, the latter are an ideal way of presenting many of the choices that IT can make available. The uses of voice synthesis may well be restricted, although new types of VDU screen are quite plausible. The 'programming', by unskilled people, of household equipment dedicated to specific tasks, involves their choosing between options presented by IT hardware. The diffusion of such technology will very much depend upon the extent to which the software provided with it requires no specialized knowledge. It is now a commonplace that software is currently an expensive bottleneck in the development of IT. Considerable efforts are going into making software production itself more easy ('the self-programming computer'), and 'user-friendly' software is also likely to become cheaper and more powerful. This is likely to mean that existing home computer programs for educational and household management purposes may be poor guides to the facilities that will be available in the future; and computer literacy may be of more use in helping people understand how IT operates and to participate in the design of the IT systems they live and work with, than in helping them to use specific devices more effectively. (It also has implications for the argument that a country should aim to exploit its comparative advantage in programming skills in order to find a niche in the global information society.)

This leads to another aspect of convenience, but in order to introduce this it is necessary first to outline briefly one other aspect of the expanding potential of computer-telecommunications systems. It has been widely noted that IT can make the creation of music, graphics and designs – for practically anything from gardens to garments – less a matter of traditional technical skills than one of being able to combine imagination and taste with elementary understanding of new IT facilities. Some forecasters see this as recreating 'Renaissance Man' (and Woman too, presumably): specialized skills will effectively be within the reach of all of us, the heritage of human knowledge will be accessible through database services ... But less grandiose prospects have also been considered. For example, the addition of cameras to home video systems may be one indicator of the beginning of the return to 'do-it-yourself' home entertainment some forecasters expect (there is a well-established trend of increased 'entertaining' of friends for meals). And IT can help inform other types of domestic production, as well as providing improved tools. In this respect the new technology gives people more control over their personal environments.

But the technology itself is rather opaque: it is easy enough to see how a watch works by looking at it, but the same is not true for integrated circuits. While most people cannot repair watches, less delicate mechanical equipment is within the grasp of many of us (car repairs, for example); but mending microelectronics equipment is another matter. One aspect of convenience that needs to be addressed is the durability and 'repairability' of equipment. For example, it might be desirable to develop self-diagnosis and modular equipment, so that faulty components can be easily replaced. As in the case of many novelties, household IT has not had the best record of servicing and consumer relations; this will have to be overcome if families are to make considerable investments in new equipment. And there will also, justifiably, be doubts and worries about the problems of being even more dependent upon electricity supplies and other utilities, and on professional repair workers.

Several other factors might inhibit the diffusion of social innovations based on IT. One factor is, paradoxically, the very rate of change in IT itself. It is likely that new hardware and software will continue to be introduced rapidly: even if there were not continuing development of the basic technology, many new products and services can be developed on the basis of existing technology. Consumers are liable to be deterred by an apparently high rate of obsolescence of equipment, and confused by a proliferation of choices. One important role might be the consultant who aids consumer choice; a new profile for consumer organizations might also develop. As well as rapid change, there is evidence that the incompatibility of different systems inhibits the diffusion of products, and it is interesting to note in this light the coordinated strategy of Japanese home computer manufacturers in respect of software (as opposed to the divergence of British suppliers).

5 The dynamics of social innovations

Drawing on numerous forecasts of potential applications of IT in the household, Tables 15.1 and 15.2 list a range of such applications, and indicate particular aspects of the technology that are most likely to be relevant to various household activities. Despite the impressive novelty of many of these innovations, it will be evident that the types of activities involved are not necessarily intrinsically different from those we are familiar with. People will continue to want to sleep, to be entertained and informed, to travel, to maintain their health and so on.

But many activities can be carried out in different ways, involving different combinations of various ingredients. It is these combinations that underlie the use of information and information services in various household activities. In considering the 'post-industrial society' debates, some researchers have stressed changes in the way that households have acquired final services. They have related socioeconomic change to shifts in the location of activities. For example, the activities may involve household production using manufactured goods, or state authorities providing benefits or establishing rights. The variety of ways in which activities can be carried out is another reason for divergence in forecasts of household and community implications of IT: many authors only emphasize one or other of these ways. Thus some studies of the implications of IT focus mainly on those for manufacturing, some on those for service industries, and some on those for households themselves. We have already outlined some applications of IT in gadgets used in domestic work: let us consider some rather different examples.

5.1 Transport

[. . .] IT could be applied extensively to transport. It could be used to increase productivity by substituting capital for labour in existing services. While driverless vehicles will not appear on the roads for quite a while, automation of ticket machines and barriers is now commonplace, usually reducing costs and in some cases increasing the efficiency of the service. This may increase demand and thus offset job losses, although if demand expansion is limited, all that may be achieved is the containment of decline. But IT can also be used in order to augment existing transport services: interactive services could aid and speed ticket booking and payment, the planning and scheduling of trips, and even the routing of some forms of public transport (for example, dial-a-ride facilities, which could be especially useful to the elderly and disabled). Travel agencies are already making extensive use of IT; its diffusion to other transport services is quite likely. IT – in the form of telephone and video facilities on buses and trains – may also affect the quality of time spent using the services. [. . .]

[Other] aspects of IT may have significant indirect implications for transport, as for other ways of life. 'Telework' and 'teleservices', for example, may reduce requirements for travel in everyday life. Some forecasters do contrast 'information-moving' to 'people-moving', but others note that to date telecommunications have not displaced travel extensively. The telephone may have displaced personal mail, but if anything it has encouraged greater mobility

Table 15.1 *Applications of advanced information technology in household activities*

Household activities	Applications of advanced information technology		
	Improved telecommunications	*Advanced microcomputers*	*'Intelligent' devices*
Formal Work			
employment	a b c d e	g h j k l	n
tax, banking	a b d	k	n
Personal Care			
nutrition	b c d	g h i k	m n o
sleep, rest	–	f i	m o
childcare	a b	f k	m o
dressing	b c	g	–
washing	–	–	m
Housework			
household cleaning	b		m
cleaning clothes	b	i	m
meal preparation	b	g h i	m n o
gardening	b d e	f g h k	m n
housing repairs	b c d e	g h	m
decoration	b c	g h	m
equipment maintenance	b e	h	m
routine shopping	b d	f l	n
non-routine shopping	b c d	k	–
Communications			
transport	a b c d e	–	m n o
telecommunications	a b c d e	i l	m n o
Entertainment			
spectator sport	b d e	–	–
participator sport	d e	h k l	m
games	a d	h l	m
performance art	b c d e	g h i l	m o
cultural facilities	b c d e	l	–
Education			
basic education	a b d e	f g h j k l	–
higher education	a b c d e	f g h j k l	–
specialized skills	a b c d e	f h i j k l	–
vocational training	a b c d e	f h i j k l	–
leisure education	a b c d e	f g h i j k l	o
Health			
health maintenance	a c d	f g h k l	n o
curative medicine	a b c d e	f g k l	m n o
emergency care	a b	f i	m

Table 15.1 *(Cont'd)*

Household activities	Applications of advanced information technology		
	Improved telecom- munications	*Advanced micro- computers*	*'Intelligent' devices*
Social Relations			
friendship and kinship	a e	k	–
political participation	a d e	h k	–
legal authorities	a b c d	–	–
voluntary associations	a b d e	k	–

Notes:

1   Interactive digitized broadband telecommunications facilities—

    a = message transmission

    b = booking, ordering, scheduling services

    c = advisory and brokerage services

    d = data base, information, telesoftware and broadcast programmes

    e = networking

2   Advanced domestic microcomputers–

    f = monitoring and sensing facilities

    g = computer-aided design

    h = computer-aided instruction

    i = control of equipment

    j = text and graphics processing

    k = record keeping

    l = specialized programmes

3   'Intelligent' domestic equipment–

    m = automated control and regulation

    n = record keeping and information-giving

    o = personalization of operations

(for example, people are able to live further from their parents because they can maintain regular contact with them). Television seems to have whetted appetites for foreign travel. But 'telework' may effect substantial changes in travel to work, just as 'teleconferencing' may affect business travel – and while these developments are often regarded as requiring extreme changes in ways of life, substantial investments in relevant equipment are being made by some US firms. Other indirect implications might come from changes in the length and organization of the working week – although impacts on business and leisure travel might diverge. [...]

5.2   Collective services

Self-servicing is less well established where such collective services as education and health are involved – although, of course, neither the physical nor the mental well-being of the population would be in an acceptable state if people did not take considerable responsibility for keeping themselves at least minimally fit and informed. Collective services are largely provided by state agencies, with some participation of private and voluntary organizations. People also take care of themselves in many everyday respects. The forecasting

Table 15.2 *Potential applications of IT in household activities*

Household activity	Illustrative potential applications of advanced information technology
Formal Work	
employment	telework
banking and tax	telebanking; computer-aided tax form-filling
Personal Care	
nutrition	monitoring nutritional standards, diets
sleep	relaxation, alarms
childcare	monitoring infant well-being, alarms
dressing	aiding choice of clothes
washing	(improved energy efficiency)
Housework	
cleaning	(improved energy efficiency in washing and drying machines)
cooking	menu assistance, automated ovens
gardening	garden planning aids
household maintenance	monitoring heat loss, damp, etc.
decoration	computer-aided design
equipment maintenance	fault-finding with sophisticated goods
routine shopping	teleshopping
non-routine shopping	teleshopping, consumer information
Communications	
transport	travel booking and route planning
telecommunications	electronic mail, interactive services
Entertainment	
spectator sport	booking seats, delivering video recordings
participator sport	booking facilities, locating partners
games	video games, computer-assisted games
performance art	delivering recorded performances, reviews
cultural facilities	electronic libraries and newspapers
Education	
basic education	instructional programmes
higher education	tele-education, teleconferencing
specialized skills	access to online databanks
vocational training	computer-aided instruction, simulations
leisure education	tele-education
Health	
health maintenance	programmes for lifestyle planning and monitoring
curative medicine	diagnostic programmes, remote counselling
emergency care	emergency alarms, improved equipment and communication in ambulances
Social Relations	
friendship and kinship	improved telephony
political participation	telecommunication aids to community association
legal authorities	online access to legal advice
voluntary associations	telecommunication between voluntary workers, clients, co-ordinators

literature suggests that there is considerable scope both for substitution in the provision of the services and for augmenting these services in significant ways.

Technological innovations in many collective services have to date predominantly involved the substitution of technology for human labour. However, there have been a number of spectacular innovations in which IT has been used to augment services – as in the case of the Open University, for example, or some advances in high-technology medicine like computer-aided tomography. Forecasters have also outlined the prospects for self-service innovations in collective services, an example being the new methods that are now becoming available for clients to interrogate computers about employment opportunities.

For example, routine health care, monitoring of one's physical well-being, and some diagnosis of the meaning of symptoms could be provided via IT. Indeed, many of these options are already available: Prestel carries some basic interactive health information, and peripheral attachments to home computers enable users to monitor heart rates and other conditions; it is easy to imagine, furthermore, current kitchen-menu programmes for home computers being combined with database systems to enable users to plan and monitor their diets, and perhaps relate these to programmes of exercise and to medical check-ups.

Such developments may seem outlandish, but consider the growing concern in keeping fit (as indicated by increased participation in sports, interest in special diets, and declining cigarette use). Would not such applications of IT represent extensions of these trends? There is bound to be opposition to these developments on a number of grounds – that they are isolating, impersonal and potentially dangerous, that they threaten professional standards, and the like. These developments are also likely to find vociferous enthusiasts, who stress the greater freedom of choice and reduction of reliance on expertise that can be made available. They might also point out that, after all, these IT-based systems are really only more contemporary, and hopefully enhanced, versions of the volumes of self-help medical advice from earlier generations, now turning musty on many a bookshelf. If there is a proliferation of new types of information and advisory services, then there may well be a requirement to establish ways of regulating them that can allow innovations to flourish while preventing exploitation and abuse.

These examples of change in health-related activities draw attention to a number of issues which were less evident in the transport case. First, attention is drawn to the fact that what is involved is a combination of a social and a technical innovation: and that these involve substantial change in the way in which people would carry out these activities if (or when) these developments come about. The technical innovation is evident enough: new types of computer, peripherals and software. The social innovation involves a change in household activities: perhaps meaning that individuals more frequently and systematically monitor and seek to improve their physical well-being, and change their habits in respect of entertainment, sport, diet and the like. Such innovations may well augment the health care available to individuals – few of us have the opportunity to consult specialists about the next meal, for example, or to choose between a whole range of alternative diets or even between different medical approaches. They may also change the way in which people deal with health problems; in some instances we may move toward consulting expert systems about troubling symptoms as a matter of course, for example. The spectre of a nation of hypochondriacs is raised by some critics of such a prospect, but others express more concern about the displacement of medical practitioners. New types of activity may be carried out, but this does not rule out some substitution of tasks previously carried out by medical specialists in the formal economy by new IT-based systems.

The second issue of interest relates to the fact that a process of change in health-related activities, involving individuals self-servicing themselves to a greater extent, could take place in a number of ways. It might take the form dubbed 'privatique' by recent French writers, being based centrally on IT ('informatique') possessed by private households, as was implicit in the examples above. Or it could involve health services augmenting their own operations, by offering online services of the type outlined. For example, rather than necessarily going to the GP's waiting room for an appointment, one might first communicate with a computer in the surgery; if its expert system determines that your symptoms are beyond the scope of routine medical advice an appointment or a home visit would be organized. Such a system might meet with favour from medical professionals, for although it substitutes for some of their work it would be freeing them of time-consuming routine consultations, making it possible to devote more attention to more serious problems that at present too often receive short shrift.

But related advice on aspects of one's lifestyle, together with a wider range of services, could also be made available in quite different ways. Advice and consultation other than contact with medical professionals might be provided online by private information services – in which case there would be a good case for careful regulation of the quality of the variety of alternative services that might be offered. Such facilities might well be developed in parallel with software purchased by households for use with their domestic computer systems (and perhaps 'downloaded' through cable media rather than being purchased on tape or disc).

As this example of health-related activities suggests, social innovations using IT can apply to very many services, and for any given class of service they could also be provided through quite different channels. Similar possibilities are envisaged by forecasters for other services: for example, the possibility of using IT to tailor education very much more closely to individual requirements, and so 'delivering' the services much more to individuals in their own homes rather than in conventional lecture halls has received much attention. Home computers are already the focus of a great deal of activity on the part of software houses, who are producing large volumes of educational software for them. Even more important, of course, is the expansion of IT in formal education. Since the 1960s, the recognition has grown that computers need not merely substitute for teachers as in 'programmed learning'. Current practices are much more oriented toward using microcomputers as a new audio-visual adjunct in conventional classes, as tools for training in the operation and use of IT, and – perhaps most significantly – as means of allowing students to develop problem-solving skills. (This latter is epitomized by the use of the instructional language LOGO, but is also implied by many simulations and specific programmes used in schools.) Educationalists are often critical of educational software as merely offering rote learning in a glamorized form, but it is clear that when the programmers have substantive knowledge of educational environments and their needs (rather than computer skills only), they have been able to make significant contributions.

In addition, computer-communication facilities are being developed to make educational access to databases a routine matter – indeed, the involvement of schools in production of the databases is a likely development, as in the current 'Domesday Book' videodisc project. Basic information and skills may be adequately conveyed by databases packaged together with microcomputers, and large increases in the storage capacity of cheap equipment are likely to expand the range of available opportunities. But online data services could well cater for the information needs of private households, public libraries and educational establishments alike. The literature contains numerous claims that such innovations will be increasingly important in formal and informal education; but in this instance, as in the case of the health innovations discussed above, it is rare to find any systematic analysis of how they might be integrated with conventional forms of service delivery. Likewise [. . .] there are relatively few attempts to relate, say, the needs for training and retraining implied by the visions of information society, to the provision of education services with the use of IT.

This raises a further point about collective services. These are services which consume large volumes of public expenditure, and thus the temptation to apply IT to rationalize these services is great. They are also services that involve large proportions of the population at any one time, and everyone at some time in their lives. Thus it is important also to consider the possibilities for augmenting them in ways that deal with the problems of the future decades. For example, the health and educational services are necessarily going to have to confront the results of change in the age structure of the population and in people's working lives. Innovations designed to cope with such changes might well be framed in the light of the potentials of IT. What is more, the public services provide opportunities to engage people in experiments concerning the acceptability and utility of IT-based change. While considerable attention has been paid to the role of private sectors centred on entertainment and specialized information in leading the 'information revolution', it is plausible that collective services also have an important role to play. Finally, the issues of regulation and also of privacy are ones that are already being confronted by collective services; their experience may have important implications for other parts of the information society. [. . .]

6   Conclusions

Our survey of the forecasting literature confirms that it is widely anticipated that market opportunities and social benefits will be associated with a wide range of new IT-based services. But a virtuous circle cannot be established merely by the potentials of IT itself: people have to see useful things to do in convenient ways and at sensible prices for demand to be forthcoming. While there is likely to be considerable continuity in the broad form of household activities, it is clear that within these there may be major innovations in ways of life. Predicting the uses and services that may prove popular in the future is difficult, because we are to a large extent hampered by our experience of the application of IT within existing ways of life, which may not be a good guide to the ways in which different changes may combine together.

While some authors offer relatively detailed and clearcut visions of the information society, their forecasts almost inevitably involve a large leap in the dark. The social innovations that actually do take place may well take quite different directions, and while it is possible to identify and account for trends in social life, there is considerable uncertainty about the specific choices that will be made with respect to various household activities. And, of course, policy decisions taken today may determine the types of decision that people make. Decisions about telecommunications infrastructure rank high here. The information society literature tends to assume that broadband digital systems will be available, enabling the development of decentralized communications and interactive services. It would be worth examining how far choices made today between different types of telecommunications infrastructure foreclose options for its future development: is innovation in IT liable to increase the options that we have here, as it does in so many areas, or are those authors correct who suggest – though they rarely elaborate their argument – that current decisions will be crucial? Whether or not development of the appropriate infrastructure is a priority remains somewhat obscure, since in some cases it is not always virtuous to be a technological pioneer – Britain does not need an IT Concorde. But what seems to be more evident is that, whatever infrastructural development does take place, it should be of such a form as to permit considerable experimentation with service innovations.

The unpredictability of the exact trade-offs that people will want to make between different ways of carrying out household activities is a major reason for needing to keep options open in this way. But this does not necessarily limit public authorities' role to providing opportunities for infrastructural development. We have already noted that public services could take something of a leading role in creating the information society by offering some facilities in attractive ways as online services: tax and medical advice, library and official databases, opportunities to relate to welfare authorities, for example. They have a role to play in establishing pilot projects and demonstration schemes, and conducting social experiments. And, given that the wider social implications of uncertain changes in people's ways of life are doubly uncertain, it is important that these experiments should be monitored so as to draw out the social costs and benefits of alternative ways of realizing the potential of IT. Both to avoid suspicions that Big Brother lies behind such projects, and to strengthen the link between technology and social need that is necessary for successful innovation, the involvement of voluntary bodies, such as community and consumer associations, would be important.

The forecasting literature often waxes eloquent on a related topic – the possibility of using IT to enhance democracy. Earlier predictions of the 'electronic town hall' and 'instant referenda' have been less prominent in the recent literature than heretofore, although further experiments along these lines are almost certain to be tried out sooner or later – by entertainment media if not by political authorities. Less glamorously, but perhaps of more substance for participatory democracy, some commentators discuss the prospects for social movements of all sorts using the networking possibilities of IT to communicate far more effectively, rapidly establishing communities of interest, locating relevant knowledge and expertise, and reaching out to wider constituencies. Some experiments along these lines are already in progress. But computer networks used by the public until now seem to be more preoccupied with 'lonely hearts' and similar services. It is possible to envisage these in the future becoming a medium for helping people 'service' each other in everyday activities – to share a car journey or babysitting, to swop skills or property, to play games or work on cultural projects.

Forecasters who have analysed trends in ways of life have, as we saw above, tended to see these as leading to the application of IT to provide more 'self-service' ways of satisfying final demand. While many have portrayed this as an unequivocal improvement in the quality of life, one that increases choice and informed decision-making, there remains a strong undercurrent of concern about possible problems associated with this trend: perhaps it rests on an excessively individualistic view of social life, and underplays the role of community in our lives. Several types of problem have been outlined in the literature. It is argued that shifting many productive activities back into the household cannot be seen as a return to the pre-industrial self-reliant family; industrialization itself has transformed family relations and the 'self-servicing' family would still remain highly integrated into the formal economy. It is feared that the integration of communities might diminish; people might become more isolated, preferring to interact with their terminals than directly with other people. It is also pointed out that women tend to bear by far the greater part of the burden of household work, and the IT-based activities show little sign of changing this: and, indeed, 'telework' might mean that employed women would have to be carrying out their keyboarding job while keeping an eye on the children. Finally, it is pointed out that – especially if the labour market becomes more dualistic – a dualism of consumers might emerge, with the better-quality services being available to those who can keep up financially or intellectually with IT, while other people might be left with shoddy and declining traditional services.

Optimistic forecasters tend to dismiss such worries. They point out, for example, that many forms of socializing have grown despite the impact of television, that telecommunications to date do not seem to have reduced people's inclination to travel (and perhaps the contrary has been true), and that IT offers unprecedented opportunities to free work from traditional stereotypes of masculine and feminine jobs. (On the one hand, for example, many industrial jobs become more like the secretarial task of keyboarding; on the other hand, kitchen equipment becomes more technically sophisticated.) But these are, they will admit, forecasts: we cannot be sure of what form social innovations will take, and it may prove to be the case that spontaneous changes will run counter to many of the aims of social policy. Already legal changes have been prompted by the uses to which video-recorders have been applied. The more cautionary forecasts cannot be dismissed merely because IT is a reason to take them seriously. Our literature review suggests that IT itself does not necessitate social changes; we need to ensure that its applications are overwhelmingly benevolent ones. The past history of major techno-logical changes has demonstrated that even where they bring massive benefits, the associated costs were often predicted. With hindsight, is it not possible that some of the worst costs of the Industrial Revolution could have been avoided while making the most of its benefits?

In discussing forecasts of the implications of IT for employment, we pointed to a strong current in the literature: that IT might be associated with a long-term reduction in employment, but that for a country like Britain to refuse to make use of IT in industry on these grounds would lead to even greater problems for employment. Perhaps something rather similar applies in the present case. The sorts of social change that have been outlined above may well cause social problems; but without some major innovations the problems may be even greater. A protectionist attitude to all of our current institutions in itself appears to be a dead-end, for it is widely agreed that public services need to be organized in a very different way to cope with the problems of the future. As private consumers, people are in any case likely to adopt social innovations pioneered in other countries, even if public policies can slow this process. Given that many services may in the future be exportable in IT-based forms, a strategy of service innovation might prove to have trade advantages for the UK economy.

Yet the risk of dualism may be involved in almost any process of social innovation linked to IT. Educational and financial circumstances mean that the benefits of new technologies are often not conveyed evenly. Even now, parts of the UK still receive broadcast services of very different qualities; if more social affairs are to be handled by means of telecommunications, then regional differences in infrastructure may come to play an important role, too. The challenge is to find socially useful and gainful applications of IT, while limiting and redressing any further disadvantages that might accrue to the already disadvantaged. This might mean, for example, that services on which people rely should not be withdrawn or allowed to run down unless the new alternatives can be made readily available. Furthermore, a number of initiatives might contain or even reverse dualistic tendencies, and again the public services might have an important role to play here, ensuring that their innovations are not restricted to relatively privileged groups: the intentions behind the Open University and the online employment information services are examples of good practice here. Other experiments could include community access to IT (making facilities available for community centres and public libraries, for example, so that new networks of common cultural, social or political interest might form); or services corresponding to needs of low-income groups (provision of emergency service systems by local authorities): or IT awareness training schemes and greater encouragement for potentially 'information-poor' groups to learn relevant skills.

PART V
The Future of the Human Spirit: Depersonalization or New Development?

Introduction to Part V

Despite the variety of perspectives and dimensions discussed in this book on the social issues of information technology, the overall impression is that we are experiencing an information revolution. Like other revolutions, it raises fundamental questions concerning the effects it will have on the human spirit. As computers enter into social life and psychological development, how will they affect the way we think, especially the way we think about ourselves? And how will they affect our modes of communication and interaction in groups, especially in relation to factors such as social hierarchies and gender differences? Will they exacerbate established patterns and social differences, or transform them? Does the computer culture threaten the very idea of the human mind and the 'self', putting us on a level with machines? Will the development of artificial intelligence lead to a mechanical view of human nature and the dominance of instrumental reason in our culture? Or can it increase our human capacity to make moral and aesthetic choices, including the choice of how we as individuals will relate to the computer? These and other questions are discussed in the papers that follow.

Kiesler, Siegel and McGuire, 'Social Psychological Aspects of Computer-mediated Communications', review research findings on social responses to computer-mediated communications. They note that the cultural conventions that normally guide social interaction are frequently missing in computer-mediated communication, and this has significant effects on people's behaviour. For example, clues to social status of participants may be missing, and normal patterns of dominance are altered. This has clear significance for social hierarchies, and for group interactions which might otherwise reflect gender differences, such as the tendency for male participants in face-to-face work groups to speak more and to dominate females.

Turkle, 'Computers and the Human Spirit', discusses some of the most profound issues concerning the effect of computers on the way we think and on how we see ourselves. She also draws on her own research into different computer cultures, illustrating how adults and children may invest their computers with quite different meanings, and have different styles of interacting with the machine.

Rosenbrock, 'Engineers and the Work that People do', writes from the perspective of an engineer about the need for engineers to see that they have a choice in how they design technology – either to minimize and eliminate workers' skill, or to enhance human abilities. He discusses some of the reasons why engineers have tended to operate with a paradigm which minimized skill rather than enhancing it. Purely economic arguments will not change this tendency, he concludes, nor is there a sufficiently widely shared set of beliefs that would provide the basis for change. His conclusion, that rejection of trivialized and dehumanized work precedes any possible rationalization, takes on a special significance in the era of the microprocessor.

Weizenbaum, 'Artificial Intelligence', takes us to social issues at the frontiers of information technology. Will fifth-generation computers, with highly developed artificial intelligence, be able to take over the functions of human intelligence? Or is there something unique about the human mind that cannot be reproduced in a machine, and so some functions which cannot be delegated? Weizenbaum's conclusion is that the relevant issues are not technical; they are ethical.

16

Social Psychological Aspects of Computer-mediated Communication

Sara Kiesler, Jane Siegel and Timothy W. McGuire

1 Introduction

Computer-mediated communication differs in many ways, both technically and culturally, from more traditional communication technologies. Technically, it has the speed (including simultaneity, if desired) and energy efficiency, but not the aural or visual feedback of telephoning and face-to-face communication. It has the adaptability of written text. Messages can be sent to groups of any size and can be programmed for such special functions as automatic copying to a prespecified distribution list. Culturally, computer-mediated communication is still undeveloped. Although computer professionals have used electronic communication for over two decades, and they make up a subculture whose norms influence computer users and electronic communication (Sproull, Kiesler and Zubrow, in press), no strong etiquette as yet applies to how electronic communication should be used. A few user manuals devote a paragraph to appropriate uses of a computer network, but generally speaking, people do not receive either formal or informal instruction in an etiquette of electronic communication. These technical and cultural issues might be organized around the following questions.

1.1 Time and information processing pressures

Does easy, rapid communication – messages exchanged literally at the touch of a key – change the quantity or the distribution or the timing of information exchanged? Availability of instantaneous electronic communication, for example, might lead people to expect immediate responses. (We have talked with a company president in Pittsburgh who sends computer mail at dinnertime asking his subordinates in Singapore for quarterly projections by breakfast.)

1.2   Absence of regulating feedback

Does communication through text alone reduce coordination of communication? In traditional forms of communication, head nods, smiles, eye contact, distance, tone of voice, and other nonverbal behavior give speakers and listeners information they can use to regulate, modify, and control exchanges. Electronic communication may be inefficient for resolving such coordination problems as telling another person you already have knowledge of something he or she is explaining (Kraut, Lewis and Swezey, 1982).

1.3   Dramaturgical weakness

Computer communication might weaken social influence by the absence of such nonverbal behavior as taking the head seat, speaking loudly, staring, touching, and gesturing (R. Kling, personal communication, May, 1983). The opportunity to hear someone's voice or to look him or her in the eye changes how bargains are negotiated or whether any real bargaining occurs (for example, Carnevale, Pruitt and Seilheimer, 1981; Krauss, Apple, Morencz, Wenzel, and Winton, 1981). When using computers to communicate, how will people compensate for the dramaturgical weakness of electronic media? For example, Hiltz and Turoff reported that computer conferees have developed ways of sending computerized screams, hugs, and kisses (in Pollack, 1982, p. D2).

1.4   Few status and position cues

Software for electronic communication is blind with respect to the vertical hierarchy in social relationships and organizations. Once people have electronic access, their status, power, and prestige are communicated neither contextually (the way secretaries and meeting rooms and clothes communicate) nor dynamically (the way gaze, touch, and facial and paralinguistic behavior communicate; Edinger and Patterson, 1983). Thus charismatic and high status people may have less influence, and group members may participate more equally in computer communication.

1.5   Social anonymity

Is electronic communication depersonalizing? Because it uses printed text, without even the texture of paper to lend it individuality, electronic communication tends to seem impersonal. Communicators must imagine their audience, for at a terminal it almost seems as though the computer itself is the audience. Messages are depersonalized, inviting stronger or more uninhibited text and more assertiveness in return. It might be especially hard to communicate liking or intimacy without writing unusually positive text. (At our university, a computer manual warns, 'Sometimes . . . users lose sight of the fact that they are really addressing other people, not the computer.')

1.6   Computing norms and immature etiquette

Because electronic communication was developed and has been used by a distinctive subculture of computing professionals, its norms are infused with that culture's special language (i.e. people talk about 'default' attitudes and 'bogus' assertions) and its implicit rejection of organizational conventionality and 8-hour workdays. In our own university as well as other organizations (Sheil, personal communication, April 1982), people using electronic mail overstep conventional time boundaries dividing office and home; they mix work and personal communications; they use language appropriate for board-rooms and ballfields interchangeably; and they disregard normal conventions of privacy (for instance, by posting personal messages to general bulletin boards). This behavior is not counteracted by established conventions or etiquette for computer communication. There are few shared standards for salutations, for structuring formal versus informal messages, or for adapting content to achieve both impact and politeness. How do people develop a communication network social structure using a technology in cultural transition? Do they import norms from other technologies? Do they develop new norms?

From a social psychological perspective, this list of questions suggests that computer-mediated communication has at least two interesting characteristics: (a) a paucity of social context information and (b) few widely shared norms governing its use. These characteristics may affect communication via computer in at least three areas. First, the lack of social feedback and unpredictable style of messages might make it difficult to coordinate and comprehend messages (Kraut and Lewis, in press). Second, social influence among communicators might become more equal because so much hierarchical dominance and power information is hidden (Edinger and Patterson, 1983). Third, social standards will be less important and communication will be more impersonal and more free because the rapid exchange of text, the lack of social feedback. and the absence of norms governing the social interaction redirect attention away from others and toward the message itself. Indeed, computer-mediated communication seems to comprise some of the same conditions that are important for deindividuation – anonymity, reduced self-regulation, and reduced self-awareness (for example, Diener, 1980; Festinger, Pepitone, and Newcomb, 1952; Forsyth, 1983, pp. 308-38).

This last point deserves some elaboration. Using traditional communication, norms, social standards, and inferences about individuals are made salient by observable social structural artifacts (such as prestige communicated through a person's dress or letterhead) and by communication itself, including nonverbal involvement (Edinger and Patterson, 1983; Patterson, 1982). However, terminals and electronic signals convey fewer historical, contextual, and nonverbal cues. Electronic media do not efficiently communicate nuances of meaning and frame of mind, organizational loyalties, symbolic procedural variations, and, especially, individuating details about people that might be embodied in their dress, location, demeanor, and expressiveness (for example, Ekman, Friesen, O'Sullivan and Scherer, 1980; Mehrabian, 1972). This situation, where personality and culture lack salience, might foster feelings of depersonalization. In addition, using the computer tends to be absorbing and conducive to quick response, which might reduce self-awareness and increase the feeling of being submerged in the machine. Thus, the overall weakening of self, or normative regulation might be similar to what happens when people become less self-aware and submerged in a group, that is, deindividuated (Diener, Lusk, DeFour and Flax, 1980; Scheier, 1976; Scheier and Carver, 1977; Scheier, Carver and Gibbons, 1981).

2   Outcomes of technology use

Most existing discussions of computers focus on the advantages of computer-mediated communication for work: fast and precise information exchange, increased participation in problem solving and decision making, and reduction of 'irrelevant' status and prestige differences (Lancaster, 1978; Linstone and Turoff, 1975; Martino, 1972). This orientation is illustrated by the following:

> The scientific literature will become unified . . . Scientists everywhere will have equal access . . . the advantage of being in a famous center of research will be substantially lessened. Scientists in obscure universities . . . will be able to participate in scientific discourse more readily. (Folk, 1977, p. 80)

Existing social psychological studies do not entirely contradict the forecasts that communicating by computer will increase participation, objectivity, and efficiency of groups and organizations. For example, any communication technology that reduces the importance of status and dominance could increase the likelihood that opinions in groups are sampled more widely. If people who are high in status usually talk most and dominate decision-making (Hoffman, 1978), then computer-mediated communication that de-emphasizes the impact of status also might increase people's consideration of minority views. If minority opinions can enhance performance, then groups could be more effective when using computers to communicate.

On the other hand, equal participation, objectivity, and efficiency sometimes interfere with important group outcomes. To be effective, rather than encouraging equal participation, group members may need to organize themselves by discovering sources of information, deciding who can be depended on, distributing work to these people, and protecting their autonomy (for example, Hackman and Morris, 1978). To be effective, rather than aiming at objectivity, groups may need affective bonds, a status distribution that helps sort out multiple objectives, and a hierarchy that determines influence, even if these behaviors interfere with 'good' decisions (Kelley and Thibaut, 1978; March and Olsen, 1976; Salancik, 1977). For accomplishing these purposes, the social structure provided by roles, norms, and status and reinforced by trust and personal engagement with others is critical.

These ideas suggest that the use of computers for communication will be more complex than is typically envisioned in the computer technology literature. We have speculated that computer-mediated communication will influence group functions involving coordination of discussion, participation and influence of dominant individuals, and normative control. In technical problem solving, then, computer-mediated groups might be disorganized, democratic, unrestrained, and perhaps more creative than groups communicating more traditionally; they might have trouble reaching consensus if the 'correct' answer is not obvious; they might not operate as cool, fast decision makers. What might be the outcome for real groups that have to deal with technical, political, and organizational tasks? Ultimately, it might depend on existing relationships. In computer-linked groups whose members are discontented and in conflict with one another, impersonal behavior might tend to polarize members, exacerbate aggressiveness, and cause negative attributions to others (for example, Gibbons and Wright, 1981; Goldstein, Davis and Herman, 1975; McArthur and Solomon, 1978; Prentice-Dunn and Rogers, 1980). However, in computer-linked groups that are on friendly, cooperative terms, impersonal behavior might actually encourage joint approaches to decision-making or negotiating (see Druckman, 1977; Pruitt and Lewis, 1975), and it could reduce self-consciousness and promote intimacy. Some of our colleagues, for example, notice that their students are more often willing to approach a professor for assistance with assignments or a potential date through electronic mail than in face-to-face encounters (Larkin, personal communication, July 1982; Welsch, 1982).

These speculations must be evaluated empirically. There are no experimental research studies published in scientific journals that focus directly on group behavior in modern computer-mediated communication, such as electronic mail. However, earlier studies of the teletypewriter lend support to the analyses we have presented. Sinaiko's (1963) experiments at the Institute for Defense Analyses indicated that 'teletype quite dramatically depersonalizes negotiations... Differences in initial positions held by negotiators converge more in a face-to-face situation, next by telephone and least when the teletypewriter is the medium of communication' (p. 18). Morley and Stephenson (1969; 1970) found that tasks requiring dependence on interpersonal or interparty considerations interacted strongly with media. Three studies that focused on group processes showed that role differentiation was diminished and more unstable in the computer-mediated cases. Moreover, frequency of participation was most equal in the teletypewriting mode, less equal with audio only, and least equal when subjects were face to face (Krueger, 1976; Strickland, Guild, Barefoot and Patterson, 1975; Williams, 1975a). Communication by teletype was both 'egalitarian' and 'disorganized' (Williams, 1977).

The findings from research on earlier technologies indicate that computer-mediated communication raises some old issues. Technologies that lacked a distinctive etiquette (teletype, for instance) and/or the opportunity to exchange a full range of paralinguistic cues (such as freeze-frame video conferencing) caused special problems for groups. In earlier advances of communication technology, people had to learn how to organize new and disparate pieces of information, and they had to learn how to behave toward one another.

Electronic communication differs from any other communication in time, space, speed, ease of use, fun, audience, and opportunity for feedback. For example, in one firm where someone posted a new product idea on the computer network, the proposition was sent in one minute to 300 colleagues in branches across the country, and, within two days, sufficient replies were received to launch a new long-distance joint project. We do not present this anecdote as though we know its precise significance, but we do mean to argue that computers are different from previous technologies. Research must discover how groups respond to the difference; how, given time, groups work out new communication traditions and rules; and what the requirements of the new communication culture will be. The answers to these questions ultimately will determine the nature of the social revolution embodied in modern communication technologies.

The rest of this article describes one approach to studying the social psychological dimensions of computer-mediated communication. In the following section, we summarize experiments on the effects on groups of simultaneous terminal-to-terminal teleconferencing and of electronic mail. Also we have begun to study underlying processes and to explore questions of external generalizability. The final section summarizes the direction of this work.

3   Studies of participation, choice, and interaction in computer-mediated groups

The purpose of our initial studies (Siegel, Dubrovsky, Kiesler and McGuire, 1983) has been to explore, experimentally, the impact of computer-mediated communication, as used in our own local computer network, on group interaction and decisions. To our knowledge, these are among the first controlled experiments using modern, fast terminals and flexible computer conference and mail software (see also Hiltz, Johnson and Turoff, 1982). We emphasized control over generalizability in the first three experiments, choosing a small group size of three. The subjects were students who had used the computer network previously. Also, we used a group task about which there is considerable knowledge, that is, the Stoner (1961) choice-dilemma problems (see, for example, Dion, Baron and Miller, 1978; Kogan and Wallach, 1964, 1967; Lamm and Kogan, 1970; Vinokur and Burnstein, 1974; Zajonc, 1969). This research was carried out in offices and rooms where terminals were already in use so as to duplicate the actual setting where communication typically takes place.

The first experiment is prototypical of the rest. The study compared three-person groups who were asked to reach consensus on a choice-dilemma problem in three different contexts; once face-to-face, once using the computer anonymously (i.e. not knowing by name who within their group was talking), and once using the computer nonanonymously. In the computer-mediated discussions, each person was separated physically from the others, and each used a computer terminal to communicate. Each group member typed his or her remarks into the computer using a program called 'Converse', which divides the screen into three or more parts and allows messages from different people to appear simultaneously and scroll independently.

The main dependent variables in all of the experiments were (a) communication efficiency, (b) participation, (c) interpersonal behavior, and (d) group choice. We derived hypotheses for the experiments both from our observations of the technology and from the social psychological literature. We tried to examine whether computer communication is depersonalizing and lacking in social structure, and we tried to test our hunches about the implications. Hence, in the first experiment we predicted that participation would be more equal in the computer-mediated communication conditions. We thought that coming to consensus would be more difficult. In carrying out pilot work, we had seen many instances of what appeared to be uninhibited behavior – subjects swearing, individuals shouting at their terminals, and groups refusing to make a group decision until a group member gave in – and as a result we systematically evaluated interpersonal interactions as revealed in the transcripts of both face-to-face and computer-mediated groups. We predicted more uninhibited behavior in computer-mediated groups. Also, we added an anonymous computer-mediated communication condition in order to explore whether not knowing specifically who was talking would increase depersonalization (for example, Williams, Harkins and Latane, 1981).

We hypothesized that choice shift would be greater when people used the computer, generally because norms are weaker and hence, group members might be less likely to simply average initial opinions or obey the initial majority. According to social comparison theory (Brown, 1965; Goethals and Zanna, 1979; Sanders and Baron, 1977) and the persuasive arguments model (Vinokur and Burnstein, 1974, 1978), choice shift may occur in groups because people compare themselves to others with extreme or novel attitudes or because they are exposed to extreme arguments they would not otherwise hear (this assumes most people have moderate initial positions). If people in computer-mediated groups, as compared to face-to-face groups, are party to a broader distribution of opinions (because participation is spread more evenly across opinions) and extreme opinions are less likely to be withheld (because behavior is less inhibited), then we would predict more choice shift in computer-mediated groups.

Our data showed, in all three experiments, that computer-mediated communication had marked effects on communication efficiency, participation, interpersonal behavior, and decision-making.

3.1 Communication efficiency

Three measures bear on communication efficiency: time to decision, number of remarks exchanged, and percentage of discussion remarks about the group choice rather than about extraneous topics (for example, school work). We found that in spite of the fact that messages arrived instantaneously, using a keyboard took time. Computer-mediated groups took longer to reach consensus than did face-to-face groups, and they exchanged fewer remarks in the time allowed them. We think groups in the computer-communication conditions took more time to reach consensus for reasons beyond technical difficulties. They might have had greater difficulties reaching agreement, judging by the vehemence of their arguments. Also, when we asked people to type out remarks that subjects had made face-to-face, we found typing time could not account for all the time taken by computer-mediated groups to reach consensus.

We found that computer-mediated groups were as task oriented as face-to-face groups. This tends to rule out the idea that groups using the computer were inefficient because they were not paying attention to the task. [. . .]

3.2 Participation, group choice, and interpersonal behavior

Based on analyses of who talked and how much they talked (i.e. the distribution of remarks among group members), group members using the computer participated more equally than they did when they talked face to face. Although one person tended to dominate in both face-to-face and computer-mediated interaction, this dominance was less strong in computer-mediated groups.

Computer-mediated groups showed significantly higher choice shift. We do not fully understand this finding. Analyses of the group process (for example, extreme positions taken, use of decision rules such as majority rule or simple averaging, or repeated stating of positions) did not reveal differences in these processes between face-to-face and computer-mediated groups. People in computer-mediated groups used a higher proportion of numeric arguments, but this tendency was uncorrelated with choice shift. Perhaps if communication using the computer was depersonalized, people felt more able to abandon their previous positions or to ignore social pressure to reach consensus.

People in computer-mediated groups were more uninhibited than they were in face-to-face groups as measured by uninhibited verbal behavior, defined as frequency of remarks containing swearing, insults, name calling, and hostile comments. [. . .] Each experiment incorporated different computer communication design features and samples. By varying technical features of the communication programs and changing subject samples, we hoped to address some plausible alternative explanations of our results. Based on these variations we did reach certain conclusions. First, from using trained and practiced subjects in Experiment 2 (and adult managers in our fourth and fifth experiments), we concluded that our findings are generalizable to adults and nonstudents as well as to undergraduate students. Second, from comparing experienced and inexperienced computer network users, we concluded that our results apply not just to novices but also to people who use computers often and for whom electronic mail and message systems as well as simultaneous discussion systems are familiar. Third, we also have compared strangers and friends and obtained similar results.

Is computer-mediated communication simply disorderly, perhaps because there is no constraint on interruptions and distracting remarks? In Experiment 2, Vitaly Dubrovsky (Dubrovsky, Kiesler and Siegel, 1983) devised a technical variation of the simultaneous computer conversation program to see whether imposing procedural order through technical features of the communication medium would increase its similarity to face-to-face communication. He designed a sequential computer conference program that forced group members to take turns speaking and to indicate to others when they wished to interrupt. Hence, the new software allowed only one person to talk at a time, and we compared how groups used this method with how they used the regular simultaneous computer conference program. The most important outcomes of this study were to establish that software developed to control the sequence of interaction is disliked and that it does not necessarily coordinate or control discussions. The effects of the computer-mediated communication programs were equal to those of computer communication in the first experiment.

Experiment 3 was intended primarily to extend the study to electronic mail, which is used extensively in most computer networks. Although electronic mail has some of the same cultural and technical characteristics as simultaneous computer conferences, it does not require communication in real time.

There is time for reflection, for composing one's thoughts, and for side discussions with only part of a group. Hence, we thought it possible that electronic mail would be relatively conflict free and would produce about the same decisions as face-to-face communication. In spite of our expectations, the findings of Experiment 3 were similar to those of the other experiments. However, uninhibited behavior was somewhat higher in the computer conference condition than in the computer mail condition.

How might we explain the results as a whole? There are at least three alternatives, having to do with (a) difficulties of coordination from lack of informational feedback, (b) absence of social influence cues for controlling discussion, and (c) depersonalization from lack of nonverbal involvement and absence of norms. We will consider each briefly. First, we can explain the greater time people took to reach consensus and the evenness of participation rates by pointing to the absence of informational feedback between speakers and listeners in the computer-mediated communication condition. That is, the usual forms of discussion control through back-channel communications (Kraut *et al.*, 1982) could not be exerted. People did not know exactly when their arguments were understood or agreed to, and consequently everyone believed they had to exert more effort to be understood. This explanation, however, does not account for the findings of greater choice shift and uninhibited behavior, except indirectly. Perhaps it was frustrating for people to be discussing a problem inefficiently; they might have become angry and, hence, more extreme in decision making and more uninhibited.

A second explanation of our findings is that in computer communication there is less influence and control of a dominant person, moderator, or leader. Lack of leadership could have caused difficulties in reaching a group decision efficiently. Without leadership, a group might ignore social norms, standards, and precedents, causing both choice shift and uninhibited behavior.

A final explanation for our results is that electronic communication involves a process of depersonalization or a redirection of attention away from one's audience. Suppose computer-mediated communication prevented personal feedback and individuating information and at the same time lacked a shared etiquette and, further, was influenced by norms from the computer subculture. This could have made group members more responsive to immediate textual cues, more impulsive and assertive, and less bound by precedents set by societal norms of how groups should come to consensus. This explanation fits our data. However, we emphasize that our own data do not provide any evidence to distinguish among these tentative and somewhat limited potential explanations.

Another issue with which we must deal is external validity, that is, to what degree our results can be generalized across people and technologies. Based on our own research and anecdotal evidence from reports of computer network behavior, we are relatively sure that our findings apply to a wide sample of both novice and experienced computer users. For example, observers of computer networks have noticed uninhibited behavior for years. In the computer subculture, the word *flaming* refers to the practice of expressing oneself more strongly on the computer than one would in other communication settings. The Defense Communications Agency, which manages the 12-year-old ARPANET, has had to police use of the network bulletin boards by manually screening messages every few days to weed out those deemed in bad taste. Nor is flaming confined to government-sponsored networks. When IBM installed the personal computer in offices and created an internal message system, VNET, to link them, a 'GRIPENET' emerged – organized complaints against management practices and policies whose form and substance deviate considerably from standard IBM culture (Emmett, 1981). Of course, whether this behavior was caused specifically by a lack of shared etiquette, by computer culture norms, or by the impersonal and text-only form of communication is not clear.

We are not so sure how our findings would apply to more sophisticated technologies, say those that include video or audio channels in electronic mail. We suspect that combining telephone with electronic mail in the same facility would decrease the differences between electronic communication and face-to-face communication, if only because the amount of feedback is increased. Based on current trends, text-only electronic communication systems will become more popular. In that case, we should study both their transient effects (those likely to disappear when the technologies are mature) and their more permanent and secondary effects. Judging from our own observations of existing networks, both kinds of change are important. For example, absence of computer etiquette is a transient problem, but it is one that raises significant policy debates over rights of computer users to privacy and freedom of exploration. A more permanent effect might be the extension of participation in group or organizational communication. This is important because it implies more shared information, more equality of influence and, perhaps, a breakdown of social and organizational barriers.

4   Implications for future research

The conceptual framework for studies of computer-mediated communication will develop mainly from studies of social process. These studies will provide either detailed descriptions of behavior or tests of alternative theoretical ideas. In our own laboratory, we have just collected additional data on the process of computer-mediated communication. In one new experiment, we asked business managers and university administrators to use simultaneous computer conferences to reach decisions involving multi-attribute risky choices (Payne and Laughhunn, in press; Tversky and Kahneman, 1981). Preliminary analyses of the decisions and the content of discussions indicate that when the managers used the computer to consider the issues, they were less effective in considering all the issues and coordinating their discussion. The findings suggest that if computer-mediated communication is used by managers to make group decisions, those decisions may differ qualitatively from decisions reached face-to-face.

In another study (Kiesler, Zubrow, Moses and Geller, 1983), we tested whether using a computer to communicate is physiologically arousing or has other affective consequences. In a 2×2 design, we manipulated anxiety (anticipation of evaluation) and computer-mediated versus face-to-face communication in a study of how two people get to know each other. In this study, we measured physiological arousal (pore size and pulse), emotionality, interpersonal attraction, responsiveness to others, self-disclosure, and other aspects of interpersonal communication. Our results suggest that computer-mediated communication is not physiologically arousing. Once again we discovered more uninhibited behavior when people communicated using the computer. We also found that although people felt more embarrassed meeting one another face-to-face, they ended up liking each other better. Because other research suggests that gaze, smiling, and other nonverbal feedback is important to establish attraction (Scherer, 1974), our data does support our hypothesis that the lack of nonverbal involvement is a critical dimension of electronic communication.

Much more work on affective and cognitive dimensions of computer-mediated communication is needed to understand the issues we raised earlier. For example, further studies of affective responses may establish whether absorption in computer messages is arousing (see Zajonc, 1965), why users are sometimes aggressive (see Goldstein et al., 1975), whether attention is submerged in messages (see McArthur and Solomon, 1978), and under what conditions people will be uninhibited (see Zillman, Bryant, Cantor and Day, 1975). The research could build on recent studies of affect in social cognition (for example, Isen, Shalker, Clark and Karp, 1978) that show how mood and emotion are connected to information processing, memory, and overt behavior using computers.

In addition to identifying behavioral dimensions of computer-mediated communications, research could reveal more about fundamental group processes, both inside and outside of computer-mediated settings. For example, social norms play a critical role in models of group decision making developed by Davis and his colleagues (for example, Davis, 1973). According to these models, changing the potential for normative influence, such as reducing face-to-face contact, changes the influence function (Stasser and Davis, 1981, p. 544). Because computers appear to alter the operation of normative influences, studies of computer-mediated decision-making might contribute to our understanding of these and other models in social psychology that invoke group pressure, persuasion, and affectively relevant processes.

The potential for developing important organizational applications from social psychological studies of computer-mediated communication is also high. One avenue of development will be experimental research that suggests new ways to use computers in education (Lepper, 1982), public affairs, and mental health. It might be possible to turn computer networks into social support networks. Second, it might be possible, through experimental research, to establish the feasibility of using electronic communication for surveys, questionnaires, and interactive polling. A group at our university is carrying out what we believe are among the first controlled experiments on using the computer to collect survey data (Kiesler and Sproull, 1984).

Finally, quasi-experimental and field studies of networks will suggest applications for long-distance collaborative work and management. For example, geographically dispersed groups of scientists and their students are currently working to develop a common computer language (Common LISP) for artificial intelligence research. The groups have used electronic mail via ARPANET with everyone participating rather than forming committees and meeting face to face (Maddox, 1982). Reportedly, electronic mail was used during one year to discuss some 232 issues. About 150 of these issues were resolved before participants came to any face-to-face meeting. Most technical questions were resolved by someone in the group communicating a solution through the network. However, questions of style, for example, about programming conventions or systems architecture, evoked conflict and flaming on the computer. These matters had to be resolved by a mediator (appointed by the groups to organize the project) or in face-to-face meetings. Nonetheless, participants in the project report they have made more progress and acquired the active contribution of many more scientists by using the network. Their experience suggests that long-distance computer-mediated group problem solving could have many useful applications. Hiltz (1984) discussed many other instances of long-distance collaboration using the experimental Electronic Information Exchange System (EIES).

Although the social responses to computer-mediated communication described in this article occur in the situation in which the communication takes place, readers should not carry away the impression that all of the social implications are short term. Some effects, such as increased lateral communication in an organization or reduction in clerical staff, might develop over a long period through the actions and attitudes of many people (Hough and Panko, 1977). Others have examined organizational effects of computers generally (Boguslaw, 1981; Danziger, Dutton, Kling and Kraemer, 1982; Whisler, 1970). Our aim has not been to delineate any particular social impact but to suggest, using our work as an example, the significance of understanding the broad range of social implications of computerization. Much of this work belongs in the field of social psychology, although the line between social psychology and other areas of psychology and social science is tenuous and arbitrary. Actually, studies of behavioral and social processes in computer-mediated communication (indeed of all computing) will be carried out best as an interdisciplinary effort.

References

Boguslaw, R. (1981) *The New Utopians: A Study of System Design and Social Change* (2nd ed.). New York: Irvington.

Brown, R. (1965) *Social Psychology*. New York: Free Press.

Carnevale, P. J. E., Pruitt, D. G. and Seilheimer, S.D. (1981) 'Looking and competing: Accountability and visual access in integrative bargaining', *Journal of Personality and Social Psychology*, 40. pp. 111-20.

Danziger, J. N., Dutton, W. H., Kling, R. and Kraemer, K. L. (1982) *Computers and Politics: High Technology in American Local Governments.* New York: Columbia University Press.

Davis, J. H. (1973) 'Group decision and social interaction: A theory of social decision schemes', *Psychological Review, 80.* pp. 97-125.

Diener, E. (1980) 'Deindividuation: The absence of self-awareness and self-regulation in group members' in P. Paulus (ed.). *The Psychology of Group Influence* (pp. 209-42). Hillsdale, NJ: Erlbaum.

Diener, E., Lusk, R., DeFour, D. and Flax, R. (1980) 'Deindividuation: Effects of group size, density, number of observers, and group member similarity on self-consciousness and disinhibited behavior'. *Journal of Personality and Social Psychology, 39.* pp. 449-59.

Dion, K. L., Baron, R. S. and Miller, N. (1978) 'Why do groups make riskier decisions than individuals?' in L. Berkowitz (ed.) *Group Processes* (pp. 227-

99). New York: Academic Press.

Druckman, D. (1977) *Negotiations: Social-psychological Perspectives.* London: Sage.

Dubrovsky, V., Kiesler, S. and Siegel, J. (1983, October) *Human Factors in Computer-mediated Communication.* Paper presented at the meeting of the Human Factors Society, Baltimore, MD.

Edinger, J. A. and Patterson, M. L. (1983) 'Nonverbal involvement and social control', *Psychological Bulletin, 93.* pp. 30-56.

Ekman, P., Friesen, W. V., O'Sullivan, M. and Scherer, K. (1980) 'Relative importance of face, body, and speech in judgments of personality and affect', *Journal of Personality and Social Psychology, 38.* pp. 270-7.

Emmett, R. (1981, November) 'VNET or GRIPENET?', *Datamation*, pp. 48-58.

Festinger, L., Pepitone, A. and Newcomb, T.(1952) 'Some consequences of deindividuation in a group', *Journal of Abnormal and Social Psychology, 47.* pp. 382-9.

Folk, H. (1977) 'The impact of computers on book and journal publication' in J. L. Divilbiss (ed.) *The Economics of Library Automation: Proceedings of the 1976 Clinic on Library Applications of Data Processing* (pp. 72-82). Urbana, IL: University of Illinois Graduate School of Science.

Forsyth, D. R. (1983) *An Introduction to Group Dynamics.* Monterey, CA: Brooks/Cole.

Gibbons, F. X. and Wright, R. A. (1981) 'Motivational biases in causal attributions of arousal', *Journal of Personality and Social Psychology, 40*, pp. 588-600.

Goethals, G. R. and Zanna, M. P. (1979) 'The role of social comparison in choice shifts', *Journal of Personality and Social Psychology. 37.* pp. 1469-76.

Goldstein, J. H., Davis, R. W. and Herman, D. (1975) 'Escalation of aggression: Experimental studies', *Journal of Personality and Social Psychology, 31*, pp. 162-70.

Hackman, J. R. and Morris, C. G. (1978) 'Group tasks, group interaction process, and group performance effectiveness: A review and proposed integration', in L. Berkowitz (ed.) *Group Processes* (pp. 1-55). New York: Academic Press.

Hiltz, S. R. (1984) *Online Scientific Communities: A Case Study of the Office of the Future.* Norwood, NJ: Ablex Press.

Hiltz, S. R., Johnson, K. and Turoff. M. (1982) *The Effects of Formal Human Leadership and Computer-generated Decision Aids on Problem Solving Via Computer: A Controlled Experiment* (Report No. 18). Newark, New Jersey Institute of Technology.

Hoffman, L. R. (1978) 'The group problem-solving process', in L. Berkowitz (ed.) *Group Processes* (pp. 101-2). New York: Academic Press.

Hough, R. W. and Panko, R. R. (1977) *Teleconferencing Systems: A State-of-the-art Survey and Preliminary Analysis* (National Science Foundation Report No. RA 770103, PB268455). Washington, DC: National Science Foundation.

Isen, A. M., Shalker, T. E., Clark, M. and Karp, L. (1978) 'Affect, accessibility of material in memory, and behavior: A cognitive loop?' *Journal of Personality and Social Psychology, 36*, pp. 1-12.

Janis, I. L. (1972) *Victims of Groupthink*. Boston: Houghton Mifflin.

Kelley, H. H. and Thibaut, J. W. (1978) *Interpersonal Relations*. New York: Wiley.

Kiesler, S. and Sproull, L. (1984) *Response Effects in the Electronic Survey*. Unpublished manuscript. Carnegie-Mellon University, Pittsburgh, PA.

Kiesler, S., Zubrow, D., Moses A. and Geller, V. (1983) *Affect in Computer-mediated Communication*. Manuscript submitted for publication.

Kogan, N. and Wallach, M. A. (1964) *Risk Taking: A Study in Cognition and Personality*. New York: Holt, Rinehart & Winston.

Krauss, R. M., Apple, W., Morencz, N., Wenzel, C. and Winton, W. (1981) 'Verbal, vocal, and visible factors in judgments of another's affect', *Journal of Personality and Social Psychology, 40*, pp. 312-20.

Kraut, R. E. and Lewis, S. H. (in press) 'Some functions of feedback in conversation' in H. Applegate and J. Sypher (eds) *Understanding Interpersonal Communication: Social, Cognitive, and Strategic Processes in Children and Adults*. Beverly Hills, CA: Sage.

Kraut, R. E., Lewis, S. H. and Swezey, L. W. (1982) 'Listener responsiveness and the coordination of conversation', *Journal of Personality and Social Psychology, 43*, pp. 718-31.

Krueger, G. P. (1976) *Teleconferencing in the Communication Modes as a Function of the Number of Conferees*. Unpublished doctoral dissertation, Johns Hopkins University, Baltimore, MD.

Lamm, H. and Kogan, N. (1970) 'Risk-taking in the context of intergroup negotiations', *Journal of Experimental Social Psychology. 6*. pp. 351-63.

Lancaster, F. W. (1978) *Toward Paperless Information Systems*. New York: Academic Press.

Lepper, M. R. (1982, August) *Microcomputers in Education: Motivational and Social Issues*. Paper presented at the 90th annual convention of the American Psychological Association, Washington, DC.

Linstone, H. A., and Turoff, M. (eds) (1975) *The Delphi Method: Techniques and Applications*. Reading, MA: Addison-Wesley.

Maddox, W. (1982) *Computer Communication in the Carnegie-Mellon University Spice Project*. Unpublished report, Carnegie-Mellon University, Pittsburgh, PA.

March, J. G. and Olsen, J. P. (1976) *Ambiguity and Choice in Organizations*. Bergen, Norway: Universitetsforlaget.

Martino, J. P. (1972) *Technological Forecasting for Decisionmaking*. New York: American Elsevier.

McArthur, L. Z. and Solomon, L. K. (1978) 'Perceptions of an aggressive encounter as a function of the victim's salience and the perceiver's arousal', *Journal of Personality and Social Psychology, 36*, pp. 1278-90.

Mehrabian, A. (1972) *Nonverbal Communication*. Chicago: Aldine.

Morley, L. E. and Stephenson, G. M. (1969) 'Interpersonal and interparty exchange: A laboratory simulation of an industrial negotiation at the plant level', *British Journal of Psychology, 60*, pp. 543-5.

Morley, L. E. and Stephenson, G. M. (1970) 'Formality in experimental negotiations: A validation study', *British Journal of Psychology, 61*, pp. 383-4.

Patterson, M. L. (1982) 'A sequential functional model of nonverbal exchange', *Psychological Review, 89*, pp. 231-49.

Payne, J. W. and Laughhunn, D. J. (in press) 'Multiattribute risky choice behavior: The editing of complex prospects', *Management Science.*

Pollack, A. (1982, May 27) 'Technology: Conference by computer', *New York Times,* p. D2.

Prentice-Dunn, S. and Rogers, R. W. (1980) 'Effects of deindividuating situational cues and aggressive models on subjective deindividuation and aggression', *Journal of Personality and Social Psychology, 39,* pp. 104-13.

Pruitt, D. G. and Lewis, S.A. (1975) 'Development of integrative solutions in bilateral negotiations', *Journal of Personality and Social Psychology, 31,* pp. 621-33.

Salancik, G. R. (1977) 'Commitment and the control of organizational behavior and belief', in B. M. Staw and G. R. Salancik (eds) *New Directions in Organizational Behavior* (pp. 1-54). Chicago: St Clair Press.

Sanders, G. and Baron, R. S. (1977) 'Is social comparison irrelevant for producing choice shifts?', *Journal of Experimental Social Psychology, 13,* pp. 303-14.

Scheier, M. F. (1976) 'Self-awareness, self-consciousness, and angry aggression', *Journal of Personality, 44,* pp. 627-44.

Scheier, M. F. and Carver, C. S. (1977) 'Self-focused attention and the experience of emotion: Attraction, repulsion, elation, and depression', *Journal of Personality and Social Psychology, 35,* pp. 625-36.

Scheier, M. F., Carver, C. S. and Gibbons, F. X. (1981) 'Self-focused attention and reactions to fear', *Journal of Research in Personality, 15,* pp. 1-15.

Scherer, S. E. (1974) 'Influence of proximity and eye contact on impression formation', *Perceptual and Motor Skills, 38,* pp. 538.

Short, J., Williams, E and Christie, B. (1976) *The Social Psychology of Telecommunications.* London: John Wiley & Sons.

Siegel, J., Dubrovsky, V., Kiesler, S. and McGuire, T. (1983) *Group Processes in Computer-mediated Communications.* Manuscript submitted for publication.

Sinaiko, H. W. (1963) *Teleconferencing: Preliminary Experiments* (Research Paper P-108). Arlington, VA: Institute for Defense Analyses.

Sproull, L., Kiesler, S. and Zubrow, D. (in press) 'Encountering the alien culture', *Social Issues.*

Stasser, F. and Davis, J. H. (1981) 'Group decision making and social influence: A social interaction sequence model', *Psychological Review, 88,* pp. 523-51.

Stockton, W. (1981, June 28) 'The technology race', *New York Times Magazine.* p. 14.

Stoner, J. (1961) *A Comparison of Individual and Group Decisions Including Risk.* Unpublished master's thesis, School of Industrial Management, Massachusetts Institute of Technology.

Strickland, L. H., Guild, P. D., Barefoot, J. R. and Patterson, S. A. (1975) *Teleconferencing and Leadership Emergence.* Unpublished manuscript, Carleton University, Ottawa, Canada.

Tversky, A. and Kahneman, D. (1981) 'The framing of decisions and the psychology of choice', *Science, 211,* pp. 453-8.

Vinokur, A. and Burnstein, E. (1974) 'The effects of partially shared persuasive arguments in group-induced shifts: A group problem-solving approach', *Journal of Personality and Social Psychology, 29*, pp. 305-15.

Vinokur, A. and Burnstein, E. (1978) 'Novel argumentation and attitude change: The case of polarization following group discussion', *European Journal of Social Psychology, 8*, pp, 335-48.

Welsch, L. A. (1982) 'Using electronic mail as a teaching tool', *Communications of the ACM, 23*, pp. 105-8.

Whisler, T. L. (1970) *The Impact of Computers on Organizations*. New York: Praeger.

Williams, E. (1975a) *The Effectiveness of Person-to-person Telecommunications Systems Research at the Communications Studies Group* (University College, Long Range Research Report 3, Reference No. LRRR 003/ ITF). (Available from Communications Studies Group, Wates House, 22 Gordon Street, London, WC1H 0QB, England.)

Williams, E. (1977) 'Experimental comparisons of face-to-face and mediated communication: A review', *Psychological Bulletin, 84*, pp. 963-76.

Williams, K., Harkins, S. and Latane, B. (1981) 'Identifiability as a deterrent to social loafing: Two cheering experiments', *Journal of Personality and Social Psychology, 40*, pp. 310-11.

Zajonc, R. (1965) 'Social facilitation', *Science, 149*, pp. 269-74.

Zajonc, R. (1969) 'Group risk-taking in a two-choice situation: Replication, extension, and a model', *Journal of Experimental Social Psychology, 5*, pp. 127-40.

Zillman, D., Bryant, J., Cantor, J. R. and Day, K. D. (1975) 'Irrelevance of mitigating circumstances in retaliatory behavior at high levels of excitation', *Journal of Research in Personality, 9*, pp. 282-93.

17

Computers and the Human Spirit

Sherry Turkle

1 Introduction

The schoolbook history of new technologies concentrates on the practical. In these accounts, the telescope led to the discovery of new stars, the railroad to the opening of new territories. But there is another history whose consequences are deep and far-reaching. A new sense of the earth's place in the solar system made it necessary to rethink our relation to God; the ability to cross a continent within days meant a new notion of distance and communication. Clocks brought more than the ability to measure time precisely; they made time into something 'divisible' and abstract.[1] Time was no longer what it took to get a job done. Time was no longer tied to the movement of the sun or the moon or to the changing of a season. Time was what it took for hands to move on a mechanism. With digital timekeeping devices, our notion of time is once more being touched by technical changes. Time is made more abstract still. Time is no longer a process; time is information.

Technology catalyses changes not only in what we do but in how we think. It changes people's awareness of themselves, of one another, of their relationship with the world. The new machine that stands behind the flashing digital signal, unlike the clock, the telescope, or the train, is a machine that 'thinks'. It challenges our notions not only of time and distance, but of mind.

Most considerations of the computer concentrate on the 'instrumental computer', on what work the computer will do. But my focus here is on something different, on the 'subjective computer'. This is the machine as it enters into social life and psychological development, the computer as it affects the way that we think, especially the way we think about ourselves. I believe that what fascinates me is the unstated question that lies behind much of our preoccupation with the computer's capabilities. That question is not what will the computer be like in the future, but instead, what will *we* be like? What kind of people are we becoming?

Most considerations of the computer describe it as rational, uniform, constrained by logic. I look at the computer in a different light, not in terms of its nature as an 'analytical engine', but in terms of its 'second nature' as an evocative object, an object that fascinates, disturbs equanimity, and precipitates thought. [. . .] .

These efforts to capture the impact of the computer on people involve me in a long-standing debate about the relationship between technology and culture. At one pole there is 'technological determinism', the assertion that technology itself has a determinative impact, that understanding a technology allows us to predict its effects. 'What does television do to children?' The question assumes that television, independent of its content or its social context, has an effect, for example that it creates a passive viewer, or that it breaks down the linear way of thinking produced by the printed word. At the opposite pole is the idea that the influence of a technology can be understood only in terms of the meanings people give it. What does it come to represent? How is it woven into a web of other representations, other symbols?[2]

My method, attentive to the detail of specific relationships with computers as they take place within cultures, provides a kind of evidence that undermines both extreme positions. Technological determinism is certainly wrong: there can be no simple answer to the question, 'What is the effect of the computer on how people think?' As we shall see, computers evoke rather than determine thinking. The consequences of interaction with them are dramatically different for different people. But the idea that what is changing is 'all in the mind' does not hold up, either. The impact of the computer is constrained by its physical realities. One such reality is the machine's physical opacity. If you open a computer or a computer toy, you see no gears that turn, no levers that move, no tubes that glow. Most often, you see some wires and one black chip. Children faced with wires and a chip, and driven by their need to ask how things work, can find no simple physical explanation. Even with considerable sophistication, the workings of the computer present no easy analogies with objects or processes that came before, except for analogies with people and their mental processes. In the world of children and adults, the physical opacity of this machine encourages it to be talked about and thought about in psychological terms.

In my interviews I heard discourse about computers being used to think about free will and determinism, about consciousness and intelligence. We shall see that this is not surprising from a philosophical point of view. But I was not talking to philosophers. I was talking to sophomores in high-school computer clubs, five year olds playing with computer games and toys, college freshmen taking their first programming course, engineers in industrial settings, and electronics hobbyists who had recently switched from building model trains to building computers from kits. In this book I report on interviews with over four hundred people, about half of them children and half of them adults. The computer brought many of them to talk about things they might otherwise not have discussed. It provided a descriptive language that gave them the means to do so. The computer has become an 'object-to-think-with'.[3] It brings philosophy into everyday life.

For children, a computer toy that steadily wins at tic-tac-toe can spark questions about consciousness and intention. For adults, such primitive machines do not have this power. Since almost everyone knows a mechanical strategy for playing tic-tac-toe, the game can easily be brought under the reassuring dictum that 'machines do only what they are programmed to do'. Tic-tac-toe computers are not metaphysically 'evocative objects' for adults.

But other computers are. Conversations about computers that play chess, about robotics, about computers that might display judgement, creativity, or which lead to heated discussions of the limits of machines and the uniqueness of the human mind. In the past, this debate has been carried on in academic circles, among philosophers, cognitive psychologists, and researchers working on the development of intelligent machines. The growing computer presence has significantly widened the circle of debate. It is coming to include us all.

Steve is a college sophomore, an engineering student who had never thought much about psychology. In the first month of an introductory computer-science course he saw how seemingly intelligent and autonomous systems could be programmed. This led him to the idea that there might be something illusory in his own subjective sense of autonomy and self-determination.

Steve's classmate Paul had a very different reaction. He too came to ask whether free will was illusory. The programming course was his first brush with an idea that many other people encounter through philosophy, theology, or psychoanalysis: the idea that the conscious ego might not be a free agent. Having seen this possibility, he rejected it, with arguments about free will and the irreducibility of people's conscious sense of themselves. In his reaction to the computer, Paul made explicit a commitment to a concept of his own nature to which he had never before felt the need to pay any deliberate attention. For Paul, the programmed computer became the very antithesis of what it is to be human. The programmed computer became part of Paul's identity as not-computer.

Paul and Steve disagree. But their disagreement is really not about computers. It is about determinism and free will. At different points in history this same debate has played on different stages. Traditionally a theological issue, in the first quarter of this century it was played out in the debate about psychoanalysis. In the last quarter of this century it looks as though it is going to be played out in the debate about machines.

The analogy with psychoanalysis goes further. For several generations, popular language has been rich in terms borrowed from psychoanalysis, terms like 'repression', 'the unconscious', 'the Oedipus complex' and, of course, 'the Freudian slip'. These ideas make a difference in how people think about their pasts, their presents, and their possibilities for change. They influence people who have never seen a psychoanalyst, who scarcely understand Freudian theory, and who are thoroughly skeptical about its 'truth'. So, when we reflect on the social impact of psychoanalysis, it makes more sense to speak of the development of a psychoanalytic culture than to talk about the truth of particular psychoanalytic ideas.[4] What fueled the development of a psychoanalytic culture is not the validity of psychoanalysis as a science, but the power of its psychology of everyday life. Freud's theory of dreams, jokes, puns, and slips allows people to take it up as a fascinating plaything. The theory is evocative. It gives people new ways to think about themselves. Interpreting dreams and slips allows us all to have contact with taboo preoccupations, with our sexuality, our aggression, our unconscious wishes.

My interpretation of the computer's cultural impact rests on its ability to do something of the same sort. For me, one of the most important cultural effects of the computer presence is that the machines are entering into our thinking about ourselves. If behind popular fascination with Freudian theory there was a nervous, often guilty preoccupation with the self as sexual, behind increasing interest in computational interpretations of mind is an equally nervous preoccupation with the idea of self as machine.

The debate about artificial intelligence has centered on the question 'Will machines think like people?' For our nascent computer culture another question is more relevant: not whether machines will ever think like people, but whether people have always thought like machines. And if the latter is true, is this the most important thing about us? Is this what is most essential about being human? [...]

2   Personal computers with personal meanings

Children use the computer in their process of world and identity construction. They use it for the development of fundamental conceptual categories, as a medium for the practice of mastery, and as a malleable material for helping forge their sense of themselves. The computer is a particularly rich and varied tool for serving so wide a range of purposes. It enters into children's process of becoming and into the development of their personalities and ways of looking at the world. It finds many points of attachment with the process of growing up. Children in a computer culture are touched by the technology in ways that set them apart from the generations that have come before.

Adults are more settled. In the worst of cases, they are locked into roles, afraid of the new, and protective of the familiar. Even when they are open to change, established ways of thinking act as a braking force on the continual questioning so characteristic of children. Family and work responsibilities and the very real constraints of social class can make it too risky to cast doubt on certainties. But there are events and objects that cause the taken-for-granted to be wrestled with anew. The computer is one of these provocations to reflection. Among a wide range of adults, getting involved with computers opens up long-closed questions. It can stimulate them to reconsider ideas about themselves and can provide a basis for thinking about large and puzzling philosophical issues.

Of course, this doesn't happen for everyone. Some people are intimidated by computers and keep their distance. Others see them merely 'as a tool' and assimilate them into their nine-to-five life. But within the world of home computer owners, within the world of virtuoso programmers known as 'hackers', and within the world of artificial intelligence experts, a community dedicated to the enterprise of building 'thinking machines' and computational theories of mind, people have taken up the computer in ways that signal the development of something new. The 'something new' takes many different forms. A relationship with a computer can influence people's conceptions of themselves, their jobs, their relationships with other people, and with their ways of thinking about social processes. It can be the basis for new aesthetic values, new rituals, new philosophy, new cultural forms.[5]

In this chapter on personal computer owners I put the emphasis on these developments by focusing on the role of the computer as a catalyst of culture formation. What joined the first generation of personal computer owners into a culture was not only that they used the same hardware, read the same magazines, and attended similarly organized users' groups, but also, as I learned, something else. They shared a quality of relationship with the computer, an aesthetic of using the computer for transparent understanding. In this chapter I show how, despite important changes in personal computers themselves, in the kinds of people who are buying them, and the uses to which they are being put, this issue of transparent understanding remains an important theme for a new generation's relationship with their machines.

2.1   The birth of a personal computer culture

In 1975 the popular symbol of 'the computer' was the IBM card, a fragile object – 'Do not fold, spindle, or bend' – an object that was to be fed into a large machine owned by a bank, a corporation, a research institution. As this book goes to press, another image dominates public awareness: a person, intense and concentrated, hunched over the keyboard of a small computer with an interactive screen display.

In 1975 the most common complaints about the computer were about billing errors ('the computer did it') and lost airplane reservations ('the computer is down'). The threat from the computer was the threat from the impersonal system that knew you only as a number. Now the threat seems all too personal, captured in the fear that a child or a spouse will get 'hooked' and become addicted to a machine.

1975 was a watershed year. Until then the number of people who kept a personally owned computer in their homes could not have exceeded a few score. Then quite suddenly things changed. A small company named MITS announced a kit for $420 containing everything one would need to build a small computer. It was called the Altair, and it started a revolution. Within a year thousands of people had bought the Altair or the spate of products that quickly followed to fill the growing demand for kits, for parts, and for ready-made small machines. Within a year thousands of people had joined computer clubs and subscribed to personal computer magazines. Within five years the number had climbed into the millions.

From the beginning, most promotional literature and popular accounts of home computer use emphasized the instrumental: how computers could teach French or help with financial planning and taxes. But from the beginning it was clear that this utilitarian rhetoric was not the source of the real excitement. I spoke at length to members of that first generation of personal computer owners, the people who bought and built small computers in the late 1970s. Some justified their purchase of a personal computer by referring to a specific job – monitoring a home heating system, keeping records for a small business, establishing an inventory for a kitchen or a toolroom – but in most cases they also described a point at which their sense of engagement with the computer had shifted to the non-instrumental. They spoke about 'cognitive play' and 'puzzle solving', about the 'beauty of understanding a system at many levels of complexity'. They described what they did with their computers with phrases such as 'building another room in my mind'. Once people actually had a computer in their home, the most interesting thing about it became the computer itself, not for what it might do, but for how it made them feel.

We saw that computers can broaden children's sense of their talents and possibilities. Computers can do something of the same sort for adults who have more entrenched ideas about what they can and cannot do, their aptitudes and ineptitudes. Many people think of themselves as incapable of doing anything technical or mathematical, and learn from their interactions with a personal computer that this simply isn't true.[...]

The computer is Janus-like – it has two faces. Marx spoke of a distinction between tools and machines.[6] Tools are extensions of their users; machines impose their own rhythm, their rules, on the people who work with them, to the point where it is no longer clear who or what is being used. We work to the rhythms of machines – physical machines or the bureaucratic machinery of corporate structures, the 'system'. We work at rhythms that we do not experience as our own. What is most striking in the story of the revolution that began with the Altair personal computer is that for many people the computer at home becomes a tool that compensates for the ravages of the machine at work. [...]

2.2   Personal computers and personal politics

When personal computers were first introduced they were most accessible to people [...] whose work experiences prepared them to use the machines (with the early models this took considerable technical expertise) and gave them a desire to exploit the machines' potential for creating worlds of transparency and intelligibility. There is something else notable about the introduction of personal computers; they came on the scene at a time of dashed hopes for making politics open and participatory. Personal computers were small, individually owned, and when linked through networks over telephone lines they could be used to bring people together. Everything was in place for the development of a politically charged culture around them.[7]

The computer clubs that sprang up all over the country were imbued with excitement not only about the computers themselves, but about new kinds of social relationships people believed woud follow in their wake. Of course there was talk about new hardware, new ideas for programming and circuit design. But there was also talk about the rebirth of ideas from the sixties, in which, instead of food cooperatives, there would be 'knowledge cooperatives'; instead of encounter groups, computer networks; and instead of relying on friends and neighbors to know what was happening, there would be 'community memories' and electronic bulletin boards. Computers, long a symbol of depersonalization, were recast as 'tools for conviviality' and 'dream machines'. Computers, long a symbol of the power of the 'big' – big corporations, big institutions, big money – began to acquire an image as instruments for decentralization, community, and personal autonomy.

Personal computers have entered the American consciousness as a new variation on the Horatio Alger story – the story of Steve Jobs and Steve Wozniak beginning with a machine in a garage and turning it into the Apple computer corporation. But in the late 1970s another mythology was also born, as resonant of the 1960s as Horatio Alger was of an earlier period: build a cottage industry that will allow you to work out of your home, to have more personal autonomy, more time for family and the out-of-doors. [...]

When in the 1960s social critic Ivan Illich searched for an image of how people could have direct access to each other – for learning, for teaching, for bypassing traditional hierarchies – he came up with a giant telephone directory and switchboard. A decade later, personal computers linked on networks provided new technical images to support such aspirations.

There was talk of harnessing computer power for networks and 'knowledge co-ops'. Some people joined with others to try to make it happen. Most did not. The more usual way in which the machine became associated with anti-establishment politics was due to a vague sense that the computer in the basement, living room, or kitchen was a window onto a future where relationships with all technology would be more immediate, where people would understand how things work, and where dependence on big government, big corporations, and big machines would end. But this vague sense did not come only from the idea that the small, personally owned computer could be of practical help in creating new political networks and decentralized information resources. Something else, less instrumental, more subjective, was at work. As the first-generation personal computer culture grew, a particular style of working with the machine evolved, and the style itself was used as a political metaphor. People imagined a computer-rich future by generalizing from their special style of relationship with home computers, a style which, as we shall see, was characterized by transparency, simplicity, and a sense of control.

For some people the railroad signifies progress; for others it signifies the rape of nature. But either way, if you want to use the railroad, you have only one choice. You buy a ticket, get on the train, and let it take you to your destination. This is not true of every technology, and with the computer it is not the case at all. [...]

The men and women I am writing about here also used the computer as an 'object-to-think-with'. But here the computer experience was used to think about more than oneself. It was used to think about society, politics, and education. A particular experience of the machine – only one of the experiences that the machine offers – became a building block for a culture whose values centered around clarity, transparency, and involvement with the whole. Images of computational transparency were used to suggest political worlds where relations of power would not be veiled, where people might control their destinies, where work would facilitate a rich intellectual life. Relationships with a computer became the depository of longings for a better, simpler, and more coherent life. Understandings in the realm of personal computers were contrasted with more diffuse understandings elsewhere. [...]

But this tone of 'pleasing populism' in the early personal computer culture was not itself unproblematic. The satisfactions that the computer offers are essentially private. People will not change unresponsive governments or intellectually deadening work through an involvement, however satisfying, with a computer in the den. They will not change the world of human relations by retreating into the world of things. There is a tension here. It would certainly be inappropriate to rejoice at the 'holistic' relationships that personal computers offer if it turns out that they serve as a kind of opiate. One thing is certain: for the technical hobbyists of that first generation, part of what made the personal computer satisfying was that it felt like a compensation for dissatisfactions in the world of politics and the world of work.

Understanding how the computer can be used in this way requires that we step back and look once again at styles of programming. The 'hard masters' among children demanded control. But here, for this community of adults, something new is added to the desire for control. Intellectual fragmentation at work and the complexity and smokescreens of political life create new pressures, and with them a desire to find transparent understanding *somewhere*. In contrasting hard and soft mastery, the issue was planning versus the pleasures of negotiation. Here another contrast is needed: risk versus reassurance.[8]

2.3   Risk and reassurance

At Indianapolis, cars zoom by in the hands of master drivers highly tuned and sensitized to the machines' response. Yet many of these drivers end up in fatal crashes. By contrast, there is another kind of automotive mastery, where pride comes from detailed knowledge of cars to help insure family safety. There is mastery in the service of the desire to operate just on the edge of disaster, and there is mastery to feel safe. Cars can kill. Computers don't. But here too there are safe programmers and 'racing-car' programmers, those who pursue risk and those who avoid it.

Risk and reassurance can be played out in programming because the computer presents two possibilities to the programmer: there is the 'local simplicity' of the line-by-line program and there is the global complexity of the dynamic processes that can emerge when the program is run. Locally, each step in a program is easy to understand; its effects are well defined. But the evolution of the global pattern is not always graspable. As soon as a program reaches a certain level of logical complexity, its behavior is no longer predictable by its programmer in any simple sense. One is dealing with a system that surprises. Depending on how the programmer brings local simplicity and global complexity into focus, he or she will have a view of the machine as completely understandable and under control or as mysterious and unpredictable, even fraught with risk. By concentrating on the local, the line-by-line, you feel in control. By concentrating on the global, you see control slip away and can then feel the exhilaration of bringing it back. [...]

Preferences in programming language and programming style are building blocks in the construction of computer cultures, in this case the culture of the first-generation hobbyist and the hacker. One might see the differences among computer cultures as expressions of differences in the typical styles of their members' personalities. For example, the incipient hacker might spend time with other hackers because of shared personality traits such as a need to assert control that is so strong, so absolute, that it can be expressed only in relation to things. But once in their company, he or she becomes integrated into a community that amplifies whatever shared features of personality brought its members together. What might have begun as an expression of individual personality develops into a social reality. [...]

2.4   The next generation

Technical hobbyists dominated the early personal computer culture: they gave that early culture a certain coherency and supported one of its dominant themes, the computer as a way to counteract feelings of political alienation and discontent in the workplace. The people who are buying their first personal computer in the 1980s are buying a different machine than was available to the first generation of owners. They are not coming to the computer during a time of heightened political awareness. And for the most part, they are not technical people.

When the personal computers first appeared, nontechnical people were intimidated and kept their distance. 'Computers' continued to be the electronic teller at the bank, the data-retrieval system at the office, the word processor on the secretary's desk. But increasingly, the computer became less compartmentalized. Millions of Americans brought them into their homes, encouraged by the increasing availability, reliability, and now portability of the machines, and encouraged, too, by their decreasing cost.[9]

Their interest is being elicited. They are inundated by articles in magazines and images on television telling them that they need a personal computer. And they believe it, even if they don't know why. Computers are being marketed by associating them with new, appealing images. For example, from the beginning, Apple had an image of being a counterculture computer. Its name and its logo suggest nature and simplicity. When IBM came into the field, it sensed the need for a strong symbol to break away from its Brooks Brothers image. Its promotions made an icon of anti-technological innocence into the trademark of its personal computer: the Charlie Chaplin tramp, Charlot with a rose.

Beyond being sold as an 'anti-technology technology,' personal computers are being presented as a technology for the young, the chic, the successful, who build their own companies and make their own schedules.

Onto such complex and ambivalent images manufacturers project more concrete promises as well: the machine will help Father with his finances, Mother with her writing, the children with their schoolwork. The machine is presented as a way of asserting status, a way of saying that this is someone who has not been left behind. Few purchases carry so much expectation. Even before the purchase is made, people start spending time 'on the computer', because the decision to buy one carries the question 'Which one?' It is unusual for people to come to a major purchase with so little prior knowledge. It is unusual for people to come to a major purchase with so little confidence in their own taste.

Just contemplating owning a personal computer means entering a new world of information to be gathered and assimilated and discussed. For most people, the portal to that new world is the personal computer store. Considering the purchase already means that one finds oneself in debates about 16K versus 64K, about disks versus tapes, about high resolution versus character graphics, about dot-matrix versus daisy-wheel printers.

There is something striking about these conversations. People seem to feel a pressure to have an opinion about all such matters. There is a reluctance to treat them as technical decisions to be left to a technical expert. Becoming fluent in this language, participating in this world, is part of what people are buying.

In the case of the technical hobbyists, the computer rarely served a truly instrumental function – the point of having the machine was the pleasure of working with it. For nontechnical users – and the typical home computer owner of the 1980s fits this description – the machines are used for a purpose: games, word processing, record keeping, reinforcing school learning. But here too, once they are in the home, personal computers get taken up in ways that signal the development of something beyond the practical and utilitarian. People buy an 'instrumental computer', but they come to live with an intimate machine. [. . .]

The first-generation home machines were easy to 'open up', to peer into and experiment with, but the new machines tend to be closed 'black boxes'. They are built as a technology to be exploited. not explored. Manufacturers, now in the business of mass marketing to consumers not likely to be experts, are worried about warranties, guarantees, and parts replacement. Hardware comes in boxes marked 'Do Not Open', 'Not User Serviceable', 'Warranty Is Void if Seal is Broken by Owner'. And if you do open the box, you find that behind the physical inaccessibility of the hardware there is a new intellectual inaccessibility. The first personal systems were built up in a modular way. You could follow function through form. With mass production, with greater compression of function on single chips, intelligibility is sacrificed to ease and cost of fabrication.

At the same time that the hardware is growing more 'opaque', a greater and more powerful variety of languages, operating systems, and other software is becoming available: text editors, file management programs, and debugging aids. Such systems give increased computing power. But the increased power does not lead to a sense of direct control where nothing stands between the programmer and the bare machine.

Despite all this, many people make active efforts to bypass the new features to get back to a more direct sense of contact. (Indeed, part of the success of the Apple II computer seems to have been due to the fact that it was designed to make it easy for people who wanted to get at its 'innards'.) As we have seen, the 'direct-control' style does not necessarily depend on physical contact with the hardware. When you program in machine or assembly language, you are typing at a keyboard. The sense of physical relationship depends on symbolic contact. [. . .]

2.5   Personal computation and personal philosophy

In this chapter I have 'tagged' two different styles of relating to the computer – one that focuses on magic, the other on transparency – by associating them with the culture of computer hackers and first-generation computer hobbyists. But these relational styles have a life of their own. They exist outside of these cultures. [. . .]

These styles enter into programming and into the computer owner's feelings about what makes the machine consequential, what makes it satisfying and 'beautiful'. I discovered that they also find expression in something else as well: how individuals use the computer to think about other questions, among them 'metaphysical' ones.

Children find in the question 'Are computers alive?' a way to talk about the line between computers and people. Adults don't. Nonetheless, they are affected by the questions that stand behind the question: 'What is life?' 'What makes us special?' 'How do computers challenge our definition of ourselves?' One way of getting adults to talk about these things is to ask not about 'life' but about the possibility of machine intelligence. And here different styles of relating to the computer correspond to different kinds of answers. [. . .]

Adults express their ideas about what computers share with people not through opinions about machine aliveness but about machine intelligence. Committed to a notion of the computer as ultimately comprehensible in terms of its 'specs,' most first-generation hobbyists ruled the enterprise of artificial intelligence out of court: 'How can you program something that can't be reduced to specs?'

Today [some] people are drawn toward a relationship with the computer equally committed to keeping it unmysterious. And this often brings them to that same position: computers are too 'mechanical' to have anything in common with mind or with life. What is powerful about the computer is placed in a different realm from the human mind. According to the aesthetic of what we might call the 'pure' hobbyist culture, human intelligence has a quality of mystery. It is precisely what cannot be reduced to specs. It is precisely what cannot be meaningfully analogized with computational processes. One computer owner put it this way: 'In a computer, no matter how fancy, all that is going on is GIGO, 'Garbage in and garbage out.' You can have all of these programs, you can even have them talking to each other, but in the end, you told them to do it. You can't have a spark of life in a computer. That spark of life in people, well, that must be God.'

Other computer cultures – for example, the culture of artificial intelligence researchers or the hacker culture. [. . .] – have very different computational aesthetics that can lead them in very different directions when they use what they know about computers to think about themselves. [. . .] Far from finding artificial intelligence irrelevant, [some] see it as an embodiment of what [they] find most exciting about the computer: the way in which unpredictable and surprising complexity can emerge from local ideas. [They] believe that if you make the system complicated enough, the simultaneous operation of millions of interacting programs might be able to create in a machine 'that sense of surprising oneself . . . that makes most people feel that they have free will, perhaps even . . . a soul'.

3   The human spirit in a computer culture

The computational model of mind is yet another blow to our sense of centrality. Copernicus and Darwin took away our special role as the center-piece of creation, but we could still think of ourselves as the center of ourselves. Now the computer culture, like the psychoanalytic culture before it, threatens the very idea of 'self'. Freud's notion of the unconscious challenges thinking about personal responsibility and life decisions. Psychoanalysis asks us to confront the fact that our choices – even and especially our most consequential choices about love and work, career and spouse – are repetitions of a primitive scenario, are determined by our earliest experiences. But the Freudian unconscious has a certain abstract quality. It allows people to slide easily between 'I am my unconscious' and the more acceptable 'I am influenced by my unconscious'.

The theorists who followed Freud reasserted an active autonomous ego, making it easier for psychoanalysis to enter the general culture as a triumph of reason over the uncivilized within each of us. The computer's threat to the 'I' is in many ways similar, but far more relentless. The computer takes up where psychoanalysis left off. It takes the idea of a decentered self and makes it more concrete by modeling mind as a multiprocessing machine. Where the Freudian vision seemed speculative to some, literary to others, the computational model arrives with the authoritative voice of science behind it – and with the prospect that someday there will be a thinking machine whose existence will taunt us to say how we are other than it.

In response, a quest has already begun for ways to hold on to an understanding of human mind as other than machine.

Joseph Weizenbaum's controversial book *Computer Power and Human Reason* argued that the computer – linear, logical, and rule-governed – encourages this kind of thinking in us and magnifies the place of instrumental reason in our culture.[10] Weizenbaum fears that the psychological theories that might be derived from artifical intelligence would lead to a flattened, mechanical view of human nature.

Weizenbaum's response is to value as most human what is most different from the computer. As emblematic of the human essence, he chooses what the computer cannot do, the things 'we know but cannot tell': the glance that a mother and a father wordlessly share as they stand over the bed of their sleeping child.

Weizenbaum is critical of some aspects of the culture of artifical intelligence. But his idea that what is essentially human is the uncodable is shared by many who are far more sympathetic to AI theories of mind. It is also expressed by many people without theoretical interests who when they meet the psychological machine define the human in opposition to it.

Psychoanalysis has taught us that resistance to a theory is part of its cultural impact. Resistance to the idea of the unconscious and the irrational leads to an alternative view of people as essentially logical beings. Resistance to a computational model of people as programmed information systems leads to a view that what is essential in the human is what is ineffable, uncapturable by language or formalism. It is as if we need to strike a balance. When we use information-processing models to explain larger and larger slices of our behavior, we seem impelled to isolate as our 'core' something we can think of as beyond information. We met this idea in Weizenbaum's assertion that the human is the uncodable, and in a more elaborated form in John Searle's argument that no matter how perfect, a computer simulation of thought is not thought, because the computer will simply be following rules that 'it' does not understand.[11]

When people give allegiance to Searle's argument, when they say that he has done 'something important' by 'taking on' artificial intelligence, they are doing more than assenting to his specific arguments. They are using Searle to help themselves reassert a set of deeply felt commitments: a commitment to a 'centered' self, to the 'real' as distinct from any simulation, to the human as unique.

Arguments about human uniqueness based on what computers can't do leave us vulnerable to technical progress and what clever engineers might come up with. Searle separates the issues. No matter what a computer can do, human thought is something else. For Searle, thought is the product of our specific biology, the product of a human brain.

When Searle talks about biology he means neurons and the chemistry of the synapse. Most people have a more personal view of what it means to be 'biological'. What makes us biological is our life cycle: we are born, we are nurtured by parents, we grow, we develop sexually, we become parents in our turn, we die. This cycle is what gives meaning to our lives. It brings us the knowledge that comes from understanding loss – from knowing that those we love will die and so will we. A being that is not born of a mother, that does not feel the vulnerability of childhood, a being that does not know sexuality or anticipate death, this being is alien. We may be machines, but it is our mortality that impels us to search for transcendence – in religion, history, art, the relationships in which we hope to live on.

There is something familiar in all of these reassertions of 'essentially human'. The response is romantic. It is provoked by the new technology, the ultimate embodiment of universal logic, just as the nineteenth-century Romantic movement was provoked by the triumph of science and the rule of reason. As a self-conscious response to Enlightenment rationalism, what Romanticism longed for was clear: feelings, the 'law of the heart'.[12]

So, too, in the presence of the computer, people's thoughts turn to their feelings. As the children tell it, we are distinguished from the machines by love and affection, by spiritual urges and sensual ones, by the excitement that attaches to heroism, and by the warmth and familiarity of domesticity. The twelve-year-old programmer David summed up these sentiments: 'When there are computers who are just as smart as people, the computers will do a lot of the jobs, but there will still be things for the people to do. They will run the restaurants, taste the food, and they will be the ones who will love each other, have families and love each other. I guess they'll still be the ones who go to church.' Adults who work closely with computers often end up with similar images. In the style of David, some find it sufficient to say that machines are reason and people are sensuality and emotion. But most find it necessary to take greater account of human reason and to seek more nuanced formulations. Then the dichotomy that David used to separate computers and people becomes a way to separate the elements of what is human. One student speaks of his 'technology self' and his 'feelings self', another of her 'machine part' and her 'animal part'.

In Greek times, the experience of the divided human was captured in Plato's image of a driver of two horses, white and black, reason and passion. The ride was uneven. With and without the computer, people have found ways to describe this uneven ride. They use different langugages: there are reason and passion, logic and emotion, ego and id. The computer makes a new contribution. Along with a new urgency, it provides a new discourse for describing the divided self. On one side is placed what is simulable; on the other, that which cannot be simulated. People who say they are perfectly comfortable with the idea of mind as machine assent to the idea that simulated thinking is thinking, but often cannot bring themselves to propose further that simulated feeling is feeling.

The new romantic reaction is not made by people who reject the computer in the way that the nineteenth-century Romantics rejected science. The reassertions of feeling and of the 'ineffable' that I speak of here come from people who have and accept the technology, not those who are fleeing from it.

In this it is different from the romanticism of the 1960s, when people set themselves in opposition to technology and rationalism. Sixties values – simplicity, self-expression, and the authenticity of pure emotion – were asserted in a global protest against cold science. Mysticism and Eastern religion were arms against instrumental reason. The computer presence gives new legitimacy to a set of values that many people did not find comfortable as long as they were associated with the East and opposed to science and reason.

Cultures are fluid, conflictual, and contradictory. The computer gives support to those who see human psychology in mechanistic terms, and also, in a paradox that is increasingly important for our culture, it is a point of reference for those who place greatest value not on rationality but on affect. We cede to the computer the power of reason, but at the same time, in defense, our sense of identity becomes increasingly focused on the soul and the spirit in the human machine.

Before the computer, the animals, mortal though not sentient, seemed our nearest neighbors in the known universe. Computers, with their interactivity, their psychology, with whatever fragments of intelligence they have, now bid for this place. We met children who seemed ready to give it to them. These children defined themselves not with respect to their differences from animals, but by how they differ from computers. Where we once were rational animals, now we are feeling computers, emotional machines. But we have no way to really put these terms together. The hard-to-live-with, self-contradictory notion of the emotional machine captures the fact that what we live now is a new and deeply felt tension.

As they grow up, will children of the computer culture follow Searle back around his circle, reasserting the primacy of biology? Will they remain where we saw them, split between a mechanical vision of intelligence and a mystical vision of pure emotion? More probably, the challenge of the computer will inspire them to invent new hybrid self-images, built up out of the materials of animal, mind, and machine.

One thing is certain: the riddle of mind, long a topic for philosophers, has taken on new urgency. Under pressure from the computer, the question of mind in relation to machine is becoming a central cultural preoccupation. It is becoming for us what sex was to the Victorians – threat and obsession, taboo and fascination.

Notes

1 See, for example, Lewis Mumford (1934), *Technics and Civilization*, New York: Harcourt, Brace and World, particularly the classic discussion of time in 'The Monastery and the Clock', pp. 12-18.

2 An example of the 'determinist' view is expressed by anthropologist Leslie White: 'Social systems are functions of technologies and philosophies express technological forces and reflect social systems. The technological factor is therefore the determinant for the cultural system as a whole.' See Leslie White (1949) *The Science of Culture*, New York: Farrar, Straus, and Giroux, p. 336. An example of the nondeterminist view is expressed by historian Lynn White: 'As our understanding of history increases, it becomes clear that a new device merely opens a door, it does not command one to enter.' See Lynn White (1966) *Medieval Technology and Social Change*, New York: Oxford University Press, p. 28.

Not all positions are as polarized. Although sociologist Daniel Bell gives a privileged status to technology as a motor of change, he describes a complex relationship between technical and social factors. See Daniel Bell (1973) *The Coming of Post-Industrial Society*, New York: Basic Books. But in the popular culture and in the popular literature on technology and its effects, the 'pure' technology-driven position is rampant. See, for example, Marshall McLuhan (1973) *Understanding Media*, New York: New American Library, John Naisbitt (1982) *Megatrends*, New York: Warner Books, and Alvin Toffler (1970) *Future Shock*, New York: Random House.

The question of technological determinism, characterized as a debate over 'engines of changes', is discussed in Langdon Winner (1977) *Autonomous Technology*, Cambridge, Mass: MIT Press, pp. 44-106. Marshall Sahlins makes a distinction related to the debate on technological determinism when he contrasts materialist/rationalist explanations and explanations that look to the centrality of symbols. See Marshall Sahlins (1976) *Culture and Practical Reason*, Chicago: University of Chicago Press.

3 My analysis of the computer as an 'object-to-think-with' grew out of my appreciation of the way several other authors discussed the relation between artifacts and thought. In particular, I was influenced by Claude Lévi-Strauss' discussion of *bricolage* in *The Savage Mind* (1968) Chicago: University of Chicago Press, Mary Douglas' discussion of objects in *Purity and Danger* (1966) London: Routledge and Kegan Paul, and Seymour Papert's description of a relationship to gears as crucial to his development as a mathematician. See Seymour Papert, 'The Gears of My Childhood,' in *Mindstorms*. Sharon Traweek's recent work on the culture of high-energy physicists in the United States and Japan includes a fascinating discussion of the relationship of physicists to their tools: see *Uptime, Downtime, Spacetime, and Power: An Ethnography of the Particle Physics Community in Japan and the United States*, unpublished PhD dissertation, University of California at Santa Cruz, 1982.

4 For a discussion of the role of psychological theories as they enter into everyday life and become materials for the construction of personal biography, see. Peter L. Berger and Thomas Luckmann (1967) *The Social Construction of Reality: A Treatise in the Sociology of Knowledge*, New York: Doubleday, Peter L. Berger, 'Towards a Sociological Understanding of Psychoanalysis', *Social Research* 31 (Spring 1965), pp. 26-41, Peter L. Berger (1963) *Invitation to Sociology: A Humanistic Perspective*, New York: Anchor. See also Jerome Bruner 'Freud and the Image of Man' in Jerome Bruner, (1962) *On Knowing: Essays For the Left Hand*, Cambridge, Mass.: Belknap. For one of the first essays sensitive to the computer as metaphor, see Ulrich Neisser, 'Computers as Tools and as Metaphors' in Charles Dechert (ed.) (1966) *The Social Impact of Cybernetics*, Notre Dame, Indiana: The University of Notre Dame Press. For a more extended discussion of my use of the term 'psychoanalytic culture' see Sherry Turkle (1978) *Psychoanalytic Politics: Freud's French Revolution*, New York: Basic Books.

5 The early hobbyist movement is best seen as a technical subculture. The literature on the sociology of subcultures offers an approach to its study and is also useful for comparative purposes. On subcultures see Howard Becker (1963) *The Outsiders: Studies in the Sociology of Deviance*, Glencoe: Free Press, and David Arnold, (ed.) (197) *The Sociology of Subcultures*, Berkeley: Glendessary Press, Paul Willis (1981) *Profane Culture*, Berkeley: University of California Press, and Hunter Thompson (1967) *Hell's Angels*, New York: Ballantine Books, deal with subcultures around a technological object, the motorbike. On machines as cultural objects, see also Robert Pirsig (1975) *Zen and the Art of Motorcycle Maintenance*, New York: William Morrow; Tracy Kidder (1982) *The Soul of a New Machine*, Boston: Little, Brown; and Frederick P. Brooks, Jr. (1979) *The Mythical Man-Month: Essays on Software Engineering*, Reading, Mass.: Addison-Wesley.

The concept of computing worlds as cultural worlds is taken up in Rob Kling and Elihu Gerson (1978) 'Patterns of Segmentation and Communication in the Computer World', *Symbolic Interaction* 1, pp. 24-43; Rob Kling and Walt Scacchi (1980) 'Computing as Social Action: The Social Dynamics of Computing in

Complex Organizations', *Advances in Computers*, Vol. 19, New York: Academic Press, pp. 150-327; Lee S. Sproull, Sara Kiesler, and David Zubrow 'Encountering an Alien Culture', unpublished manuscript (August 1983); Shoshanna Zuboff (1982) 'New Worlds of Computer Mediated Work', *Harvard Business Review* 60, pp. 142-52; Sherry Turkle (1980) 'Computer as Rorschach', *Society* 17, pp. 15-24; and Sherry Turkle (1982) 'The Subjective Computer: A Study in the Psychology of Personal Computation', *Social Studies of Science* 12, pp. 173-205. Some of the material on first-generation users that appears in this chapter was presented at the 1980 meetings of the International Federation of Information Processors; see Sherry Turkle (1980) 'Personal Computers and Personal Meanings', in S. H. Lavington (ed.), *Information Processing* 80, New York and Amsterdam: North Holland.

6 See Karl Marx, 'Machinery and Modern Industry' in Robert C. Tucker (ed.), (1978) *The Marx-Engels Reader*, New York: Norton, pp. 291ff.

7 The political charge on the early personal computer movement was only one aspect of its cultural life. Its strongest roots as an organized movement were in the California Bay Area. There it grew up with role-playing fantasy games, with holistic health, and with humanistic psychology. Many of these themes emerged in the discourse of early personal computer utopians, in the early literature of the hobbyist movement, and in the proceedings of the first generation of personal computer 'Faires', sponsored by the organizers of the San Francisco Homebrew Computer Club.

8 The distinction between risk and reassurance brings us into a discussion of the psychology of programming for adults. On this subject see Gerald M. Weinberg (1971) *The Psychology of Computer Programming*, New York: Von Nostrand Reinhold. For more recent work, see Beau Shiel (1981) 'The Psychological Study of Programming', *ACM Computing Surveys* 13,1, pp. 101-41, and Richard E. Mayer (1981) 'The Psychology of How Novices Learn Computer Programming', *ACM Computing Surveys* 13,1, pp. 121-41. Mayer's study is part of a growing literature on novice programming. See also E. Solloway (1981) 'Cognition and Programming: Why Your Students Write Those Crazy Programs', *Proceedings of the National Education Conference*; E. Solloway, K. Ehrlich, J. Bonar and J. Greenspan (1982) 'What Do Novices Know About Programming', in B. Schneiderman and A. Badre (eds), *Directions in Human-Computer Interactions*, Hillsdale, N.J.: Ablex; and Sproull *et al.*, 'Confronting an Alien Culture'.

9 For a quantitative study of the factors that lead this next generation to buy a home computer, see Everett M. Rogers, Hugh M. Daley, and Thomas D. Wu (October 1982) 'The Diffusion of Home Computers: An Exploratory Study', Institute for Communication Research, Stanford University.

10 Joseph Weizenbaum (1976) *Computer Power and Human Reason: From Judgment to Calculation*, San Francisco: W. H. Freeman.

11 John Searle (1980) 'Minds, Brains and Programs', *The Behavioral and Brain Sciences* 3, pp. 417-24.

12 On the Romantic reaction to science see Walter Jackson Bate (1961) *From Classic to Romantic: Premises of Taste in Eighteenth Century England*, New York: Harper and Row; M. H. Abrams (1977) *The Mirror and the Lamp*, New York: Oxford University Press; and Alfred North Whitehead (1953) *Science and the Modern World*, New York: Macmillan.

18

Engineers and the Work that People do

Howard Rosenbrock

1 Introduction

The phenomenon which I wish to discuss in this paper can be illustrated by a plant which was making electric light bulbs in 1979. Production was 800 bulbs an hour, of the type having a metallized reflector and the components of the glass envelope were made elsewhere. They travelled on a chain conveyor around the plant, which occupied an area about 30 feet by 10 feet and was quite new. It was noisy, and the large room which housed it was drab, but conditions otherwise were not unpleasant.

The plant was almost completely automatic. Parts of the glass envelope, for example, were sealed together without any human intervention. Here and there, however, were tasks which the designer had failed to automate, and workers were employed, mostly women and mostly middle-aged. One picked up each glass envelope as it arrived, inspected it for flaws, and replaced it if it was satisfactory: once every $4\frac{1}{2}$ seconds. Another picked out a short length of aluminium wire from a box with tweezers, holding it by one end. Then she inserted it delicately inside a coil which would vapourize it to produce the reflector: repeating this again every $4\frac{1}{2}$ seconds. Because of the noise, and the isolation of the work places, and the concentration demanded by some of them, conversation was hardly possible.

This picture could be matched by countless other examples, taken from any of the industrialized countries. Beyond the comment that the jobs were obviously bad ones, and that something should have been done about them, we are not likely to be surprised or to feel that the situation was unusual. Yet, as I shall hope to show, what has been described is decidedly odd.

2 A design exercise

To prepare the way, let us take one of the jobs, say the second one, and suppose that in a first year engineering degree course it was proposed, as a design exercise, to automate it. Picking up bits of wire out of a box is obviously too difficult, but we can easily avoid it. Let the wire be taken off a reel by pinch rollers and fed through a narrow tube. At the end of the tube, let it pass through holes in two hardened steel blocks. Then we can accurately feed out the right length, and by displacing one of the steel blocks we can shear it off. If this is all made small enough, it can enter the coil, so that when the wire is cut off it falls in the right place.

So far, so good, but the coil may perhaps not be positioned quite accurately. Then, if we cannot improve the accuracy, we shall have to sense its position and move the wire feeder to suit. Perhaps we could do this by using a conical, spring loaded plunger, which could be pushed forward by a cam and enter the end of the coil. Having found its position in this way, we could lock a floating carriage on which the plunger and wire feeding mechanism were mounted, withdraw the plunger, and advance the wire feeder.

There would be scope here for a good deal of mechanical ingenuity, but of a kind which might not appeal to all of the students. 'Why not,' one of them might ask, 'why not use a small robot with optical sensing. The wire feeder could be mounted on the robot arm, and then sensing the position of the coil and moving the arm appropriately would be a simple matter of programming.'

An experienced engineer would probably not find much merit in this proposal. It would seem extravagant, using a complicated device to meet a simple need. It would offend what Veblen[1] calls the 'instinct of workmanship', the sense of economy and fitness for purpose. Yet the student might not be discouraged. 'All that is true,' he might say, 'but the robot is still economically sound. Only a small number of these plants will be made, and they will have to bear the development costs of any special device we design. Robots are complicated, but because they are made in large numbers they are cheap, while the development costs will be much less.'

After a little investigation, and some calculation, it might perhaps turn out that the student was right. A plant might even be built using a robot for this purpose. What I would like to suggest, however, is that this would not be a stable solution. It would still offend our instinct of workmanship. The robot has much greater abilities than this application demands. We should feel, like the robot specialist[2] that 'To bring in a universal robot would mean using a machine with many abilities to do a single job that may require only one ability.'

As opportunity served we might pursue one of two possibilities. We might in the first place seek to find some simpler and cheaper device which would replace the robot. Alternatively, having a robot in place with capacities which had been paid for but were not being used, we might attempt to create for it a task which more nearly suited its abilities. It might, for example, be able to take over some other task on a neighbouring part of the line. Or we might be able to rearrange the line to bring some other suitable task within the reach of the robot. At all events, as engineers we should not rest happy with the design while a gross mismatch existed between the means we were employing and the tasks on which they were employed.

3   The application

The drift of this fable will have become clear. For robot, substitute man or woman, and then compare our attitudes. This I will do shortly, but first let me extend the quotation which was given above[2]: 'However, it is less obvious that robots will be needed to take the place of human beings in most everyday jobs in industry . . . .To bring in a universal robot would mean using a machine with many abilities to do a single job that may require only one ability.' There is a curious discrepancy here between the apparent attitudes to robots and to people, and it is this which I wish to explore.

It will be readily granted that the woman whose working life was spent in picking up a piece of aluminium wire every $4\frac{1}{2}$ seconds had many abilities, and was doing a job which required only one ability. By analogy with the robot one would expect to find two kinds of reaction, one seeking to do the job with a 'simpler device', and the other seeking to make better use of human ability. Both kinds of reaction do exist, though as will be seen, with a curious gap.

First, one cannot read the literature in this field without stumbling continually against one suggestion: that many jobs are more fitted for the mentally handicapped, and can be better done by them. The following are some examples.

Slight mental retardation . . . often enables a person to do tedious work which would handicap a 'normal' worker because of the monotony.[3]

The US Rubber Company has even pushed experimentation so far as to employ young girls deficient in intelligence who, in the framework of 'scientific management' applied to this business, have given excellent results.[4]

The tasks assigned to workers were limited and sterile . . . the worker was made to operate in an adult's body on a job that required the mentality and motivation of a child. Argyris demonstrated this by bringing in mental patients to do an extremely routine job in a factory setting. He was rewarded by the patients' increasing the production by 400 per cent.[5]

Mike Bayless, 28 years old with a maximum intelligence level of a 12 year old, has become the company's NC-machining-centre operator because his limitations afford him the level of patience and persistence to carefully watch his machine and the work that it produces.[6]

Swain[7] remarks that 'The methodological difficulties of using this . . . approach to the dehumanised job problem cannot be glossed over' the meaning of which, one hopes, is that society would utterly reject it. Nevertheless, the quotations should alert our instinct of workmanship to the gross misalignment between human abilities and the demands of some jobs. A much more respectable response to this misalignment is the one which appeals to many technologists and engineers – that is, to carry the process of automation to the point where human labour is eliminated.

This becomes easier in manual work as the robot becomes cheaper and more highly developed. So, for example, in the manufacture of automobile bodies spot-welding is now regularly done by robots, and spray-painting also will soon cease to be a human occupation. Similar possibilities for eliminating human labour in clerical work are opened up by the microprocessor.

When it is applied to jobs which are already far below any reasonable estimate of human ability, there can be no objection on our present grounds to this development. Difficulties begin when we consider jobs that demand skill and the full use of human ability. To automate these out of existence in one step is never possible. They have to go first through a long process of fragmentation and simplification, during which they become unsuitable for human performance.

The mismatch between jobs and human abilities has also been approached from the opposite side by social scientists. Seeing the under-use of human ability, they have developed their techniques[8] of job enlargement, job enrichment, and of autonomous groups. These take existing jobs, and redesign them in a way which makes more use of the human abilities of judgement and adaptability. For example, in an autonomous group the allocation of tasks among its members is not imposed from outside but is left to the group itself to decide. The jobs that result can be better matched to human abilities, within the usually severe constraints of the technology. As Kelly[9] has noted, the opening which is given for the exercise of judgement and adaptability within the group may account for some of the increased productivity that has been observed.

These, then, are the techniques available to us for eliminating the mismatch between jobs and human abilities. There are two which reduce the abilities deployed, one of them inadmissible and the other stemming from engineering. There is a group of techniques which seek to use the abilities of people more fully, and these stem from the social sciences. So far as I know there are no others of significance; and what is remarkable is that engineers and technologists have not produced any methodology for using to the full the abilities and skills of human beings.

The designer of the lamp plant, for example, had made its operation automatic wherever he could do so conveniently. Where he could not, he had used human beings. He might perhaps have used robots, and if so he would have been concerned to use them economically and to make full use of their abilities. He felt, it appears, no similar concern for the full use of human abilities. We may say, paradoxically, that if he had been able to consider people as though they were robots, he would have tried to provide them with less trivial and more human work.

4   A paradigm

The conclusion we have reached discloses the oddity which was mentioned at the beginning of this paper. It is one that becomes more strange the more one considers it, and we are bound to ask how it arises.

The question has two parts: how do individual engineers come to adopt the view we have described, and how did this originate and become established in the engineering profession? As to the individual, engineers in my experience are never taught a set of rules or attitudes which would lead to this kind of view, nor do they base their actions on a set of explicit principles incorporating it. Instead, we have to imagine something like the 'paradigm' discussed by Thomas Kuhn.[10] This is the name he gives, in the sciences, to a matrix of shared attitudes and assumptions and beliefs within a profession.

The paradigm is transmitted from one generation to another, not by explicit teaching but by shared problem-solving. Young engineers take part in design exercises, and later in real design projects as members of the team. In doing so, they learn to see the world in a special way: the way in fact which makes it amenable to the professional techniques which they have available. Paradigms differ from one specialization to another within engineering, so that a control engineer and a thermodynamicist, for example, will see a gas turbine in slightly different ways. Effective collaboration between them will then demand a process of mutual re-education, as many will have discovered from this or other kinds of collaboration.

Seen in this way, as a paradigm which has been absorbed without ever being made fully explicit, the behaviour of the lamp-plant designer becomes understandable. We still have to ask how this paradigm arose. This is a question which deserves a more extended historical study than any I have seen. Tentatively, however, I suggest the following explanation, which has been given elsewhere[11] in somewhat greater detail.

Looking back at the early stages of the industrial revolution we tend to see the early machines as part of one single evolution. Examples of the machines themselves can be found in museums, and in looking at them we see the family resemblance which they all bear, deriving from the materials that were used and the means by which they were fashioned. They were made of leather and wood, and of wrought and cast iron, and in all of them these materials were fashioned in similar ways.

What I wish to suggest is that there were in fact two quite different kinds of machine, similar only in their materials and their construction, but with opposed relationships to human abilities. One of them can be typified by Hargreaves's spinning-jenny, which he invented for his own or his family's use. It is a hand-operated machine, deriving from the spinning wheel, but allowing many threads to be spun at the same time. To use it demands a skill, which is a natural development from the skill needed to use the spinning wheel. This skill in the user is rewarded by a great increase in his productivity. Samuel Crompton's spinning-mule was a similar kind of machine, and even when it was driven mechanically it needed the skilled cooperation of the spinner.

The other type of machine can be typified by the self-acting mule which was invented by Richard Roberts in 1830. What Roberts set out to do was not, like Hargreaves or Crompton, to make skill more productive. Rather he set out to eliminate skill so that the spinner was no longer needed except to supervise a set of machines. Fragments of his job remained, such as mending broken threads, or removing thread which had been spun. These jobs were given largely to children, and they began to resemble the jobs around the lamp-making plant.

For reasons which were valid enough in the early nineteenth century, and which are well documented by Ure[12] and Babbage,[13] the second course proved more profitable for the inventor and the manufacturer than the first. When the engineering profession arose later in the century it therefore inherited only one attitude to the relation between machines and human skill, which is essentially the one described above.

Whether this attitude is appropriate at the present time is something which I should question. In a broad economic sense, the under-use of human ability is clearly a loss. Some of the reasons which made it nevertheless profitable for an early manufacturer no longer apply with the same force. Unskilled labour is still cheaper than skilled, but much less so than it was at an earlier period.

Once only skilled workers could strike effectively, but the less-skilled now, by their numbers, may have even greater industrial strength.

Under present conditions, the motivation of workers may be a major preoccupation of managers. By 'quality circles' or other means they may strive to engage the abilities of the workers outside their jobs. By the social scientists' techniques of job-redesign they may seek to make the jobs themselves less repugnant to human ability. For engineers to spend effort and money at the same time on fragmenting jobs and reducing their content seems neither rational nor efficient, if there is any alternative.

5   An alternative paradigm

If Hargreaves and Crompton could develop machines which collaborated with the skills of workers in the eighteenth century can we not do the same in the twentieth century, using the incomparable power and flexibility of new technology? A major difficulty is that the problem is not generally posed as a choice between two alternative routes along which technology could develop. The engineering paradigm is not explicit, and it prevails not by a conscious choice, but by suppressing the ability to see an alternative.

It is therefore useful to construct an example to show how a valid choice could indeed be made. This is not easy. At least 150 years of engineering effort have been given to one alternative, while the other has been ignored. One path is therefore broad, smooth and easy, the other narrow, difficult and rough. The example, however, need not be taken from engineering. What has been said applies equally to all technology, and will take on a new force as the advance of the microprocessor affects ever newer and wider areas.

What proves easiest is to choose as example an area where high skill exists, and where the encroachment of technology upon skill has hardly yet begun. In this way, both possible routes which technological development could follow are placed upon an equal basis. Following an earlier account, the example of medical diagnosis will be used.

Feigenbaum[14] has recently described a computer system called PUFF for the diagnosis of lung diseases. It uses information about patients obtained from an instrument and from their past history. The information is matched against a set of 'rules' which have been developed by computer scientists in collaboration with medical specialists. In the rules is captured the knowledge of the physician, part of which he was explicitly aware of knowing. Another part was knowledge which he used unconsciously and which only became explicit as he compared his own response with that of the computer.

Though still in an early stage of development, the system gave agreement of 90 to 100 per cent with the physician, according to the tests which were used. There is no difficulty in supposing that this and similar systems can be improved until they are at least as good as the unaided physician.

One way in which they might be used is to make the skill in diagnosis of the physician redundant. The computer system could be operated by staff who had not received a full medical training, but only a short and intensive course in the computer system and its area of application. There might then be no difficulty in showing that the quality of diagnoses was as good as before, and possibly even better. The cost would be reduced, and a better service could be offered to the patient.

Alternatively, diagnosis might still be carried out by the physician, but he could be given a computer system to assist him in his work. Much that he had carried in his mind before would now be in the computer, and he would not need to concern himself with it. The computer would aid him by relieving him of this burden, and would allow him to carry on his work more effectively.

Under this second system, the physician would usually agree with the computer's diagnosis, but he would be at liberty to reject it. He might do so if, for example, some implicit rule which he used had not yet found its way into the computer system; or if he began to suspect a side effect from some new drug. Using the computer in this way, the physician would gradually develop a new skill, based on his previous skill but differing from it. Most of this new skill would reside in the area where he disagreed with the computer, and from time to time more of it might be captured in new rules. Yet there is no reason why the physician's skill in using the computer as a tool should not continually develop.

This is all speculation, but I believe not unreasonable speculation. Which of these two possible routes would be the better? The first leads, step by step, towards the situation typified by the lamp plant. The operators, having no extensive training, can never disagree with the computer, and become its servants. In time, the computer might be given more and more control over their work, requesting information, demanding replies, timing responses and reporting productivity. A mismatch would again arise between the abilities of the operators, and the trivialised tasks they were asked to perform. Social scientists might then be invited to study their jobs, and to suggest some scheme of redesign which would alleviate the monotony or the pressure of the work.

The second path allows human skill to survive and evolve into something new. It cooperates with this new skill and makes it more productive, just as Hargreaves's spinning-jenny allowed the spinner's skill to evolve and become more productive. There seems no reason to believe that this second path would be less economically effective than the first.

The example can be readily transposed into engineering terms. It applies with little change to the future development of computer-aided design. It suggests also that if we re-thought the problem, the operator's job on an MC machine tool need not be fragmented and trivialised, to the point where 'slight mental retardation' becomes an advantage. The task of making a part, from the description produced by a CAD system, could be kept entire, and could become the basis of a developing skill in the operator.

As I have said elsewhere,[15] the task of developing a technology which is well matched to human ability, and which fosters skill and makes it more productive, seems to me the most important and stimulating challenge which faces engineers today. If they are held back from this task, it will not be so much by its difficulty, as by the need for a new vision of the relation between engineering and the use of human skill. That I should pose such a problem to engineers will indicate, I hope, the very high position which I give to the role of engineering.

6   Postscript

My paper could end at that point, but some readers may (and I hope will) feel a sense of unease. The argument which is developed above is in essence a broadly economic one. The skills and abilities of people are a precious resource which we are misusing, and a sense of economy and fitness for purpose, upon which we justly pride ourselves as engineers, should drive us to find a better relation between technology and human ability.

Yet economic waste is not the truest or deepest reason which makes the lamp plant repugnant to us. It offends against strong feelings about the value of human life, and the argument surely should be on this basis.

I wish that it could be, but my belief at present is that it cannot, for the following reasons. To develop such an argument we need a set of shared beliefs upon which to build the intellectual structure. Medieval Christianity, with its superstructure of scholastic philosophy, would once have provided the framework within which a rational argument could have been developed. By the time of the Industrial Revolution, this had long decayed, and nineteenth century Christianity did not unequivocally condemn the developments I have described.

Marxism provides an alternative set of beliefs, and a philosophical superstructure, and it utterly condemns the misuse of human ability: but only when it is carried on under a capitalist system. If it is carried on under socialism then Marxism seems not to condemn it unequivocally, and those are the conditions under which Marxism can have the greatest influence. In support, it is only necessary to say that the lamp plant was in a socialist state, and is in no way anomalous there.[16]

Humanism might serve as another possible basis, with its demand[17] 'that man make use of all the potentialities he holds within him, his creative powers and the life of the reason, and labour to make the powers of the physical world the instruments of his freedom'. This indeed underlies much of the thought in the social sciences, yet again it seems that no conclusive argument can be based on it.

The difficulties are twofold. First, no system of beliefs is as widely disseminated as industrial society. Therefore if a conclusive argument could be based on one system of beliefs, it would have only a limited regional force. Secondly, and almost axiomatically, if there is a system of beliefs from which some of the prevalent features of industrial society can be decisively condemned, it will not be found as the dominant set of beliefs in an industrialized country.

My own conclusion is that rejection of trivialized and dehumanized work precedes any possible rationalization. Tom Bell[18] tells the following story of his mate who, day after day, sharpened needles in Singer's Clydebank works. 'Every morning there were millions of these needles on the table. As fast as he reduced the mountain of needles, a fresh load was dumped. Day in, day out, it never grew less. One morning he came in and found the table empty. He couldn't understand it. He began telling everyone excitedly that there were no needles on the table. It suddenly flashed on him how absurdly stupid it was to be spending his life like this. Without taking his jacket off, he turned on his heel and went out, to go for a ramble over the hills to Balloch.'

No very large part of the population so far has turned on its heel and gone for a ramble over the hills, though a mood akin to that does exist. If industrial society ever comes to be decisively rejected, it seems to me that it will be in this way and for these reasons, rather than as the result of a logically-argued critique. The thought, if valid, takes on a special significance at the present time, when we are engaged in determining the kind of work which men and women will do in the era of the microprocessor.

References

1 Thorstein Veblen (1898) 'The instinct of workmanship and the irksomeness of labour', *American Journal of Sociology*, Vol.4, No.2, pp. 187-201.
2 George, F.H. and Humphries, J.D. (eds) (1974) *The Robots are Coming*, p. 164. NCC Publications.
3 Swain, A.D. (quoting M.L. Tinkham, 1971) 'Design of industrial jobs a worker can and will do' in Brown, S.C. and Martin, J.N.T. (eds) (1977) *Human Aspects of Man-Made Systems*, p. 192. Open Univ. Press.
4 Friedmann, Georges (1955) *Industrial Society*, p. 216. Free Press of Glencoe.
5 Herzberg, Frederick (1966) *Work and the Nature of Man*, p. 39. World Publishing Co.
6 *American Machinist*, July 1979, Vol. 123, No.7, p. 58.
7 Swain, A.D. loc.cit.
8 Drake, Richard I. and Smith, Peter J. (1973) *Behavioural Science in Industry*. McGraw-Hill.
9 Kelly, John E. (1978) 'A reappraisal of sociotechnical system theory', *Human Relations*, Vol.31, pp. 1069-99.
10 Kuhn, Thomas S. (1970) *The Structure of Scientific Revolutions*, passim, but especially pp. 181-7. Univ. Chicago Press.
11 *New Technology: Society, Employment and Skill* (1981), Council for Science and Society.
12 Ure, Andrew (1835) *The Philosophy of Manufactures*. London: Charles Knight, also *The Cotton Manufacture of Great Britain* (1836). London: Charles Knight.
13 Babbage, Charles (1832) *On the Economy of Machinery and Manufactures*, reprinted 1963. N. York: Kelley.
14 Feigenbaum, Edward A. (1979) 'Themes and case studies of knowledge engineering' in D. Michie (ed) *Expert Systems in the Micro-electronic Age*, pp. 3-25. Edinburgh Univ. Press.
15 Rosenbrock, H.H. (1977) *The Future of Control, Automatica*, Vol.13, pp. 389-92. Pergamon.
16 Haraszty, Miklós (1977) *A Worker in a Worker's State*. Penguin Books.
17 Maritain, Jacques (1939) *True Humanism*, p. xii. Geoffrey Bles, Centenary Press.
18 Meacham, Standish (1977) *A Life Apart*, p. 137, quoting Tom Bell. Thames and Hudson.

19

'Artificial Intelligence'

Joseph Weizenbaum

The question I am trying to pursue here is, 'What human objectives and purposes may not be appropriately delegated to computers?' We can design an automatic pilot, and delegate to it the task of keeping an airplane flying on a predetermined course. That seems an appropriate thing for machines to do. It is also technically feasible to build a computer system that will interview patients applying for help at a psychiatric out-patient clinic and produce their psychiatric profiles complete with charts, graphs, and natural-language commentary. The question is not whether such a thing *can* be done, but whether it is appropriate to delegate this hitherto human function to a machine.

The artificial intelligentsia argue, as we have seen, that there is no domain of human thought over which machines cannot range. They take for granted that machines can think the sorts of thoughts a psychiatrist thinks when engaged with his patient. They argue that efficiency and cost considerations dictate that machines ought to be delegated such responsibilities. As Professor John McCarthy once put it to me during a debate, 'What do judges know that we cannot tell a computer?' His answer to the question – which is really just our question again, only in different form – is, of course, 'Nothing.' And it is, as he then argued, perfectly appropriate for artificial intelligence to strive to build machines for making judicial decisions.

The proposition that judges and psychiatrists know nothing that we cannot tell computers follows from the much more general proposition subscribed to by the artificial intelligentsia, namely, that there is nothing at all which humans know that cannot, at least in principle, be somehow made accessible to computers.

Not all computer scientists are still so naive as to believe, as they were once charged with believing, that knowledge consists of merely some organization of 'facts'. The various language-understanding and vision programs, for example, store some of their knowledge in the form of assertions, i.e. axioms and theorems, and others of it in the form of processes. Indeed, in the course of planning and executing some of their complex procedures, these programs compose subprograms, that is, generate new processes, that were not explicitly supplied by human programmers. Some existing computer systems, particularly the so-called hand-eye machines, gain knowledge by directly sensing their environments. Such machines thus come to know things not only by being told them explicitly, but also by discovering them while interacting with the world. Finally, it is possible to instruct computers in certain skills, for example, how to balance a broomstick on one of its ends, by showing them how to do these things even when the instructor is himself quite incapable of verbalizing how he does the trick. The fact, then, and it *is* a fact, that humans know things which they cannot communicate in the form of spoken or written language is not by itself sufficient to establish that there is some knowledge computers cannot acquire at all.

But lest my 'admission' that computers have the power to acquire knowledge in many diverse ways be taken to mean more than I intend it to mean, let me make my position very clear:

First (and least important), the ability of even the most advanced of currently existing computer systems to acquire information by means other than what Shank called 'being spoonfed', is still extremely limited. The power of existing heuristic methods for extracting knowledge even from natural-language texts directly 'spoonfed', to computers rests precariously on, in Winograd's words, 'the tiniest bit of relevant knowledge'. It is simply absurd to believe that any currently existing computer system can come to know in any way whatever what, say, a two-year-old child knows about children's blocks.

Second, it is not obvious that all human knowledge is encodable in 'information structures', however complex. A human may know, for example, just what kind of emotional impact touching another person's hand will have both on the other person and on himself. The acquisition of that knowledge is certainly not a function of the brain alone; it cannot be simply a process in which an information structure from some source in the world is transmitted to some destination in the brain. The knowledge involved is in part kinesthetic; its acquisition involves having a hand, to say the very least. There are, in other words, some things humans know by virtue of having a human body. No organism that does not have a human body can know these things in the same way humans know them. Every symbolic representation of them must lose some information that is essential for some human purposes.

Third, and the hand-touching example will do here too, there are some things people come to know only as a consequence of having been treated as human beings by other human beings. I shall say more about this in a moment.

Fourth, and finally, even the kinds of knowledge that appear superficially to be communicable from one human being to another in language alone are in fact not altogether so communicable. Claude Shannon showed that, even in abstract information theory, the 'information content' of a message is not a function of the message alone but depends crucially on the state of knowledge, on the expectations, of the receiver. The message 'Am arriving on 7 o'clock plane, love, Bill' has a different information content for Bill's wife, who knew he was coming home, but not on precisely what airplane, than for a girl who wasn't expecting Bill at all and who is surprised by his declaration of love.

Human language in actual use is infinitely more problematical than those aspects of it that are amenable to treatment by information theory, of course. But even the example I have cited illustrates that language involves the histories of those using it, hence the history of society, indeed, of all humanity generally. And language in human use is not merely functional in the way that computer languages are functional. It does not identify things and words only with immediate goals to be achieved or with objects to be transformed. The human use of language manifests human memory. And that is a quite different thing than the store of the computer, which has been anthropomorphized into 'memory'. The former gives rise to hopes and fears, for example. It is hard to see what it could mean to say that a computer hopes.

These considerations touch not only on certain technical limitations of computers, but also on the central question of what it means to be a human being and what it means to be a computer.

I accept the idea that a modern computer system is sufficiently complex and autonomous to warrant our talking about it as an organism. Given that it can both sense and affect its environment, I even grant that it can, in an extremely limited sense, be 'socialized', that is, modified by its experiences with its world. I grant also that a suitably constructed robot can be made to develop a sense of itself, that it can, for example, learn to distinguish between parts of itself and objects outside of itself, that it can be made to assign a higher priority to guarding its own parts against physical damage than to similarly guarding objects external to itself, and that it can form a model of itself which could, in some sense, be considered a kind of self-consciousness. When I say therefore that I am willing to regard such a robot as an 'organism', I declare my willingness to consider it a kind of animal. And I have already agreed that I see no way to put a bound on the degree of intelligence such an organism could, at least in principle, attain.

I make these stipulations, as the lawyers would call them, not because I believe that what any reasonable observer would call a socialized robot is going to be developed in the 'visible future' – I do not believe that – but to avoid the unnecessary, interminable, and ultimately sterile exercise of making a catalogue of what computers will and will not be able to do, either here and now or ever. That exercise would deflect us from the primary question, namely, whether there are objectives that are not appropriately assignable to machines.

If both machines and humans are socializable, then we must ask in what way the socialization of the human must necessarily be different from that of the machine. The answer is, of course, so obvious that it makes the very asking of the question appear ludicrous, if indeed not obscene. It is a sign of the madness of our time that this issue has to be addressed at all.

Every organism is socialized by the process of dealing with problems that confront it. The very biological properties that differentiate one species from another also determine that each species will confront problems different from those faced by any other. Every species will, if only for that reason, be socialized differently. The human infant, as many observers have remarked, is born prematurely, that is, in a state of utter helplessness. Yet the infant has biological needs which, if he is to survive at all, must be satisfied by others. Indeed, many studies of orphanages have shown that more than his merely elementary physical needs must be satisfied; an infant will die, if he is fed and cleaned but not, from the very beginning of his life, fondled and caressed – if, in other words, he is not treated as a human being by other human beings.[1]

A catastrophe, to use Erik Erikson's expression for it, that every human being must experience is his personal recapitulation of the biblical story of paradise. For a time the infant demands and is granted gratification of his every need, but is asked for nothing in return. Then, often after the infant has developed teeth and has bitten the breast that has fed him, the unity between him and his mother is broken. Erikson believes this universal human drama to be the ontogenetic contribution to the biblical saga of the Garden of Eden. So important is this period in the child's life that

a drastic loss of accustomed mother love without proper substitution at this time can lead [under otherwise aggravating conditions] to acute infantile depression or to a mild but chronic state of mourning which may give a depressive undertone to the whole remainder of life. But even under the most favorable circumstances, this stage leaves a residue of a primary sense of evil and doom and of a universal nostalgia for a lost paradise.

[These early stages] then, form in the infant the springs of the basic sense of trust and the basic sense of mistrust which remain the autogenic source of both primal hope and of doom throughout life.[2]

Thus begins the individual human's imaginative reconstruction of the world. And this world, as I said earlier, is the repository of his subjectivity, the stimulator of his consciousness, and ultimately the constructor of the apparently external forces he is to confront all his life.

As the child's radius of awareness, coordination, and responsiveness expands, he meets the educative patterns of his culture, and thus learns the basic modalities of human existence, each in personally and culturally significant ways ... *To get* ... means to receive and to accept what is given. This is the first social modality learned in life; and it sounds simpler than it is. For the groping and unstable newborn organism learns this modality only as it learns to regulate its organ systems in accordance with the way in which the maternal environment integrates its methods of child care ....

The optimum total situation implied in the baby's readiness to get what is given is his mutual regulation with a mother who will permit him to develop and coordinate his means of getting as she develops and coordinates her means of giving .... The mouth and the nipple seem to be the mere centers of a general aura of warmth and mutuality which are enjoyed and responded to with relaxation not only by these focal organs, but by both total organisms. The mutuality of relaxation thus developed is of prime importance for the first experience of friendly otherness. One may say ... that in thus *getting what is given*, and in learning to *get somebody to do* for him what he wishes to have done, the baby also develops the necessary ego groundwork *to get to be* a giver.[3]

What these words of Erikson's make clear is that the initial and crucial stages of human socialization implicate and enmesh the totality of two organisms, the child and its mother, in an inseparable mutuality of service to their deepest biological and emotional needs. And out of this problematic reunification of mother and child – problematic because it involves inevitably the trauma of separation – emerge the foundations of the human's knowledge of what it means to give and to receive, to trust and to mistrust, to be a friend and to have a friend, and to have a sense of hope and a sense of doom.

Earlier, when speaking of theories, I said that no term of a theory can ever by fully and finally understood. We may say the same thing about words generally, especially about such words as trust and friendship and hope and their derivatives. Erikson teaches us that such words derive their meanings from universal, primal human experiences, and that any understanding of them must always be fundamentally metaphoric. This profound truth also informs us that man's entire understanding of his world, since it is mediated by his language, must always and necessarily be bounded by metaphoric descriptions. And since the child 'meets the educative patterns of his culture,' as Erikson says, 'and thus learns the basic modalities of human existence, each in personally and culturally significant ways,' each culture, indeed, each individual in a culture, understand such words and language, hence the world, in a culturally and personally idiosyncratic way.

I could go on to describe the later stages of the socialization of the individual human, the effects of schooling, marriage, imprisonment, warfare, hates and loves, the experiences of shame and guilt that vary so radically among the cultures of man, and so on. But that could be of no help to anyone who is not already convinced that any 'understanding' a computer may be said to possess, hence any 'intelligence' that may be attributed to it, can have only the faintest relation to human understanding and human intelligence. We, however, conclude that however much intelligence computers may attain, now or in the future, theirs must always be an intelligence *alien* to genuine human problems and concerns.

Still, the extreme or hardcore wing of the artificial intelligentsia will insist that the whole man, to again use Simon's expression, is after all an information processor, and that an information-processing theory of man must therefore be adequate to account for his behavior in its entirety. We may agree with the major premise without necessarily drawing the indicated conclusion. We have already observed that a portion of the information the human 'processes' is kinesthetic, that it is 'stored' in his muscles and joints. It is simply not clear that such information, and the processing associated with it, can be represented in the form of computer programs and data structures at all.

It may, of course, be argued that it is in principle possible for a computer to simulate the entire network of cells that constitutes the human body. But that would introduce a theory of information processing entirely different from any which has so far been advanced. Besides, such a simulation would result in 'behavior' on such an incredibly long time scale that no robot built on such principles could possibly interact with human beings. Finally, there appears to be no prospect whatever that mankind will know enough neurophysiology within the next several hundred years to have the intellectual basis for designing such a machine. We may therefore dismiss such arguments. The part of the human mind which communicates to us in rational and scientific terms is itself an instrument that disturbs what it observes, particularly its voiceless partner, the unconscious, between which and our conscious selves it mediates. Its constraints and limitations circumscribe what are to constitute rational – again, if you will, scientific – descriptions and interpretations of the things of the world. These descriptions can therefore never be whole, anymore than a musical score can be a whole description or interpretation of even the simplest song.

But, and this is the saving grace of which an insolent and arrogant scientism attempts to rob us, we come to know and understand not only by way of the mechanisms of the conscious. We are capable of listening with the third ear, of sensing living truth that is truth beyond any standards of provability. It is *that* kind of understanding, and the kind of intelligence that is derived from it, which I claim is beyond the abilities of computers to simulate.

We have the habit, and it is sometimes useful to us, of speaking of man, mind, intelligence, and other such universal concepts. But gradually, even slyly, our own minds become infected with what A.N. Whitehead called the fallacy of misplaced concreteness. We come to believe that these theoretical terms are ultimately interpretable as observations, that in the 'visible future' we will have ingenious instruments capable of measuring the 'objects' to which these terms refer. There is, however, no such thing as mind; there are only individual minds, each belonging, not to 'man', but to individual human beings. I have argued that intelligence cannot be measured by ingeniously constructed meter sticks placed along a one-dimensional continuum. Intelligence can be usefully discussed only in terms of domains of thought and action. From this I derive the conclusion that it cannot be useful, to say the least, to base serious work on notions of 'how much' intelligence may be given to a computer. Debates based on such ideas – for example, 'Will computers ever exceed man in intelligence?' – are doomed to sterility.

I have argued that the individual human being, like any other organism, is defined by the problems he confronts. The human is unique by virtue of the fact that he must necessarily confront problems that arise from his unique biological and emotional needs. The human individual is in a constant stage of becoming. The maintenance of that state, of his humanity, indeed, of his survival, depends crucially on his seeing himself, and on his being seen by other human beings, as a human being. No other organism, and certainly no computer, can be made to confront genuine human problems in human terms. And, since the domain of human intelligence is, except for a small set of formal problems, determined by man's humanity, every other intelligence, however great, must necessarily be alien to the human domain.

I have argued that there is an aspect to the human mind, the unconscious, that cannot be explained by the information-processing primitives, the elementary information processes, which we associate with formal thinking, calculation, and systematic rationality. Yet we are constrained to use them for scientific explanation, description, and interpretation. It behoves us, therefore, to remain aware of the poverty of our explanations and of their strictly limited scope. It is wrong to assert that any scientific account of the 'whole man' is possible. There are some things beyond the power of science to fully comprehend.

The concept of an intelligence alien to certain domains of thought and action is crucial for understanding what are perhaps the most important limits on artificial intelligence. But that concept applies to the way humans relate to one another as well as to machines and their relation to man. For human socialization, though it is grounded in the biological constitution common to all humans, is strongly determined by culture. And human cultures differ radically among themselves. Countless studies confirm what must be obvious to all but the most parochial observers of the human scene: 'The influence of culture is universal in that in some respects a man learns to become like all men; and it is particular in that a man who is reared in one society learns to become in some respects like all men of his society and not like those of others.'[4] The authors of this quotation, students of Japanese society who lived among the Japanese for many years, go on to make the following observations:

In normal family life in Japan there is an emphasis on interdependence and reliance on others, while in America the emphasis is on independence and self-assertion . . . In Japan the infant is seen more as a separate biological organism who from the beginning, in order to develop, needs to be drawn into increasingly interdependent relations with others. In America, the infant is seen more as a dependent biological organism who, in order to develop, needs to be made increasingly independent of others.

The Japanese baby seems passive, and he lies quietly with occasional unhappy vocalizations, while his mother, in her care, does more lulling, carrying, and rocking of her baby. She seems to try to soothe and quiet the child, and to communicate with him physically rather than verbally. On the other hand, the American infant is more active, happily vocal, and exploring of his environment, and his mother, in her care, does more looking at and chatting to her baby. She seems to stimulate the baby to activity and to vocal response. It is as if the American mother wanted to have a vocal, active baby, and the Japanese mother wanted to have a quiet, contented baby. In terms of styles of caretaking of the mothers in the two cultures, they get what they apparently want . . . a great deal of cultural learning has taken place by three-to-four months of age . . . babies have learned by this time to be Japanese and American babies in relation to the expectations of their mothers concerning their behavior.

[Adult] Japanese are more 'group' oriented and interdependent in their relations with others, while Americans are more 'individual' oriented and independent . . . Japanese are more self-effacing and passive in contrast to Americans, who appear more self-assertive and aggressive . . . Japanese are more sensitive to, and make conscious use of, many forms of nonverbal communication in human relations through the medium of gestures and physical proximity in comparison with Americans, who predominantly use verbal communication within a context of physical separateness.

If these distinct patterns of behavior are well on the way to being learned by three-to-four months of age, and if they continue over the life span of the person, then there are very likely to be important areas of difference in emotional response in people of one culture when compared with those in another. Such differences are not easily subject to conscious control and, largely out of awareness, they accent and color human behavior. These differences . . . can also add to bewilderment and antagonism when people try to communicate across the emotional barriers of culture.[5]

Such profound differences in early training crucially affect the entire societies involved. And they are, of course, transmitted from one generation to the next and thus perpetuated. They must necessarily also help determine what members of the two societies know about their worlds, what are to be taken as 'universal' cultural norms and values, hence what in each culture is and is not to be counted as fact. They determine, for example (and this is particularly relevant to the contrast between Japanese and American social norms), what are private as opposed to public conflicts, and hence what modes of adjudication are appropriate to the defense of what human interests. The Japanese traditionally prefer to settle disputes, even those for which relief at law is statutorily available, by what Westerners would see as informal means. Actually, these means are most often themselves circumscribed by stringent ritualistic requirements that are nowhere explicitly codified but are known to every Japanese of the appropriate social class. This sort of knowledge is acquired with the mother's milk and through the whole process of socialization that is itself so intimately tied to the individual's acquisition of his mother tongue. It cannot be learned from books; it cannot be explicated in any form but life itself.

An American judge, therefore, no matter what his intelligence and fairmindedness, could not sit in a Japanese family court. His intelligence is simply alien to the problems that arise in Japanese culture. The United States Supreme Court actively recognized this while it still had jurisdiction over distant territories. For example, in the case of Diaz v. Gonzales, which was originally tried in Puerto Rico, the court refused to set aside the judgment of the court of original jurisdiction, that is, of the native court. Justice Oliver W. Holmes, writing the opinion of the Court, stated

> This Court has stated many times the deference due to understanding of the local courts upon matters of purely local concern. This is especially true when dealing with the decisions of a Court inheriting and brought up in a different system from that which prevails here. When we contemplate such a system from the outside it seems like a wall of stone, every part even with all the others, except so far as our own local education may lead us to see subordinations to which we are accustomed. But to one brought up within it, varying emphasis, tacit assumptions, unwritten practices, a thousand influences gained only from life, may give to the different parts wholly new values that logic and grammar never could have got from the books.[6]

Every human intelligence is thus alien to a great many domains of thought and action. There are vast areas of authentically human concern in every culture in which no member of another culture can possibly make responsible decisions. It is not that the outsider is unable to decide at all – he can always flip coins, for example – it is rather that the *basis* on which he would have to decide must be inappropriate to the context in which the decision is to be made.

What could be more obvious than the fact that, whatever intelligence a computer can muster, however it may be acquired, it must always and necessarily be absolutely alien to any and all authentic human concerns? The very asking of the question, 'What does a judge (or a psychiatrist) know that we cannot tell a computer?' is a monstrous obscenity. That it has to be put into print at all, even for the purpose of exposing its morbidity, is a sign of the madness of our times.

Computers can make judicial decisions, computers can make psychiatric judgments. They can flip coins in much more sophisticated ways than can the most patient human being. The point is that they *ought* not be given such tasks. They may even be able to arrive at 'correct' decisions in some cases – but always and necessarily on bases no human being should be willing to accept.

There have been many debates on 'Computers and Mind'. What I conclude here is that the relevant issues are neither technological nor even mathematical; they are ethical. They cannot be settled by asking questions beginning with 'can'. The limits of the applicability of computers are ultimately statable only in terms of oughts. What emerges as the most elementary insight is that, since we do not now have any ways of making computers wise, we ought not now to give computers tasks that demand wisdom.

Notes

1 See especially the work of Spitz, R. A. (1945) 'Hospitalism' in *Psychoanalytic Study of the Child*, Vol. 1.
2 Erikson, E. (1963) *Childhood and Society*, 2nd ed., pp. 79, 80. New York: W. W. Norton.
3 Ibid., pp. 75-6.
4 Caudill, W. and Weinstein, H. (1967) 'Maternal Care and Infant Behavior in Japan and in America', *Psychiatry* 32, pp. 12-43. Reprinted in C. S. Lavatelli and F. Stendler (eds) *Reading in Child Behavior and Development*, 3rd ed., 1972, p. 78. New York: Harcourt Brace Jovanovich.
5 Ibid., pp. 80 *et seq.*
6 Diaz v. Gonzales, 261 US 102 (1923), Per Holmes, O. W. I owe this reference to Professor Paul Freund of the Law School of Harvard University.

List of Contributors

Bessant, John, Department of Business Management, Brighton Polytechnic.

Bissell, Chris, Faculty of Technology, Open University.

Campbell, Duncan, *New Statesman.*

Child, John, Management Centre, University of Aston.

Connor, Steve, journalist and writer.

Dutton, William H., Associate Professor of Communications and Public Administration, Annenburg School of Communications, University of Southern California. Visiting Fulbright Scholar at University of West London, 1986-87.

Finnegan, Ruth, Faculty of Social Sciences, Open University.

Freeman, Christopher, Science Policy Research Unit, University of Sussex.

Gershuny, Jonathan, Department of Humanities and Social Sciences, University of Bath.

Guy, Ken, Science Policy Research Unit, University of Sussex.

Jayaweera, Neville D., World Association for Christian Communication, London.

Kiesler, Sara, College of Humanities and Social Sciences, Carnegie-Mellon University.

Kling, Rob, Department of Information and Computer Sciences, University of California, Irvine.

McGuire, Timothy W., College of Humanities and Social Sciences, Carnegie-Mellon University.

Melody, William H., Economic and Social Research Council, London and Simon Fraser University.

Miles, Ian, Science Policy Research Unit, University of Sussex.

Monk, John, Faculty of Technology, Open University.

Pool, Ithiel de Sola, late of Massachusetts Institute of Technology.

Robins, Kevin, Department of Languages and Culture, Sunderland Polytechnic.

Rosenbrock, Howard, Control Systems Centre, University of Manchester Institute of Science and Technology.

Rush, Howard, Department of Business Management, Brighton Polytechnic.

Salaman, Graeme, Faculty of Social Sciences, Open University.

Siegel, Jane, College of Humanities and Social Sciences, Carnegie-Mellon University.

Smith, Stephen, Kingston Polytechnic and Faculty of Technology, Open University.

Street, Brian V., School of Social Sciences, University of Sussex.

Thompson, Kenneth, Faculty of Social Sciences, Open University.

Turkle, Sherry, Massachusetts Institute of Technology.

Webster, Frank, Department of Sociology, Oxford Polytechnic.

Weizenbaum, Joseph, Department of Computer Science, Massachusetts Institute of Technology.

Wield, David, Faculty of Technology, Open University.

Index